Semantic Syntax

For my son Raj

Semantic Syntax

Pieter A. M. Seuren

BLACKWELL
Publishers

Copyright © Pieter Seuren 1996

The right of Peter Seuren to be identified as author of this work has been asserted in accordance with the Copyright, Designs and Patents Act 1988.

First published 1996

2 4 6 8 10 9 7 5 3 1

Blackwell Publishers Ltd
108 Cowley Road
Oxford OX4 1JF, UK

Blackwell Publishers Inc.
238 Main Street
Cambridge, Massachusetts 02142, USA

British Library Cataloguing in Publication Data

A CIP catalogue record for this book is available from the British Library.

Library of Congress Cataloging-in-Publication Data

Seuren, Pieter A. M.
   Semantic syntax / Pieter A.M. Seuren.
     p. cm.
   Includes bibliographical references (p.   ) and index.
   ISBN 0–631–16005–1 (alk. paper). — ISBN 0–631–16006–X (pbk. :
alk. paper)
    1. Semantics.   2. Grammar, Comparative and general—Syntax.
3. Generative grammar. I. Title.
P325.5.G45S48   1997
415—dc20   96–11834
                                        CIP

Camera-ready copy supplied by the author
Printed in Great Britain

This book is printed on acid-free paper

Contents

Preface

This book is meant not only for theoretical linguists but also for computational linguists. It presents a family of rule systems for four European languages (and a small one for Turkish) to convert semantic analyses of sentences, expressed in an orthodox variety of Predicate Calculus, into well-formed syntactic surface structures that can be fed directly into a proper morphology. In other words, the rule systems map semantic analyses of sentences onto syntactic surface structures. Since these rule systems, in addition, provide a formal definition of well-formedness of sentences, they are grammars in the accepted sense of the term. The theory underlying and constraining the rule systems presented in this book is called Semantic Syntax (SeSyn). It is a direct continuation of what used to be called, since the late '60s, Generative Semantics. Since, however, what it presents is not a semantics but a syntax, the name Generative Semantics must be considered a misnomer. For that reason I decided, in the early '70s, on the name Semantic Syntax, as it offers a syntactic theory that is closely connected with semantic analyses.

Those familiar with the market of present-day linguistic theories will be struck by the apparent unorthodoxy of the SeSyn rule systems, which often play havoc with principles thought to be well-established (like X-bar-theory). On the other hand, they may well be struck as well by their unusual degree of empirical success. The SeSyn rule systems produce the desired surface structures with great formal precision, so much so that they cry out for implementation. (In fact, the rule systems for English and Dutch have been implemented in Prolog by Henk Schotel, and other implementations and expansions are under way.) Whether they produce the surface structures aimed at in a way that makes optimal use of generalizations over available facts is, as always, open to debate. Progress in this respect is the gist of science. Many areas in the rule systems presented can and will be drastically improved and extended, not only at the ends that have been left fraying, but also right at the centre. (For example, I am myself not at all happy with the treatment of copula verbs and other verbs of being. But one has to make stops at certain moments to share the findings with the community.) On the whole, however, the rules work well and in ways that provide insight, not only into the structures of the languages concerned but, to the extent that this is feasible, of language structures in general. As a result, the rule systems can easily be extrapolated to further facts and to other languages. In fact, the similarities among the rule systems for the various languages dealt with are striking, even if it is premature as yet to try to define them formally.

It is useful to realize, in this context, that the history of theoretical linguistics over the past century is characterized mainly by the desire to achieve the status of a 'real science' (physics usually serving as the model).

Some, often overestimated but in fact quite limited, progress has undeniably been made in this respect, especially since the advent of Transformational Grammar, initiated by Harris and further developed and marketed by Chomsky in the '50s. This development made language empirically accessible from the grammatical angle: a few central empirical problems were formulated, the status of data became somewhat clearer, some formal properties of possible explanatory theories were worked out and a discussion arose as to the causal and ontological properties of such theories. The sociological climate, however, did not change accordingly. With the numbers of practising linguists steadily increasing large sections of the field have become riddled with fads and fashions, complete with coteries ('citation clans'), trendsetters and ephemeral jargon, at the expense, of course, of normal serious scholarship. Often ill-supported claims are presented as 'proofs'. Serious argument and judgment have come to count less than clan membership. For students, the subject often appears to begin with the latest dissertation. As long as this climate prevails linguistics cannot be said to have achieved the status of a respectable, mature science where results are cumulative.

It is useful to realize as well that modern linguistic studies, with all their ramifications and applications and despite the often highly pitched aims and, in some cases, a rich supply of funds, have not achieved a single formally explicit and factually adequate syntactic description of a natural language. This is not universally known. One still comes across statements like 'there are relatively few problems attached to particular constructions or linguistic phenomena' (Hutchins (1986:267-268), uttered, ironically, as part of an overenthusiastic eulogy of the Eurotra machine translation project which had just started at the time and has since proved to be a sad and costly failure, not least because of failing theories). Patience and a delicate touch create better conditions for good results than crass confidence in the latest technical or theoretical developments (or claims). I cannot and do not, of course, pretend that the final word on syntax is in this book, but I think I can say that the analyses presented clear a significant piece of syntactic ground, and do so in a way that not only provokes thought and, I hope, leads to insight but also opens the way to much improved practical applications.

When, in the late '60s, I started work in the framework of Semantic Syntax I felt that the insights that had been gained in the context of Generative Semantics were strong and extremely promising, much more so than the results produced by what seemed to me the retrograde development of its main rival, Autonomous Syntax. Meanwhile, of course, Generative Semantics fell on hard times. Some even declared it dead. The present book is proof that it is not. While developing further and testing, over the years, the syntactic notions and methods first broached in the heyday of Generative Semantics I came to see very clearly both the power and the beauty of the system that emerged. It took shape not by the imposition of any flamboyant overriding formal principle that has to be carried through till the bitter end, as too often found in linguistic theories. Rather, if anything like such a principle emerged it was because it was proving its empirical mettle. We know, or should know, from experience that language always puts paid to dogmatic a priori principles.

Semantic Syntax allows more room for induction. It takes the view that the first thing to do is look at the facts of language with an uncluttered mind and formulate small and cautious hypotheses, supported by whatever factual knowledge, familiarity and experience is available. Only then does one stand a chance of finding out how the constructions in natural languages really work. We know, of course, that in the vast majority of cases there is no way of proving formally that a particular description or analysis is the correct one. But we know equally well that analyses that keep being confirmed from often unexpected quarters and at the same time have a high degree of generality in terms of formal apparatus and coverage of facts do acquire, in a very real sense, a ring of truth. And if such analyses begin to be numerous one gets the feeling of being somehow on the right track. This is the experience I have systematically had when working on European and other languages. The same rules, rule systems and principles kept recurring with only minor switches in rule ordering or in directionality parameters (like left or right adoption). The principle of AUX-formation, for example, proved surprisingly uniform across languages, despite considerable surface differences (e.g. *do*-support in English). Interesting variations were found in the behaviour of modals: the modality of futuricity appears to be naturally attracted by the tenses, and other modalities often follow, to differing degrees. The results are now sufficiently confirmed for me to feel that what I have developed over the past twenty-five or so years should, finally, be presented in the form of a book, though one never feels that the result is final in whatever sense.

The syntax is limited, in this volume, to sentence syntax: categorial phrases, in particular Noun Phrases, are hardly dealt with. Given these limitations, it not only defines wellformedness conditions of sentences, it is also, and above all, a formal mapping of semantic analyses of sentences, expressed in Predicate Calculus structures, onto their surface structures. As such it finally does what was implicitly presupposed in all philosophies and theories since Plato holding that the meanings of sentences are not written on their faces but are hidden behind the surface. Theories of deep structure meaning go back to classical Antiquity, but the programme inherent in them, the programme of formally defining the relationship between surface and semantic structure, has not been tackled until quite recently. Semantic Syntax is part of that effort. It maps semantic structures onto corresponding surface structures, and this generative system provides the grid for efficient parsing strategies. Its theoretical strength is expressed in its potential with regard to improved formal translation procedures and other natural language processing applications.

In presenting this book I have the perhaps pretentious hope of being able to transfer to the reader the experience of being somehow on the right track. If that hope is fulfilled interesting wider perspectives will no doubt open up for the philosophy of man and his mental life, for the vastness as well as the limitations of language, and also for practical applications in this new era where the computer is penetrating into so many spheres of life. But this latter hope is secondary and conditional, as wider perspectives, whether philosophical or practical, are the usual corollary of any new fruitful insight into an important and general matter. The hope of such perspectives will have to be given up the moment the supposed insight turns out to be a delusion. So I am, for the moment, putting all my money on the actual theory and machinery. The rest will no doubt follow, but is of less immediate concern (though, clearly, application of the theory to the practicalities of natural language processing techniques provides invaluable empirical testing). My immediate concern is to get the facts of syntax straight and to do so convincingly and in a formal framework, while trying continually to complete and streamline the syntactic systems that define the forms of languages and to discover more and better generalizations for them. And since what I am presenting is made to have a proper semantics I have a commitment to seeing that realized as well, in the same way, getting the semantic facts right without too much regard for formal a-prioris or sociological parti pris. The overall picture inevitably follows, when there is enough to look back on. In the end, I believe, any sound theory will prove its value by its empirical success, including practical applications, as well as by its internal coherence, and its natural linkage to other disciplines looking at the same facts from a different angle.

The structure of the book is simple. The introductory chapter 1 provides some historical and intellectual context to SeSyn and prepares the reader for the actual stuff. Chapter 2 provides formal definitions of the main notions and operations of SeSyn. The chapters 3, 4, 5 and 6 contain core grammars of English, French, Dutch and German, respectively, with some vocabulary. They show the actual working of SeSyn, and provide, in addition, solutions to a number of stubborn syntactic problems. Chapter 7, finally, deals with a few left-overs that deserve fuller treatment but could not get it owing to limits of space and time. Among this unfinished business is a rudimentary syntax of Turkish (7.6), showing that SeSyn fits that language quite naturally. I feel a little guilty about not having included a section on parsing, since that is among the issues that require immediate attention now. But, having grown up in the generativist camp, I am not a specialist on parsing techniques, and I considered it too hazardous to venture unprepared into that territory. Fortunately, I have a number of PhD students who are working on that.

In the Preface to *Methods in Structural Linguistics* of 1951, Zellig Harris wrote: "This book is regrettably not easy to read. ... Anyone who wants to use these methods or to control them critically will have to work over the material with paper and pencil, reorganizing for himself the examples and general statements presented here." I must, regrettably, make these words my own (though pencils are not used so much any more). Grammar, like all formal science, is not easy.

As this book is, in a way, a synthesis of work done, on and off (mostly on), over many years, it is difficult to acknowledge specific persons who have helped and stimulated me during that long period. But I can, and hereby do, mention a specific group, the group that is, scattered over time, of all those students who, through the years, gave me their curiosity, interest, criticisms and helpful comments. As for more recent years, it is easier to single out those who have contributed to the coming about of this book. I must mention, in the first place, Henk Schotel, who contributed many useful thoughts and spotted all kinds of weaknesses that had escaped my own less acute eye. His computer implementation of my rule systems for English and for Dutch (Schotel 1994) has proved of great value. Others must be thanked for their careful reading of earlier drafts and their critical comments. Among these I must make special mention of Nicolas Nicolov, of Sofia and Edinburgh, who saved me from many inaccuracies. A separate word of thanks is due also to Dan Cristea, of the Computer Science Department of the University "Al.I.Cuza" of Iaşi in Romania. He forced me to make my notions of tree and rule more precise and more formal. Then, I want to thank my friend and colleague Zaharin Yusoff, of the Universiti Sains Malaysia in Penang, and his graduate students, whose keen interest and searching questions spurred me into making a start with the actual writing of this book and who kept me on the alert while I was writing it. In this connection I wish to express my gratitude towards the Universiti Sains Malaysia in Penang, Malaysia, for providing me repeatedly with the opportunity to write large parts of this book as a visiting scholar. Finally, I wish to mention the Netherlands Organization of Scientific Research (NWO), who advanced this work by granting the funds for adequate computer and printing equipment.

Nijmegen, January 1996   P.A.M.S.

CHAPTER 1

Introduction

1.1 Some historical and methodological backgrounds

If one were to divide the history of Transformational Generative Grammar (TGG), short as it is, into two main periods one would no doubt place the main break around 1970. Generative Semantics clearly belongs to the first period, and its lone offshoot Semantic Syntax is therefore to be regarded as a continuation of that tradition. It is the result of a consistent application of most of the central notions developed in TGG from its first beginnings until about 1970. This first phase in the growth of TGG is characterized by relatively many dramatic and highly important developments, whose relevance and importance have tended to be played down or even ignored in much of the literature that has appeared since 1970. Since Semantic Syntax has much in common with dominant trends in TGG as it was until 1970, and hardly anything with its dominant trends after that year, it seems worthwhile to retrace the early developments in a quick survey.

1.1.1 The birth of Generative Grammar

The origins of TGG lie in the theory of grammar outlined in Bloomfield's book *Language* (1933). It was Leonard Bloomfield (1887-1949) who introduced the now omnipresent tree structures into the theory of grammar. In taking hierarchically ordered constituent analyses, i.e. tree structures, as the main notion in the analysis of linguistic structures, Bloomfield was most probably inspired by Wilhelm Wundt, whom he greatly admired in his younger years. Wundt was, in the spirit of his days, driven by the ideal of a grand synthesis of psychology, linguistics and logic to account for the workings of the human mind, an ideal which he shared in principle with his illustrious American colleague William James. Wundt proposed the notion of tree structure as the basis of both linguistic and psychological structural analysis in various places (1880:53-71; 1900:vol.2,320-355; 1901:71-82). In his *An Introduction to the Study of Language* of 1914, Bloomfield does not mention the Wundtian tree structures explicitly, but one notices the idea on pp. 61 and 110, where Wundt's ideas are clearly present. (Wundt defends the idea, considered less bold in his days than in ours, that binary branching, or hypotaxis, represents a more advanced stage in the development of a language than multiple branching, or parataxis.)

Although Bloomfield gave up Wundt for behaviourism around 1920, the notion of tree structure must have gone on fermenting in his mind. For after the merely fleeting references to it in his (1914), it is the basis of his theory in his *Language* of 1933, where all linguistic structures are analysed exclusively in however, one big question looming large and looking ominous: on what grounds is one to assign a particular tree structure to any given sentence, clause or phrase? Although tree structures seemed fruitful and inspiring at the time and have proved their value a thousand times since, Bloomfield himself was unable to provide a satisfactory answer to this one prior, dominating question. He could not specify any sound and operationally viable criteria for the precise assignment of tree structures to sentences and parts of sentences. His grounds for assigning tree structures or for preferring one structure assignment over another were still purely intuitive.

It was this question of the proper criteria for tree structure assignment which, in the '40s and early '50s, mainly occupied the fairly large circle of Bloomfield's students and followers. Some, headed by Kenneth L. Pike and mostly belonging to an organization of American Protestant missionaries (which earned them the nickname of 'God's truth linguists'), pursued Bloomfield's intuitive approach. They were, as good Christians, antibehaviourists and took tree structures to be a reality in what was, for them, the 'mind'. Not being used to thinking in terms of routinely performed computational mental procedures that are strictly inaccessible to awareness or introspection, they hoped to find the correct answer to the question of the motivation of tree structures by introspectively consulting their own linguistic 'conscience'. The ultimate motivation of a given tree structure assignment was thus some hoped for intuitive consensus or agreement among linguists.

Others sought a principled methodology for the proper assignment of tree structures on more formally based grounds of simplicity of description. They were, in principle and to differing degrees, behaviourists and instrumentalists in the sense that linguistic structural analyses need not, in their view, correspond to any 'mental' or otherwise hidden reality. For them, a tree structure assignment was nothing but a way to control the available data (the 'corpus'). Introspection was considered totally unscientific. Instead, a *simplicity criterion* was proposed: the simplest way to 'control the data' is to be preferred. As these linguists allowed for, and even took obvious delight in, all kinds of clever juggling with symbols and formulas, they were nicknamed the 'Hocus-Pocus linguists' by their opponents. Prominent among this group were Rulon S. Wells, Charles F. Hockett and Zellig S. Harris.

Zellig Harris played a crucial role in the development of what was to become the new paradigm of Generative Grammar, and later of Transformational Generative Grammar. At the end of his *Methods in Structural Linguistics* (1951:366-373) Harris pointed out that those tree structures should be preferred that were generated by the simplest and most economical set of generative rules. From then on Harris and his students, among whom Noam Chomsky, concentrated on the generative *rule system* rather than on *individual tree structures* for the correct answer to the motivation question. It was their aim to formulate a finite set of rules that would specify, by means of algorithmic generation, all and only the well-formed or grammatical sentences of the language L under description in the simplest, i.e. most sentences of the language L under description in the simplest, i.e. most economical possible, way. These rules together form the *grammar* of L. Since the set of well-formed sentences of any natural language is denumerably infinite, the grammar of any natural language must contain some form of recursion, allowing (part of) the rule system to re-apply to its own output. (Early rule systems of the '50s achieved recursion mainly by so-called 'generalized' transformational rules that combined non-recursive outputs of the Formation Rules into complex structures. But in the early '60s transformational linguists became convinced that grammars gain in simplicity and generality if it is stipulated that the only form of recursion allowed in the rule system is S-recursion, i.e. embedding of sentential structures. This insight has since proved to be extremely fruitful in many different ways, even though it is not often mentioned in contemporary grammatical literature.)

1.1.2 The birth of Transformational Generative Grammar

The new orientation towards rule systems rather than individual tree structures gradually led to the insight that it pays off, in terms of economy of description, to generate sentences in stages: first, the Formation Rules generate so-called Deep Structures (DS), which are then transformed into Surface Structures (SS) by Transformational Rules (T-rules). But this was not how it started. In the early '50s, the linguists who worked in this tradition were struck by structural similarities and analogies in different sentence types: active and passive, assertive and interrogative, positive and negative sentences. It was thought that greater economy could be achieved by letting Formation Rules generate only skeletal structures, the so-called kernel sentences, without any indication as to active or passive voice, without negation, without question words or markers, and such like. The T-rules would then introduce the necessary modifications and combinations to get the variety of actual Surface Structures. Nowadays this is thought a little naive. Since Katz & Postal (1964), about which more in a moment, it has been commonly accepted that there is no principled reason for including, for example, tense indicators or quantifiers into the 'skeletal' deep structures and excluding negation or question and voice markers: the Formation Rules generate the lot, and the notion of 'kernel' has disappeared from the theory.

Yet many of the T-rules and concomitant principles that were first discovered in the relatively primitive context of the '50s have since proved useful or even indispensable for a variety of approaches, including Semantic Syntax. Without these rules and principles the practitioners of these theories would be at a loss to get the description of syntactic constructions right. Which suggests that those early developments did have real substance.

As this new insight of the usefulness of T-rules broke through, the need was felt for some wider reflection. The reflection was carried out mainly on two fronts. The first was to do with the philosophical and methodological foundations of linguistic theory. The second was about the formal mathematical properties of rule systems (grammars).

1.1.2.1   Methodological reflections: adequacy and psychological reality

The main propagator of TGG in those years was Noam Chomsky, whose interest extended not only to the rule system or grammar itself but equally to the general methodological and philosophical aspects of language study. Reflecting on the nature of language and the ontological interpretation of grammatical rule systems he adopted, in the early '60s, the distinction, first made by Ferdinand de Saussure (1857-1913) at the beginning of the century, between *langue* and *parole*, or linguistic *competence* and linguistic *performance*. In this perspective, a generative grammar can be seen as a reconstruction-by-hypothesis of a speaker's competence in his native language. Thus conceived a grammar is a realist, not an instrumentalist, theory of certain cognitive functions in the human mind. Consequently, questions of psychological plausibility and psychological reality became relevant and were mooted both by psychologists and by linguists.

Even more importantly, this new notion of a generative rule system as an explicit account of a native speaker's competence to use his language properly also threw light on the hitherto neglected aspect of meaning. Owing to the extraordinary influence of behaviourism in virtually all the human sciences, the study of meaning had been banned from the more formally oriented approaches to language and grammar as being 'mentalistic' and hence 'unscientific'. By 1960, however, it became widely recognized that behaviourism had outlived itself. Its basic assumption had been that all human behaviour could be causally explained by either direct physical causation or else a simple mechanism of stimulus association calling forth substitute responses ('conditioning'). When it became generally accepted that this was woefully inadequate as a theoretical basis for an explanatory theory of human behaviour, behaviourism suffered an almost instantaneous collapse and was replaced by the new paradigm of Cognitive Science, which lives by the much richer assumption that the bulk of human behaviour, to the extent that it is not due to direct physical causation or (in few cases) to conditioning, is to be explained as the result of complex computing processes in the mind, which began to be seen as a gigantic, stunningly efficient computing plant.

The new approach was thus explicitly antibehaviouristic, Chomsky himself being one of the protagonists in bringing about the downfall of behaviourism (Chomsky 1959a). Most of the computing machinery in the mind was now taken to be stowed away in special sealed compartments, inaccessible to any form of awareness or introspection. The introspective method of testing theories or structures, favoured by the God's truth linguists (and by the majority of European structuralists) was thus abandoned entirely. The only role left for 'intuition' was now the native speaker's ability to distinguish intuitively between well-formed and ungrammatical sentences and, more fundamental in the eyes of some, between possible meanings of sentences. (However, the question of how to tap or measure these native speakers' 'intuitions' has still not been answered in anything like a satisfactory way.)

The rejection of introspectivism meant that a different and better method was called for. This was found in the age-old adage known as 'Ockham's razor': *Do not multiply your assumptions beyond the minimum necessary.* In other words, the simplest theory must prevail among those theories that have staked out a reasonable claim in the field. In practice this implies a tiered or multilayered criterion of simplicity. First, there is *descriptive simplicity*: among competing and, as far as has been tested, factually adequate grammars of the same language the simplest and most compact grammar, with the highest yield in grammatical sentences, should be the one preferred. At a higher level we have *crosslinguistic simplicity*: good grammars of different languages should differ minimally from each other. A general theory of grammars can be seen as a theory of the species-specific predisposition of humans for human language, i.e. the much debated innate language faculty. The existence of such an innate language faculty is plausible anyway, on independent and partially a priori grounds. Human language in general represents a very particular choice, to be discovered empirically, from the infinite range of formally possible languages. Philosophically, this development meant a considerable shift from empiricism, the philosophy favoured in the human sciences until the early '60s, in the direction of rationalism, though the issues were not always fully understood or adequately rendered (Chomsky 1966; Aarsleff 1970).

A final and highest level of application of the simplicity criterion may be called *interdisciplinary simplicity*. That is, both general linguistic theory and grammars of specific languages should fall in, as much as possible, with what other disciplines have to offer in the way of adequate and successful descriptions and analyses of structures and processes in the human mind. In particular, if a linguistic theory A fits in better with what one may reasonably regard as good psychology than another linguistic theory B, A will, or should, carry the day. This criterion reflects the ideal of a maximally compact body of scientific knowledge in general.[1]

The philosophical basis of modern TGG is thus firmly cognitivistic. It has taken over, though in a much improved and more sophisticated way, the realism and the antibehaviourism from the God's truth linguists, and the simplicity criterion from the Hocus-Pocus school.

The grammarian's life would probably be easier if the psycholinguists had succeeded in developing independent experimental procedures to test the adequacy or correctness of the grammarian's rule systems. However, the psychological 'underground' character of grammars has, so far, been an obstacle: fully automatic routine procedures are difficult to tap experimentally. Even so, however, the realist position commits the linguist to peaceful trading with the psycholinguists, and vice versa. Relevant hard results of psycho-

---

[1] This ideal differs essentially from that of 'Unified Science' as developed in the '30s. The Unified Science movement was based on a variety of philosophical materialism that sought to reduce all science to physics, sacrificing the autonomy of the separate sciences to an all-embracing Physics (cf. Fodor 1975:9-26).

linguistic experiments have to be respected by the linguist. On the other hand, if the linguist comes forward with a machinery that carries out the job to a high degree of satisfaction, the psycholinguist should accept that as a constraining factor in his own theorizing. For example, if a linguistic theory successfully treats lexical items as semantic predicates with an underlying phonology, with a set of grammatical instructions (rules, labellings, etc.) and with a well-defined argument frame, then this should, in principle, be taken into account in any psycholinguistic theory of grammatical encoding, such as Levelt (1989:235-283). An interesting and fruitful dialogue will then come about between linguists and psycholinguists against the double backdrop of psycholinguistic and linguistic theory formation. This point, however, is not pursued in this study.

1.1.2.2 Formal properties of grammars: the Chomsky Hierarchy

What, then, constitutes the range of formally possible languages just referred to? Here we have a second area where deeper and more precise insights were required. What is the generative power of different algorithmic rule systems or grammars? In a number of publications (e.g. Chomsky & Miller 1958; Chomsky 1959b,c; Chomsky & Schützenberger 1963), a hierarchy of grammars was developed, now commonly called the Chomsky Hierarchy. The hierarchy is based on a few selected mathematical properties of production rules. Four mathematical types of generative grammar are distinguished, according to the restrictions imposed on the rules (and hence on the structures generated) by the mathematical rule properties selected. We shall limit ourselves here to only a brief and informal characterization of the four types. For more details the reader is referred to the publications mentioned, and to Levelt (1974, Vol.I,II).

Type-3 grammars, also called Finite State Grammars or Regular Grammars, are the most restricted type. The rules are all rewrite rules of the type $\alpha \rightarrow \beta$, where α consists of one symbol only (i.e. $|\alpha| = 1$), and β consists of one or two symbols (i.e. $|\beta| = 1$ or 2), and where, if $|\beta| = 2$, either always the righthand or always the lefthand symbol is rewritable by another rule (possibly recursively), and if $|\beta| = 1$, β is either itself a terminal symbol (i.e. a symbol that is not rewritten by any rule) or directly rewritable into a terminal symbol. Regular Grammars are thus always binary branching and always either right-branching or left-branching.

A simple and trivial example of a regular grammar is G_{WN} (grammar of written numbers), which generates all written natural numbers (N stands for 'number', and D for 'digit'):

G_{WN}:   (i) $N \rightarrow D(N)$
         (ii) $D \rightarrow \{0,1,2,3,4,5,6,7,8,9\}$

G_{WN} generates, for example, the number 10748, with the structure as in (1) (if tilted a little clockwise, (1) shows the familiar shape of a tree structure):

(1) N——N——N——N——N
     | | | | |
     D   D   D   D   D
     1   0   7   4   8

Regular grammars assign a uniformly linear structure to all output strings. From the point of view of structural analysis they are, therefore, not very interesting. On the other hand, they have the advantage of simplicity from a mathematical point of view. They were widely used in the late '40s and '50s in the context of Information Theory (Shannon & Weaver 1949; Wilson 1954), where tree structure was considered trivial and the main burden of explanation was placed on transitional probabilities from a given string of length n to any new symbol. The lower the probability of a symbol B occurring given a string α, the higher the 'entropy' of B, and hence the higher the degree of 'meaningfulness' of B. If α has length 1 (i.e. if $|\alpha| = 1$), then the statistical approximation of the probability of the occurrence of B is called a second order approximation. If $|\alpha| = 2$, then the statistical approximation of the probability of the occurrence of B given α is a third order approximation, and so on: if $|\alpha| = n$, the statistical approximation of the probability of the occurrence of B given α is an $n+1$th order approximation. The idea was that, with a sufficiently high value for n, this method would generate enough good sentences of L to count as a viable generative grammar of L. This idea was debunked in Chomsky (1957) and other works.

Type-2 grammars, also called Context-Free (CF) grammars, consist of rewrite rules likewise of the type $\alpha \rightarrow \beta$, where α consists again of one symbol only (i.e. $|\alpha| = 1$), but where β consists of $1 \leq n$ symbols (i.e. $|\beta| \geq 1$) (and where $\emptyset$ is among the symbols available). As with regular grammars, the application of a rule in a CF-grammar automatically and by definition leads to the generation of a bit of tree structure. But the resulting tree structures are no longer monotonically right-branching or monotonically left-branching. Instead, CF-grammars impose no restrictions on the trees generated, as long as no crossing branches are allowed to occur. It is easy to see that regular grammars are a specific subclass of CF-grammars, and hence the languages generated by regular grammars, the regular languages, are a proper subset of the languages generated by CF-grammars, the CF-languages.

Type-1 grammars are even less restricted than type-2 grammars. They are called Context-Sensitive (CS) grammars. Again, they consist of rewrite rules of the type $\alpha \rightarrow \beta$, but now $|\alpha| \geq 1$ and $|\beta| \geq 1$ and $|\alpha| \leq |\beta|$. Chomsky (1959b) adds the further restriction (which makes these grammars properly 'context-sensitive') that α must contain precisely one symbol A which is replaced by a substring α_2 of β ($|\alpha_2| \geq 1$). In the Chomsky version, CS-rules can thus be written in the format $A \rightarrow \beta \ / \ \alpha_1 - \alpha_3$, or: A can be rewritten as β only if A occurs in the context $\alpha_1 - \alpha_3$ (where α_1 and α_3 can be null). It is, again, easily seen that CF-grammars are a proper subset of CS-grammars, and analogously for the languages generated by them.

Bloomfield had, of course, no idea of the mathematical aspects of grammatical theory. But one can say with full justification that his idea of grammar was implicitly that of a CS-grammar but with a limited amount of context-sensitive rules (largely in the morphology). Only rarely does he transgress the boundaries of a CS-grammar, as when he proposes rules for the introduction of single morphemes (later called 'portmanteau' morphemes) replacing two or more underlying morphemes, such as the past tense form *went* which derives from *go* + PAST (Bloomfield 1933:223).

Type-0 grammars, finally, are unrestricted rewrite systems: any rule $\alpha \rightarrow \beta$ is allowed, without any restriction on α or β. CS-grammars are obviously a proper subset of type-0 grammars, and likewise for the languages generated by them. The theoretical problem with type 0 languages that are not also of type 1 is that they risk not being parsable (decidable) by a finite apparatus, which makes them less attractive as models for human languages. In Levelt's words (1974,Vol.II:39) 'the step towards type-0 models for natural languages must not be taken lightly.' Yet this step was taken in the theory of TGG.

Transformational grammars (T-grammars) are 'mixed' in that they consist of a base consisting standardly of CF Formation Rules, and a set of transformation rules or T-rules. The T-rules take as input one or more tree structures (generated by the base or already transformed by some T-rule) and deliver one output tree. In most current models of T-grammar (but not, for example, in Tree-Adjoining Grammar (Joshi et al. 1975)), each T-rule takes one input structure and delivers one output structure. The structures generated by the base are called Deep Structures (DS). Those resulting from the T-rules are called Surface Structures (SS). T-grammars, in particular those of the type presented in Chomsky (1965), exceed the limits imposed by CS-grammars, and are therefore strictly speaking of type 0.

The theoretical danger was not immediately seen. Peters & Ritchie (1973) pointed out that the existing transformational literature, including Chomsky's *Aspects* of 1965, suffered from a dangerous lack of constraints on what is and what is not allowable as a transformational operation. Mathematically, the notion of transformation is so wide and unconstrained as to be of little empirical value if applied without checks. Some kind of charter or constitution was needed constraining the construction of grammars beyond the point already reached. Only then can one reasonably speak of an empirically justifiable theory of the innate human language faculty. Moreover, the addition of further universal constraints on grammars may well bring natural languages back into the class of parsable (decidable) languages. The criterion of crosslinguistic simplicity thus became directly relevant to the actual practice of analysing and describing linguistic constructions.

It became clear that formal linguistic analyses and descriptions should be constrained by a universal 'charter', whose interest and importance did not primarily lie in its mathematical properties, but rather in the *empirical* restrictions imposed. In order to formulate such universal restrictions on rules and grammars one has to dig into the heavy clay of natural language and see what treasures are hidden there. Formal a prioris are less helpful since language always turns out to be different from what one expects it to be, and more complex as well. Knowledge of formal systems is useful to determine one's position in mathematical space. But inductive delving into the ecological reality of language is necessary if one wants to find out about it.

1.1.3 The birth of the transformational Cycle

One fruitful universal constraint discovered just before 1970 was the insight that the T-rules should be divided into two classes, the *cyclic* and the *postcyclic* rules. The cyclic rules are to be applied cyclically through the tree, starting with the most deeply embedded S and climbing up through successive Ss until the top-S has been dealt with. This system of S-cycles provided a solution to frequent situations where, given two T-rules T_1 and T_2, T_1 must precede T_2 in some constructions whereas the inverse order is required for others. When it was found that the required order of application corresponded regularly with depth of S-embedding the notion of the cycle was born (see McCawley (1970) for a clear exposé).

By 1970 the syntax of a natural language L was thus considered to consist of two main components, the *Formation Rules* generating DSs and the *Transformational Component* consisting of T-rules generating SSs. The Transformational Component was divided into the *Cycle* and the *Postcycle*. The Cycle generates Shallow Structures (ShS); these are input to the Postcycle which generates SSs. All this is, of course, generally known. Even so, however, it is useful to point out those elements in the early history of TGG that have proved to be of particular value in the development of Semantic Syntax. As will become clear in the following pages, Semantic Syntax has maintained these distinctions and the principles underlying them.

1.1.4 The birth of Generative Semantics

In 1964 the philosopher J.J. Katz argued that 'mentalism' should be restored in linguistics, in the sense that a grammar should be conceived of as a piece of software for the brain's hardware. In 1963, he and J.A. Fodor published an article in *Language* proposing that a reconstruction-by-hypothesis of a native speaker's linguistic competence should encompass not only his ability to distinguish well-formed sentences from ungrammatical strings, but also his ability to comprehend the *meanings* of the sentences concerned. This view is, of course, so obviously correct that one wonders how anyone could have thought of a theory of linguistic competence without immediately considering facts of meaning. On the other hand, however, it was also embarrassing given the total lack of anything approaching a semantic theory in linguistics. Behaviourism had created a climate in which anything to do with meaning had of necessity to remain foggy and unanalysed. Whereas TGG had provided a reasonably fruitful way of tackling questions of syntax, it was still totally in the dark about how to approach semantic phenomena in an empirically satisfactory way. For linguists, meaning was still cloudy stuff. Knowledge of logic or model-theory was virtually unheard of in linguistic circles.

It was in this semantically barren context that Katz and Fodor proposed, in 1963, that a *Semantic Component* should be added to the already existing Syntactic Component. The Semantic Component should consist of 'Projection Rules' taking syntactic structures as input and delivering something called 'Semantic Representations' or SR (our 'Semantic Analysis' or SA). More precisely, the proposal was that for each sentence S, its DS and its SS should both be input to Projection Rules, which would then deliver the SR of S. The total 'integrated' system should thus provide for each S a pair <SS,SR> of its Surface Structure and its Semantic Representation. Figure 1 shows the structure of a linguistic description à la Katz & Fodor (1963).

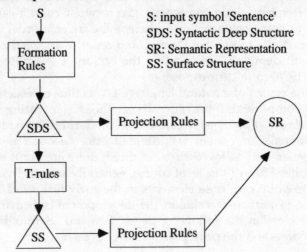

S: input symbol 'Sentence'
SDS: Syntactic Deep Structure
SR: Semantic Representation
SS: Surface Structure

Figure 1   Integrated linguistic description (Katz & Fodor 1963)

Katz & Fodor (1963) was followed in 1964 by Katz & Postal's *An Integrated Theory of Linguistic Descriptions*. In this book it is argued that syntactic descriptions gain significantly in simplicity and generality if it is postulated that all semantic information of a sentence S is already contained in its DS, so that the T-rules merely have a formal effect, neither adding nor taking away semantic information. The only semantic effect of T-rules is now that they may bring about ambiguities. This constraint of *semantic invariance of T-rules*, Katz and Postal argued, pays off in the syntax as it makes for better and wider generalizations to be captured by the T-rules. Figure 2 gives a schematic representation of this concept of 'integrated linguistic description'.

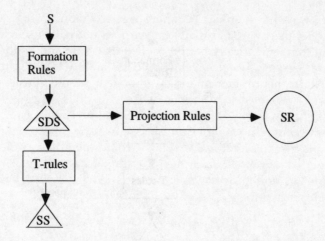

Figure 2 *Integrated linguistic description (Katz & Postal 1964)*

This courageous publication was widely acclaimed, and quickly accepted as presenting the correct approach. Yet there still were serious gaps. The most important gap consisted in the fact that the notion of Semantic Representation was virtually undefined. The nature, structure and function of SRs were still largely opaque, despite unconvincing efforts by Katz, Fodor and Postal to provide clarity. Not until the late '60s did McCawley show, in various articles (put together in McCawley 1973), that the only rational concept of SR is one in which SRs are themselves, again, linguistic structures, but formulated in some formal, presumably logical, language that makes them particularly fit for further semantic interpretation, whatever that might be. The same idea was developed independently in Seuren (1969:219-224).

This insight had a dramatic effect on linguistic theory building. It began with the realization that if SRs are syntactic structures and if Deep Structures carry all semantic information, then there is no reason to distinguish the two. A number of young linguists decided, therefore, about 1967, that the whole semantic component as proposed in Katz & Postal (1964) could be dispensed with: Deep Structures *are* Semantic Representations and no rules are required to link the two. A grammar of a language L is thus nothing but a set of Formation Rules generating the presumably near-universal DS/SR-structures, and a set of T-rules converting these into Surface Structures. This theory of grammar was called 'Generative Semantics', a somewhat unfortunate misnomer, as was said in the Preface, since it is not a semantic but a syntactic theory. The term 'Semantic Syntax' is therefore to be preferred (Seuren 1972a). The overall structure of this theory is shown in fig.3.

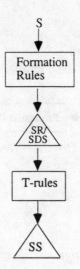

Figure 3   *Linguistic description according to Generative Semantics*

Around 1970 the linguistic world somehow felt as if it had come home from years of straying. Generative Semantics reconciled TGG with the ancient tradition, originating with Plato, according to which (surface structures of) sentences are nothing but the, often misleading, garments of thought. The real thing behind sentences is their meaning, represented by linguistic structures that are at the same time input to a well-defined system of transformational rules yielding precisely all and only the well-formed sentences of the language in question. Moreover, since the postulated DS/SR-structures were, and are, thought to be cast in terms of some workable variety of modern Predicate Calculus, linguistic theory and modern logic could and should be integrated as parts of one great theory of linguistic communication.

This was a wholesome experience for those concerned, as linguistics and logic had been sadly estranged from each other since logic had gone mathematical and modern Predicate Calculus had been introduced in the early 1900s. Generative Semantics contained the promise of a renewed and well-motivated rapprochement between linguistics and logic. This, together with the newly forged links with the world of psychology, raised hopes of a belated realization of the great synthesis of logic, linguistics and psychology envisaged by early psychologists and philosophers such as Wilhelm Wundt and William James. The publication, in 1971, of Steinberg & Jakobovits' Reader *Semantics. An Interdisciplinary Reader in Philosophy, Linguistics and Psychology*, bears witness to the spirit of those days.

1.1.5 Autonomous Syntax and X-bar theory

Unfortunately, however, it turned out that this linguistic spring had come too early. It was quickly superseded by a grim isolationist winter. Within TGG there was a faction of opponents to Generative Semantics, known as *Autono-*

mous Syntax, headed by Noam Chomsky. He made expert use of the many vulnerable spots of Generative Semantics and reverted to a strictly structuralist non-semantic ('autonomous') model of syntactic description. Generative Semantics was, of course, highly vulnerable. Its practitioners had little or no knowledge of logic and model-theoretic semantics. They were as unfamiliar with general philosophical and psychological notions of meaning as any other linguist of those days. They were also optimistic and courageous, even a little heady with the newly discovered semantic space.[2] As a result, the descriptions and analyses produced by them occasionally took liberties with the rules of sober discipline and method.[3] This undeniable fact was used by Chomsky and others to debunk the whole Generative Semantics approach, instead of only its more baroque and less controlled manifestations. The critique was thus as uncontrolled as the object criticized.

It is true, as has been pointed out, that TGG, in its actual practice, was insufficiently constrained. This fact was brought home forcefully by Peters & Ritchie (1973), whose criticism applied to the bulk of the transformational literature before 1970, including the many analyses preceding the split-up of TGG into Generative Semantics and Autonomous Syntax. Autonomists now censured Generative Semanticists for their undisciplined rule writing, declaring the whole edifice of Generative Semantics unsound and worthless. Meanwhile, however, autonomists implicitly admitted the beam in their own eye by starting a wild scramble for universal constraints on grammars. Since 1970 these have appeared in rapid succession while the concomitant theories were presented under a variety of names, the latest ones being 'Government and Binding', 'Principles and Parameters', and 'Minimalism'.

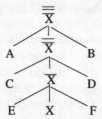

Figure 4   General structure of a categorial expansion in X-bar theory

Despite the never ending succession of modifications required as new data, often from newly explored languages, came to light, there have been a few constant factors in the development of Autonomous Syntax since 1970. Probably

[2] The clearest expression of this giddiness is found in the jocular *Fragestellung* prefacing Ross's unpublished but immensely popular (1967) *Constraints on Variables in Syntax*, published as *Infinite Syntax!* in 1986.

[3] By far the most prominent representative of Generative Semantics was James McCawley, whose syntactic analyses were invariably sustained by a powerful intuition coupled with profound insights. Even he, however, occasionally fell victim to the flower-power attitude that prevailed more than it should have. By appealing too easily to 'brute force' whenever a proposed rule system would show unruly behaviour, he made himself too easy a victim of all too facile criticisms.

the most fundamental of these is the adherence to X-bar theory, developed mainly by Jackendoff in his study on X-bar Syntax, published in 1977 but in circulation long before that. Roughly, this theory amounts to the hypothesis that all syntactic structures are categorial expansions under one of the main category symbols, largely V(erb), N(oun), A(djective), P(reposition) or Infl(ection). Full sentences are V-expansions, NPs are N-expansions, PPs are P-expansions, and AUX is an Infl-expansion. Each expansion is of the general form presented in fig.4. The left and right branches represent modifiers and/or complements, which may be filled, possibly again by a categorial expansion, or may remain empty.

Thus conceived, an S (i.e. V-expansion) acquires a large number of hierarchically ordered structural positions. According to Autonomous Syntax, a T-rule can only move an element upward in the tree from bottom right to top left, whereby the element moved must find an empty side branch to sit on. When moved it leaves a trace in its original position. This central idea was refined in a number of different ways, and other subtheories were added.

X-bar theory is a working hypothesis with a strong intellectual appeal, due to its generality and simplicity. If linguistic structures could indeed all be captured in this universal mould such a fact would give rise to far-reaching questions about the organization of the human mind and its processes. Unfortunately, however, it seems too aprioristic. Its empirical success has so far been less than convincing, and the extent of its real success may well be attributable to the proliferation of structural positions it allows for. In any case, in Semantic Syntax it has so far not seemed useful to make use of X-bar theory in any of its current varieties. In fact, it violates the principle of categorial expansion, since the rules allow for a non-branching NP-node directly and uniquely dominating an S-node, as shown in 3.8.1 (cf. Seuren 1989). Needless to say, Semantic Syntax differs fundamentally from the developments in Autonomous Syntax in every conceivable way. It has, at least in its present state, no X-bar theory and no traces and, in general, none of the constraints now current in MIT-based syntactic theory. Instead it has its own, radically different, charter for the writing of grammars (see also 1.1.7).

1.1.6 The demise of Generative Semantics?

As the adherents of Autonomous Syntax regrouped around Chomsky and set out in hot pursuit of universal constraints based on X-bar theory (and lately the minimalist theory), the Generative Semanticists, on the whole, felt cowed by the scorching criticisms poured upon them by the autonomists. The violence of the rhetoric was such that participants and bystanders failed to notice that no other argument was brought to bear than the lack of universal constraints in many of the then current Generative Semantics analyses. It was forgotten that the same criticism applied to Autonomous Syntax, and that the criticism could mean nothing more than that steps should be taken to avoid all too baroque rules or rule systems, without, for the moment, any fatal implications for the sinning theories themselves. There thus arose a spurious consensus[4] to the effect that Generative Semantics was fundamentally misguided and in any case dead.

From a sociological point of view it certainly seemed dead. Generative Semantics did not regroup and the movement disappeared from the scene of theoretical linguistics. Most of its leading practitioners began to make themselves familiar with semantics and logic, eschewing the noisy political arena. Some stayed with grammar, others concentrated on other aspects of language. There was thus no longer a Generative Semantics movement, only individuals carrying on their own research. The ideas, however, did not die. On the contrary, they keep coming back in various ways and places. For example, in computational linguistics (which seems to be upstaging standard theoretical linguistics), and in particular in machine or machine-aided translation, practical needs lead back to precisely those concepts that were central in Generative Semantics. These practical needs thus support the theoretical insights, as they show empirical superiority. (It is shown in 6.6 and 7.5 that some of the well-known problems in machine translation are naturally solved in terms of Semantic Syntax.) Contemporary forms of Autonomous Syntax appear less interesting to these scientists as the structural frames provided by X-bar and/or the minimalist theory do not seem to fulfil any useful function in either the formal reconstruction of the human ability to communicate by means of linguistic signs or any practical applications.

That Generative Semantics was ousted without any serious academic argument and only on the basis of rhetoric and sociological manipulation has recently been confirmed by Huck and Goldsmith, who write in their Preface (1995:ix):

> But while the Generative Semanticists unquestionably faced theoretical obstacles of various sorts, there are also good reasons to believe that the demise of their program was not a consequence of theoretical weakness. Indeed we will argue in what follows that it is not possible to find, internal to the idea of Generative Semantics as it was evidently originally understood by Lakoff, McCawley, Postal and Ross, adequate grounds to explain its widespread abandonment in the 1970s. We will be concerned to evaluate the linguistic evidence on its own terms, paying particular attention to the theoretical assumptions that underlay the various critiques, and will conclude that one must turn to external explanations to account adequately for what transpired.

It is fair to say that the issue should be decided by the measure of descriptive and crosslinguistic empirical success and of interdisciplinary integration of the approaches involved. It is also fair to say that the developments that have emanated from MIT over the past twenty years have not excelled in either empirical success or interdisciplinary integration. The embarrassing persisting presence of large contingents of counterexamples made it necessary to put up defences without continuously revising the principles and the rule system. These defences, however, had to be methodologically unsound since counter-

---

[4] This consensus was fuelled by Newmeyer's (1980) partisan account of the career of Generative Semantics, which, as was convincingly argued by McCawley (1980), bears little resemblance to the facts of history and seems based on odd notions of what constitutes sound scientific methodology.

evidence is and remains counterevidence as long as the rule system has not been repaired. And if repairs are nothing but patches they inexorably weaken the system. An appeal to incorrect observation, performance errors, substandard or dialectal usage, or a distinction between 'core' and 'periphery' grammar (a distinction that seems to vary with the emergence of counterevidence), or ruling counterevidence out of court unless accompanied by an alternative theory are, though well-known, methodologically aberrant strategies for steering clear of counterevidence. They reveal an inherent weakness with regard to the most elementary requirement of any scientific theory, compliance with all the relevant known facts.

The empirical claims made by Semantic Syntax are substantial and at least as well supported by all relevant known facts as those put forward by contemporary autonomists. We refrain here from a detailed comparative evaluation of these two approaches, mainly because this book is meant as an introduction to Semantic Syntax, not as an exercise in comparing grammatical theories. Moreover, if Semantic Syntax is to be set off against the latest developments at MIT, other theories of grammar are equally entitled to a careful and detailed discussion, and this would require a volume in its own right. So what we do here is present a system of grammatical analysis, and those users of this book who feel so inclined will then be able to evaluate the theory presented here against its competitors, such as Lexical Functional Grammar, Tree Adjoining Grammar, Head-driven Phrase Structure Grammar, Categorial Grammar, Dependency Grammar, or whatever serious theory is on the market. It will then become clear how Semantic Syntax compares with other existing theories of grammar, whether of linguistic or formal semantic origin, as regards coverage of facts, simplicity and generality.

1.1.7 Methodological differences with post-1970 Chomsky

As has been said, those familiar with the methodological views propagated by Chomsky and his followers since about 1970 will notice substantial differences between those views and the methodology advocated here. Our methodology is far more inductive and assigns paramount importance to factually accurate analyses and descriptions. The formulation of general principles is considered a high and important, perhaps the most important, theoretical goal. But it can be attained only through a thorough knowledge of and familiarity with linguistic facts combined with an ability to handle formalisms competently and in a creative and flexible way.

It has now become clearly visible, and is also widely recognized, that the developments that have been taking place at MIT in this respect over the past twenty-five years have placed undue emphasis on formal unification of rules and principles at the expense of an adequate coverage of the facts. This raises serious questions as to the empirical and theoretical value of these developments. One would not be far off the mark if one maintained that virtually all the attempts at universalization and unification undertaken in

Chomskyan circles since about 1970 have proved speculative and without empirical substance.

Though it looks as if we are beginning to understand the transformational processes linking SAs with surface structures in a variety of languages, we still know relatively little about the universal properties of the trees and rules involved. Especially in the Postcycle, many of the rules formulated to describe and analyse syntactic structures in a given language are carefully tailored to fit the facts and thus may appear to some degree ad hoc. Yet it often happens that identical, or very similar, rules, constraints and principles are needed for the description of other languages, which makes us feel that perhaps what seemed ad hoc at first sight may turn out not to be so after all.

Our knowledge of the broader underlying abstract and formal regularities is still in a primitive stage. If more were known in this respect, the rules, first found and formulated inductively, could probably be reformulated largely in terms of general abstract notions and some rules might even prove unnecessary as they would be seen to follow automatically from general principles. When we design a grammar we thus try to generalize over grammatical rules in what is in principle the same way we try to generalize over facts of language. In terms of section 1.1.2.1, the practical need is felt to proceed from descriptive to crosslinguistic simplicity. The present book is as much an attempt at a factually correct and compact description of languages as an attempt at unearthing such general formal principles and notions as will help to achieve maximal simplicity for grammars.

The method followed bears all the bootstrapping characteristics of scientific induction. After thorough inspection of large sets of data in a few languages, tentative descriptions and analyses were developed. These became more and more daring as they proved successsful. It was then felt that the grammars thus devised were cutting the patterns of the languages concerned 'at the seams'. Thus it became time to try and make the formalism used more precise and more unified. As this book will make clear, we are, at the moment, in the middle of that process. But it will be noted that unification is never attempted at the expense of an adequate coverage of the data.

1.2 Surface semantics and compositionality

Although it is the syntactic aspects that are mainly emphasized in this book, a few words must be said about the semantic aspects as well. Despite the profound differences between MIT-based linguistics and Semantic Syntax, they have in common the distinction between semantic analyses ('Logical Form' in MIT terminology) and surface structures, and the idea that any empirically viable semantics must be grafted onto the semantic form of sentences. The distinction between semantic structures and surface sentences, central in these theories, is defended on empirical grounds of coverage of facts, simplicity and generality. Semantic Syntax defends this distinction not only from a semantic point of view, as Autonomous Syntax does, but also because it maintains, with even probable, that both SAs and SSs are subject to 'autonomous' structural constraints). It is, in other words, a central element in the theory of Semantic Syntax as well as in other forms of TGG that the semantics of a language takes as input not the surface structures but the semantic analyses corresponding to the sentences of the language in question. TGG thus rejects surface semantics.

This rejection is, however, not universally accepted. A whole crop of new approaches to syntax has recently sprung up in the wake of the application of logical model-theory to linguistic structures. The application of semantic methods developed in logic to the facts of natural language was due mainly to the American logician Richard Montague, who developed his ideas in this respect in the '60s. It was Montague who proposed that a semantic theory of natural language should be grafted directly onto the surface structures of sentences. Montague proposed to regard the surface structures of English as a 'formal language', i.e. a language with a model-theoretic interpretation of the kind developed in modern logic, in the tradition of Tarski and Carnap (Montague 1970, 1973). The typical procedure was to delimit a (rather trivial) 'fragment' of the language (English) which would not pose too many problems. Initially, the question of how to extrapolate from the 'fragment' to the language as a whole was not seriously considered. Later, however, much greater sophistication was achieved.

This development is known as 'Formal Semantics', but despite its name it is directly relevant to the theory of grammar or syntax. In fact, a variety of syntactic theories have recently been developed in the wake of Formal Semantics. Due to the considerable influence of Formal Semantics and of those syntactic theories that take their cue from it, the rejection of surface semantics defended by transformational grammarians (who have never earned a good reputation in semantic matters) has been decidedly out of favour with anyone in the business of semantically motivated grammatical theory. It is, therefore, an uphill task to argue against surface semantics.

1.2.1 The notion of compositionality

In order to clarify these points it is necessary first to consider the notion of compositionality. This notion is central in semantic theory, and it is so for an obvious and straightforward reason. But let us see first what is meant by this term. The original notion of compositionality, which is also the one we adopt here, is both conservative and minimal:[5]

---

[5] The principle of compositionality originates with Frege, who formulated it for *Bedeutung* (1906:302) in a context where this term can be understood as either 'extension' or 'meaning': '<Definitions> require knowledge of certain primitive elements and their signs. Using these, the definition puts together a group of signs according to certain rules, in such a way that the *Bedeutung* of this group is determined by the *Bedeutungen* of the signs used'. (This would falsify Janssen's claim (1993) that Frege himself never formulated the principle.)

(2) A compound expression is semantically compositional just in case its meaning is a function of the meanings of each constituent part and from the position of these parts in the structure at hand.

That is, the structure is meant to function as a computational frame or 'abacus', and the independently given meanings of the ultimate constituents are fed into it. The final value resulting at the top of the tree structure should specify the meaning of the structure as a whole. How the structure has come about is not at issue. It may have rained on us from heaven. In natural language, the structures one encounters are the tree structures that have been central to the discussion from the beginning. This is just as well, because a compositional calculus has a natural preference for tree structures. The crucial point is that tree structures branch out from the single top node ('root') to the terminal elements ('leaves'), via the 'branches'. The calculus can thus assign primitive semantic values to the leaves. One of the leaves under a common dominating node is given a function as its semantic value, so that it can take the values of the other leaves as input and deliver the output to the common dominating node. This output can then again serve as input to a brother node whose semantic value is a function, and the resulting value can again be passed on to the node above, and so on until the central top node is reached. Its final value is the semantic value of the whole structure.

Cyclic compositional treatment is common in arithmetic, with either *constituency trees* or *dependency trees*. The formula $(7 \times 8) + 2$ can be represented as a constituency tree, as in (3), or as a dependency tree, as in (4):

Both structures are compositional, since the value of the whole formula can be computed from the values of their constituents and the positions they occupy. The symbols × (multiplication) and + (addition) represent functions from pairs of numbers to numbers. In (3) the double numerical input required for the function ×, <7,8>, results in the value, 56. This is assigned as value to N_1. Now we have the required double input for the function +, viz. <56,2>, which yields 58. In the dependency tree (4), the function signs dominate the input signs. Dependency trees are standardly used in mathematics. In linguistics, there is some debate as to the empirical superiority of the two kinds of tree, since they differ in the actual structures they assign and in the structures they can assign. The position taken here is that constituency trees, as introduced by Wundt and developed by Bloomfield and others, are better suited to the needs of both syntactic and semantic theory than dependency trees. For grammar, this preference is based on experience, but above all on the fact that dependency trees are totally unsuitable for the expression of the grammatical regularities we wish to capture in the theory. The transformational apparatus which is central to Semantic Syntax requires constituency trees, not dependency trees. This is said, of course, with all due respect for those linguists who take a different view. At the end of the day, it will no doubt be clear which was the better choice.

Either way, compositional calculi are necessary if an infinite number of different finite structures are to be given a value by means of a finite set of calculus rules. This is so not only for the set of natural numbers, which is infinite though each of its members is of finite length and has a numerical value, but also for natural languages: a language can be regarded as an infinite set of finite strings, each with a semantic value. The crucial role of the notion of compositionality in a semantic theory is now easy to see. Some notion of compositionality is necessary, though not sufficient,[6] if one wants to explain how speakers can comprehend an unlimited, mathematically speaking infinite, set of different sentences while having only a finite amount of machinery at their disposal.

But at the same time, if one wants to approach this problem impartially, one had better work with a minimal notion of compositionality and refrain from building in alien elements which require justification on independent grounds. Yet this seems to have happened in Partee et al. (1990). On p.318 the authors define the meaning of a compound expression as 'a function of the meanings of its parts *and of the syntactic rules by which they are combined'*. One may, of course, as the authors of the book in question do, impose on syntax the semantically based constraint known as 'rule-to-rule semantics', which gives each syntactic rule a semantic counterpart. This will then disallow all semantically neutral transformational rules (except those that do not result in any structural change), and will thus ban our theory of Semantic Syntax, and a few other competitors, from the start. But then it should be made clear that this constraint is unconnected with the a priori necessity of a compositional semantic calculus. Clearly, the theory of syntax favoured in Partee et al. (1990) is very different from, for example, the theory proposed here. But it cannot be thought superior simply because it incorporates a non-necessary element into the mathematically necessary notion of compositionality. Partee et al. (1990) does not present the mathematically necessary minimal notion. It incorporates that notion but adds a non-necessary element to motivate one out of a multitude of possible theories of syntax. As the notion of compositionality has nothing to do with specific empirical constraints on the rules of syntax, there seems to be no good reason for incorporating the latter into a definition of the former. One is understandably reluctant to be ruled out on the strength of a mere definition.

---

[6] Full and integrated comprehension of uttered sentences is, as is well known, heavily underdetermined by the semantic information carried by the sentences in virtue of their systematic linguistic properties. Contextual and background knowledge are often called upon to provide the additional information required for full comprehension. This, however, is an aspect we shall not go into here.

1.2.2 No surface semantics

Any attempt at grafting a calculus of meaning specifications directly onto surface structures makes for serious but unnecessary, and therefore unwanted, complications. In fact, Montague-style theories, where this strategy of *surface semantics* is followed, often feel the need to cut surface structures down to a semantically manageable size, undoing, for example, what is usually called AUX-INVERSION or *do*-INSERTION in English interrogative or negative sentences, or eliminating semantically irrelevant copies of the negation from the structure at hand. Such procedures are in fact transformational, and any theory that allows for them gives way to the Deep Structure semantics as it is defended by transformational grammarians.

The problems with surface semantics are general and profound. What to do, for example, with phenomenon of copying ('spread')? NEGATION COPYING in one form or another is common in the languages of the world. If interpreted literally, the Cockney sentence *'E ain't never been no good to no woman, not never* would mean 'he has at some time been some good to some woman', which is clearly not what this sentence means. Or take the following sentence of the West African Kwa language Akan (Akuapem dialect): *Me-de aburow mi-gu msu-m* (Schachter (1974:258)). In a word-by-word translation this sentence says 'I poured the corn *I* go into the water', but its actual meaning is 'I poured the corn into the water', based on an underlying grammatical structure (with the serial verb 'go') 'I poured the corn *it* go into the water'. The grammatical machinery is perfectly clear: the original semantic subject *it*, resuming the object *the corn* of the Main Verb *pour*, has been deleted (under standard conditions) and the original subject *I* of the higher verb has been copied for the subordinate verb. This is a case of syntactic Subject Copying, clearly a rule without any semantic import, but syntactically necessary for a proper description of this dialect of Akan. Since observations like these are easily multiplied for any language (cf. Seuren 1985:61-110 for a long list of cases), it seems sound strategy to reject direct surface semantics and to revert to the traditional view that meanings tend to hide behind semantically misleading surface structures.

This amounts to saying that surface structures are, as a matter of principle, not compositional. Surface structures are unfit for semantic treatment other than via structural, non-semantic reduction to their Semantic Analyses. Any attempt at grafting a semantic calculus directly onto surface structures will either fail or be unduly complex.

Nowadays, the grammatical theories that have developed out of the Montague tradition have achieved greater sophistication than pristine Montague grammar. They are now serious candidates from the point of view of linguistic complexity and empirical adequacy, which makes them interesting competitors, whose proponents should not feel the need to rely on spurious a priori claims derived from impure notions of compositionality. Instead, let empirical success be the decisive factor, measured against the criteria of descriptive, crosslinguistic and interdisciplinary simplicity.

1.2.3 The overall architecture of the theory

Semantic Analyses are formulated in a logical language. They are so called because they are taken to be maximally transparent and, above all, (largely) compositional. They provide the most regular input to a calculus specifying their meanings. Yet, all that has been said about semantics in the preceding sections still does not answer the question of what kind of compositional calculus is envisaged for the specification of sentence meanings. In Montague Formal Semantics, which is a direct application of logical model-theory, the view is that the tree structure of a sentence (whether 'surface' or 'deep' is immaterial at this point) is the abacus with which to compute the truth-value of a sentence S given a 'world' W and an interpretation of the language L to which S belongs. The output of such a computation is thus a truth-value. By generalizing over the infinite set of all possible worlds, the output at the top of the tree (the S-node) becomes a specification of the truth-value of S for each possible world, i.e. a function from possible worlds to truth-values. This can be looked upon as a specification of the truth-conditions of S, specifying what has to be the case for S to be true in any world. This brand of semantics takes the shortest possible route between language and any 'world' with respect to which the language is to be interpreted. It does not take into account the mediating role of cognition in the comprehension of sentences.

In our view, ignoring cognition condemns semantics to a non-empirical enterprise. The semantic analysis and description of sentences is better served with a cognitive detour. Since sentences are not interpreted in isolation but, clearly, in context, an SA is considered to be mapped first onto a cognitive 'discourse domain', a working memory which has open access to, and merges with, available contextual and background knowledge (Seuren 1985). Each newly uttered sentence in the discourse is added ('incremented') to the discourse domain. It is only from discourse domain structures that the truth-conditional leap is made to any 'world', whether real or imagined.

The overall architecture of the theory can thus be represented as in fig.5 (*KB* stands for 'knowledge base', *D* for 'discourse domain', *I* for 'incrementation procedure', *E* for 'expression procedure', *G* for 'grammar', and *P* for 'parser'). Note that *I* and *E*, and *P* and *G* overlap but are not identical.

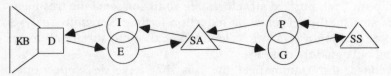

Figure 5   *Overall architecture of the theory*

The part which primarily concerns us is the mapping from SA via G to SS:

Figure 6   *The generative part of Semantic Syntax*

1.3 Some general properties of the rule system

Semantic Syntax has pursued the course that was set out by McCawley in the late '60s and early '70s. The general idea is that theoretical decisions and hypotheses that have proved their value in syntax so far should be applied as much as possible to less visible, more abstract parts of the syntax, the main motivation being Ockham's razor, the principle of maximal empirical profit for minimal theoretical expenditure. This strategy of applying the rules and constraints of more directly accessible syntax to the more abstract parts we call the *Streamline Principle*. It is apparent, for example, in the assignment of well-known cyclic rules not only to surface verbs but to all SA-predicates, which now include not only all lexical content words but also all logical operators. The result is a uniform and streamlined set of syntactic rules relating logical structures to Surface Structures.

1.3.1 The architecture of G

The rule systems in Semantic Syntax are essentially *generative*. First, Semantic Analyses (SA) of sentences are constructed according to the context-free Formation Rules, defining their wellformedness conditions. A transformational system maps these onto the corresponding Surface Structures (SS). No *parsing* procedure has been developed yet, though a start has been made. The parsing procedure will presuppose the generative system but follow its own principles. It will use certain formal features of surface sentences, such as tense markings and categorial word labels, to set up chunks of SA on the basis of information from the Lexicon and the generative rules. A generative re-run of the reconstructed SA will test the parsing result if necessary.

The Semantic Syntax rule system is divided into three main components:

(a) (context-free) Formation Rules generating Semantic Analyses (SA);
(b) the Cycle, generating Shallow Structures (ShS) from SAs;
(c) the Postcycle, generating Surface Structures (SS) from ShSs.

There are, moreover, transition processes. Thus, it would seem that some *precyclic tree-editing* will be needed between (a) and (b) (see note 4 to chapter 3). Then, it has proved necessary, for the languages that have been investigated, to formulate a few *corollaries* between the Cycle and the Postcycle. These are to do with categorial relabellings, the default insertion of particles or complementizers, the delimitation of the AUX-area in V-clusters and similar operations. Since these can be called 'transformational' only in a weak sense they have not been included among the postcyclic transformations.

The surface structures are input to the morphology and phonology, left out of account almost entirely in this book. The only claim regarding morphology and phonology implicit in the architecture as given is that the rules in these two components receive their input from the syntax, without any feedback or tracking mechanisms. Nothing is implied about the relationship or possible interaction between morphological and phonological rules.

The hierarchical system of the three components is presented in fig.7.

$$1. \text{ Formation rules } \rightarrow \text{ SA (Semantic Analysis)}$$
$$\downarrow$$

SYNTAX $$3. \text{ Cycle } \rightarrow \text{ ShS (Shallow Structure)}$$
$$\downarrow$$
$$4. \text{ Postcycle } \rightarrow \text{ SS}$$

$$\downarrow$$
MORPHOLOGY $\rightarrow$ PHONOLOGY

Figure 7   *Overall structure of Semantic Syntax*

1.3.2 The General Format: VSO or SOV

The (context-free rewrite) Formation Rules, as well as the argument structures specified for predicates in the lexicon are subject to a *General Format* constraint, based on McCawley's (1970) hypothesis that all languages of the world have an underlying structure of either Verb-Subject-Object (VSO) or Subject-Object-Verb (SOV). McCawley showed that the machinery of the cyclic T-rules is considerably simplified and streamlined under this hypothesis — a finding that has since been confirmed abundantly. The *general format constraint* specifies that every S-structure consists of a predicate (V) accompanied by its argument terms, each with its specific *argument function*. In 'open syntax' (as distinct from the internal syntactic analysis of semantically complex lexical predicates), there are between zero and three argument terms and thus argument functions. If there is none, some languages require a dummy subject (e.g. English 'it'). If there is one, it is the subject. If there are two, the first is the subject and the second is normally the direct object. If there are three, the first is the subject, the second is normally the indirect object, and the third is normally the direct object, as in *give (Ann, Joe, the book)*. We say 'normally' because lexical semantic properties of the predicate in question may result in different argument functions. For example, in many languages the equivalents of the two-term verbs *help* or *follow* treat the second argument term as an indirect object, not, as in English, as a direct object (see also the following section, 1.3.3). In all cases, the subject and direct object terms can be either NP or S (even an NP over a fully tensed S). The middle (normally indirect object) term can only be NP.

In some languages, the 'deep' VSO-languages, V precedes the argument terms, in others, the 'deep' SOV-languages, the terms precede V. Some languages, notably German, and to a lesser extent Dutch, though probably best analysed as deep VSO, have certain features that are typical of deep SOV-languages. Such features are considered to be archaic remnants of an older deep SOV-stage of the languages concerned. No language has SAs of the form SVO (or NP-VP). The NP-VP-structure required in the SSs of many languages (e.g. the languages of Europe) results automatically from the cyclic treatment of the tenses, as will be shown.

The General *SA-Format* for the sentences of deep VSO-languages is specified by the following constraint, presented as a threefold rewrite rule:

(5)   V + (NP/S)

SA-Format: S →   V + NP/S + NP/S

                                V + NP/S + NP + NP/S

1.3.3 Thematic functions versus argument functions

There is no straightforward correspondence between argument functions such as subject, direct or indirect object and *thematic functions*, often called 'thematic roles', such as 'agent', 'patient', 'beneficiary' or the like, though it does seem that grammatical subjects, and direct and indirect objects, with their standard case assignments, act as some sort of prototypical focus for such thematic functions. There can be no doubt that thematic functions play an important part in the machinery of language, in particular in the organizational principles that govern or constrain the shape of lexical argument frames. However, what role they play, if any, in grammar proper is not clear. There are serious reasons for assuming that argument functions alone are not sufficient to catch the regularities found in syntactic processes. It seems, for example, that the subject term of true intransitive verbs (also called, unappealingly, 'unaccusatives' in a particular school), such as *arrive, die, be born*, may, in some languages, show different syntactic behaviour from that of quasi-intransitive verbs (called 'unergatives' in that school, equally unappealingly), such as *sleep, laugh, jump* or *live*. These latter verbs allow for paraphrases with an internal object, such as, respectively, *have a sleep, have a laugh, take a jump, have a life*. Yet whether the syntactic phenomena that have been observed in this connection are indeed adequately explained by the distinction between 'unaccusatives' and 'unergatives' is very much a moot point, due to the lack of independent criteria for the distinction.

In similar fashion, in the Dutch and French PREDICATE RAISING (PR) constructions syntactic differences are observed which cannot be explained on the basis of argument functions alone (see 4.4.3 for French and 5.4 for Dutch). In the French PR construction, the embedded S must be passivized when the lexical verb assigns the thematic function 'actor' to its subject, while the active form is allowed when the lexical verb of the embedded S assigns the thematic function 'recipient' to the subject. This is shown in the sentence pair (6a,b). In (6a) the embedded S contains the recipient verb *voir* ('see'), and may thus remain active, though the passive is also allowed, with a corresponding change in meaning. In (6b), on the other hand, the embedded verb *réparer* ('repair') is actor-oriented and must therefore be passivized.

(6) a. Je ferai   voir la lettre à (par) Paul
         I make-FUT see the letter to (by) Paul
         'I will let Paul see the letter'

    b. Je   ferai   réparer la voiture par (*à) Paul
          I make-FUT repair the car   by (*to) Paul
          'I will let Paul repair the car'

Similar examples are found in Dutch PR constructions:

(7) a. Ik zal Paul de brief laten zien / Ik zal de brief aan Paul laten zien
         I will Paul the letter let see / I will the letter to Paul let see
         'I will let Paul see the letter'

    b. Ik zal Paul het hout laten halen / *Ik zal het hout aan Paul laten halen
          I will Paul the wood let fetch / I will the wood to Paul let fetch
          'I will let Paul fetch the wood'

In (7a) the NP *Paul*, semantic subject of the recipient verb *zien* ('see'), may occur as an external dative, with the preposition *aan* ('to'), but this is not possible in (7b), with the embedded actor-oriented verb *halen* ('fetch').

Examples such as these suggest that notions like 'recipient' or 'actor oriented' verb should occur in syntactic rules and descriptions. We must admit, however, that the lexical semantic notions required for an adequate treatment of such phenomena are simply not available in anything like a reliable form. No adequate theory of lexical semantic analysis and classification has so far been developed. What we have is fragmentary and still largely ad hoc. Given this situation, it seems wise to keep in mind that lexical classification according to types of thematic functions will probably be required in syntax. Meanwhile one has little choice, for the moment, but to keep them out of any implementable rule system.

Such a limitation does not cripple the grammatical theory too much. Descriptions in terms of argument functions alone can already do a great deal of work. Time and again, it turns out that, within the machinery of actual grammar, a characterization in terms of subject, direct object and indirect object, depending merely on the number and the position of the terms in question and without any mention of thematic roles, has a high explanatory value in accounting for certain classes of phenomena. A case in point is the English verb *pay*, whose full argument frame contains a subject, an indirect object and a direct object (*pay the money to the doctor*). Yet *pay* may drop one or both of its object terms. When it drops the indirect object (*pay the money*) the remaining term is still direct object, but when it drops the direct object (*pay the doctor*) the remaining term becomes direct object and loses the status of indirect object despite the fact that its thematic role remains unaffected. *Pay* is not unique in this respect. Verbs like *teach*, *serve* etc. show the same pattern. Other languages, like French or Dutch, also have classes of verbs that behave in this manner (see section 4.3.1 for French examples). Moreover, in French PREDICATE

RAISING constructions involving recipient embedded verbs, the same pattern shows up there in open syntax (*J'ai fait manger la viande à Pierre; J'ai fait manger la viande; J'ai fait manger Pierre*).

Cases such as these show that argument functions play an explanatory role in syntax. The same may be expected of thematic functions. Unfortunately, however, the theory of thematic functions and of corresponding lexical classifications has not, so far, been developed to the point of being usable in fully explicit, implementable syntactic rule systems.

1.4 SAs as a way of representing sentence meaning

So far, we have stressed the functional character of SA-structures in terms of the syntactic rules that convert them into surface structures. There is, however, also the question of their general suitability to represent meanings. This question has a certain urgency as alternative semantic representation systems are available, especially in psycholinguistics and computational linguistics (see 1.4.5). As has been pointed out, our SAs are characterized by the systematic application of Predicate-Argument structure (PAS), not only for main lexical predicates, but also for sentential operators that may appear in all kinds of guises in surface structures: as adverbs, particles, affixes, prepositional phrases or what not. We feel that this type of SA-structures is more adequate and better suited to represent meanings than any of the existing alternatives. To support this claim we shall first specify the overall structure of SAs posited for the European languages generally. (To what extent this structure can be extrapolated to become a true universal is a question we cannot answer until more languages have been analysed.)

1.4.1 The overall structure of SAs for European languages

Since tenses, logical operators and all kinds of adverbial adjuncts (including prepositional phrases) are derived from predicates in SA-structure it is useful, at this stage, to give a schematic account of the way in which this is done. Figure8 (overleaf) gives the skeletal frame of SA-structures.

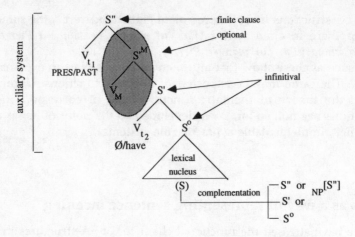

Figure 8   *Skeletal frame of SA-structures*

Within the SA-tree we distinguish between an *auxiliary system*, which contains the tenses, the logical operators and the adverbials, and a *lexical nucleus*, which contains the main lexical predicate (verb, adjective or NP) and the appropriate arguments. One of these may again be an S-structure, in which case we speak of complementation. Embedded complement-Ss are of three types: S" (i.e. an S with the complete two-tense system), S' (i.e. an S with only one tense, which can only be t_2), or an S° (i.e. an S without any tense). Each of the three types can be headed by an NP-node (which gives it NP-status, manifested by special grammatical properties). S' and S° embeddings lead to surface infinitivals if not headed by NP, and to participials or gerunds if headed by NP. Languages without infinitivals, such as Modern Greek and most Balkan languages, lack the possibility of NP-less S' or S° complement clauses.

The shaded area between t_1 and t_2 is optional and reserved for the modal complex, i.e. any future tense operator plus, in some languages, a number of modal auxiliaries. (It will be obvious that the insertion of the modal complex in this position automatically accounts for the defective paradigm of modals in some languages, English in particular.) Logical operators and adverbials belong to the S"-complex, the S'-complex, or the S°-complex. Accordingly, they are inserted above, between or below the tenses and modals. Each of the three types of complement-S may attract any logical operator or adverbial belonging to the complex defined for the type in question. That is, an S'-complement is free to take an adverbial of the S'-complex, etc.

1.4.2 The status of predicate argument structure: the 19th century debate

Perhaps the most striking feature of Semantic Syntax is the heavy use made of Predicate-Argument Structure. All lexical elements are considered to be predicates, labelled 'V', at SA-level, and only the surface verbs keep that category throughout. All logical operators, including negation, the quantifiers, *and* and *or*, are treated as predicates. So are the tenses, prepositions and all kinds of adverbs or adverbials. The lexicon of each language determines the surface category of these predicates. Some will become prepositions, others become verbs, adjectives, adverbs, particles, affixes, determiners, and so on, the appropriate category change taking place along with the transformational treatment.

This strategy is also due to McCawley, who made proposals to this effect in various publications in the late '60s and early '70s (collected in McCawley 1973). It fits into what has been called the Streamline Principle above: rules and processes found to occur in readily accessible parts of syntax are postulated also for the deeper strata of syntax. The SA-Format as specified in (5) above is thus applicable throughout the whole of SA-structures, including those parts that specify tenses, modalities, prepositional adjuncts, adverbials of any kind, etc.

One advantage of this application of the Streamline Principle is that it contributes to the building of a common semantic basis for translation equivalents in different languages even though they differ radically in surface structure. Consider, for example, the English sentence *He could have eaten*, which translates in French as *Il aurait pu manger*. Although a competent human translator has no problem in translating this, closer inspection quickly reveals radical structural differences that are not immediately transparent. Similar problems occur, for example, with sentences like *He has just left*, which corresponds to French *Il vient de partir*, or *He is reportedly ill*, which can be rendered in French as *On dit qu'il est malade*. Or *He likes to sing*, which translates in Dutch as *Hij zingt graag*, with *zingt* ('sings') as the finite verb form, and the adverb *graag* ('with pleasure') as an adverbial modifier. Such cases are not exceptional. The languages of the world show vast structural differences for the expression of identical or near-identical meanings. In Finnish, for example, the negation is best described as an auxiliary verb: it takes affixes for person and number, but the past tense (not the present tense) is expressed on the main verb, which becomes a past participle, as in, for example, (8) (Hellwig 1991):

(8)   Minä   e-n   osta-nut   polkupyörä-ä
       I   not-1SG buy-PAST PARTICIPLE bicycle-PARTITIVE
       'I did not buy the bicycle'

The Turkish sentence (9) (see 7.6 for a rudimentary grammar of Turkish) translates literally as 'the man in-s the house'. Here, the postposition *de* ('in') acts as the main surface predicate:

(9)   Adam   ev- de- dir
       man   house-in-3SG-PRES
       'the man is in the house'

Since an underlying semantic analysis in terms of PAS neutralizes these differences, it provides an important part of the common semantic basis required for an explicit account of translation relations.

Traditionally, PA-analyses usually took the form of a primary distinction between Subject and Predicate, based on grammatical surface form and supported by traditional (Aristotelian) logic. Around 1850, however, philosophers and linguists began to query the validity or relevance of this old logico-grammatical distinction.[7] They felt that if the notions of Subject and Predicate had linguistic relevance they should also have some psychological reality. In the intellectual climate of the day, a great deal of speculation arose about what 'subject' and 'predicate' should or could amount to in actual, 'living' linguistic communication. Around the end of the 19th century, it was not uncommon to make a distinction between a grammatical, a logical and a psychological subject-predicate analysis. At the time, this threefold distinction was central to the debate on the nature of language. Unfortunately, this whole episode in the history of linguistics has been largely forgotten. It is revived here not least because the issues discussed in those days turn out to be highly significant in the present context.

Consider the example given in Steinthal (1860:101): 'Coffee grows in Africa'. In Steinthal's view, a logician could not but say 'that *Africa* expresses the concept to which *coffee grows* is subordinated. Logically speaking the sentence runs "the growing of coffee takes place in Africa".' (Soon after it became fashionable to speak of 'psychological', rather than 'logical' subject and predicate.) Another group of examples centred on contrasted constituents, as in *SCOTT wrote Ivanhoe*, or *Scott wrote IVANHOE*. Authors of the day agreed that the contrasted element should be regarded as some sort of predicate. Some (e.g. Wegener 1885:20; Gardiner 1932:273) spoke of 'logical predicate', others (e.g. Paul 1880:285) of 'psychological predicate'. All agreed that the grammatical analysis of the sentence fails to show the 'true predicate' (Sechehaye 1926:127). Quantified elements were likewise regarded as (non-grammatical) predicates. An example is Meyer-Lübke (1899:352): 'From the point of view of logic, there can be no doubt that in the sentence *Il arrive deux étrangers* <i.e. 'two foreigners are arriving'> the part *il arrive* is subject and *deux étrangers* is predicate.' One can hardly fail to notice the parallelism between what those authors saw as non-grammatical (psychological or logical) predicates and what are treated as abstract predicates at SA-level in Semantic Syntax.

The whole debate was, however, seriously flawed by a terrible lack of clear definitions and of workable operational criteria. It may well be that this is why de Saussure, who taught in this period, remained totally silent on this issue (though his students Bally and Sechehaye took an active part in the debate). One is inclined to infer that de Saussure preferred to dismiss the whole issue as fruitless and ill-defined, and to make an entirely new start.

---

[7] See Elffers-Van Ketel (1991) for a thorough survey of this episode in the modern history of linguistics.

Kalepky (1928:20) decried the confusion and the apparent lack of substance in the debate: 'Eine derartige Wirrnis schreit förmlich nach Abhilfe' ('Such a confusion cries out formally for relief'). It was therefore quite natural that a few authors tried to develop alternative ways of analysing sentences, other than in terms of subject and predicate or PAS. The most important development in this respect goes back to Franz Brentano, who proposed a 'thetic' sentence structure as both opposed and complementary to classical PAS, which he termed 'categorical'. This idea was taken over and developed further by the Swiss philosopher Anton Marty, who taught at Prague at the beginning of the century, and then by Vilém Mathesius, who made it one of the central elements in the early years of the Prague Linguistic Circle (founded in 1926). He introduced the term *Functional Sentence Perspective* (FSP), meant to cover semantic features of sentences that seem to escape analysis in terms of PAS, in particular the phenomena that suggest a distinction between the *topic* and the *comment* of a sentence (see Sasse (1987) for an excellent survey). After World War II, this idea was taken up again in the school of Petr Sgall and Eva Hajičová in Prague.

To show the reality of a topic-comment modulation in sentences, few examples will do better than the following, taken from a political pamphlet circulated during the change-over from Communism in Czechoslovakia in 1989 (Hajičová & Panevová 1993:60):

(10)   There is good news and there is bad news. The good news is that the Czechs are staging a revolution. The bad news is that the revolution is being staged by the Czechs.

Though the point is both obvious and important it does not rule out an analysis in terms of PAS. Modern formal developments have brought about a dramatic increase in the scope of such analyses, way beyond what Brentano, Marty or Mathesius thought possible. The NP *a revolution* in (10) represents an existential quantifier and is therefore a deep predicate (section 7.1). It is the highest lexical predicate of the *that*-clause, which says that the set of things the Czechs are staging has a member in common with the set of revolutions. Not so in the last sentence of (10). Here, the highest lexical predicate of the *that*-clause is *by the Czechs*, and the clause says that the staging of the revolution is by the Czechs (see 3.5). Given the general principle that higher operators, including negation, affect the highest lexical predication in their scope there is nothing strange in using the operators *the good news is* and *the bad news is* over different but truth-conditionally equivalent predications. Analogously, a sentence like *Scott did not write Ivanhoe* is likely to convey a different message from *Ivanhoe was not written by Scott*. In *He didn't take the train for fun*, the denial applies to the Prepositional Phrase *for fun*. And in *He didn't make many mistakes* it is the numerousness of the mistakes, expressed in the quantifier *many*, that is denied. A precise study of the machinery of Semantic Syntax will show how the correct structures are produced.

A formal analogy can now be established between various forms of clefting and the occurrence of contrastive accents in 'canonical' sentences. The canonical sentence *SCOTT did not write Ivanhoe* corresponds with the cleft sentence *It isn't SCOTT who wrote Ivanhoe*. Likewise, *Scott did not write IVANHOE* corresponds with *It isn't IVANHOE that Scott wrote*. All these sentences are derived from an SA that has a cleft structure, with the contrasted element as the highest predicate under the negation: 'not [be Scott (the x who wrote Ivanhoe)]' for the first pair and 'not [be Ivanhoe (the x that Scott wrote)]' for the second. In Semantic Syntax a simple transformational process turns this into *SCOTT did not write Ivanhoe* or *It isn't SCOTT who wrote Ivanhoe*, and *Scott did not write IVANHOE* or *It isn't IVANHOE that Scott wrote*, respectively (see section 7.2.2). In this analysis no FSP or thetic structure is required as an alternative to PAS. A similar example is *I always teach in room 7*, which normally does not mean that it is always the case that I teach in room 7, but rather that when I teach it is always in room 7. This is caught by the cleft SA-structure: 'always [be room 7 (the x that I teach in)]', where *room 7* is the highest lexical predicate under *always*, and thus most directly affected by it. The machinery of Semantic Syntax turns this into *I always teach in room 7*. (See 7.2.2 for a discussion of clefts and contrastive or emphatic accents as a means of highlighting constituents.)

The obvious advantage of Semantic Syntax is that it provides a principled formal basis for the phenomena so widely discussed before the advent of structuralist linguistics. The notions of 'psychological' or 'logical' subject and predicate, and the 'thetic' structures in FSP-theory which aim at an alternative for PAS, were never provided with anything like a satisfactory theoretical basis, and could therefore hardly be integrated into formal grammar or formal semantics. They remained largely intuitive, a fact which has prevented the phenomena concerned from gaining the prominence they clearly deserve. To the extent that Semantic Syntax, with its emphasis on PAS, succeeds in accounting for these phenomena, it can be considered to be a formalization of the intuitions that inspired the inventors of the notions of (psycho)-logical subject and predicate and of the proponents of FSP-theory.

1.4.3 The general nature of predicate argument structure

This leaves us with the question of what predicate and arguments 'really' are. The question is of some urgency because there is no a priori reason why one should apply the same terms 'predicate', 'subject', '(direct or indirect) object' to structural elements at the level of grammatical, psychological and/or logical analysis.[8] In brief, our answer is as follows. Whenever, in the litera-

---

[8] The modern notion of PAS derives directly from Frege and applies to SA-structures. At SA-level a PAS is the expression of a formal inclusion relation: the n-tuple of argument term extensions is represented as an element in the extension of the predicate. *John likes the book* expresses the fact that the pair of entities called 'John' and 'the book, i.e. $\langle[\![$ John $]\!],[\![$ the book $]\!]\rangle$, is a member of the set of pairs of individuals such that the first likes the second. If a term extension is of set-theoretical order n the predicate extension for that term is necessarily of order $n+1$. Individuals are 0-order elements, sets of individuals are 1st order elements, sets of sets of individuals 2nd order elements, etc. The predicate *like* is a 1st order predicate with respect to both its terms, which takes individuals as exten-

ture discussed in the previous section, a different PAS is assigned to the grammatical and the logico-psychological level of analysis there is always a paraphrase, taken to be a more precise and more analytical rendering of the meaning of the sentence in question, which has the presumed logico-psychological predicate as the grammatical predicate, and likewise for the subject and (direct or indirect) object.[9] Therefore, what unites the notions 'predicate' and 'argument' at the different levels of analysis is their use in *grammatical* structure, at the level of surface structure or at that of the intuitive paraphrase.

In grammar, the general, unifying notion of subject and other argument terms is *positional*: they are defined at SA-level by their positions in expansions of S, as indicated in section 1.3.2 above. The predicate, at SA-level, is always S-initial or S-final, depending on the language type, and is semantically defined. In terms of model-theoretic semantics, it is defined by the fact that it denotes a function from argument term extensions to truth values. In terms of discourse semantics the predicate denotes a function from denotations of argument terms to increments.

Surface structure predicate and argument terms are often, perhaps even prototypically, those of the lexical nucleus, the tenseless S^o of fig.8 in 1.4.1 above. The lexical nucleus tends to act as a matrix structure incorporating the abstract elements of the auxiliary system, and to some extent also Vs and subject-NPs of infinitival complement clauses. This is why, at least in prototypical cases, the subject term of the lexical nucleus figures as the surface grammatical subject, and likewise for the other argument terms. In such cases, it was felt by the 19th and early 20th century authors discussed in 1.4.2, there is congruity in PAS between the grammatical and the logico-psychological levels. Their discovery was that in many cases there is no such congruity. This gave rise to the questions they asked. And although they often provided answers that we may now consider insightful, we must admit that, on the whole, the problem transcended their theoretical powers. We must also admit that little progress has been made in this respect in modern linguistic theory.

The answer envisaged in Semantic Syntax is that the intuitive paraphrases presented by the older scholars should be regimented into a semantically analytical language, the language of SAs. The grammar then relates the SAs to their corresponding surface structures. This provides a principled and empirically solid basis for the distinction between congruent and incongruent cases (with sentence intonation, which is always congruent, as empirical

---

sions. (When a term extension is a set of individuals, as when it is a plural term, the predicate is automatically upgraded to 2nd order for that term. Predicates can be upgraded but never downgraded.) The predicate *disperse* is a 2nd order predicate with respect to its subject as it cannot take less than sets of individuals as subject term extensions. At SA-level, quantifiers are 2nd or higher order predicates as they express properties of (pairs of) sets of (sets of) individuals.

[9] There is a hierarchy of argument terms (Keenan & Comrie 1977; Comrie 1981:149-153; 169-174): subject > direct object > indirect object. This hierarchy has not, so far, been formally defined in the general theory of syntax, but the many instances where it is seen at work leave no doubt about its reality.

support). It moreover enables us to extend the analysis into the more abstract regions of analysis in terms of modern predicate calculus, with quantifiers, tenses, and other operators as predicates over propositional structures.

In this way, ordinary negation and other truth-functional operators are considered to be predicates over proposition expressions. A proposition expression S takes a particular possible fact F (and not, as in Fregean semantics, a truth-value) as its extension. (Any statement of an inclusion relation refers to a possible fact.) When S is uttered as an assertive speech act the speaker commits himself to an inclusion of F in the class of realized possible facts, i.e. to the truth of S. If S is placed under negation the new proposition expression states that F belongs to the class of unrealized possible facts, and that new possible fact is then the object of the speaker's commitment. In analogous ways and in accordance with the Streamline Principle, all 'abstract' logical, modal and attitudinal operators are considered to be predicates in the theory of Semantic Syntax.

For a PAS to be true it must *correspond* to reality, but it does not *mirror* it. Term extensions often refer to real world entities via a complex interpretative formula: the average London cabdriver or the government's policy on poverty are not real world entities. Yet in language they are treated as if they were, and they are even quantified over. Sentences containing such terms can have a truth value only in virtue of a powerful intermediate cognitive machinery providing, if all goes well, a proper reduction to real entities. A state of affairs can be truthfully described in any number of PA-structures. Instead of *The dog barked* we can say *The thing that barked is/was a dog.* Languages and speakers make their choices in this respect, and linguistics has the task of reconstructing which choices they make. If sentence structure imposes constraints on ontology or vice versa, they are remote and indirect.

1.4.4 The non-universality of SAs and universal meaning

All theories within the general framework of TGG have claimed some more or less universal status for SAs ('Logical Form'), without, however, being very specific about this question. Yet it appears that SAs are far from universal. This results not only from the analyses of different languages such as English, French, German and Dutch (and Turkish in 7.6), which require different but closely related SAs as input to the T-rules, but also from an analysis of specific cases that have proved problematic for formal translation procedures, such as those presented in section 1.4.2.

SAs are subject to the constraints embodied in the Formation Rules of each single language, and these differ in ways which are interesting and intriguing but make it impossible to consider them or their SA-output structures universal. The Formation Rules devised so far prove empirically successful, which is a forceful argument for keeping them. But they are not identical across languages. The structural differences found between translation-equivalent sentences are often due to different Formation Rule systems. That being so, the question arises at what level the formal link between translation-equivalent sentences should be established.

A possible answer to this question might be the assumption of an even deeper and more universal level of meaning representation at which different languages can barter their translation equivalents. We shall argue in section 7.5 that the assumption of such a level of semantic representation, a *Deeper Semantic Analysis* or DSA, can only provide a partial answer to the problem of 'universal meaning' in that it is probably useful for the formulation of some translation equivalents for a given set of languages. Other than that, translation equivalents are to be sought at deeper levels of cognition which have so far proved resistent to formal treatment. It is probably correct to say that anything like DSA, if viable, can do no more than represent a skeletal, mainly truth-conditional part of language-neutral meaning in terms of a tree structure and without a systematic analysis of lexical meaning. But translation equivalents are probably bartered mostly at deeper levels where precise satisfaction conditions for predicates come into play as well as conditions to be met by wider discourse, context of utterance and world knowledge. It is precisely because there is, as yet, no way of opening up these deeper levels to formal treament that a formal theory of translation and its correlate, a formal translation procedure, are still beyond our grasp.

Even so, there seems to be a point in constructing meaning representations that are neutral between given particular languages. Such representations will fulfill a limited role in providing a reliable exchange of meaning equivalents for certain categories of non-trivial cases. (In doing that they will be of use in machine-aided translation programs, but they will be inadequate as a basis for fully formalized translation procedures.) For a relatively language-neutral DSA to do a good job it has to take away from the language-specific SAs whatever is of no semantic consequence. For example, a predicate may become an adverb in the surface structures of one language, but a morphological verb in those of another, so that it must be 'plugged in' in different positions in the SAs of the respective languages. SAs must therefore be considered to contain more information than is required for the stark semantics of the sentences they represent. The semantic redundancy of SAs appears likewise from the scope relations of operators occurring in the auxiliary systems of natural languages. Tense predicates, for example, as well as many adverbial and prepositional predicates, may occur above, between or below other predicates such as the modals, negation or quantifiers without any real semantic difference. This would show that some operator combinations in SAs are mutually insensitive to scope: they have identical scope relations with respect to other operators or operator groups. Yet the grammar of each individual language must assign each operator a specific structural position in the SAs of that language.

SAs are thus seen to be overspecific with regard to meaning specifications: their tree structure may be more hierarchical than is necessary and certain structural choices may be induced by the grammar of the language concerned.

The overall architecture of the theory as depicted in fig.5 above would thus have to be extended with an intermediate level of language-neutral semantic representation as part of the incrementation procedure I. This aspect of semantic representation and processing is discussed in section 7.5.

1.4.5 Alternative ways of representing sentence meaning?

The question may well be asked whether the PAS-based SA-structures that are input to the Semantic Syntax rule systems are the best available. Should they not be replaced with a different system of semantic representation that does the job more efficiently? The answer to this question will depend on what one wants meaning representations to do. We assume here that a meaning representation of a sentence S of a language L has to satisfy two broad conditions:

(a)   It must be an adequate input to (output from) a semantic machinery that specifies the full semantic contribution (truth-conditional and other) of S in all of its meanings.

(b)   It must be an adequate input to (output from) a syntactic machinery generating all and only the well-formed sentences of L for the meanings specified.

A meaning representation is thus an interface between the syntax and the semantics of L. Note that a meaning representation does not necessarily have to be entirely disambiguated itself. It may still contain ambiguities, as long as the semantic machinery to which it is input does the further disambiguating that is required. For example, a sentence like (De Rijk 1974):

(11)   I no longer remember the names of my students

is ambiguous in that it means either 'I have forgotten the names of my students' (the constant reference reading) or 'I used to know the names of the students I had in the past but nowadays I do not know the names of the students I have now' (the variable reference reading). Whether this ambiguity has to be resolved at the level of meaning representation or 'higher up' in the semantic machinery is a question that has no a priori answer. Any reasonable answer will depend on the actual semantic machinery and the way it links up with meaning representations. In other words, the answer to this and similar questions is largely theory-dependent. And since we do not have, as yet, a well-established semantic machinery we do not have an answer to this question either. Which means that we cannot use sentence disambiguation as a criterion by which to judge meaning representation systems.

The same question presents itself with respect to the syntactic machinery. But here we do have a syntactic machinery for the kind of meaning representation we use. The combination of Semantic Syntax and SAs works well, and to the extent that it does we have an argument for our SA-structures as an adequate system of meaning representation. That is, we think that there is a syntactic advantage in having meaning representations that have the form of a hierarchical tree structure and are formulated in what is essentially the

Predicate-Argument-Structure-based language of modern predicate calculus (with definite descriptions, anaphoric pronouns and a few other additions).

From this vantage point we can review other ways of representing meanings. One may ask, for example, whether it would not be better to work with thematic functions (roles) rather than with functional notions like subject and (in)direct object? We have argued, in section 1.3.3 above, that thematic roles are not optimally suitable as semantic input to syntactic rule systems, even though they are likely to be of value at other levels of lexical semantic description. The question is relevant since thematic functions are an element in the *conceptual graph* (CG) method of semantic representation (Sowa 1984), which, in one form or another, has gained wide acceptance in Artificial Intelligence and Computational Linguistics.[10] According to Sowa, 'conceptual graphs form a knowledge representation language based on linguistics, psychology, and philosophy' (1984:69), the triad of disciplines that stood at the cradle of modern semantics.

Sowa (1984:8) traces the origin of the CG method to the 'existential graphs' designed by the American philosopher Charles Sanders Peirce at the end of the 19th century 'as a graphic notation for symbolic logic'. In its present form, the CG method consists of two parts, a CG representation for logical structure, and a CG representation for lexical structure. In the logical graphs for propositional calculus only 'not' and 'and' are represented, the former as '¬', the latter as zero. Thus, for example, 'not (p and q)' comes out as fig.9a, and 'p or q' as fig.9b, with the 'or'-operator defined in terms of 'not' and 'and' in the standard way (Sowa 1984:138):

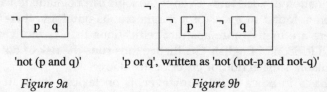

'not (p and q)'   'p or q', written as 'not (not-p and not-q)'

Figure 9a   *Figure 9b*

A similar device is presented for the predicate calculus structures, where only the existential quantifier is used, represented as zero, and the universal quantifier is expressed in terms of the existential quantifier and negation, i.e. by standard conversion. Variable binding is indicated by a dotted line from the quantifier to the position of the variable, as in fig.10 (Sowa 1984:141; note that the second occurrence of PERSON is in fact the bound variable):

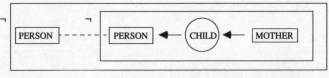

Figure 10   *CG for 'Every person has a mother'*

[10] I am indebted to Nicolas Nicolov at Edinburgh for stimulating discussions on conceptual graph theory.

Apart from what happens within the innermost of the two boxes, the lexical nucleus, the actual apparatus for the representation of the scope relations of quantifiers and propositional operators, and for the system of variable binding, is hardly an improvement on the standard Russellian syntax of predicate calculus. To be blunt but precise, the logical notation presented in Sowa (1984) is awkward compared with the standard notation, and without good arguments for its introduction the case for the Sowa notation is weak. Note also that the only reason for not expressing the propositional operator 'or' and the universal quantifier is notational as it is felt to be difficult to represent these operators graphically. Finally, and most importantly, the Sowa logical notation is just a disguised form of tree structure notation, with the operators representing the left branch and the boxes the right branch of an expansion. In this respect it does not differ from the linear Russell notation where the brackets reflect tree constituency. On the whole, one may say that the logical notation system found in Sowa (1984) has no advantages and only disadvantages.[11]

CG theory, moreover, appears liberal with its reifications, which figure freely in what are called 'logical translations' of sentences. Quantification is allowed over such entities as 'instances of flying', which can only be mental constructs. Consider, for example, how *The possible person Julian is flying to Mars* is 'translated into modal logic' (Sowa 1984:175): '◊∃x(PERSON (Julian) ∧ FLY(x) ∧ PLANET(Mars) ∧ AGNT(x,Julian) ∧ DEST(x,Mars))', to be read as 'it is possible that there is an x such that there is a person called Julian and x is an instance of flying and there is a planet called Mars and the agent of x is Julian and the destination of x is Mars'. Even if the logic can be made to work and an interpretation is found in terms of a parsimonious ontology, there is still the fact that there are many more abstract reifications than is motivated by the grammar and lexicon of English. CG theory thus runs the risk of not providing the best available satisfaction of criterion (b) above.

The emphasis in Sowa (1984), however, is on lexical predicate-argument relations. Here thematic functions play a central role, in the form of 'conceptual relations'. Let us look at a few examples. First consider figs.11-13:

Figure 11   CG for the phrase 'man biting dog' (Sowa 1984:8)

---

[11] Regarding the logic, there are some further less satisfactory details. For example, the negation sign '¬' is found not only as a propositional operator, as in figs.8 and 9, but also as an operator over conceptual relations, as in Sowa (1984:71, fig.3.2), where a circle contains the 'negated' conceptual relation '¬ ABUT'. The status of '¬' is thus ill-defined.

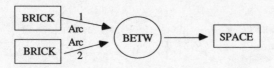

Figure 12   Triadic relation 'a space is between a brick and a brick' (Sowa 1984:72)

Figure 13   CG for the proposition 'the cat sitting on a mat' (Sowa 1984:78)

Sowa's comment is as follows (pp.70-72): The boxes (square brackets) contain concept representations, the circles (round brackets) 'conceptual relations'. An arc is an arrow linking a box with a circle. The arcs represent 'logical associations in the brain, not the actual shapes of the neural excitations'. Conceptual relations may have any number of arcs, although the most common ones are dyadic. Some, like the *past tense marker* (PAST) or the *negation* (NEG), are monadic; others, like *between* (BETW), are triadic; and others may have an arbitrary number of arcs. For *n*-adic relations, the *n*th arc is drawn as an arrow pointing away from the circle, and all the other arcs are drawn as arrows pointing towards the circle. If $n \geq 3$, the arrows pointing towards the circle are numbered from 1 to *n*-1. Moreover, each conceptual graph asserts a single proposition (p.78).

Here, a few observations and questions are in order. First, the set of conceptual relations seems to contain not only thematic functions like 'AGENT', 'OBJECT, 'STATE', 'LOCATION' but also object language words like *between*, to be realized as such in the corresponding sentence. True, the example in fig.12 harks back to a complex 'CG for an arch', defined as 'two standing bricks and an arbitrary object lying across the bricks' (Sowa 1984:71, fig.3.2), but this interpretation does not seem to fit the general statement that each CG 'asserts a single proposition', since an arch is hardly the assertion of a proposition. In general, the status of the conceptual relations is unclear: one looks in vain for a general definition of this category.

Then, the interpretation of the notion 'arc' remains obscure. To say that 'arcs represent logical associations in the brain' does not entail much. Nor is it clear what the meaning is of the direction of arrows from or towards the conceptual relations. While fig.13, which has all arrows pointing to the right, may be read as 'the cat is in a state of sitting on the mat', one would expect fig.11 to be readable as, e.g., 'the man is acting as a biter of the dog', which would have all arrows pointing to the right as well.

Moreover, while the arrows symbolize *n*-adic relations of certain kinds associated with conceptual relations (circles) no account is given of the *n*-adic relations entered into by lexical verbs. One can get, for example, a CG like fig.14 (based on Sowa 1984:78,92,134,175), where nothing indicates what the lexically defined argument terms are of the main verb *eat*.

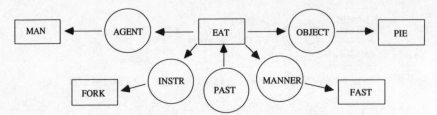

Figure 14   CeG for "man ate pie with fork fast"

For all one knows, FORK and FAST are argument terms just like MAN and PIE. This is unsatisfactory in any theory that aims at relating meaning representations with grammatical surface sentences. What seems to be happening is that all kinds of modifiers, adjuncts and operators, which are neatly distinguished and assigned scope in the Auxiliary System of Semantic Syntax, are attached to the main verb (the 'head'; Sowa 1984:78) indiscriminately. The hierarchical relations of the modifiers, adjuncts and operators, remain largely unexpressed, although their expression is indispensable in any adequate theory that links semantic representations with surface structures (see 3.5). Consider, for example, a sentence like:

(12)   John stupidly did the job cleverly   (=(18e) in section 3.5)

In Sowa's non-hierarchical treatment the two adverbs would have a parallel status with respect to the concept DO, and the CG would run the risk of expressing an internally contrary proposition.

Moreover, one wonders why PAST or BETWEEN are not concepts but concept relations, or why PAST has an arrow going into the box for EAT, while all the other connections are outgoing arrows. And why is PAST not represented as a propositional operator, as one would expect from a semantic point of view? Generally, there seems to be no systematic theory for the tenses.

This method of semantic representation leads to a proliferation of conceptual relations that are unlikely to have any function at all in the grammatical system of the language. Thus one finds (Sowa 1984:415-419), a motley collection of conceptual relations, some of which represent lexical items, others abstract notions, and most of which have no grammatical significance. The list includes items like ACCOMPANIMENT, CHARACTERISTIC, CHILD, DESTINATION, INITIATOR, LINK, MATERIAL, METHOD, NAME, PART, PATH, RESULT, SOURCE, SUPPORT, SUCCESSOR, UNTIL.

Considering, moreover, that there seems to be no principled distinction between definite and quantified terms, and that the CG theory of quantification (Sowa 1984:137-149), insofar as it works, appears to be a notational variant of the standard theory, there is no escaping from the conclusion that conceptual graphs are far from ideal either as a system for representing meanings or as input to a grammar turning them into well-formed surface structures. Compared with conceptual graphs, PAS-type semantic representations as used in Semantic Syntax are a model of regularity, whose expressive power and semantic precision greatly exceeds that of conceptual graphs.

Similar critiques can be formulated for other alternatives, which all have in common that they concentrate primarily on the representation of lexical meaning structures at the expense of higher operators like quantifiers, negation, tenses, aspects, modalities, adverbial or prepositional modifiers, in short those elements that are accounted for in the auxiliary system of the grammar and are most in need of hierarchical tree structures.

Leaving aside for the moment the question of whether thematic functions are useful or not in a meaning representation system that must act as input to (output from) the syntax, we can say that the CG method tries to represent grammatical relations in a non-tree-like fashion, by means of boxes, circles and arrows that form networks but not trees. But we have seen that tree hierarchies are indispensable for the whole auxiliary apparatus of a sentence, and that for some of this part of the grammar, to the extent that it is explicit, the CG method is in fact nothing but a disguised form of tree structure representation. The question then is: why should we graft a non-tree method of representation onto one that already has tree structure? The question is the more pressing as we already have a satisfactory method for representing meanings, i.e. the tree structures of standard predicate calculus, with predicate argument structure rendered likewise in tree-like fashion. Not only does it look as if the wheel is being reinvented, but the problem of relating semantic representations to sentences (surface structures) is made unnecessarily complex. For the tree structures of predicate calculus are the same kind of algebraic objects as the tree structures of surface structures, which simplifies the rule system required for mapping the two kinds of structure onto each other enormously. The introduction of a notational variant expressed in algebraic objects of a different kind, whether for semantic analyses or for surface structures, requires strong independent arguments. For conceptual graph theory these have not been presented.

1.5 Prelexical syntax and other aspects of lexical meaning

The function of the lexicon is not represented in fig.7 above. The lexicon is, in principle, a set of semantic predicates, each with its argument structure, its surface category, the T-rules induced by it, the lexical processes and derivations it allows for, and, of course, a description of its semantic and socio-linguistic (interactive) conditions and of its phonological form or forms. The syntactic function of the lexicon is expressed by the fact that some Formation Rules refer to the lexicon, which transplants the lexically specified argument structure of a predicate into the SA-tree under construction. SAs thus draw on the lexicon when so told by the Formation Rules.

There is one aspect of the lexicon not treated in this book although it falls in with the system of SA meaning representation proposed here. This is the possibility of applying 'prelexical' syntactic analyses to semantically complex predicates. This possibility is explored in the theory of *prelexical syntax*, introduced by McCawley in the late '60s. Prelexical syntax is a theory of internal lexical structure based on the rules and processes of ordinary 'open' syntax, at least for a general, non-specific part of the meaning description. A distinction can often be made between a more general and a specific part. Thus, for example, the verb *assassinate* has a general part corresponding to 'cause to die' and a specific part requiring that the subject of 'die' is human, that the death is brought about unlawfully and with malice aforethought (i.e. murder), and that the person was murdered on account of his or her prominent position in public life. The general part often allows for an analysis in terms of a syntactic construction under a V-node, i.e. as a V-island, put together accor- ding to well-known rules and processes of open syntax, though not necessarily the open syntax of the language concerned in the period concerned. Prelexical syntax is thus a further manifestation of the Streamline Principle mentioned earlier.

Prelexical syntax may be expected to simplify the General Format given in (5). Indirect objects, for example, may turn out to be products of prelexical syntax. Take the verb *show*, which can be analysed as 'cause to see', whereby the indirect object figuring in the argument structure of *show* represents the original subject of the embedded verb *see*. If all indirect objects can be reduced that way and if other types of middle NP are likewise seen to result from prelexical processes the *General Format* no longer needs to specify the middle NP in the third line of (5). Other examples are impersonal weather verbs. They must probably be specified as V without a semantic subject term so that a dummy NP[it] must be inserted. Prelexical syntax can relieve this inelegant feature if the rule of SUBJECT INCORPORATION (SI) is invoked, which occurs in the open syntax of some languages. Muravyova (1992) reports SI for intransitive sentences in the Paleosiberian language Chukchee, which has sentences of the form 'grass appeared', i.e. with an overt subject, next to sentences 'it grass-appeared', with the semantic subject 'grass' morpho- logically incorporated into an impersonal verb form. Thus, an English sentence like *It is raining* need not be ultimately derived from a structure lacking a subject term if the lexical predicate *rain* is given a prelexical analysis 'V[fall NP[rain]]'.[12] With Prelexical Syntax, the *General Format* can hopefully be simplified to V + NP/S + (NP/S). But, as has been said, we shall leave prelexical syntax out of account in this book.

Another fruitful application of our system of SA-structure for the repre- sentation of sentence meanings is found in the systematic representation of concepts. This can be of help in the question of the recognition of the possible meanings of nominal compounds (Coolen 1995). As is well-known, the semantic relation between the members of nominal compounds varies considerably from one compound to another, and the question is how speakers recognize the proper meaning even for novel compounds presented in isolation, i.e. without

[12] This is also the normal way of expressing the proposition 'it is raining' in most Creole languages. For example, Mauritian Creole and the Surinamese Creole language Sranan say, respectively: *Lapli pe tôbe* and *Alen e fadon*, both meaning literally 'rain is falling'.

embedding context. Consider, for example, the following common and novel noun-noun-compounds:

(13)a. butcher's knife   f.   carving knife   k. room knife
   b. bread knife   g.   cutting knife   l. evening knife
   c. kitchen knife   h.   dream knife   m. belief knife
   d. breakfast knife   i.   pocket knife
   e. table knife   j.   guillotine knife

Clearly, the semantic relations between the first and second members of the compounds vary a great deal, and in the case of (13k-m) they are even unclear. It has been proposed that conceptual structure, background knowledge or context plays a role, each individually or in conjunction. But it is not known what the restrictions are on possible semantic relations within compounds, nor what enables the hearer to identify them.

Suppose we classify the head of the compounds in question, the word *knife*, as denoting an INSTRUMENT. This enables us to assign it a place in a schematic SA-structure as follows:

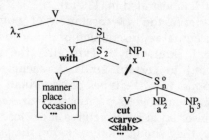

Figure 15   *Schematic SA-structure for the concept 'knife'*

At SA-level, prepositions are two-place predicates, with a matrix S as subject term and the prepositional object as object NP-term. (The cyclic rules of OBJECT INCORPORATION and LOWERING ensure the proper syntactic treatment.) The object NP-term (NP_1) contains the variable bound by the lambda operator. Therefore, fig.15 reads as 'class of things x such that with x ... an individual *a* cuts (carves, stabs, etc.) an object *b*.' The line interruption stands for possible adverbials of the type 'manner', 'place', 'occasion' and the like, which the grammar allows between an instrumental *with*-adverbial and S_n^o containing the lexical nucleus. Such adverbials will find a place under S_2 or any further S between S_2 and S_n^o. S_n^o, moreover, contains the verb *cut*, which stands for the prototypical (default) action performed with a knife. But less prototypical actions can be performed with knives as well, such as carving, stabbing, cleaning nails, and the like. These are given between angled brackets in fig.15. Finally, the verb of S_n^o takes a standard lexically defined argument structure, which, for *cut*, is a subject-NP and a direct object NP, represented in fig.15 as NP_2 and NP_3, respectively. These parameters again require a value.

The point is now that the first member of each interpretable compound in (13) can be the value of one of the parameters specified in the conceptual representation for 'knife' as given in fig.15. Thus, *butcher's* in (13a) fills the subject position of NP_2 in S_3^0. *Bread* in (13b) fills the direct object position in S_3^0. *Kitchen* in (13c) and *pocket* in (13i) fill the position of place adverbial, as does *dream* in (13h). *Breakfast* and *table* in (13d,e) function as occasion adverbials, as does *guillotine* in (13j). *Carving* and *nail cleaning* in (13f,h) are alternatives for the default *cut*, while *cutting knife* in (13g) sounds odd because expressing the default is redundant.

In all these cases one or more choices can be made from the available options with the help of general encyclopaedic or background knowledge about knives and anything connected with them. Encyclopaedic knowledge must provide a plausible scenario, in the sense that, with the first compound member as the value for a given parameter in the concept representation, a situation must be depicted that is recognized as well-known or regularly occurring. When this recognition is there the compound is readily interpretable. When, however, our world knowledge at the moment of interpretation fails to provide such a scenario either no interpretation or only a doubtful one comes forth, as demonstrated in (13k-m).

If this theory is viable the interpretation of nominal compounds is *constrained* by the conceptual representation of the head noun and *screened* by available encyclopaedic knowledge. Typically, the parameters that are available are restricted to certain kinds. It seems worth investigating whether these correspond with the types of adverbials that are insertable in SA sentence structures in analogous positions. High sentential operators, for example, can only be inserted in SA structures at or close to the very top of the SA tree. Consequently, they should not be among the possible insertions in a conceptual tree like fig.15, as they fall outside the frame provided. This seems to be borne out by the facts: (13m), for example, if it allows for an interpretation at all, cannot be interpreted as 'that which is believed to be a knife'. (We have, of course, *a makebelief knife*, but there *makebelief* is an adjective.) And a *rumour criminal*, if anything at all, cannot be 'one who is rumoured to be a criminal'. If this is generally so, which would have to be checked, it would follow that no parameters are available for *knife* that would require a structural position in the concept representation of fig.15 outside the syntactic frame provided. It would be worth exploring if this is a general constraint on compound interpretation and similar cases where conceptual structure can be taken to constrain the interpretation.

CHAPTER 2

Some formal properties of grammars, trees and rules

2.1 Introductory[1]

Before the reader embarks on reading this chapter a warning is in order. This chapter is not meant to be read in the ordinary sense. Its main purpose is to serve as a reference text for the later chapters. Readers already familiar with concepts and techniques in transformational grammar will need it less than novices, who will have to spend some time getting used to the terms and techniques employed. Even they, however, are well-advised not to try and master this chapter before they set out on chapter 3. Instead, they should begin with the following chapter, which provides a gentler introduction into the matter, and look up technical terms and formal operations in the present chapter. This way the process of assimilation will be less demanding.

There is, however, also an important theoretical point to this chapter. It is thanks to the precise way in which the general notions are defined here that Semantic Syntax achieves the degree of compactness and uniformity in the syntactic description of the various languages shown in the following chapters. The universality of grammar starts at ground level.

2.2 Nodes, constituents, expansions and areas

In 1.3.2 of the previous chapter the general format for Verb-first languages of the Formation Rules that generate SA-structures was specified as follows:

$$V + (NP/S)$$

SA-Format: $S \rightarrow$ $V + NP/S + NP/S$

$$V + NP/S + NP + NP/S$$

This SA-Format is useful as far as it goes. It acts as a filter on structures generated by the Formation Rules. But in order to show up the underlying regularities in the rules (which were devised to show up the regularities detectable in the language), more information is needed on nodes, trees and operations on trees. This information will be provided in terms that may seem unnecessarily close to implementation. Their point, however, is not the imposition of some specific class of possible implementations but only, more modestly, to provide a set of notions precise enough to describe and analyse the

[1] In writing this chapter I was very much helped and stimulated by my Romanian colleague Dan Cristea, whose one-month stay at Nijmegen was entirely taken up with hours of concentrated work, interrupted by intensive discussions, on the issues discussed here.

operations occurring in the grammars of the languages described to an acceptable degree of formal precision.

Let us consider a tree to be a set of nodes and of relations of nodes, each node being characterized by a *tag* and by its values on a number of parameters. Each node is obligatorily specified for the parameters of *category, parent-node, right* and *left brother* under the same parent, and *lexical filler* or *dependents* (the two being mutually exclusive), and optionally also for possible *features*. There are three kinds of features, rule features, which only occur with categorial nodes (see 2.6), plus-minus features, only occurring with non-categorial nodes, and neutral features, occurring with either. Thus, the general structure of a node specification for a node tagged N_i is as follows, with P, Q, R, S and T as appropriate variables. The value for all parameters except 'category' may be zero ($\emptyset$).

$$N_i - \quad \text{cat=P} \qquad \text{('cat': category)}$$
$$\text{p=}N_j \qquad \text{('p': parent)}$$
$$\text{rb=}N_k \qquad \text{('rb': right brother)}$$
$$\text{lb=}N_l \qquad \text{('lb': left brother)}$$
$$\text{d=}N_m,...,N_x \quad \text{or: fill=Q} \quad \text{('d': dependent nodes; 'fill': lexical filler)}$$

optional: fe=[+/-R] or: fe=[s] or: rulf=<T> ('fe': feature; 'rulf': rule feature)

At SA-level the only categorial node (see 2.6) is V: all lexically filled nodes have the category value 'V' (predicate). The category value may be changed during the Cycle by means of NODE CATEGORY CHANGE (see 2.5). Many predicates bring along from the lexicon a rule feature inducing a cyclic rule. Rule features are removed when the rule in question starts to operate. When a cyclic rule results in a V-cluster through attraction of material from outside, any remaining rule features are inherited by the new cluster.

The parameters for parent, right/left brother and dependents define the local surroundings of the node. They express the two mathematical properties in terms of which tree structures are defined: dominance and precedence. They will be called the node's *connections*. When there is no reason to specify both left and right brother connections, connections are given in terms of right brother only.

For example, for a V-node tagged N_2 whose parent is an S-node tagged N_1, whose left brother is $\emptyset$, whose right brother is N_3 — cat=NP, and which is lexically filled by *believe*, with the rule feature <SR> (SUBJECT RAISING), the specification is as in (1a):

(1)a. N_2 —   cat=V
$$\text{p=}N_1$$
$$\text{rb=}N_3$$
$$\text{lb=}\emptyset$$
$$\text{fill=believe}$$
$$\text{rulf=<SR>}$$

That the parent node N_1 is an S and the right brother an NP, is not specified for N_2. (In rule specifications, however, category conditions on connections are normally expressed.) If the parent S-node, N_1, has no parent and no right or left brother but it has the three dependent nodes N_2, N_3 and N_4, the specification of N_1 is:

(1)b. N_1 —   cat=S
$\qquad\qquad$ p=$\varnothing$
$\qquad\qquad$ rb=$\varnothing$
$\qquad\qquad$ lb=$\varnothing$
$\qquad\qquad$ d=N_2 - N_3 - N_4

A definition is needed, moreover, of the concept of *constituent* or *subtree*. We define, first, the notion of *parent of nth degree*, or p^n. The parent connection has been defined already, but only for the immediate parent (dominance) relation. The notion can be generalized by saying that the connection expressed by the parameter 'p' is the first degree parent connection or p^1. In other words, simple 'p' is to be read as 'p^1'. In order to say that the (immediate) parent connection of a node N_i is the node N_j we use the expression: $N_i.p=N_j$, which is thus equivalent to $N_i.p^1=N_j$. Now, if $N_j.p^1=N_k$, then N_k is the second degree parent of N_i: $N_i.p^2=N_k$. And so on recursively: if $N_k.p^1=N_l$ then $N_i.p^3=N_l$. The relation p^0 automatically holds between any node and itself. As a general term for 'parent of degree n' ($n \geq 0$) we shall use the term *ancestor*. The notion of *dominance*, used informally so far, can now be formally defined: a node N_a *dominates* a node N_b just in case N_a is an ancestor of N_b. If $N_a \neq N_b$ N_a *properly dominates* N_b. In practice, however, the term *dominate* is understood in the sense of *properly dominate*, just as *subset* is normally understood as *proper subset*.

The definition of the concept *constituent* or *subtree* is now simple. Any node N_a in a tree dominates its unique *constituent* or *subtree*, which consists of the total set of nodes that have N_a as their common ancestor. This corresponds to the intuitive notion of a constituent in a tree structure according to which a constituent is formed by the dominating node N_a plus all the nodes that are connected by a downward path from N_a down to the lexically filled bottom nodes ('leaves'). Note that the node dominating a constituent (N_a) is part of the constituent, as it stands in the relation p^0 to itself. Moreover, a lexically filled node is a *minimal constituent*.

Then, if a node N_a dominates a node N_b the constituent dominated by N_b is a *subconstituent* of the constituent dominated by N_a. Normally, one only speaks of a subconstituent when $N_a \neq N_b$. In that case the constituent dominated by N_b is a *proper subconstituent* of the constituent dominated by N_a.

The notion *expansion* is also useful: an *expansion* is the amount of structure consisting of a parent node and its dependents: [P:A-B-C], where P is the parent node and A, B, C the dependent nodes.

A further notion is needed, especially in connection with the formation of the auxiliary constituent. This is the notion of *area*, defined as follows:

An *area* is a constituent C minus a subconstituent D of C

Any constituent or subconstituent thus forms an area (when D=Ø), but we normally speak of an area only when D≠Ø. An area A has an *entrance*, which is the parent connection of N_c dominating C, and an *exit*, formed by the parent connection of N_d dominating D. If D=Ø the node N_k, such that $N_d.p=N_k$ in cases where D≠Ø,[2] adopts a temporary node EXIT (to the right if C is right-branching; to the left if C is left-branching — see 2.7.1.1 and 2.8 below). Figure 1 shows an area of the type needed for the formation of the auxiliary (finite verb) constituent AUX. C is the constituent dominated by the parent node of $_{Aff}$[PRES] ('Aff'=Affix). D is $_V$[$_V$[have]$_{PaP}$[eaten]] ('PaP' = Past Participle). The entrance is the connection to the highest V; the exit is the connection to the subtracted subconstituent $_V$[$_V$[have]$_{PaP}$[eaten]]. Note, however, that areas may have a Ø entrance and/or exit. The heavy line connecting the V-nodes in fig.1 is the *spine* of the V-cluster (see 2.8).

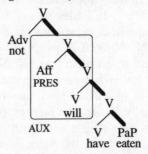

Figure 1   *The auxiliary area for the V-cluster in 'He will not have eaten'*

The rationale for the singling out an area A lies in the fact that A may deviate from its surroundings in certain important ways, for example in that A is to become a separate (sub)constituent or a separate morphological word (with different structural properties, such as a different directionality of branching; see 2.8 below). Sometimes also, a postcyclic rule requires that an area A be moved about. In the chapters to follow areas will be used mainly in connection with operations around the area called 'Auxiliary' (AUX).

2.3 Downgrading of S-nodes

We stipulate that if, by any rule, an S(entence) is stripped of its subject constituent it is automatically demoted to the status of Verb Phrase (/S): i.e. a defective S. But note that an /S still counts as S for all rules unless the rule contains a specification to the contrary. This we shall call DOWNGRADING 1. It reflects the theoretical statement that an S without a subject term is defective. Then, again automatically, any S or /S that comes to lack, by any

---

[2] 'N_n.[parameter]=[value]' is to be read as 'the [parameter] of N_n is [value]'. Thus, '$N_i.rb=N_k$' stands for 'the right brother of N_i is N_k'. 'N_n — [parameter]=[value]', on the other hand, means 'the node N_n such that its [parameter] is [value]': 'N_i — cat=NP' thus means 'the node N_i such that its category is NP'.

rule anywhere, a constituent labelled 'V' ceases to exist: the S-node or /S-node is erased and all dependent material is re-attached higher up (the precise formal definitions of these operations are given below). This second automatic operation is called DOWNGRADING 2. It reflects the theoretical statement that an S without a V is impossible. These two forms of DOWNGRADING have proved to be systematically fruitful in the analysis and description of syntactic structures. Formal definitions are given in 2.7.1.4.

2.4 Argument functions

Besides the node specifications given, a procedure is needed to determine what makes a constituent do duty as an argument function (AF), i.e. as subject (SU), direct object (DO) or indirect object (IO). In section 1.3 it was said that the AFs SU, DO or IO are based primarily on the number and position of the argument terms. That is, no parameters other than connections are needed for the definition of AFs: in VSO structures, the first NP or S after V is subject; the last NP or S is direct object provided there is also a subject; any NP between subject and direct object is the indirect object. This is the default definition of AFs. Sometimes, however, as with Passive, AF definitions are not possible in terms of just the connections though they are needed. Moreover, a term may be assigned an AF feature on lexical grounds. In many languages, for example, the object of verbs meaning 'help' is an IO, even if there is no DO. The AF features stick to the argument terms as long as they are not modified by some rule, and are activated when necessary. The default assignment of AF features on the basis of connections alone is as follows:

(2)a.   [**SU**]:   A subject is a constituent dominated by a node

$$N_i \text{ — cat=[NP or S] such that there is a node}$$
$$N_j \text{ — cat=V}$$
$$p=S$$
$$rb=N_i$$

b.   [**IO**]:   An indirect object is a constituent dominated by a node

$$N_i \text{ — cat=NP such that there are nodes } N_j \text{ and } N_k \text{ where } N_j.fe=[SU]$$
$$\text{and} \quad N_k\text{— cat=[NP or S]}$$
$$p=S$$
$$lb=N_i$$
$$rb=\emptyset$$

c.   [**DO**]:   A direct object is a constituent dominated by a node

$$N_i \text{ — cat=[NP or S] such that there is a node}$$

N_j — cat=[NP] or:	N_j — cat=[NP or S]
p=S	p=S
rb=N_i	rb=N_i
lb=N_k — cat=NP or S	lb=N_k — cat=V
fe=[IO]	fe=[SU]

According to these definitions the first NP or S after V is subject. If there is a subject the last NP or S of the dominating S is direct object. Any middle NP between subject and direct object is indirect object. As has been said, the features [SU], [DO] and [IO] stick to their arguments throughout the derivation, unless they are changed in virtue of some rule.

Argument functions may change in the course of the cyclic treatment of the complementation system. Thus, for example, in PREDICATE RAISING (PR, one of the main rules of the complementation system in languages like Dutch, German and French; see 2.7.4.1), the lower subject of an embedded transitive object clause becomes the middle NP of the higher S. In cases where the grammar redefines the AF-features according to the AF definitions given above, the old subject is, from there on, treated as indirect object (provided it satisfies the independently given thematic restrictions on indirect objects).[3] But if the object-S is intransitive, as in fig. 2b, its original subject ends up as direct object, simply because of the number of argument terms that occur with the derived complex V-island. These processes are shown schematically (with RIGHT ADOPTION) in fig. 2.

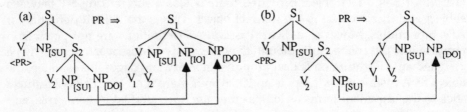

Figure 2   PREDICATE RAISING (PR) with (a) transitive and (b) intransitive
object clause

The French verb *faire* ('do','make','let') clearly shows these processes (see 4.4.3 for details). Consider, for example, the sentences (3a-c).

(3)a.   Il   a   v[fait   partir]   Albert
        he has   made leave   Albert
        'he made Albert leave'

   b.   Il   a   v[fait   voir]   la lettre   à Albert
        he has   made see   the letter   to Albert
        'he made Albert see the letter; he showed Albert the letter'

   c.   Il   a   v[fait   réparer]   la voiture   par Albert
        he has   made repair   the   car   by Albert
        'he had the car repaired by Albert

---

[3] That is, the term in question must allow for the thematic function 'beneficiary'. A sentence like *Il fera trouver sa solution au problème* ('he will make sure that the problem finds its solution') is ungrammatical because the NP *le problème* is not interpretable as a beneficiary. One has to say instead something like *Il fera de sorte que le problème trouve sa solution* ('he will act in such a way that the problem finds its solution').

Without tenses, the underlying structure of (3a) contains an embedded *intransitive* object clause: S_0[$_V$[faire]$_{NP}$[il]$_{S_1}$[$_V$[partir]$_{NP}$[Albert]]]. PREDICATE RAISING of $_V$[partir] results in an S_0 with a complex V-island $_V$[faire partir] ('make leave'), the original higher subject-NP *il* plus $_{NP}$[Albert], which is assigned the feature [DO] in virtue of (2) above. (3b) results from underlying S_0[$_V$[faire]$_{NP}$[il]$_{S_1}$[$_V$[voir]$_{NP}$[Albert]$_{NP}$[la lettre]]], i.e. with a *transitive* lower S. Now PR results in an S_0 with the V-island $_V$[faire voir] ('make see') and the original higher subject-NP *il* plus two new NPs: *Albert* and *la lettre*. (*Albert* is then turned into the PrepPhrase *à Albert* by DATIVE EXTRACTION.) Application of (2) above now results in the assignment of the features [DO] and [IO] to *la lettre* and *Albert*, respectively. The grammar allows this as the subject of *voir* ('see') has the thematic function 'recipient', and IOs are appropriate bearers of 'recipient' roles.

Not so in (3c), where the lower verb, *réparer* ('repair'), has an actor subject. With the corresponding active object-S PR would give *Il a fait réparer la voiture à Albert*, which means 'he had Albert's car repaired' and where *à Albert* has a different SA origin. In (3c), the lower S *must* be passivized, probably because datives are precluded from expressing 'actor' roles.

2.5 Elementary operations

Transformational rules and other well-regulated forms of tree surgery are packages, routines, of elementary operations on nodes. A precise description of the rules and other routines therefore requires a precise statement of the elementary operations involved. Five elementary operations seem to be needed.

(A)   **NODE DETACHMENT**
       When a node N_d is detached its connections to parent and brothers are erased and stored in a routine memory. Its connections to its dependents or its lexical filler are left untouched.

Since the lexical filler or dependent connections of a detached node are left intact, a detached node still is the ancestor of a constituent or an area. This constituent (area) is called the *detached constituent (area)*. Detached constituents (areas) may be either thrown away (deleted) or re-attached somewhere else. Intuitively one may regard the erasure of a connection as an operation whereby a connection in a tree is cut. NODE DETACHMENT thus leads to the cutting out of a constituent or area from a tree.

(B)   **NODE ERASURE**
       When a node N_e is erased its connections to its parent, brothers and dependents are erased and stored in a local memory. N_e is thrown away.

The normal procedure, in such a case, is for the dependent node or nodes to be re-attached higher up (see below). The two operations of NODE ERASURE and

RE-ATTACHMENT HIGHER UP figure together in the routines of TREE PRUNING and DOWNGRADING 2. A lexically filled node cannot be erased, but it can be detached and the detached constituent can be deleted. NODE ERASURE thus never involves a constituent or area. Only the node itself is removed. Constituent deletion, as in the rule SUBJECT DELETION (SD), involves NODE DETACHMENT, not NODE ERASURE.

(C)   **NODE ATTACHMENT**
    A node N_a is attached if it gets new connections to its parent and
    brothers.

N_a is attached *to an existing node* N_e when N_a takes the parent connection to N_e, which then automatically takes the corresponding dependent connection to N_a. For ATTACHMENT TO AN EXISTING NODE it must be specified where exactly N_a is to be plugged in under N_e, e.g. by specifying its new right brother connection to any of the dependents of N_e, or to none, in which case N_a ends up to the far right of the dependents of N_e. ATTACHMENT TO AN EXISTING NODE is either to a new position or to an existing position from which a constituent has been detached. That is, when a node N_a is attached to an existing node N_e in a new position the following takes place:

   any string of nodes α - β such that $N_e.d=\alpha$ - β $\rightarrow$ α - N_a - β and
   $N_a.p=N_e$ (α and β are possibly null strings of nodes)

If α is null N_a is *left-attached*. If β is null N_a is *right-attached*. If neither α nor β is null, N_a is *centre-attached*.

   If N_a is left-attached then $N_a.rb=X$ (X is the leftmost node in β).
   If N_a is right-attached then $N_a.rb=\varnothing$ and $X.rb=N_a$
      (X is the rightmost node in α).
   If N_a is centre-attached then:
   any nodes X,Y such that $X.rb=Y$ $\rightarrow$ $X - rb=N_a$ and $N_a - rb=Y$
      (X is the rightmost node in α; Y is the leftmost node in β).

When a node N_a is attached to an existing node N_e in a position from which a node N_d has been detached N_a takes over, as specified in (C) above, the old parent and brother connections from N_d (which have been kept in a routine memory).

A string γ of brother nodes $N_1,...,N_n$ ($1 \le n$) is re-attached *higher up* when their parent connection has been erased through removal of higher structure H (i.e. the common parent node N_p or an area A). $N_1,...,N_n$ take over the parent connection of N_p or of the node N dominating A. If $H=N_p$ only N_n takes over the brother connections of N_p. If H is an area A γ can only consist of one node N_s, which takes over the brother connections of N_a. That is, the exit and the entrance of A are linked up.

More precisely, when a node N_p is erased or an area A dominated by N_a is removed the string of dependents $N_1,...,N_n$ ($1 \le n$) of N_p or the node N_s

dominating the subconstituent subtracted from the constituent dominated by N_a is re-attached higher up. This involves the following steps:

any node $X \!-\! d\!=\!\alpha \!-\! N_{p/a} \!-\! \beta \;\rightarrow\; X \!-\! d\!=\!\alpha \!-\! \gamma \!-\! \beta$
(α, β may be $\varnothing$; $N_{p/a}$ is N_p or N_a; γ is $N_1,...,N_n$ or N_s)
any node $N_i \in N_1,...,N \;\rightarrow\; N_i \!-\! p\!=\!Y$
(Y is the parent node of $N_{p/a}$)
any node $X \!-\! rb\!=\!N_{p/a} \;\rightarrow\; X \!-\! rb\!=\!Z$
(Z is the leftmost node of γ)
any node X such that $N_{p/a}.rb\!=\!X \;\rightarrow\; Y \!-\! rb\!=\!X$
(Y is the rightmost node of γ)

(D)   **NODE COPYING**
When a node N_m is copied N_m is detached and a new node N_c is created. N_c copies the category value of N_m and takes the parent and brother connections of N_m, and takes N_m as its sole dependent. N_m takes N_c as parent.

More precisely:

Create $N_c \!-\! cat\!=\!X$ (X is the old category value of N_m)
$\qquad\qquad p\!=\!Y$ (Y is the old parent connection of N_m)
$\qquad\qquad rb\!=\!Z$ (Z is the old right brother connection of N_m)
$\qquad\qquad d\!=\!N_m$
Then: $X \!-\! d\!=\!\alpha \!-\! N_m \!-\! \beta \;\rightarrow\; X \!-\! d\!=\!\alpha \!-\! N_c \!-\! \beta$ (α and β may be $\varnothing$)

For example, in the nonce tree (a) in fig. 3, N_m is to be copied, giving (b):

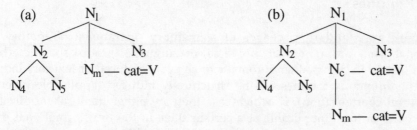

Figure 3   Node copying

The net result is, simply, that N_c is inserted on the line connecting N_m with its parent, taking over the category value.

(E)   **NODE CATEGORY CHANGE**
The category value of the node in question is changed according to an independently given specification.

This operation is trivial and needs no further comment.

2.6 Some definitions

At this point it is useful to introduce a few terminological definitions:

(1) A node X is **filled** if X is a C-node with a filler. X is **lexically filled** if the filler is phonologically realized (non-zero) and C ≠ Aff (i.e. 'Affix').

(2) **Categorial node (C-node)**: any node whose category value allows for a lexical filler.

(3) **Lexical C-node**: any lexically filled C-node, where C ≠ Affix or Clitic.

(4) **Lexical constituent (LC)**: any constituent $_C[a]$ where C is a lexical C-node, and any constituent $_C[_C[a]_A[b]]$ or $_C[_A[b]_C[a]]$, where:
$_C[a]$ is an LC and $_A[b]$ is an α-Affix or α-Clitic, with the spine on the α-side (α is the variable for left or right branching; see 2.8).

(5) **C-cluster**: any subtree dominated by a C-node.

(6) **C-island**: any C-cluster containing only C-nodes or lexical C-constituents

NB: The definition of *spine* is given below, in 2.8. For the moment, the following non-definitional description will do:

(7) **Spine**: a connection between a parent node P and a dependent node D (marked by a heavy line) indicating the directionality of the expansion: if the expansion is left-branching, the spine is on the left, and likewise for the right.

2.7 Routines

Routines are standard packages of elementary operations, obligatory or optional. They are, moreover, universal or language (group) specific. They differ further in being either automatic or category-induced or lexically induced. The automatic routines can be structurally induced (applicable given a structural configuration), in which case they are either nonlocal (applicable anywhere) or local (applicable at a certain stage in the transformational process). Or they can be procedurally induced (applicable in a larger routine, i.e. as subroutines). Subroutines, i.e. procedurally induced routines, like the two forms of ADOPTION, are local or nonlocal, but always universal and obligatory. Category-induced and lexically induced routines are all local. The former are found mostly in the Postcycle, the latter in the Cycle. Local routines are often called (transformational) rules. The nonlocal routines are known as conventions or standard procedures. This produces the following schema:

Routines:

type	subtype	local	universal	obligatory
automatic	procedurally induced	+/-	+	+
	structurally induced	+/-	+/-	+/-
category-induced		+	+/-	+/-
lexically induced		+	+/-	+/-

Figure 4   *Classification of routines*

2.7.1 Procedurally induced routines

2.7.1.1 ADOPTION

An important procedurally induced routine is called ADOPTION. It applies whenever a node X has to attract a subtree Y as part of a rule specification. This makes it non-local. Since ADOPTION seems to apply in the grammars of all languages it is classified as universal. And as there seems to be no other way of attaching a subtree to a node it is classified as obligatory.

When X adopts Y then: (a) NODE COPYING of X to X',
                             (b) DETACHMENT of Y,
                             (c) ATTACHMENT of Y to X'.

The ATTACHMENT is to the left (LEFT ADOPTION) or to the right (RIGHT AD-OPTION) of X'. The variable α is used for right or left: α-ADOPTION.

Thus, in the (sub)tree (4a) $_V$[let] right-adopts $_V$[go] in virtue of the rule PREDICATE RAISING (PR) induced by *let*. The result is first (4b) then (4c):

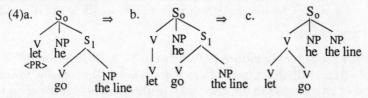

Note that the subject of the embedded object-S_1, $_{NP}$[the line], has been re-attached higher up after the automatic erasure of S_1 due to the removal of its V (DOWNGRADING 2). In its new position it is no longer a subject but a direct object. Note also that the rule feature <PR> disappears as soon as the rule in question, predicate raising, starts operate. This rule feature is thus not in-herited by the new V-cluster.

Or consider (5a), where OBJECT INCORPORATION (OI) involves the RIGHT-ADOPTION of $_{NP}$[Paris] by $_V$[in]. After OI the rule LOWERING (L) must still be applied. The remaining rule feature <L> now attaches to the whole new V-cluster:

(5)a. S_0 OI $\Rightarrow$ b. S_0

V S_1 NP   V S_1
in   Paris
<OI.L> V   NP
    live he   V   NP V   NP
                                 in Paris live he
                                        <L>

Occasionally it happens (as with DATIVE EXTRACTION; 2.7.2.2) that two subtrees Y and Z are to be adopted simultaneously, one to the left and one to the right. In that case NODE COPYING takes place once, and both ATTACHMENTS are made to the one new copy.

2.7.1.2 SURFACE CATEGORY ASSIGNMENT

Another procedurally induced routine is SURFACE CATEGORY ASSIGNMENT (SCA). This involves one or more applications of NODE CATEGORY CHANGE. SCA is obligatory whenever an SA-predicate is listed in the lexicon as belonging to a surface category different from V. It occurs typically as a corollary of any cyclic RAISING or LOWERING of the SA-predicate in question. When this RAISING or LOWERING involves a single lexical constituent $_V[X]$, SCA, if required, changes the category value 'V' into the surface category specified in the lexicon for X. If, however, the RAISING or LOWERING involves a two-layered V-cluster, as in (5), where LOWERING applies to the cluster $_V[_V[in]_{NP}[Paris]]$, SCA assigns phrase status to the copy node dominating the cluster, besides assigning the correct surface category to the original V. Since *in* is listed in the lexicon as a surface category preposition, this cluster becomes a PP, with the preposition *in* and its object-NP *Paris*. No provision seems needed for the application of SCA to V-clusters with more than two layers. SCA will be involved again in the internal grammar of NPs, which is not discussed here.

2.7.1.3 TREE PRUNING

Four further procedurally induced routines are TREE PRUNING 1, 2, 3 and 4 (the notion of TREE PRUNING goes back to Ross (1969)). They apply automatically at the end of any routine in the grammar, leading to the erasure of superfluous nodes that may have remained after all the operations of the routine have been carried out. They are nonlocal, universal and obligatory.

Informally, TREE PRUNING 1 is formulated as follows:

Any non-branching node of category C directly dominating another node also of category C is erased and the latter node is re-attached higher up.

More formally:

TREE PRUNING 1:
For any nodes X, Y such that X.cat=C and X.d=Y and Y.cat=C:
(a) ERASURE of X,
(b) RE-ATTACHMENT of Y higher up.

The second form, TREE PRUNING 2, is very much like TREE PRUNING 1 and amounts, informally, to the following:

Any non-branching and not lexically filled node of category C directly dominated by another node also of category C is erased and its dependent node is re-attached higher up.

More formally:

TREE PRUNING 2:
For any nodes X,Y,Z such that X.cat=C and Y.cat=C and X.d=Z and X.p=Y:
    (a) ERASURE of X,
    (b) RE-ATTACHMENT of Z higher up.

The third variety of TREE PRUNING required in Semantic Syntax, TREE PRUNING 3, is informally defined as follows:

Any non-branching categorial node that is not lexically filled is erased and its dependent node is re-attached higher up.

The list of categorial nodes (i.e. nodes that allow for lexical filling) includes, inter alia: V(erb), N(oun), NP,[4] A(djective), Adv(erb), P(reposition), Pa(st)P(articiple), Pr(esent)P(articiple), Aff(ix). A more formal definition is:

TREE PRUNING 3:
For any nodes X,Y such that X.cat=C and C∈L and X.d=Y (where
'L' is the set of category values that allow for lexical filling):
    (a) ERASURE of X,
    (b) RE-ATTACHMENT of Y higher up.

TREE PRUNING 4 is trivial and consists in the erasure of any node that has neither a lexical filler nor any dependents:

TREE PRUNING 4:
For any node X that lacks a value for either *fill* (lexical filler) or *d* (dependent(s)), erase X.

2.7.1.4 DOWNGRADING

In section 2.3 above two forms of DOWNGRADING were introduced. These, too, are procedurally induced routines, nonlocal, universal and obligatory. DOWNGRADING 1 applies automatically to any S-node whenever its subject dependent is detached and either re-attached elsewhere or deleted. It turns the S-node into a node labelled /S (=VP). Formally we say:

---

[4] For the moment, NPs are considered possible categorial nodes, and are thus allowed to take lexical fillers (e.g. pronouns). As the internal syntax of NPs is developed further this anomaly will have to be removed.

DOWNGRADING 1:

For any node X such that X.cat=S and X.d=V - α (α may be Ø; α does not contain a subject-node):

NODE CATEGORY CHANGE: X — cat=S → X — cat=/S.

DOWNGRADING 2 consists in the deletion of S or /S whenever the V-dependent is no longer dominated by S or /S:

DOWNGRADING 2:

For any node X such that X.cat=S or X.cat=/S and X.d=α (α may be Ø; no node of α dominates V with no S or at most one /S in between):

    (a) ERASURE of X,

    (b) RE-ATTACHMENT of α higher up.

2.7.2 Structurally induced routines

We shall now discuss three structurally induced routines, IT (for English), DATIVE EXTRACTION and MINCE. All three are local, and may therefore be called rules. DATIVE EXTRACTION and MINCE are obligatory. Only MINCE stands a chance of being universal.

2.7.2.1   IT

The rule IT, traditionally called EXTRAPOSITION or CLAUSE EXTRAPOSITION, is part of the Cycle in English grammar and consists in the creation of a dummy NP *it*, which is inserted into an S° in subject position under certain conditions. The main condition on IT is that the S° in question has a sentential subject term. The rule IT has the effect of preventing the sentential subject term from functioning as a grammatical subject, replacing it by a dummy $_{NP}$[it]. The original sentential subject is moved to object position if it is not already there (cf. the external-S-constraint; Ross 1967, 1986). IT has a clear functional motivation: the grammar of English (and many other languages) requires a not too heavy NP-subject in Surface Structure. This requirement of a surface NP-subject follows from, or is anyway in accordance with, the obligatory rule feature <SR> (SUBJECT RAISING) of the highest tense operator of a fully tensed sentential structure, since SR can only affect an NP-subject and not an S-subject (see 2.7.4.2.1). The rule IT is therefore obligatory when the subject is a bare S, not headed by an NP-node. But IT also applies when the subject-S is dominated by an NP-node. In such cases the functional explanation is probably the grammar's dislike for heavy sentential structures in subject terms. Although dummy *it* also occurs with infinitival complements (e.g. *It pleases me to eat early*), the rule IT is formulated here as a structurally induced rule only for fully tensed S" and $_{NP}$[S"] constituents. In other cases it may, perhaps, be regarded as lexicon-driven.

The rule IT is obligatory for a subject-S" without an NP-node. With a subject of the form $_{NP}$[S"] the rule is not obligatory but preferred. It seems that this preference can be overridden under conditions to do with the topic-comment modulation of sentences. Unfortunately, these conditions are not entirely clear. They can anyway not be formulated in terms of the syntax alone. It must be assumed that discourse-semantic topic-comment properties are somehow reflected in the syntax in such a way that certain rules, like IT, are made sensitive to them. In section 7.2 below, which deals with contrastive accents and cleft constructions, we will be a little more specific. Here we must be content with an incomplete formulation of the application conditions of the rule. We say that when a subject-clause $_{NP}$[S"] functions as topic IT is obligatory. But when a subject-clause $_{NP}$[S"] functions as comment IT is probably best regarded as optional.

The formal definition of structurally induced IT is as follows (for lexically induced IT the condition on γ is simply that γ be a sentential subject):

> IT: (cyclic)
> For any node S_c^o — d=[V - γ - α] (γ is S_d — d=[NP - /S - β] or
> $_{NP}$[S_d — d=[NP - /S - β]]; α and β may be $\varnothing$):
> > (a) create N — cat=NP
> > > fill=it
> > (b) INSERT N into S_c^o to the immediate right of V.

The condition S_d — d=[NP - /S - β] ensures that the subject-S is fully tensed, since only fully tensed Ss assume the NP-/S form. Schematically, IT is demonstrated in fig.5, where 'α' stands for any, possibly null, further dependents of S_c. (Non-null α is found, for example, in *It seems to me that you are right*, where the subject-S has been moved across α, *to me*.)

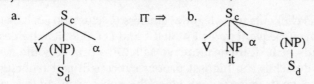

Figure 5   *Schematic representation of IT*

2.7.2.2 DATIVE EXTRACTION

The rule DATIVE EXTRACTION (DE) occurs as a rule of the Cycle in the grammar of all Romance languages. Subject to certain conditions, it turns an internal dative, i.e. an indirect object standing between the subject and the direct object terms, into an external dative, i.e. a prepositional object to the right of the direct object. Languages like English or Dutch have both internal and external datives, but, as has been shown by many investigators (e.g. Green 1974), there are notable semantic differences between the two. Accordingly, the two kinds of dative have different base-origins in these languages: the internal dative is generated as an NP between the subject and direct object

terms, while the external dative is generated the way prepositional phrases
normally are. In the Romance languages, however, only vestiges of an internal
dative are left (especially in their pronominal clitic systems) and the
external dative has become the standard surface cast for what is the middle
NP-term in VSO-structures (for a more detailed discussion see 3.6 and 4.3.1).

The formal definition of DE (as for French; see 4.3.1) is as follows:

> **DATIVE EXTRACTION:**   (cyclic)
> For any node S_c — d=[V - [NP_1 or S] - N_D - [NP_3 or S]]
>   (N_D — cat=NP
>   fe=[+Dative,-Clitic]):
>   (a) create N_V — cat=V
>   fill= à
>   rulf=<OI,L>
>   (b) adoption by S_c of N_V to the left and N_D to the right.

Diagrammatically, DE is demonstrated in fig.6:

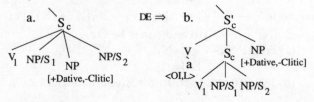

Figure 6   Dative   extraction

The rules OBJECT INCORPORATION and LOWERING subsequently produce an S_c
with the dependents [V - NP or S - NP or S - $_{PP}[_P[$à$]_{NP_{[+Dative]}}[X]]]$.

2.7.2.3 MINCE

MINCE (postcyclic) cuts up categorial clusters (C-clusters) such as the V-cluster
resulting from subsequent cyclic RAISINGs and LOWERINGs. It does not cut into
AUX, C-islands or lexical constituents. MINCE is probably the last rule of the
Postcycle. It detaches the highest proper subconstituent (subcluster) of a C-
cluster situated on its spine (except when this subconstituent is part of AUX or a
C-island or a lexical constituent) and re-attaches it on that side of its original
parent node on which it has been detached, i.e. left or right. MINCE applies
until all C-(sub)clusters have been processed:

> MINCE (with right-attachment; postcyclic):
> For any node C — d=α - D (C dominates a maximal C-cluster;
> D dominates a C-cluster but not AUX or a lexical constituent or a C-
> island; α is a non-null string of one or more nodes):
> (a) DETACH D
> (b) RE-ATTACH D to X such that C.p=X, to the right of C.

2.7.3 Category-induced routines

Category-induced routines are transformational rules, in the Cycle or in the Postcycle. When in the Cycle, they apply after the lexically induced rules. An example of a postcyclic category-induced routine is AFFIX HANDLING (AH). COPULA INSERTION (CI) is an example of a cyclic category-induced routine. They are discussed in the following two subsections.

2.7.3.1 AFFIX HANDLING

AH takes as input a C-cluster with one or more affixes branching off the spine. The immediately following lexical constituent right-adopts the affix (leading to a new lexical constituent; see 2.6). It keeps applying until all successive affixes have been processed. Some affixes cause the new lexical constituent to be relabelled. For example, the affixes PRES or PAST relabel the new constituent as FV ('finite verb'); $_{Aff}$[EN] and $_{Aff}$[ING] relabel the new constituent as PaP (past participle) and PrP (present participle), respectively. The new label is mentioned in the rules or the lexicon, wherever appropriate. Formally, the definition of AH is as follows:

> **AFFIX HANDLING:**   (postcyclic)
> For any node A — cat=Aff and A — rb=L (L is a lexical constituent), or A — rb=B and B — d=L - C or C - L (B and C are not lexical constituents or C is a lexical constituent but on a spine):
> L RIGHT-ADOPTS A.

AH, applied twice, is exemplified as follows for the French V-cluster corresponding to *ferait voir*: ('would let see (third person singular)'):

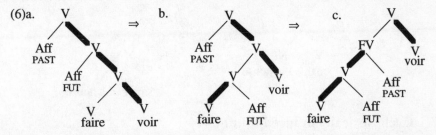

(6)a.   b.   c.

AH applies first to $_{Aff}$[FUT]: its right brother $_V$[$_V$[faire]$_V$[voir]] is, though a V-island, not a lexical constituent but it dominates two lexical constituents, one of which, $_V$[voir], is on a spine. Therefore, the non-spine lexical constituent, $_V$[faire], right-adopts $_{Aff}$[FUT], as shown in (6b) (one V-node gets pruned: TREE PRUNING 1). Note that $_V$[$_V$[faire]$_{Aff}$[FUT]] is now a lexical constituent, so that the right brother of $_{Aff}$[PAST] now dominates two lexical constituents, one of which, $_V$[voir], is on a spine and one, $_V$[$_V$[faire]$_{Aff}$[FUT]], is not. The latter now right-adopts $_{Aff}$[PAST], with the result as shown in (6c). The subcluster $_{FV}$[$_V$[$_V$[faire]$_{Aff}$[FUT]]$_{Aff}$[PAST]] of (6c) is now all left-branching, as shown by the spine that runs on the left hand side. This structure is input to the morphology, which will produce the form *ferait* (if in the third person singular). The top of the V-cluster is, however, right-branching, despite appearances, and produces the separate word *voir*. (See 2.8 and 2.11 for further discussion.)

2.7.3.2 COPULA INSERTION

For languages with a copula verb for adjectival and NP-predicates, a cyclic rule COPULA INSERTION (CI) is assumed, which makes the parent S^o-node of a V_{Adj} or V_{NP} predicate left-adopt the copula verb *be* under certain conditions, which may differ somewhat from language to language. In general, the main condition is that the parent node of V_{Adj} or V_{NP} be, at that stage in the Cycle, a full S (not /S), and, moreover, the V_{Adj} or V_{NP} in question must, after application of all lexically induced cyclic rules, still be in the original position (see 3.7.3.2). When V_{Adj} and V_{NP} undergo PREDICATE RAISING on the newly created S^o-cycle SCA turns them into Adj and NP, respectively.

Formally, this process is represented as follows:

> **COPULA INSERTION:** (cyclic)
> For any node C — cat=S, C — d=V_{adj} - α or C — d=V_{NP} - α
> (α is a non-null string of one or more nodes):
> (a) create a node N — cat=V_{cop}
> fill=be
> rulf=<L_V>
> (b) C LEFT-ADOPTS N.

For example, the partial SA-structure (7a) is transformed into (7b):

2.7.4 Cyclic lexically induced routines

Lexically induced routines are transformational rules whose applicability depends on specific lexical items. Some such routines are cyclic, others are postcyclic. The postcyclic lexically induced rules are not specified in the lexicon but in the Postcycle. The lexically induced routines (rules) of the Cycle are specified in the lexicon for the lexical items in question, which are always of the category V (deep verb or predicate). On each S-cycle the cyclic rules are put into action by the highest V-node of the S in question, which carries the rule features. Usually, this V-node is lexically filled. Sometimes, however, the V-node has adopted other material, as in the case of OBJECT INCORPORATION. In that case the rule features pass on to the copy node dominating the new V-constituent.

The most important group of lexically induced rules are those of the Cycle. Apart from a few minor rules (like the PARTICIPLE rules for English), they form a compact set of only a handful of rules which have a high degree of universality. We call these the *standard cyclic rules*. These are the rules we shall consider in this section. They are divided into four classes, cyclic RAISING, cyclic LOWERING, cyclic DELETION and cyclic INCORPORATION. The range of application of the cyclic RAISING rules is limited to either the V or the subject-NP of the embedded subject or object clause of the inducing V. The cyclic LOWERING rules can affect only the inducing V itself, which is lowered into its argument clause. The cyclic DELETION rules may affect only the subject-NP of the embedded object clause of the inducing V. Cyclic INCORPORA-TION incorporates, by α-ADOPTION, the object-NP or object-S into the V-consti-tuent.

2.7.4.1   Cyclic SUBJECT RAISING and PREDICATE RAISING

There are two forms of RAISING: SUBJECT RAISING (SR) and PREDICATE RAIS-ING (PR). The former raises the subject, the latter the V-constituent of the embedded subject or object S.

The formal definition of SR is as follows:

> **SUBJECT RAISING:**   (cyclic)
> For any node S_c — d=V - α - S_d' - β or S_c — d=V - α - S_d^o - β
> where V.rulf=<SR> (α, β are possibly null strings of nodes):
> (a) DETACH the node N—cat=NP, N—p=S_d' or S_d^o and N—fe=[SU],
> (b) ATTACH N to the immediate left of /S_d' or /S_d^o,
> (c) redefine AF features for nodes under S_c according to (2) in 2.4.

NB: S': S with only one tense (i.e. V_{t_2}),
          S^o: S without tense (see 2.11 below).

Note that SR does not apply with S"-argument-Ss. (fully tensed). When it does apply, i.e. with argument S' or argument-S^o, it requires an NP-subject: when no NP-subject is found the rule blocks and the generation process is aborted. An S" is fully tensed and becomes a full clause with a finite verb originating as AUX (see 2.10 below). An S' or S^o cannot contain AUX. They end up, in principle, as infinitives. SR, SD and PR typically produce infinitival complements. Languages that lack infinitives, such as most Balkan languages, tend not to have these rules.[5]

---

[5] The loss of infinitives is a well-known areal phenomenon that originated from early Medieval Greek and spread into the Balkans from the 4th Century onward (Joseph 1983). One can imagine that locals copied and loan-translated the linguistic habits (such as the replacement of infinitives by fully tensed clauses) of Greek travelling merchants who spoke the language of prestige. Although SR, SD and PR seem inappropriate for non-infinitival languages, Modern Greek appears to allow for a form of SR from a fully tensed object clause, as is demonstrated by the following sentence, taken from a folk song:

> Thélo ton ánthropo na échi   kardiá ('I want a man to have a heart')
> (I) want the(ACC) man that (he) has (a) heart

SR puts the subject-NP of an embedded subject or object S' or S° in the position of its own S, which is now downgraded to /S as it has lost its subject term. This /S moves one position to the right. This applies equally to SUBJECT-TO-SUBJECT RAISING and to SUBJECT-TO-OBJECT RAISING (Postal 1974). The former raises the subject of a subject clause to subject position, the latter raises the subject of an object clause to object position. The regularity is obvious: subjects of subject clauses become new subjects, while subjects of object clauses become new objects. Thanks to the deep VSO format (McCawley 1970), this regularity can be expressed in one single rule. The two forms of SR are shown in (8a) and (8b), respectively:

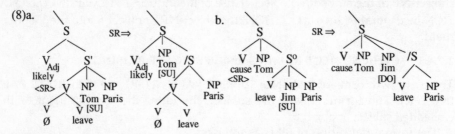

SUBJECT RAISING is also part of the routine called TENSE ROUTINE, which is responsible for the surface NP-/S (i.e. SVO) structure of the sentences of all SVO-languages. TENSE ROUTINE consists of the cyclic rules of SUBJECT RAISING and LOWERING (L), induced by the highest tense operator (V_{t_1}: PRES or PAST). See 2.7.4.2.1 below for further discussion.

SR as defined above selects the NP — fe=[SU], i.e. the subject NP, of the lower S as the NP to be raised. This pre-empts problems for the passive construction in many languages other than English, which define the subject of the passive sentence as the NP marked as direct object of V in the lexical argument structure. Structural equivalents of English *She was given a book* are thus ruled out in those languages and only structures like *A book was given (to) her* are allowed. This is taken care of by the provision in the SR rule definition that the lower subject be raised, not just the first NP after V. Note that the formulation of Passive in English ensures the proper re-assignment of the feature [SU] to the passive sentence (see 3.7.1).

PREDICATE RAISING (PR) has been mentioned and illustrated a number of times already. It consists in the ADOPTION by the inducing V of the V-constituent of an embedded partially tensed or untensed subject or object clause, leading to a V-island. The formal definition is as follows:

In colloquial Latin this construction is frequently attested as well (Terence, *Adelphi* 874):

Illum   ut vivat   optant   ('They want him to live')
him (ACC) that he-live they-wish

(This observation is due to Sanctius, *Minerva*, 1587; see Breva-Claramonte (1983:217); Kühner & Stegmann (1955, vol.II:579-582) gives over a hundred attested examples.) Note that Latin complement infinitival constructions are rather restricted as relatively few verbs induce SR or SD.

PREDICATE RAISING: (cyclic)

For any node $S_c — d=V - \alpha - S_d' - \beta$ or $S_c — d=V - \alpha - S_d^o - \beta$

where V.rulf=<PR> (α, β are possibly null strings of nodes):

    (a) DETACH the node N — cat=V, N — $p=S_d'$ or S_d^o,

    (b) the node V — $p=S_c$ α-ADOPTS N,

    (c) SCA and AF feature re-assignment as required.

Again, if the inducing V has an S" as subject or object its rule feature <PR> remains inoperative: PR applies only to an argument S' or S°. Note that AF features of S_c-arguments may be re-assigned, depending on the specifications for the language and for the S_c-verb concerned. Thus, the old subject may become indirect object, but it may also be assigned DO-status (see 4.4.3).

English has hardly any PR. Only rare lexicalized combinations, e.g. $_V$[[let][go]] (see fig.2 and (4) above), reflect PR in English. All RAISING in the English complementation system is SR. German and Dutch, on the other hand, have no SR in their complementation systems. They rely entirely on PR. French, finally, is of a mixed type: it has SR from embedded subject clauses and PR from embedded object clauses.

PR often forms lexicalized combinations with a specialized meaning even in languages that do not, or no longer, have PR in their productive syntax. In Malay, for example, one finds the lexicalized V-island $_V$[$_V$[beri]$_V$[tahu]] meaning 'inform, tell', usually written as one word but transparently composed of the two verbs *beri* ('give') and *tahu* ('know'). In Malay syntax, however, PR is hardly productive. It may be present in, for example:

(9)a.   Saya membawa masuk orang itu
        I   bring   enter   man-the
        'I brought the man in'

Masuk is both a verb ('enter') and an adverb ('in(to)'), though its origin is clearly verbal. If interpreted as a deep verb but recategorized as adverb, according to (c) of the definition of PREDICATE RAISING, it allows for the following PR-derivation (the subject term $_{NP}$[saya] is subsequently raised out of this S-structure as a result of the TENSE ROUTINE; see 2.7.4.2.1). If *masuk* is not recategorized but considered to remain a verb, PR also runs without a fault:

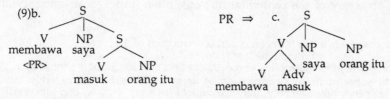

(9)b.   PR ⇒   c.

In the same way one can derive English constructions like:

(10)a.   I $_V$[$_V$[brought] $_{Adv}$[down]] the ladder
    b.   He $_V$[$_V$[put] $_{Adv}$[forth]] a proposal
    c.   You $_V$[$_V$[rang] $_{Adv}$[up]] my friend

where the adverbial part of the V-cluster has been recategorized from V.[6]

2.7.4.2 Cyclic LOWERING

Cyclic LOWERING can affect only the inducing V-constituent itself, detaching it and incorporating it into its argument-S. The 'landing site', the place of re-attachment in the lower S, may vary and is one of four categories. First, if the element to be lowered binds a variable in the lower S, as with quantifiers (see 7.1), the landing site is the first occurrence of the bound variable in the lower S. Otherwise the landing site is one of three categories, to be specified in the lexicon for every predicate inducing LOWERING. Elements may lower onto the V-constituent of the lower S (by α-ADOPTION, i.e. left adoption if the syntax is right-branching, and right adoption if the syntax is left-branching), thus helping to build up a V-cluster. Then, predicates (such as the negation word in Dutch and German, and in older forms of English)[7] may be swept to the far right of the lower S (though checked by previously lowered scope-bearing operators; see 7.1). Finally, an element may be lowered onto its own argument S, thus leaving the structure intact and, where applicable, causing only a category change in virtue of SURFACE CATEGORY ASSIGNMENT (2.7.1.2).

The definition of LOWERING is as follows (with an open parameter for the landing site):

> LOWERING: (cyclic)
> For any node N — cat=V and N — p=S_c, where $S_c.d = \alpha - S_d - \beta$ or
> $S_c.d = \alpha - /S_d - \beta$ or $S_c.d = \alpha -$ $_{NP}[S_d] - \beta$, and N — rulf=<L>
> (α, β are possibly null strings of nodes):
> (a) DETACH the node N,
> (b) RE-ATTACH N in the appropriate position (variable or lexically specified),
> (c) apply SURFACE CATEGORY ASSIGNMENT (SCA) if necessary.

LOWERING is typical of the logical operators such as negation and the quantifiers, and also of other, nonlexical, more abstract operators of the auxiliary system, that is, those operators that define tense (and aspect), quantification, negation and other sentential modifiers. These tend to be incorporated into the matrix structure of the sentential nucleus, often undergoing category change.

---

[6] One may speculate that the counterpart constructions of the type:
    (i)   He brought the ladder down
might originate from the application of SUBJECT DELETION to $_S$[bring-he-the ladder$_x$ $_S$[down-x]], with subsequent recategorization of *down* as Adverb. Alternatively (and more conservatively), however, one may list verbs like *bring down* as complex verbs in the lexicon, with specific rules applying to them.

[7] It is often said that this position of the negation word is a remnant of the pristine SOV-status of these languages, as the negation would go for the sentence-final verb. This is, however, incorrect (see 5.8). English, Dutch and German negation (*not, niet, nicht*) originated as *ne-ought, ne-iet, ne-icht*, respectively, meaning 'not something', the negative element *ne* being a copy of the main negation *ne* that stood with the verb, not at the end of the sentence. In time original *ne* got lost and *ne-ought, ne-iet, ne-icht* took over its function. The final position of the negation is thus due to the final position of the direct object.

The LOWERING rules are the converse of the RAISING rules, which are central in the complementation system and make for incorporation of lower subjects or V-constituents of partially tensed embedded argument-Ss into the nucleus.

It may be asked why the distinction is made anyway between PREDICATE RAISING with RIGHT/LEFT-ADOPTION and LOWERING onto the lower verb in the other direction, as the result appears to be identical. This is, however, only so in some cases. If PR is always replaced by L the re-attachment higher up of the arguments of the lower V-constituent will go wrong. And this re-attachment is essential for the grammar to work properly. If, on the other hand, L is always replaced by PR the treatment of Quantifiers, of Prepositional Phrases as well as the TENSE ROUTINE will go wrong as the arguments of the lower V-constituent will now be re-attached higher up. Both rules are thus indispensable, even if they sometimes lead to identical output structures. In such cases we choose between PR and L on grounds of elegance and regularity.

2.7.4.2.1 *The* TENSE ROUTINE: *from VSO to NP-/S*

We will now consider the TENSE ROUTINE, referred to several times above. This is the routine associated with the highest tense operator, t_1, which is either PRES (present) or PAST. (For the use of two tenses see 2.11 below.) PRES and PAST are defined as inducing the rules SUBJECT RAISING and LOWERING. They must be applied in that order, since in the inverse order, L followed by SR, the latter rule can no longer be applied. TENSE ROUTINE, in particular the rule SUBJECT RAISING, causes the structural change from a VSO format to an NP-/S structure.

The procedure is sketched in fig.7 (a is any string of nodes). Structure (a) is changed by SR into (b), which is at half station between VSO and NP-/S. Subsequent LOWERING produces (c), which is purely NP-/S. Note that LOWERING involves LEFT-ADOPTION by the lower V-constituent. Also note that after LOWERING the tense operator changes category from V to Aff(ix).

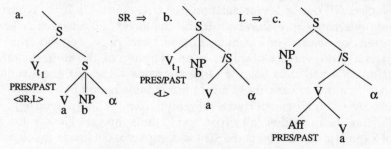

Figure 7 TENSE ROUTINE

Interestingly, the difference between surface SVO (= NP-/S) and surface VSO order in different languages of the world can now be accounted for by the assumption that the grammars of the VSO languages simply lack the rule feature <SR> for the t_1-operator. Without this rule feature the surface NP-/S structure of the SVO languages does not come about. This fits in with the well-known fact that both VSO and SVO languages have a right-branching syntax

(though often a left-branching morphology) and have therefore a number of
central syntactic properties in common, as against the SOV languages, which
are left-branching in their syntax as well as their morphology.

2.7.4.3 Cyclic DELETION

Only subject-NP-constituents of embedded (usually object) clauses may be
deleted in the Cycle. We therefore speak of SUBJECT DELETION (SD). SD is
one of the major rules of the Cycle in all languages that have infinitives. The
application of the rule feature <SD>, induced by a given verb, is subject to a
few conditions. First, the deletion is bound by a so-called *controller*, an NP-
argument term either of the higher V (VERTICAL SUBJECT DELETION) or of a
brother subject-S (HORIZONTAL SUBJECT DELETION). VERTICAL SD is
traditionally known as EQUI-NP-DELETION, found in sentences like *Tim wants
to leave* (=(13a) below) or *Tim told Tom to leave* (=(13b) below). HORIZONTAL
SD occurs typically with prepositional predicates, leading to sentences like
Tim died by swallowing poison (=(13c) below), where the semantic subject of
swallow has been deleted. With HORIZONTAL SD the controller can only be
the subject term. With VERTICAL SD the controller is an argument term of the
higher V, either the subject term or the indirect object (middle) term. Which
of the two it will be is a question about which a great deal has been written
since Rosenbaum (1967), but no satisfactory general account has been provided
so far. We shall let the matter rest here, and assume that the control relation
of SD is specified in the lexicon for each VERTICAL-SD-inducing verb: subject-
to-subject or middle term-to-subject.

SD can be applied only if the *anaphoric reference condition* is fulfilled: the
subject-NP-constituent that is up for deletion must have anaphoric referential
identity with respect to its controller. The referential identity is expressed in
tree structures by subscripting the controller's NP-label with a variable
symbol $(x, y,$ or $z)$ and providing the same variable symbol as filler for the
lower subject NP that is up for deletion (see (13a-c) below). If the controller is
a definite referring expression both it and the lower subject must refer to the
same reference object. For example, in *John wants to go*, derived from 'want
$John_x$ [go x]', the subject of *go*, x, is an anaphor of the definite referring
expression *John* and thus has the same reference value. If the controller is a
quantified term the lower subject must be a variable bound by its controller, as
in *Everybody wants to go*, derived, roughly, from '[all x [person x]] [want x
[go x]]'. Here the quantifier [all x [person x]] binds the variable x in the matrix
S [want x [go x]].[8] Since *want* is the SD-inducing verb, the lower x, subject of *go*,
is deleted.

---

[8] In effect, this sentence is true just in case all (relevant) individuals satisfy the function
[want x [[go x]]. This means that this function becomes a true sentence whenever the name
of one of the individuals in question is substituted for (the first occurrence of) x. For
quantified controllers, anaphoric referential identity is thus just a generalization over a
class of individuals.

If the lower subject fails to satisfy the anaphoric reference condition SD does not apply. In English, in such cases, SUBJECT RAISING tends to apply instead, as with, for example, English *expect* and *want* (see 3.1.2). These verbs are specified for the rules SD / SR, meaning that SD must be tried first, but if the lower subject fails to satisfy the anaphoric reference condition SR applies, taking the lower subject out of its S and reducing this S to /S. One thus finds regular pairs of sentences like the following:

(11)a. Tim wants/expects to find a job
    b. Tim wants/expects Tom to find a job

If a verb is specified for SD and no alternative is given, the embedded S' or S⁰ must have a dependent variable for subject, or else the sentence cannot be processed: [tell I John$_x$ $_{S0}$[leave Dick]] is ill-formed from the start.

As has been known from the earliest days of Transformational Grammar, /S-structures embedded under surface verbs become infinitivals (see 2.12). In English, these /S-infinitivals are usually preceded by the particle *to*. Only certain verbs embed object infinitivals without *to*. Perception verbs, for example (*see*, *hear*, *feel*, etc.) take object infinitivals without *to*, like, idiosyncratically, the verbs *make* and *let*.

(12)a. Tom saw Tim (*to) tame the horse
    b. Tom heard the butcher (*to) kill the pigs[9]
    c. Tom made Tim (*to) leave the house
    d. Tom let Tim (*to) leave the house

The modal auxiliaries (*can, will, may, must*, etc., but not *ought*) likewise do not allow for *to* to precede the following infinitival: *I can (*to) walk*. But the modal auxiliaries are not, as in traditional transformational analyses, considered to take /Ss as object terms. Instead, the modals are defined to take LOWERING onto the lower verb (by LEFT-ADOPTION), so that no /S-structure arises. For the modals one should, therefore, not expect the occurrence of *to*.

A further condition on SD is that the lower S whose subject-term is to be deleted must not have more than one tense, i.e. must be either S' or S⁰. This same condition applies, as has been shown, to SUBJECT RAISING and PREDICATE RAISING, but not to LOWERING. Therefore, embedded S' or S⁰ structures will, if affected by cyclic RAISING or DELETION rules, either be downgraded to /S (by SR or SD) or disappear altogether (by PR). The overall effect is that S's or S⁰s in an argument position to a commanding verb, i.e. as sentential complements, totally or partially merge with the embedding S, thus reducing the (often deep and steep) S-hierarchy of the input SA-structure. But embedded S"-structures, i.e. fully tensed Ss, are impervious to cyclic RAISING or DELETION rules. They develop into full clauses usually preceded by a complementizer.

---

[9] Notice the difference with *-ing* complements. In (12b) Tom is more likely to have heard the pigs than the butcher. But in:
    (i) Tom heard the butcher killing the pigs
it must be the butcher Tom heard. Cf. note 22 in chapter 3.

The cyclic RAISING and DELETION rules are typical of the complementation system of the syntax, but the auxiliary system is served mainly by LOWERING rules which are not, as has been said, subject to the condition that their argument-S may contain at most one tense: elements may be lowered into fully tensed Ss. This means that higher auxiliary structure, which tends to contain the more abstract and logical elements of the sentence in question, is integrated more fully into the lexical matrix S than complement-Ss, which maintain more of the original S-hierarchy.

(13a-c) represent the two forms of SUBJECT DELETION, VERTICAL SD and HORIZONTAL SD:

(13)a. VERTICAL SD controlled by higher subject:

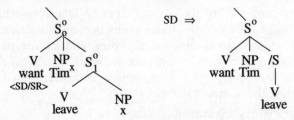

b. VERTICAL SD controlled by higher middle term (indirect object):

$$S^o_o \Rightarrow S^o$$

```
        S°o                      SD ⇒        S°
     ╱  |  |  ╲                            ╱  |  |  ╲
    V  NP NPx  S°1                        V  NP  NP  /S
   tell Tim Tom  ╱ ╲                     tell Tim Tom  |
   <SD>       V   NP                                   V
            leave  x                                 leave
```

c. HORIZONTAL SD controlled by subject in matrix subject clause (under prepositional V):

```
         So                  SD ⇒              S
      ╱   |   ╲                            ╱   |   ╲
   VPrep  S'    NP                      VPrep   S'      NP
    by   ╱ ╲     |                       by    ╱ ╲       |
 <SD,OI,L> V NPx  S1                  <OI,L>  V  NP      /S
         die Tim  ╱ ╲                        die Tim    ╱ ╲
               ╱  |  ╲                               V     NP
              V  NP  NP                           swallow poison
           swallow x poison
```

The formal definition of subject deletion can be given as follows:

SUBJECT DELETION: (cyclic)

For any node S_c—d=V - α - S_d^o/S_d' - β or S_c—d=V - α - $_{NP}[S_d^o]/_{NP}[S_d']$ - β where V.rulf=<SD> (α, β are possibly null strings of nodes), if α or β contains NP_x or S — d=V - NP_x - γ and $[S_d^o/S_d'$ or $_{NP}[S_d^o]/_{NP}[S_d']]$—d=V - $_{NP}[x]$ - δ (γ, δ may be $\varnothing$):

   (a) DETACH the node $_{NP}[x]$,
   (b) DELETE the detached constituent.

2.7.4.4 Cyclic INCORPORATION

Cyclic INCORPORATION is the rule whereby an argument NP-term is incorporated into the inducing V-constituent. By far the most common form of IN-CORPORATION is OBJECT INCORPORATION, found with great frequency in both the open syntax and in lexical word formation processes of all or most languages of the world. In English, nominalizations and adjectival *-ing*-participles may naturally include NP-objects, as in *bear hunting, beer consuming*, and verbs may be extended to include an original object, as in *take care of, keep tabs on, pay attention to*, etc. In Dutch, incorporated objects act as verbal particles: *Ik ben wezen koffie-drinken* ('I went to have coffee'). SUBJECT INCORPORATION is a great deal rarer, but it has been reported for natural phenomena in the Paleosiberian language Chukchee (Muravyova 1992; see 1.3.1), where sentences like 'it grass-appeared' exist besides 'grass appeared'. (As was said in 1.3.1, the suggestion naturally offers itself that SUBJECT INCORPORATION underlies the lexical formation of impersonal weather verbs in English and many other languages, but this point will not be further discussed here.)

As OBJECT INCORPORATION (OI) is obviously present in both open syntax and word formation processes, the Streamline Principle, introduced in 1.3, justifies its introduction into the less obvious and more abstract parts of the syntax, provided it does useful work. And here we find, as has been shown several times above, that it fits in naturally with the analysis of Prepositional Phrases. Prepositions are treated as verbs (predicates) in SA-structures, but English and many other languages prefer to say, for example, *Coffee grows in Africa*, rather than 'the growing of coffee INs Africa', with the mock surface verb *IN* and *Africa* as direct object. Yet in the 19th century a number of perceptive linguists, such as Steinthal (1861:101, referred to earlier in 1.3.2) felt that in a sentence like *Coffee grows in Africa* the highest predicate is really *IN*, and not *grow*. We can now say that Steinthal was right after all: in our analysis the SA predicate is indeed the predicate *in*, marked for 'Preposition' as surface category, and taking a sentential subject term and an NP-object, which is cyclically incorporated into the predicate through OI. The extended V-constituent is subsequently to undergo LOWERING into the subject S, which is the nuclear matrix structure of the sentence and has *grow* as its lexical verb.

Further applications of OI in cyclic syntax, again combined with LOWER-ING, are found with subordinating sentential conjunctions such as *because*, *although*, *if*, which take a fully tensed $_{NP}[S"]$ as object term (see 7.4), and with the treatment of quantifiers (see section 7.1). As regards quantifiers, we may quote a 19th century linguist, this time Meyer Lübke (1899:352), who felt that a quantifier like *two* in *Two foreigners arrived* is the 'deep' predicate, with *arrived* as the 'deep' subject. As was pointed out in 1.3.2, the formal means to give substance to these intuitions were not available to the linguists, philosophers and psychologists who engaged in discussions of this nature, which thus petered out unresolved in the '20s of this century. Now, however, such formal means are available in abundance, both in logic and in linguistics, and we are making use of them.[10]

The formal definition of OBJECT INCORPORATION is as follows:

> **OBJECT INCORPORATION:**   (cyclic)
> For any node N_i — cat=[NP or S] d=V - [NP or S] - (NP) - N_i - α
> where V.rulf=<OI> ($\alpha \neq N_k$ — cat=[NP or S] or α is null):
> (a) DETACH the node N_i,
> (b) V α-ADOPTS N_i.

SVO and VSO languages have a preference for right-adoption; SOV languages prefer left-adoption. The surface category change is probably best associated with the subsequent lowering of the extended V-constituent.

2.8 Directionality and spines[11]

One of the deeper factors that appear to play a regulating role in the building up of tree structures and the processes they undergo is *directionality of branching*. What precisely this role is and what notions would describe this role adequately is still far from clear, but enough has become visible for us to devote some attention to the subject.

It has been known for some time that languages seem to have a preference for left-branching or right-branching structures in specific areas of their grammars. (Centre-branching, though mathematically possible, does not seem

[10] In Russellian Predicate Calculus, quantifiers function as higher order predicates (i.e. predicates over sets, or sets of sets, or sets of sets of sets, etc., of individuals). In the more adequate newer theory of Generalized Quantification, quantifiers function as higher order predicates over pairs of sets (of sets, etc.) of individuals. In this theory, the sentence *Two foreigners arrived* is analysable, roughly, as 'the set of those who arrived [overlapped to the extent of at least two individuals with] the set of foreigners', i.e. with the set of arrivers referred to in subject position, the set of foreigners referred to in object position, and 'overlapped to the extent of at least two individuals with' representing the quantifying predicate *two*. It turns out that this kind of analysis is tailor-made for Semantic Syntax: the predicate *two* first incorporates the object by OI; LOWERING then makes the whole extended V-constituent land at the position of the bound variable (see section 7.1).

[11] The term 'spine' is due to Henk Schotel, who noticed the spine as something that deserved further scrutiny.

to be a useful notion in grammatical theory.) The difference between the two directionalities seems obvious. One would think that right-branching structures can always be recognized by the fact that it is always the right hand side node that splits up again, whereas left-branching structures are defined by the fact that it is the left node that does so, as shown in fig.8.

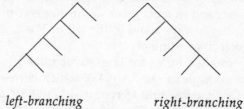

Figure 8   *left-branching*   *right-branching*

In reality, however, both the diagnosis and the definition of branching directionality is less obvious. Sometimes a surface expansion branches out from somewhere in the middle while it is otherwise clearly part of a right-branching, or of a left-branching component of the grammar. In such expansions the left or right branching directionality is not visible. To assume centre-branching as a separate setting just for these cases (see note 12 for an example) would be disproportionate and would complicate the theory unnecessarily. Then, simple binary expansions do not have enough structure to show their branching directionality, even though they may well have one. Moreover, an element that belongs in, say, a left-branching part of the grammar may find itself, through the accidents of its transformational history, in a right-branching expansion. In the grammar of English, for example, a node that was labelled V in SA may be recategorized as an Affix as a result of LOWERING. As long as it was a V it belonged to syntax and thus to right-branching grammar, but as an Affix it is part of morphology and thus of left-branching grammar. Yet as long as the derivation is syntactic no morphological structures arise, and the Affix node will therefore, though part of left-branching grammar, find itself in a right-branching context. This fact has certain consequences, which will be discussed below. There is thus more to branching directionality than meets the eye.

We may assume that in the grammar of every language there are one or more settings for directionality. The languages with only one setting for all parts of the grammar are rare. Turkish, for example, seems to be left-branching throughout. But most languages are more or less mixed between right and left branching. Thus, English, Dutch, French and other European languages are predominantly right-branching in the syntax but mainly left-branching in the grammatical (or flectional) morphology, though not necessarily in the lexical (or derivational) morphology. German flectional morphology is again largely left-branching, but the syntax likewise shows many left-branching characteristics, next to features that point to right-branching, which suggests that German syntax has a directionality problem (see chapter 6).

The distinction between deep Verb-first languages — a category that includes VSO and SVO or NP-/S languages — and deep Verb-last (mostly SOV) languages reflects a difference in branching directionality at the level of the Formation Rules. In Verb-first languages the Formation Rules generate right-branching, but in Verb-last languages they generate left-branching structures. The recursive subject-Ss in Verb-first languages always stand to the right of the V-constituent, and in most cases no further constituent follows.[12] In Verb-last languages they always stand to the left of V and are usually not followed by any other (object) constituent.

Thus, the Formation Rules for English (chapter 3) generate right-branching structures. An example is the SA (14a), which corresponds to *Tom wouldn't have left*. The Cycle, consisting of repeated LOWERING plus TENSE ROUTINE and PaP (the Past Participle rule) subsequently produces the Shallow Structure (14b), where the S-hierarchy has been transformed into an equally right-branching V-cluster hierarchy. The heavy lines in the expansions are called *spines*. Spines are used to indicate the directionality of an expansion: if an expansion is right-branching the spine is on the right, and analogously for left-branching expansions. In lexical expansions with a complement-S the spine connects the dominating S-node with that S. If there is no complement-S there is no spine.

(14)a.

S''^{ADV} — V_{Adv} not <I> — S'' — V_t^1 PAST <SR,L> — S^{MOD} — V_{Mod} WILL <I> — S' — V_{t_2} have <PaP,L> — S^0 — V_{Verb} leave — NP Tom

CYCLE ⇒

b.

S — NP Tom / S — V — Adv not / V — Aff PAST / V will / V have — Aff EN — V leave

The right-branching of the V-cluster (in (14b)) is due to the consistent LEFT-ADOPTION specified for each LOWERING rule in the English lexicon for the items concerned (see 3.1). If we now assume that there is a *right-branching setting* for the elements concerned we no longer need to specify for each

[12] Only with certain predicate classes, such as those that end up as prepositions, as subordinating conjunctions like *because, while, since* and with quantifiers does the recursive S-node dominating the matrix-S have a right brother. In principle, prepositional predicates take S + NP (see for example (5a,b) above), and subordinating conjunction predicates take S + ₙₚ[S]. In all these cases the cyclic rules induced are OBJECT INCORPORATION and LOWERING.

LOWERING rule that it takes LEFT-ADOPTION: the simple mention LOWERING ONTO LOWER V would suffice and other simplifications in the rule formulations would follow. The converse is true for PREDICATE RAISING: when a lower V is raised by PR in a right-branching context it is RIGHT-ADOPTED by the higher V, thus securing, again, right-branching.

More generally, we may assume an α-setting (i.e. a setting for left or right branching) for specific categories in the grammar. In the grammar of English the word categories (Verb with its derivatives PaP and PrP, Noun, Adjective, Adverb, Preposition, and the like) will be set for right-branching, and so will be the category S and its derivative /S. But morphological categories like Affix will have a setting for left-branching.

For the Formation Rules this means that at most one right/left-branching S-node will occur on the right/left hand side, or in the centre, of every expansion. An S-expansion will not normally contain both an object-S and a subject-S, as this would upset the directionality. In fact, in the languages looked at so far, whenever a lexical verb has both a subject and an object clause the subject clause is invariably factive (its truth is presupposed; also, in these cases, *that* can be replaced by *the fact that*), which means that the S is dominated by an NP-node (see Seuren 1985:408):

(15)   (The fact) that he grinned suggested/meant/proved that the butler knew about the theft.

Likewise for subordinating conjunction predicates such as *because, although, while*, etc. These are defined as taking a matrix-dominating S as subject term and an $_{NP}[S'']$ as object term (see 7.4), and indeed their clauses are all factive. Prepositional predicates may take an $_{NP}[S^o$ or $S']$ as object, as shown in (13c) above, leading to a prepositional *-ing* phrase. But the NP is never absent in the expansion [S: V_{Prep} - S - NP]. Only in coordination constructions (with *and, or, but, for*, etc.) will two parallel S-terms occur, leading to a double spine. In such cases, a special set of rules comes into operation, the set of CONJUNCTION REDUCTION rules (see 7.3).[13]

For the Cycle and Postcycle the assumption of an α-setting implies that when an element A attracts an element B, both occurring in α-branching expansions and both having the same α-setting (A_R and B_R, or A_L and B_L), B must stay to the same side of A: if B is on the left of A it is LEFT-ADOPTED, and if it is on the right of A it is RIGHT-ADOPTED. For clarity's sake, the notion of 'being to the left/right side of' is defined as follows:

> B is to the left/right of A just in case it has an ancestor that is a (not necessarily immediate) left/right brother of an ancestor of A.

---

[13] A problem is posed by the conjunction *if*. *If*-clauses are, obviously, not factive, yet they are subordinated to the main clause, unlike conjunction and disjunction constructions. Perhaps a prelexical analysis in terms of 'in the event that' will bring relief. Note that conditional constructions manifest themselves in rather different ways in the languages of the world and often have idiosyncratic features. They are also 'secondary' in the sense that they come about later on in the history of a language as a regrammaticalization of an originally semantically transparent construction (Stassen 1985).

(Note that every node is its own ancestor: see 2.2. above).

When an element set for, say, left-branching, finds itself in a right-branching expansion, its position is called *anomalous*. Elements in anomalous position tend to undergo treatment that removes the anomaly. Thus the Affix constituents in fig.1 or in (6a), (14b) or (16a) find themselves in an anomalous position, since Affixes are set for left-branching, while the expansions they occur in are right-branching, as indicated by the spines. The rule of AFFIX HANDLING results in the Affix constituent ending up in a left-branching expansion, as shown in (6b,c) and (16b-d). Similar phenomena are observed for lexical verbs in German, which are marked for left-branching but are placed in right-branching expansions by the Formation Rules.

In fig.9, attraction of B_R by A_R is demonstrated for B_R to the left of A_R (in this case LOWERING) and B_R to the right of A_R (in this case RAISING). Both A_R and B_R are in a non-anomalous position (though that makes no difference for the result). Analogously in fig.10 for B_L to the left of A_L (RAISING) and B_L to the right of A_L (LOWERING). No account is taken of any node erasure due to PRUNING. Clearly, if, by any rule whatsoever, A attracts B and A and B are of the same directionality then B is α-adopted on the side it came from. This is so regardless of whether B is in an anomalous position. A cannot be in an anomalous position, as anomalously placed elements cannot attract other elements but must themselves be moved. The resulting structure remains of the same directionality.

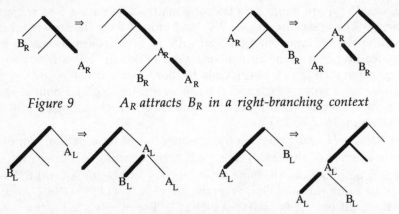

Figure 9 A_R *attracts* B_R *in a right-branching context*

Figure 10 A_L *attracts* B_L *in a left-branching context*

If, however, a node A attracts a node B but they are set for different directionalities, then B crosses over to the other side and the new expansion takes on the directionality of B. This is demonstrated in figs.11 and 12, respectively, where B is moved from an anomalous to a non-anomalous position.

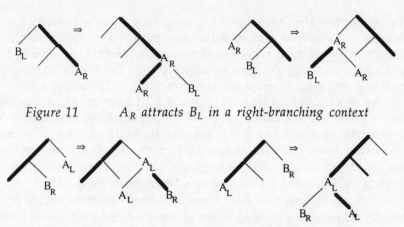

Figure 11 A_R *attracts* B_L *in a right-branching context*

Figure 12 A_L *attracts* B_R *in a left-branching context*

The figs.9-12 are schematic examples showing the effects of α-directionality settings on rules and trees. A real life example is (16). The V-cluster in (16a) occurs in the derivation of the sentence *Tim went* after the postcyclic rule of *DO*-SUPPORT but before AFFIX HANDLING (AH). $_{Aff}$[PAST] is in an anomalous position, as it is set for left-branching while the position it has tumbled into is right-branching owing to the fact that it was $_V$[PAST] before the LOWERING operation and verbs are set for right-branching in English grammar. SURFACE CATEGORY ASSIGNMENT has thus created a directionality anomaly for $_{Aff}$[PAST]. (16a) is thus similar to the first example in fig.11, but for the fact that the two nodes involved are brothers. After AFFIX HANDLING, i.e. in (16d), the Affix-constituent has found its proper left-branching place: it is no longer part of the syntax but has become part of the morphology, as befits a constituent labelled 'Affix'. Consequently, the constituent $_V$[$_V$[go]$_{Aff}$[PAST]] can now be turned into the word *went*:

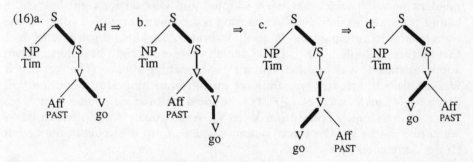

Note that $_V$[$_{Aff}$[PAST]$_V$[go]], i.e. the V-cluster as it figures in (16a), is not a lexical constituent, whereas after AH, i.e. as in (16d), it is a lexical constituent (see 2.6 above). The difference is important for a number of reasons, for example because the next rule, MINCE, will cut up V-clusters but will save lexical constituents.

To render the directionality of a branching visible even if the actual amount of tree structure is too small to show it, we have introduced the notion and the notation of *spine*, represented, whenever relevant, as a heavy line in a tree diagram showing the directionality: a right hand side spine indicates right-branching, and likewise for left-branching. An example similar to but somewhat more elaborate than (16) is (6) in 2.7.3.1 above, where the V-cluster in (6c) is partly left-branching and partly right-branching, even though on the face of it the cluster looks left-branching throughout. The spine notation corrects this erroneous impression. In fact, the left-branching part of this cluster is turned into the morphologically complex word *ferait*, whereas the remaining right-branching part becomes the separate word *voir*.

The notion *spine* can now be defined as follows (where α stands for left or right; the directionality (α-branching) of a node N may change as a result of SURFACE CATEGORY ASSIGNMENT induced by the rule that led to the expansion in question):

> A *spine* is a connection between a parent node P and a dependent node D satisfying either of the following conditions:
>
> (a) P.cat=[S or /S] and D.cat=[S or /S],
>
> or (b) P has a binary expansion and one of its dependents, B, has been adopted and was set for α-directionality before the adoption, and D is on the α-side of the expansion.

NB: The concatenated spines of the same directionality under a single dominating node N are the spine of the constituent dominated by N.

When this definition is applied to (6a-c) above, repeated here as (17a-c) with subscripts to the V-nodes, we see that (17a) is a constituent with a spine: V_3 satisfies condition (b) since it branches and immediately dominates the dependent node V_4 which has been adopted and was set for right branching before adoption, so that the V_3-expansion is a constituent with a spine on the right hand side, running from V_3 to V_4. V_2 branches again and has a dependent that has been adopted, viz. $_{Aff}$[FUT], which was set for right branching before adoption since it was labelled V in a right-branching syntax. (The fact that it was relabelled 'Aff' and was thus set for left branching after adoption will become relevant as soon as $_{Aff}$[FUT] is adopted again in virtue of a later rule.) There is, therefore, a spine from V_2 to V_3. Analogously for V_1, which has a spine running to V_2. The three combined spines form the spine of the verbal cluster dominated by V_1.

In (17b), the V_1-constituent has a shorter spine: it is the line connecting V_1 with V_3 covering only two expansions. But the subconstituent dominated by V_4 now has its own spine, this time on the left hand side, connecting V_4 with V_5.

In (17c) the V_1-constituent has an even shorter right hand side spine, the line connecting V_1 with V_2. Here the V_1-spine covers only one expansion, but there is a subconstituent dominated by FV_3 which has its own left hand side spine.

(17)a.

V_1

Aff
PAST

V_2

Aff
FUT

V_3

V_5
faire

V_4
voir

⇒   b.

V_1

Aff
PAST

V_2

V_4

V_5
faire

Aff
FUT

V_3
voir

⇒   c.

V_1

FV_3

V_4

V_5
faire

Aff
PAST

Aff
FUT

V_2
voir

2.9 The auxiliary system and the complementation system

Besides the great distinction, in the syntax of a natural language, between the Cycle and the Postcycle, there is another useful distinction. We can divide the grammar roughly into two main parts, the first of which is the *auxiliary system* and the second the *complementation system*. This distinction is not entirely identical for all languages. Tense elements seem to belong to the auxiliary system of any language. But certain elements, in particular modal predicates, that are part of the auxiliary system of language A may belong to the complementation system of language B. Thus, modal predicates are part of the auxiliary system of English, but belong to the complementation system of Dutch, as appears from their defective paradigm in English and their full paradigm in Dutch. (Obviously, the syntax of many languages contains further sections, such as, notably, the special rule systems that cover conjunction reduction or comparison of degrees. These are not at issue here.)

The distinction between these two main subsystems of the grammar of a language turns on the notion of *matrix* or *lexical nucleus* (Seuren 1969). The lexical nucleus of an SA-structure is the first subject-S from the top that does not command a tense without intervening S, whose V-constituent is a categorial node, i.e. has a lexical filler (Verb, Adjective, Noun, or, as is possible in Turkish, a Preposition), and which is not to undergo LOWERING onto its argument-S. The V of the first nucleus becomes the main predicate of the surface sentence. The matrix (nucleus) forms the main frame of the surface sentence or clause. This V attracts the tenses and other auxiliary elements. But an argument term of this V may itself be an S-structure, an embedded complement (subject or object) clause, which in turn contains a nucleus, possibly preceded by higher auxiliary material. Its top is the argument S-node in question. And so on, recursively. Each nucleus with its higher auxiliary material forms a *sentence unit*. A main clause thus forms a sentence unit down to any possible embedded complement clause, which starts a new sentence unit. For convenience we mark successive sentence units with subscripts.

Logical operators, such as *not*, the quantifiers, *and* or *or*, are semantically 'stacked': they have semantic scope according to their position relative to each other within the auxiliary hierarchy. Their semantic scope is reflected in their syntactic behaviour (see 7.1). Other operators, such as adverbials of time and place, have 'floating' scope with respect to the logical operators. Semantically, they are sensitive only to sentence-unit membership. Even so, their hierarchical position is reflected in their syntactic behaviour (see 3.5).

The nucleus of a sentence unit seems to exert an influence upon its higher auxiliary environment as well as upon its embedded complement clauses. The tendency is for the nucleus to attract and draw into itself both higher and lower structure, thus reinforcing itself and weakening or even abolishing higher and lower structure. The higher, auxiliary structure contains, roughly, the tenses and aspects, negation and other logical operators, as well as sentential and verbal modifiers. In the transformational Cycle, auxiliary elements tend to be lowered, and lower complement elements tend to be raised into the nucleus (especially when the complement clause is not or only partially tensed). The rules that deal with the formation and transformation of structure above the nucleus belong to the auxiliary system, while the treatment of complement sentence units comes under the complementation system.

2.10 AUX

In the earlier days of Transformational Grammar a great deal was written about a complex of phenomena to do with the so-called auxiliary elements in English. This complex comprises the behaviour of the modals (with their defective paradigm: no perfective tenses, no infinitive, no participles), the conditions under which a dummy verb *do* is inserted (*do*-support), the composition of the tenses and of the passive and the progressive forms, the placement of adverbs, subject-verb inversion and the like. The inversion facts, in particular, gave rise to the notion of an *auxiliary constituent*, usually called 'AUX', that could be moved about by certain rules. However, no satisfactory answer was found to the question of the status of such a constituent: was it to be considered part of the Verb Phrase, or a separate, third, constituent between the subject-NP and the VP? Later versions of TGG kept struggling with these problems, but no solution has so far been presented that can claim more than low-level descriptive adequacy.

Against this background the treatment of AUX presented here is novel. AUX originates not as a constituent but as an area of the V-cluster that results from subsequent LOWERINGS onto the V-constituent through the cyclic rules of the auxiliary system. At Shallow Structure level, an area of the V-cluster is defined as the AUX-area. This area subsequently separates itself from the V-cluster to become a constituent on its own, due to the postcyclic rule of AFFIX HANDLING. But before this happens the AUX-area may be called upon to determine the position of elements to be inserted (e.g. negation), or it may be moved about by postcyclic rules such as QUESTION FORMATION. Only if this procedure is followed, as part of the overall system, will all the relevant facts (QUESTION FORMATION, *DO*-SUPPORT, tag formation, defective paradigm of the modal auxiliaries, reduction of *not* to *n't*, placement of negation and other adverbs, etc.) fall into place with a minimum of effort.

The delimitation of the AUX-area, in English as well as in the other languages that have been studied and were found to need an AUX-area (the languages of Western Europe do, but not, for example, Turkish), proceeds according to a general procedure. To carry out this procedure we provide the successive V-nodes in the spine of a V-cluster that has n-1 expansions with subscripts 1 to n, starting from the top. We follow the convention that a constituent dominated by a node N is called the constituent **N** (i.e. in bold face).

Delimitation of the AUX-area:
- Find the parent node V_i ($1 \leq i < n$) of the $_{Aff}$[PRES/PAST]-node (or, if the language has a subjunctive: the $_{Aff}$[SUBJ]-node) in the V-cluster.
- Find the node V_j ($i < j \leq n$) such that
  (i) V_j is the α-side brother of some Affix node,
  (ii) V_j does not immediately dominate any Affix node,
  (iii) every V_{j-k} ($1 \leq k \leq (j-i)$) immediately dominates an Affix node.
- **AUX = V_i - V_{j+1}**. If V_j is lexically filled V_{j+1} = Ø.

This procedure of delimiting the AUX-area applies at any stage of the Post-cycle up to AFFIX HANDLING, but further elements adjacent to AUX may be added to AUX in virtue of special rules (as with negation in English or the clitics in cliticizing languages). When AFFIX HANDLING applies the AUX-area is fixed: no elements can leave or enter this area, though internal restructurings, such as those brought about by AFFIX HANDLING, are allowed.

Let us consider a few examples to demonstrate the AUX delimitation procedure. All examples represent possible structures of English or other languages. First consider (18):

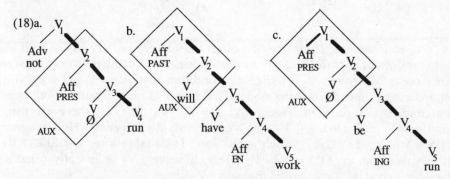

There is right hand side directionality throughout, as shown by the spines. In (18a), n=4 and $V_i=V_2$, as V_2 is the parent node of the highest Affix node in the cluster. Therefore, i=2. Now determine V_j ($2 < j \leq 4$). The only candidate is V_3: V_3 is the right brother of an Affix node, it does not immediately dominate an Affix node, and every V_{3-k} ($1 \leq k \leq (3-2)$) dominates an Affix node (k=1), and V_2 immediately dominates an Affix node. Therefore, **AUX = V_2 - V_4**.

In (18b), n=5 and $V_i=V_1$. V_j ($1 < j \leq 5$) is either V_2 or V_5: both have an Affix as a left brother of and neither is the parent of an Affix. But the condition that every V_{j-k} ($1 \le k \le (j-1)$) immediately dominate an Affix is met only by V_2. Hence, $V_j = V_2$ and $\textbf{AUX} = \textbf{V}_1 - \textbf{V}_3$.

Now consider (18c). Again, $n=5$ and $V_i = V_1$. V_j ($1 < j \le 5$) is again either V_2 or V_5. Both are the right brother of an Affix and neither directly dominates one. And again, the condition that every V_{j-k} ($1 \le k \le (j-1)$) immediately dominate an Affix node is fulfilled only by V_2. Hence, $V_j = V_2$ and $\textbf{AUX} = \textbf{V}_1 - \textbf{V}_3$.

Due to the fact that in English (and other Germanic languages) futurity is expressed by means of a modal verb placed between V_{t_1} and V_{t_2}, and not by a morphological future tense in that position, only the tense operator V_{t_1}, filled by either PRESENT or PAST (see 2.11), can have a morphological effect on the finite verb. Consequently, V-clusters in these languages can contain only one tense Affix, though other, participle forming Affixes may occur further down the V-cluster, as shown in (18b,c). In the Romance and the Slavonic languages, however, futurity is normally expressed by means of a further morphological marking on the finite verb form, which translates as a further optional tense Affix in a three-tense rule system and hence in the V-clusters. French, for example, allows for V-clusters as shown in (19):

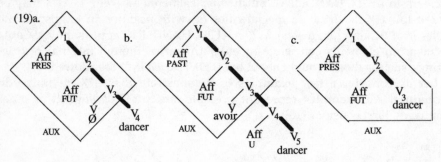

In (19a), $n=4$ and $i=1$. There are two candidates for V_j, i.e. V_2 and V_3: both are right brothers of an Affix node, but only V_3 does not immediately dominate an Affix node. Moreover, V_3 satisfies the condition that every V_{j-k} ($1 \le k \le (j-i)$) immediately dominate an Affix node: if $j=3$ then $k=1$ or $k=2$, and in both cases the condition is fulfilled. Hence, $\textbf{AUX} = \textbf{V}_1 - \textbf{V}_4$. In (19b) there are three candidates for V_j, viz. V_2, V_3 and V_5, but only V_3 survives. Hence again, $\textbf{AUX} = \textbf{V}_1 - \textbf{V}_4$. For (19c), which is the form (19a) takes after Ø-DELETION, the result is, again, $\textbf{AUX} = \textbf{V}_1 - \textbf{V}_4$. Here, however, $\textbf{V}_3$ is lexically filled so that $\textbf{V}_4 = \emptyset$ and AUX comprises the entire V-cluster.

For English, this method of delimiting AUX in conjunction with a proper selection and a proper linear ordering of the postcyclic rules will yield precisely the correct results, as will be illustrated in the following chapter, provided account is taken of one interesting further phenomenon. The postcyclic rule of ADVERB PLACEMENT (AP) detaches any node $_{Adv}$[not] above AUX (more precisely, AP detaches the Adverb area consisting of $\textbf{V}_h$, where V_h is the parent node of $_{Adv}$[not], minus $\textbf{V}_i$) and re-inserts $_{Adv}$[not] (or rather, the Adverb area in question) at the exit of AUX. (18a), for example, will thus be turned into (20) (where, later, Ø will be replaced by the dummy verb *do*, due to Ø being separated from its Main Verb *run*):

(20)

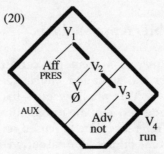

According to the AUX-delimitation procedure spelt out above, ₐdv[not] with its dominating V_3 does not become part of the AUX-area. And indeed, in more formal varieties of English this is what one finds. There one finds sentences like *Did he not run?* or *Can she not stay?* or *Would the man not have surrendered?*, with AUX proposed leaving behind the following *not*. However, in virtually all sociolects of modern spoken English one finds this construction only with emphatic negation. In spoken English, the normal non-emphatic negation is suffixed to AUX and reduced to *n't*. This can only mean that when, in modern spoken English, non-emphatic ₐdv[not] stands immediately below AUX in the V-cluster it becomes part of AUX and is subsequently reduced to *n't* (a procedure which is reminiscent of the cliticization of the French negation particle *ne*, which also becomes part of AUX — see below and 4.3.1). This fact is represented in (20), where the heavy frame delimits the formation of AUX in modern spoken English, while the older, more formal construction results from AUX as delimited by the light line.

A similar phenomenon occurs in the languages that have clitic pronouns. In these languages, under certain conditions, unstressed personal pronouns in non-subject position, as well as certain other elements such as the NEG1-element *ne* in French, are moved to a position just before (above) AUX and are then called 'clitics'. Clitics normally become part of AUX, even though the AUX-delimitation procedure contains no provision for that. In French, for example, one finds preverbal clitic clusters like *ne-lui-en* in (21a). Together with the finite verb form *auriez* ('(you) would have')they form the AUX-area:

(21)a. Vous ne   lui   en   auriez   pas   parlé avec plaisir
      you NEG1 to-him/her of-it would-have NEG2 spoken with pleasure
      'You wouldn't have spoken to him/her about it with pleasure'

   b. Ne   lui   en   auriez-vous pas   parlé avec plaisir?
      NEG1 to-him/her of-it would-have-you NEG2 spoken with pleasure?
      'Wouldn't you have spoken to him/her about it with pleasure?'

The question-form (21b) shows that AUX has been fronted, complete with the clitics.[14]

2.11 The double (treble) tense analysis

A central element in the rule system for certain languages, such as the languages of Europe, is the so-called *double tense analysis*, now widely accepted among linguists. This analysis goes back to Reichenbach (1947), where a distinction is made between the pragmatically given time of speaking S, the cognitive time **R** ('reference time') focused on in the text, and the time E ('event time') of the actual or possible situation (event or state of affairs) expressed.

For the grammar of English and related languages, the following rough semantic rules hold. The use of the simple present tense expresses a cognitive configuration where the time of speaking is represented as coinciding with the focus time and with the event time: $S=R=E$. The simple past expresses the cognitive configuration $S>R=E$ ('>' stands for 'posterior to'). $S=R>E$ is expressed by the present perfect, and $S>R>E$ by the pluperfect.

The Formation Rules express the Reichenbach system by the introduction of two tenses, V_{t_1} and V_{t_2}. V_{t_1} stands for the relation between S and R, V_{t_2} for that between R and E.[15] V_{t_1}, is 'deictic': it refers the proposition to be expressed to a discourse-defined moment or time span, either the moment of speaking or a time set in the past. Thus, V_{t_1} is filled by 'PRES' or 'PAST'. If a tense is morphologically expressed, it is recategorized as 'Affix'.

The second, V_{t_2}, is relational: it expresses a relation of simultaneity or precedence between the discourse-defined time resulting from V_{t_1} and the time of the situation (event or state of affairs) described in the proposition expressed by the matrix-S. In many languages V_{t_2} also carries perfective aspect, sometimes, as in Mauritian Creole (Seuren 1995), durative aspect as well. For the European languages the two possible values for V_{t_2} are 'SIMULTANEOUS' and 'PRECEDING'. These languages use Ø (deleted later; English sometimes realizes it as the dummy verb *do*) for 'SIMULTANEOUS' and a perfective auxiliary verb (*have* in English) for 'PRECEDING'. But languages with morphological perfective tenses, such as Latin, apply SURFACE CATEGORY ASSIGNMENT to relabel V_{t_2} as 'Affix' as well.

The aspectual aspect of V_{t_2} is probably best described as the presence of an existential quantifier: it says that at the time defined by V_{t_1} there is (was) or has (had) been, either a moment or a time span such that the situation described in the matrix-S takes (took) place or obtains (obtained) at that

[14] In fact, the processes involved in French questions are quite complex, so much so that a new periphrastic form has been developed for most types of question, which is now used preferentially.
[15] McCawley (1973:257-272) was the first to apply the double tense analysis to the description of a natural language, in this case English, in the context of TGG.

moment or during that time span. Whether the t_2-operator expresses existential quantification over a moment (point event) or over a stretch of time depends on various factors, in particular on whether the matrix-S expresses an event or a state of affairs. This again seems to depend largely on the semantics of the main predicate in the matrix-S in combination with possible adverbial or prepositional operators above it.

The emphasis in this system falls on tense, not on aspect. The reason is that the three main aspects 'durative', 'momentaneous' (or 'aorist') and 'perfective' (or 'resultative'), as well as the additional 'iterative', seem to be describable as semantic entailments of the t_2-operator together with the matrix-S and its higher adverbial and/or prepositional operators. The details, however, are complex and will not be gone into any further here.

As a semantics of tense and aspect this is, of course, intolerably rough and primitive. It is well-known that grammatically corresponding tenses vary considerably from a semantic point of view among different languages, and in ways that are often extremely hard to describe even at an ad hoc descriptive level (see 7.5 for some discussion). The question is, therefore: what is the significance of such rough semantics as is brought along by the Reichenbach system? This question is relevant and difficult to answer. Yet it is not our concern here to provide a semantics of tenses and aspects. All that is aimed at is a maximally regular, non-ad-hoc way of generating the linguistic manifestations of tense and aspect. The double tense analysis seems to answer this purely grammatical question in an empirically satisfactory way. If this fact is taken seriously it will have a constraining effect on any proper semantics of tenses and aspects. The syntactic analysis provides, so to speak, a mould for any semantics to fit into, and it challenges any semantic theory to do so.

Many semantic tense and/or aspect differences are probably best attributed to language-specific differences in the cognitive preparation of linguistic messages. For each specific language certain cognitive elements need to be foregrounded and made explicit as grammatical or lexical elements in the message to be formulated, a fact that makes itself felt with particular force in the selection of tenses, not only with respect to the European languages but quite generally for all natural languages.[16] Malay, for example, is highly indulgent in that it places few requirements on the foregrounding of time-related cognitive elements. The European languages, on the other hand, are much more demanding in this respect, and show vast differences among themselves. The question is if and how the different semantic systems can be shown to find their expression through the double tense system based on Reichenbach's **S-R-E** relations.

As has been said, futurity is expressed in English and other Germanic languages by means of a modal auxiliary (*will, shall* for English). Some languages, however, have a morphological future tense. This difference does not seem to affect the SA-analysis of tenses. In all cases there is an optional

---

[16] Needless to say, differences of this kind are a formidable obstacle to any fully automatic machine translation procedure.

middle predicate whose primary function seems to be the expression of futuricity. In English, the optional middle predicate position has attracted other modals as well. In French and German, this position appears to be reserved exclusively for the expression of futuricity. In Dutch, this position is apparently empty: futuricity is expressed by means of the ordinary main verb verb *zullen*.[17] The fact that futuricity is expressed in some languages by means of a morphological affix, and not as a (modal) verb, is irrelevant at this level of analysis: the grammars of the languages concerned will take care of that.

Whether the optional middle element is called 'tense' or 'modality' is largely a terminological issue: 'tense' seems preferable if this position can be filled only by futuricity, more so if futuricity is expressed morphologically and no adverbials are possible between it and t_2. Any other fillers of the middle position will be modalities of possibility and/or necessity (epistemic or agentive). Not wishing to decide, in this context, between 'tense' or 'modality', we shall use the non-committal notation t_m ('modal tense').[18]

A comparison of the tense, modality and aspect systems of different languages reveals that the position between V_{t_1} and V_{t_2}, if filled at all, is primarily reserved for the expression of futuricity. But languages often attract other modals to that position as well. Sometimes a special S-type jumps directly from S" to S°, bypassing S'. Examples are the English *be-to* construction (3.7.3.1), or the French construction with *venir de* + infinitive (4.1.3). They fill the combined positions of V_{t_m} and V_{t_2}. The superscript for this S-type is MAUX (middle auxiliary).

It thus appears that all languages have the rule schemata of (22) in common. (ii) and (iii) are optionally present in the grammar of a language, due to the fact that (i) optionally allows for S^M and/or S^{MAUX}, besides S'. S^{MAUX} is special in that it jumps directly to S°, bypassing S':

(22)   (i)   S "   → V_{t_1} + (S^M), (S^{MAUX}), S'

(ii) S^M → V_{t_2} + S'

(iii) S^{MAUX} → V_{Maux} + S°

(iv)   S'   → V_{t_2} + S°

(v)   S°   → V_{LEX} + ... ⟨lexical argument frame⟩

These rules set up a skeletal frame for the auxiliary system in any language (see 1.4.1 and 3.1). Additional adverbial elements, including negation, as well

---

[17] The verb *zullen* ('shall, will'), which expresses futuricity, functions as a normal lexical Main Verb, with a full paradigm, including the infinitive:
(i) √ Ik hoop het te zull-en   klaren
      I hope it to shall-INF manage   ('I hope that I shall manage')
In German, however, the verb *werden*, when expressing futuricity, fills the position between t_1 and t_2, and cannot, therefore, occur in the infinitive, though other modals can:
(ii) * Ich hoffe, es schaffen zu werd-en
       I hope it manage to shall-INF ('I hope that I shall manage')
[18] For a discussion of the modal character of futuricity, see, for example, Bybee & Dahl (1989:90-94), Comrie (1985), Dahl (1985), Lyons (1977:809-823), Ultan (1978).

as prepositional modifiers and quantifiers are woven into this structure in ways that are to some extent language-specific.

Many languages, including Malay and, typically, the Creole languages, express the tenses and often also the modalities by means of preverbal particles (mostly of verbal origin) so that no tense morphology is involved in the formation of the finite verb form. In these languages the same double (treble) operator system is at work: t_1 is clearly a tense operator, filled by either PRES or PAST, and t_2 is a mixed tense-aspect operator, filled by 'SIMUL-TANEOUS' or 'PRECEDING' and sometimes one or two aspectual operators. In most or all of these languages, the middle term, t_m, can be filled by one or more modal operators, including operators expressing (different kinds of) futuricity. In Creole linguistics it is customary to speak of the 'TMA-system', which expresses tense, modality and aspect in that order. The TMA-system is deemed characteristic for creole languages.[19] In fact, this prominent general feature of Creole languages illustrates the thesis put forward in Seuren & Wekker (1985) that Creole surface structures show a high degree of semantic transparency. Provided the t_2-operator is indeed mainly responsible for the aorist, durative and perfective aspects, the TMA system can be considered to be the direct result of the simple LOWERING of t_1, t_m and t_2 onto the lower V.

It is found, time and again, that the double tense analysis, with an optional intermediate position for the modalities, achieves a non-trivial level of descriptive adequacy in the description of individual languages. In the following chapters this will be illustrated for a small number of west European languages and for Turkish (7.6). Excursions into other languages keep confirming the success of this analysis.[20] It may therefore be assumed that the double tense analysis also achieves a nontrivial level of success at the higher level of crosslinguistic adequacy.

2.12 The complementation system

A doubly tensed S (i.e. S") contains a t_1, besides a t_2 or V_{Maux}, and possibly an intermediate t_m. An S" always leads to a finite verb form in the corresponding surface structure, since t_1 is responsible for finite verb forms. An S^M contains a t_m and a t_2. A singly tensed S, i.e. S', only contains a t_2, and, obviously, an untensed S, i.e. S°, contains no tense at all. S's and S°s correspond to infinitival

[19] See Seuren (1981) for the TMA-system in Sranan, the Creole language of Surinam, and Seuren (1995) for the TMA system of Mauritian Creole.

[20] Hellwig (1991) contains an analysis of the auxiliary system of Finnish in terms of Semantic Syntax. As is well known (e.g. Meillet & Cohen 1952:304), Finnish and related languages treat negation as a (defective) verb, which in itself is curious confirmation of the theory. Cf. also Sommer (1972:101) on the Australian language Kunjin: "The most frequently used negative is *aNañd,* 'no, not, nothing', but there are good reasons for the proposal that *aNañd,* is a verb." Or Meillet & Cohen (1952:496) on the Dravidian languages: "<the suffix *-a-* > est probablement le résidu d'un verbe indépendant; en tout cas la négation peut s'exprimer aussi par un verbe 'ne pas exister' *(h)al-* ou *(h)il-*."

and (if headed by NP) gerundive constructions in the corresponding surface structures. Occasionally, an S^o disappears altogether due to, often idiosyncratic, processes of VERB DELETION. In modern English, VERB DELETION is limited to the verb *be*, which may be dropped in certain specific positions, as in *She seemed intelligent* or *I expected you here*. But Shakespearian English has sentences like *I must away*, where *go* has been deleted under strict lexically controlled conditions. German and Dutch allow for more forms of idiosyncratic VERB DELETION, as is demonstrated in the German sentences of (23):

(23) a. Er wollte weg <gehen>   c. Das will ich <haben>
         he wanted away <go>   that want I   <have>
         'he wanted to go away'   'I want to have that'

     b. Dann bin ich hinein <gegangen>
         then am I inward <gone>
         'then I went in'

The difference between an S'- and an S^o-embedding can be partly diagnosed by testing if the embedded infinitival can occur in a perfective tense. If it does the embedding originates as an S'; if it does not the embedding may be an S^o. In English an embedded S' can be constructed with the verb *have* followed by a Past Participle, whereas S^o fills positions that disallow tensed infinitives or participles. Examples from English are given below.

This analysis makes for a simple, adequate and universally valid distinction between three possible levels of S-embedding under a lexical verb (complementation). Complement subject or object Ss as specified in the lexicon for each lexical predicate are either fully tensed (S" or $_{NP}$[S"]) or partially tensed (S' or $_{NP}$[S']) or untensed (S^o or $_{NP}$[S^o]). In general, $_{NP}$[S'] and $_{NP}$[S^o] lead to participials or nominalizations. Remarkably, embeddings of S^M-clauses do not seem to occur anywhere. The same goes for S^{MAUX}-clauses: S^M or S^{MAUX} is always part of an S"-structure, whether as a main clause or as a complement clause, but no lexical predicate is ever subcategorized for the embedding of S^M or S^{MAUX} in subject or object position.[21]

In English, a complement-S" is introduced by the default complementizer *that* (unless the clause is under a Que(stion) operator). The English predicates *assert* or *deny*, for example, can take an object-S, but only a fully tensed $_{NP}$[S"]. *That*-clauses which pronominalize as *it*, and not as *so*, are considered to be under an NP-node. Consequently, these verbs are subcategorized for $_{NP}$[S"] in object position. Other predicates take object clauses that pronominalize as *so*: *I believe so; So it seems*. These take simple S" as an option. The aspectual predicate *happen*, is subcategorized for S' in subject position, as is shown by

---

[21] This regularity is dramatically confirmed by Mauritian Creole, which has PRES or PAST for t_1, *pu* or *va* for modal futurity, and Ø, perfective *fin*, durative *pe* or temporally preceding *deza* as possible fillers for t_2. All these operators end up at surface level as preverbal particles, in the usual Creole way. Remarkably, Ø, *fin*, *pe* and *deza* do occur in infinitivals, i.e. embedded S'-structures, but *pu* and *va* do not. They can only occur in finite clauses, i.e. S"-structures, just like the English modals. See Seuren (1995) for details.

the well-formed *She happens to have finished her meal*. Other predicates again, such as *continue, make,* or *tell*, only allow for untensed infinitives, as in *She continued to drive* or *The smell made her eat,* or *She told me to leave.* Tensed infinitives are ungrammatical here: **She continued to have driven; *The smell made her have eaten, *She told me to have left.*

Some predicates, such as *believe* or *expect*, allow for both S" and S', i.e. a *that*-clause or a, possibly tensed, infinitive. *Believe,* moreover, also allows for $_{NP}$[S"], as is shown by the possibility of *it*-pronominalization: *I believe it,* which occurs next to *I believe so,* though with a subtle semantic difference (see 3.8.1). The perception verbs *see* and *hear* may choose $_{NP}$[S"] or S" or S^o (*I saw that she left; I saw her leave; *I saw her have left, I saw it; so I saw;* and likewise for *hear*).[22]

Obviously, when a lexical verb is subcategorized for an embedded S", S' or S^o (with or without NP), the expansion of these S-nodes requires a return to the Formation Rules. An S" re-enters the Formation Rules at the rule that has S" as the symbol to be rewritten, with the associated optional adverbial and/or prepositional additions. In English, a specification of a complement S" in a lexical argument frame implicitly allows for the selection of an S" with the adverbial superscript ADV_2: a complement-S" may also be S"^{ADV2} and thus re-enter at Formation Rule (1b) in 3.1.1.[23] Analogously, a complement S' may also be S'^{ADV2} and enter rule (2b), and a complement S^o may be S^{oADV3} and enter rule (3c) in 3.1.1.

Sometimes, a complement-S can only occur under its commanding verb as a untensed infinitive or participial, yet it does allow for ADV_2 operators like *not* or *tomorrow*, as in (24):

(24)a. This made me not go
   b. I told him to leave tomorrow

where the verbs *make* and *tell* do not allow for tensed complement infinitives. This is a problem, as an embedded S^o should not be allowed to take an ADV_2 operator. To solve this problem, tenseless embedded Ss that allow for class 2 adverbials are described as S'-embeddings with the obligatory selection of Ø for the second tense, expressed as the subscripted feature Ø. This way the expansion of the embedded S can, for English, enter Formation Rule (2b) or (2c) of 3.1.1. Accordingly, such embeddings are marked in the lexical argument frame as S$'_ø$.

In other cases, however, the possibility of class 2 adverbials over embedded tenseless Ss is disallowed. Perception verbs, for example, do not allow for a

---

[22] The lexicon in 3.1.2 contains the specifications as given above. See chapter 3 for further details. See also note 11 above.

[23] The highest classes of adverbials, V_{Advo}, V_{Adv1} and V_{Prepo}, V_{Prep1}, are traditionally called Sentence Adverbials. They are in many ways exceptional, for example because their occurrence in subordinate clauses is highly restricted. They are also exempted from the principle that a complement-S of any rank allows for the associated optional adverbial and/or prepositional additions. That is, a complement-S" may be S"^{ADV2}, as has been said, but not S"^{ADVo} or S"^{ADV1}.

class 2 adverbial over the complement-S, which is obligatorily tenseless, as shown in (25), which, if anything, is jocular:

(25)   ?*I definitely heard the clock not strike

We say that such verbs take genuine S^o-embeddings, and they are marked as such in their lexical specification (see 3.1.2 for *see, hear*). Genuine S^o-embeddings do allow for class 3 (manner) adverbials, but cannot take the superscripts for the progressive form or the passive voice.

Note that this machinery automatically excludes the occurrence of the S^{MAUX}-option in either S' or S^o-embeddings, as this option requires a return to S" in Formation Rule (1c). This explains the ungrammaticality of (26a), despite the wellformedness of (26b):

(26)a.   *I have caused Tom to be to arrive tomorrow
  b.   Tom is to arrive tomorrow

As was said in 2.9 above, complement-Ss, especially S's and S^os , are often subject to certain rules whose effect tends to be a reduction of the hierarchical S-embedding structure that is typical of SAs and a concomitant 'fattening' of the matrix-S. For complement S's and S^os this effect is achieved by a small variety of means: the deletion of the subject-NP or its raising into the matrix-S, both resulting in the downgrading of the embedded S to /S, or the raising of the lower predicate resulting in the abolition of the S-node dominating the complement clause. *In general, all embedded S's and S^os are either downgraded to /S or the dominating S-node disappears.* The three main rules singly or jointly leading to this effect are SUBJECT DELETION (SD), SUBJECT RAISING (SR) and PREDICATE RAISING (PR), the latter two in competition with each other. SD occurs normally in all languages that have infinitives, irrespective of the choice between PR and SR.

Languages tend to choose or to waver between SR and PR. English is almost entirely an SR-language, German and Dutch have no SR at all in their complementation system: PR does all the RAISING work there. In French some verbs induce PR (especially *faire*, though even this prototypical PR-Verb sometimes stoops to SR; see section 4.4.3 and Seuren 1972b) and others take SR. In French subject clauses, it seems, only SR is found, while in object clauses PR is the dominant rule, with a few cases of SR. The French-based Mauritian Creole wavers in interesting ways between SR and PR, even for the same verbs, depending on grammatical conditions (Seuren 1990, 1995). It would seem that the choice between PR and SR in the complementation system of a language provides a basis of classification and comparison. This suggests the introduction of a RAISING parameter in the general theory of complementation. Each individual language will then be assigned a position on this parameter between PR and SR.

CHAPTER 3

The English auxiliary and complementation system

3.1 Some basic machinery

Before the reader sets out to study the Formation Rules as they have been formulated for English it is useful to call to mind what was said in the sections 1.4.1 and 2.11 regarding the skeletal frame for SA-structures in the languages studied so far. The skeletal structure of SAs is as in fig.1 (repeated from 1.4.1):

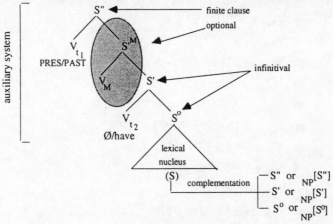

Figure 1   Skeletal frame of SA-structures

The highest tense (PRES or PAST) is responsible for finite verb forms. S-structures from bare S' downward, become infinitival or participial. The shaded area is optional and can be selected only when PRES or PAST has been selected first. In French and German V_M is the future tense, which seems to be the primary filler of this position. In English this position has attracted the other modals as well, besides the future *will* and *shall*. Note that this position in the SA-tree automatically accounts for the defective paradigm of the English modals, which lack perfect tenses, participles and infinitives. S' is obligatory, except with the Middle Auxiliary Verbs (V_{Maux}; see 2.11) where S' is left out, as these verbs jump directly to S^o, skipping S'.

Ss embedded in the lexical nucleus S^o are complement-Ss. They occur, in principle, in six versions: $_{NP}[S'']$, S'', $_{NP}[S']$, S', $_{NP}[S^o]$, and S^o (see 1.4.1 and 2.12). The first two result in finite clauses, the others in infinitivals or participials.

Besides this skeletal structure, which is easily recognized in the rules, there are optional adverbial, prepositional and quantificational additions, which can be 'plugged' into the skeletal structure of the auxiliary system at different heights. Their position in the structure determines their logical scope: the higher they occur, the larger their scope (see 3.5 and 7.1). It is these optional additions that give the Formation Rules their somewhat forbidding appearance. Even so, their treatment in the present system is only provisional and partial.

In order to limit the complexity of the system on first acquaintance, verbs with particles (*put down*) or with prepositional objects (*think of*) are not considered in the rule system and do not figure in the lexicon.

3.1.1 The main Formation Rules

(1)a. $S''^{ADV_0} \rightarrow V_{Adv_0} + S''^{ATTR}/S''^{ADV_1}/S''^{ADV_2}/S''$

$\quad\quad$ **or:** $V_{Prep_0} + S''^{ATTR}/S''^{ADV_1}/S''^{ADV_2}/S'' + NP$

or b. $S''^{ATTR} \rightarrow V_{Attr} + S''^{ADV_2}/S''$

or c. $S''^{ADV_1} \rightarrow V_{Adv_1} + S''^{ADV_2}/S''$

$\quad\quad$ **or:** $V_{Prep_1} + S''^{ADV_2}/S'' + NP$

or d. $S''^{ADV_2} \rightarrow V_{Adv_2} + S''^{ADV_2}/S''$

$\quad\quad$ **or:** $V_{Prep_2} + S''^{ADV_2}/S'' + NP$

$\quad\quad$ **or:** $V_Q + NP[\hat{}x+S''^{ADV_2}/S''] + NP$

or e. $S''\quad\quad \rightarrow V_{t_1} + S'^M/S_0^{MAUX}/S'$

(2)a. $S'^M\quad\quad \rightarrow V_M + S'^{ADV_2}/S'$

b. $S'^{ADV_2} \rightarrow V_{Adv_2} + S'^{ADV_2}/S'$

$\quad\quad$ **or:** $V_{Prep_2} + S'^{ADV_2}/S' + NP$

$\quad\quad$ **or:** $V_Q + NP[\hat{}x+S'^{ADV_2}/S'] + NP$

c. $S'\quad\quad\quad \rightarrow V_{t_2} + S_0^{PROGR}/S_0^{ADV_3}/S_0^{PASS}/S_0^{DEX}/S^0$

(3)a. $S_0^{MAUX} \rightarrow V_{Maux} + S_0^{ADV_3}/S_0^{PASS}/S_0^{DEX}/S^0$

b. $S_0^{PROGR} \rightarrow V_{Progr} + S_0^{ADV_3}/S_0^{PASS}/S_0^{DEX}/S^0$

c. $S_0^{ADV_3} \rightarrow V_{Adv_3} + S_0^{ADV_3}/S_0^{PASS}/S_0^{DEX}/S^0$

$\quad\quad$ **or:** $V_{Prep_3} + S_0^{ADV_3}/S_0^{PASS}/S_0^{DEX}/S^0 + NP$

d. $S_0^{PASS} \rightarrow V_{Pass} + S_0^{PASSPrep}/S_{0[PASS]}^{DEX}/S_{0[PASS]}^0$

e. $S_0^{PASSPrep} \rightarrow V_{PrepPass} + S_{0[PASS]}^{DEX}/S_{0[PASS]}^0 + NP_{[SUV_{LEX}]}$

f. $S_0^{DEX}\quad \rightarrow V_{PrepDex} + S_{0[DEX]}^0 + NP_{[IOV_{LEX}]}$

g. $S^0\quad\quad\quad \rightarrow V_{LEX} + \langle lex.arg.frame\rangle$ **or:** $V_{NP} + NP$

(4)a. $NP\quad\quad \rightarrow :x/\hat{}x + S^{NOM}$ **or:** x **or:** X_{WH}

b. $S^{NOM}\quad\quad \rightarrow V_{Nom} + NP[x]$ **or:** $V_{Adj} + S^{NOM}$

3.1.2 Some lexicon

SA-cat	Fillers	Surface cat	Cyclic rules
V_{Advo}	so, moreover, therefore, then, ...	Adverb	L_S
V_{Attr}	Que, Foc	X: see 3.2.1	L_S
V_{Adv1}	fortunate, alleged, admitted, moreover, ...	Adverb	L_S
V_{Adv2}	normal, often, usual, clever, moreover, ...	Adverb	$L_{S/V}$
	not, EMPH, always, just, never, soon, ...	Adverb	L_V
	today, yesterday, tomorrow, soon, ...	Adverb	$L_{S/right}$
V_{Adv3}	fast, careful, good, clever, stupid, ...	Adverb	L_{right}
V_{Prepo}	as regards, ...	Prep	OI,L_S
V_{Prep1}	in, on, at, with, about, to, ...	Prep	OI,L_S
V_{Prep2}	in, on, at, with, about, to, during, near, ...	Prep	$OI,L_{S/right}$
	by, in, after, on, before, ...	Prep	$OI,SD,L_{S/right}$
V_{Prep3}	in, at, with, about, for, over, ...	Prep	OI,L_{right}
$V_{PrepPass}$	by	Prep	OI,L_{right}
$V_{PrepDex}$	to	Prep	OI,L_{right}
V_{t1}	PRES, PAST	Affix (AH → FV)[1]	SR, L_V
V_M	will, may(not +may → cannot), shall, (not +must → need +not), can,...	Verb	L_V
V_{t2}	Ø	Verb	L_V
	have	Verb	PaP, L_V
V_{Maux}	be, [V[be] Prt[going]]	Verb	SR
V_{Progr}	be	Verb	PrP, L_V
V_{Pass}	be	Verb	PaP, L_V
V_{Cop}	be	Verb	PR
V_Q	all, every, a, some, most, ...	Det	OI,L_{var}

V_{LEX}:

SA-cat	Fillers	Argument frame	Surface cat	Cyclic rules
V_{Nom}	house, cat, child, mouse, book, ...	+ NP	Noun	— —
V_{Adj}	small, red, old, round, ...	+ NP	Adj	— —
V_{Adj}	probable, possible, true, ...	+ NP/$_{NP}$[S"]	Adj	— —
V_{Adj}	(un)likely	+ NP/S'/$_{NP}$[S"]	Adj	SR
V_{Adj}	rumoured	+ NP/S'/$_{(NP)}$[S"]	Adj	SR
V_{Adj}	due	+ NP/S'	Adj	SR
V_{Adj}	eager, ...	+ NP$_x$ + S$'_\emptyset$	Adj	SD

[1] When the postcyclic rule of AFFIX HANDLING is applied the V over Aff is relabelled FV (finite verb).

V_{Adj} easy$_1$, hard$_1$, tough$_1$, ...	+ NP/S'$_{ø[PASS]}$	Adj	SR
V_{Adj} easy$_2$, hard$_2$, tough$_2$, ...	+ NP$_x$ + S'$_{ø[PASS]}$	Adj	SD
V_{Verb} please	+ NP + NP$_{x[DO]}$ +$_{NP}$[S'']	Verb	——
V_{Verb} laugh, sleep, run, ...	+ NP	Verb	——
V_{Verb} read, eat, drink, write, follow$_1$, ...	+ NP (+ NP)	Verb	——
V_{Verb} give, sell, ...	+ NP (+ NP) + NP	Verb	——
V_{Verb} follow$_2$, make sense, ...	+ NP/$_{NP}$[S'']	Verb	——
V_{Verb} seem, appear, ...	+ S'/S''	Verb	SR
V_{Verb} tend, ...	+ S'	Verb	SR
V_{Verb} happen, ...	+ NP/S'	Verb	SR
V_{Verb} continue$_1$, start$_1$, ...	+ NP/S'$_ø$	Verb	SR
V_{Verb} continue$_2$, start$_2$, go, ...	+ NP$_x$ + S'$_ø$	Verb	SD
V_{Verb} need, ...	+ S°	Verb	SR
V_{Verb} believe, ...	+ NP + NP/S'/$_{(NP)}$[S'']	Verb	SR
V_{Verb} think, ...	+ NP + S'/S''	Verb	SR$_{subj}$
V_{Verb} expect, ...	+ NP$_x$ + NP/S'/$_{(NP)}$[S'']	Verb	[SD/SR]
V_{Verb} want, like, ...	+ NP$_x$ + NP/S'$_ø$	Verb	[SD/SR$_{obj}$]
V_{Verb} try, ...	+ NP$_x$ + NP/S'$_ø$	Verb	SD
V_{Verb} help$_1$	+ NP + S°	Verb	SR$_{obj}$,[-to]
V_{Verb} help$_2$	+ NP + NP$_{x[DO]}$ + (S°)	Verb	SD,([-to])
V_{Verb} tell, ...	+NP +NP$_x$ +NP/S'$_ø$/S''/$_{NP}$[Q$_{ue}$+S'']	Verb	SD
V_{Verb} know, ...	+ NP + NP/S'/$_{NP}$[S'']/$_{NP}$[Q$_{ue}$+S'']	Verb	SR
V_{Verb} cause, ...	+ NP + NP/S'$_ø$	Verb	SR$_{obj}$
V_{Verb} make, ...	+ NP + NP/S'$_ø$	Verb	SR, [-to$_{act}$]
V_{Verb} assert, deny, ...	+ NP + NP/$_{NP}$[S'']	Verb	——
V_{Verb} see, hear, ...	+ NP + NP/$_{(NP)}$[S'']/S°	Verb	SR, [-to$_{act}$]

3.1.3 Cyclic rules

NB: The cyclic rules are identical for the languages dealt with in this book. But for lexical differences and occasional details, they are not repeated for the other languages.

(1) LOWERING (L): Detach the inducing V-constituent and lower it into its argument-S. The landing site is defined in the lexicon (by the subscript to the rule feature L). L$_{right}$ does not cross an embedded S, but may cross an embedded /S. Adverbs may stop before a PP.

(2) SUBJECT RAISING (SR) (only if V$_{<SR>}$ has argument-S' or S°): Select the NP to the right of lower V marked [SU]. Place this NP-constituent in the position of its own S. Move this S (which is now /S) one position to the right.

(3) PREDICATE RAISING (PR) (only if V$_{<PR>}$ has argument-S' or S°): V$_{<PR>}$ α-adopts the V-constituent of the embedded argument-S.

(4) SUBJECT DELETION (SD) (only with object S'/S° or $_{NP}$[S'/S°]): Select the NP to the right of lower V marked [SU]. If this NP is of the form $_{NP}$[x] and is controlled by an NP-argument **(a)** of the inducing V itself **(vertical SD)** or **(b)** of its subject-S **(horizontal SD)**: delete $_{NP}$[x].

NB: Horizontal SD is limited to prepositional predicates such as *by*, *in*, *after*, *before*, etc., followed by a, possibly tensed, gerund.

(5) IT: (structure-driven when V of S° has subject (original) S" or $_{NP}$[S"]; otherwise lexically induced): Create new $_{NP}$[it]. Attach $_{NP}$[it] to the immediate right of V. The S"or $_{NP}$[S"] to the immediate right of $_{NP}$[it] is moved to direct object position if not already there, still marked [SU].

(6) OBJECT INCORPORATION (OI): $V_{<OI>}$ α-adopts its object-NP.

(7) COPULA INSERTION (CI) (structure-driven): S° directly above V_{Adj}, Adj or V_{NP} α-adopts V_{Cop}[be].

(8) PAST PARTICIPLE (PaP): The highest lexically filled non-spine V-node in the V-cluster of the argument-S α-adopts $_{Aff}$[EN]. With postcyclic AFFIX HANDLING the V-node directly above Aff is relabelled 'PaP'.

(9) PRESENT PARTICIPLE (PrP): The highest lexically filled non-spine V-node in the V-cluster of the argument-S α-adopts $_{Aff}$[ING]. With postcyclic AFFIX HANDLING the V-node directly above Aff is relabelled 'PrP'.

3.1.4 Corollaries

(1) SURFACE CATEGORY ASSIGNMENT (SCA) is a corollary of the application of any cyclic rule affecting a V-node whose surface category is different from V. SCA results in the replacement of the category label V of the element affected by the surface category label specified in the lexicon.

(2) Definition of AUX-area (AUX-FORMATION): AUX is the constituent **C** dominated by the parent node of the $_{Aff}$[PRES/PAST]-node A in a V-cluster minus the subconstituent **D**. **D**=∅ if the α-side brother **B** of the lowest $_{Aff}$[PRES/PAST/FUT]-node is lexically filled. If B branches **D** is the subconstituent dominated by the rightmost dependent of B.

NB1: AUX is redefined according to the above procedure after treatment of ∅ (postcyclic rules (1) and (5)), and, for languages with V-cluster clitics (e.g. French), after CLITIC MOVEMENT. AUX is then fixed and is an island: no material may be moved into or out of AUX, but internal changes are allowed.

NB2: In English, AUX may incorporate *not* after postcyclic rule (2).

(3) *To*-INSERTION is a corollary at the end of the Cycle of /S-constituents not containing AUX, unless the V-constituent under the parent of /S is marked [-to]: Select the immediate parent-node P of the highest (leftmost) filled V-node in the V-cluster. P left-adopts the Particle node $_{Prt}$[to].

(4) *That*-INSERTION is a corollary at the end of the Cycle of S" or $_{NP}$[S"] constituents occurring as argument term to a lexical predicate: S" left-adopts $_{Comp}$[that].

3.1.5 Some postcyclic rules (to be applied in the order given)

(1) $\emptyset$-*be*-DELETION: If the right brother of $_V$[$\emptyset$] equals or directly dominates $_V$[be] delete $_V$[$\emptyset$]. Redefine AUX according to Corollary (2).

(2) ADVERB PLACEMENT (AP): For any Adverb area A of the V-cluster above AUX:

a. If A contains $_{Adv}$[not] or $_{Adv}$[EMPH]: Detach the subarea A_{sub} of A defined by the parent node of the highest occurrence of $_{Adv}$[not] or $_{Adv}$[EMPH], whichever is highest, and re-attach A_{sub} at the exit of AUX. (The sequence *not-EMPH* overrides the PPI default filter; see section 3.4.) ($_{Adv}$[not], if at the EXIT of AUX, and not immediately followed by $_{Adv}$[EMPH], may become part of AUX.)

b. If A does not contain $_{Adv}$[not] or $_{Adv}$[EMPH] and AUX does not end in $\emptyset$ or is V-cluster final: Detach A and re-attach at the exit of AUX.

(3) QUESTION FORMATION:

a. $_X$[Q_{ue}] right-adopts $_C$[WH] (any WH-constituent) in scope of $_X$[Q_{ue}] but not in $_{NP}$[S] or complement question. If no $_C$[WH] is available, $_X$[Q_{ue}] right-adopts $_{y-n}$[$\emptyset$] in main questions and $_{y-n}$[if/whether] in complement questions. X is $_C$[WH]/AUX//S or $_C$[WH]/$_C$[WH] (see 3.2.1).

b. AUX//S right-adopts the nearest AUX.

(4) FRONTING:

a. $_X$[Foc] right-adopts any major constituent $_C$[+Foc], except S, /S$_o$, AUX, and *not*. X is $_C$[+Foc]/$_C$[+Foc] (see 3.2.1).

b. If $_C$[+Foc] contains negation X is $_C$[+Foc]/AUX//S, except when $_C$[+Foc] is marked [SU] (see 3.2.1). If X is $_C$[+Foc]/AUX//S, the node above $_X$[Foc] right-adopts AUX.

　　NB: If $_C$[+Foc] is a subject *that*-clause dummy $_{NP}$[it] (cyclic rule (5)) is deleted.

(5) *Do*-SUPPORT: For any V-cluster: $\emptyset$ not followed directly by a V-node filled by a surface lexical verb is replaced by the dummy verb *do*. Otherwise $_V$[$\emptyset$] is deleted, in which case redefine AUX according to Corollary (2).

(6) AFFIX HANDLING (AH): If the right brother B of $_{Aff}$[a] is a lexical constituent B RIGHT-ADOPTS $_{Aff}$[a]. (Affixes belong in left-branching structures and are, therefore, suffixed.) If B directly dominates a lexical constituent X not on the spine (i.e. on the left hand side), X right-adopts $_{Aff}$[a]. V over $_{Aff}$[PRES/PAST] is relabelled 'FV' (finite verb). V over $_{Aff}$[EN] is relabelled 'PaP'. V over $_{Aff}$[ING] is relabelled 'PrP'.

(7) MINCE: Detach the highest subsonstituent on the spine of any C-cluster. Re-attach the detached subconstituent to the right of its parent. Never detach structure belonging to AUX or to a C-island or to a lexical constituent.

3.1.6 How to use the machinery

3.1.6.1 Notation

The Formation Rules are context-free rewrite rules. The rewriting of a symbol is an *expansion*. All S-expansions in the Formation Rules, as well as the lexical argument frames, conform to the General SA-Format (see 1.3.2 and 2.2). The rules only impose additional collocational restrictions on the SAs of English sentences, beyond those imposed by the General Format.

Alternative expansions are indicated by '**or**' for whole expansions, by an oblique stroke '/' for single symbols (or occasionally by round brackets). The first symbol to be rewritten is either S''^{ADV_0} (rule (1a)), or S''^{ATTR} (rule (1b)), or S''^{ADV_1} (rule (1c)), or S''^{ADV_2} (rule (1d)), or S'' (rule (1e)). A symbol in an expansion of the form '$_{NP}[a]$' specifies the obligatory filler a of the NP.

The Formation Rules are heavily superscripted and subscripted. Some subscripts do not occur in the Formation Rules: numerical subscripts under S-nodes and /S-nodes. They serve to distinguish complement-Ss. When a lexical verb takes an S-argument, a higher subscript is assigned. Each subscript marks a *sentence unit*. They stay during the Cycle, unless the S-node in question is erased owing to DOWNGRADING 2. If there is no complement-S the numerical subscript is not used (for details see 3.8).

Subscripts to V-nodes have different functions. Some, as in V_{Prep}, indicate the surface category of the predicate in question. These are kept until the Cycle enacts SURFACE CATEGORY ASSIGNMENT.

The subscript in V_{LEX} is a variable ranging over Nom (Noun), Adjective and Verb: when a lexical predicate is selected in virtue of Formation Rule (3g) it may belong to any of these three categories. When a V_{LEX} is selected, it will be a V_{Nom} or a V_{Adj} or a V_{Verb}, and these subscripts are kept until SCA.

The superscripts in S^o, S', S'^M and S'' are maintained until the end of the Cycle but only for full S-nodes, not for /S-nodes. When an S-node is erased due to LOWERING and subsequent PRUNING the receiving S takes on the higher superscript of the erased S-node ($S^o < S' < S'^M < S''$). This ensures that when the cyclic treatment of a complement clause is completed the subsequent cyclic rules of the higher sentence unit can still recognize the original rank of the complement embedding, which may be crucial to further cyclic treatment. When an S-node is eliminated through PREDICATE RAISING it and its rank superscript disappear.

The S-superscripts ADV_n, MAUX, PROGR, DEX and PASS disappear once their S-cycle is completed and their S-node has been erased. The superscript NOM for a nominal S (S with a noun as predicate) is not discussed here, as the grammar of NPs is left out of account. The superscripts correspond with the class from which the predicate of the S in question has to be selected. This class is indicated as a subscript to the predicate (V) (except for Que and Foc, which are special; see 3.2.1). The superscripts PASS and DEX become features to further S-expansions and finally to the lexical verb selected (see 3.1.6.2).

The S-superscripts are either single or double. The first superscript is always ″,′ or °. It indicates the tense of the S to be expanded, as has been explained above. The second superscript governs the insertion into the skeletal tense structure of modalities, adverbial or prepositional phrases, negation, quantifiers, progressive aspect, passive voice, external dative and the like. They are subtypes of S″, S′ and S°. The modality subtype appears, in certain ways, to be more central to the tense system than the others. For that reason it has been made part of what is called the 'skeletal' structure (see 3.1 above). For the actual machinery, however, this makes no difference.

The correspondence mentioned above between superscripts of S-symbols and subscripts of the V-symbol in their immediate expansion is limited to the rightmost superscript. Thus, the second superscript in S''^{ADV2} or S'^{ADV2} corresponds with the subscript in V_{Adv2}, in V_{Prep2} and in V_Q. The second superscript in $S°^{PROGR}$ corresponds with the subscript in V_{Progr}, etc. In bare S″, S′ and S°, the superscript corresponds with the V in the immediate expansion. The double prime (″) stands for an S with two tenses and corresponds with V_{t_1} (the first tense, i.e. PRES or PAST). The single prime (′) stands for an S containing one single tense and corresponds with V_{t_2}, which, for English, is either Ø ('simultaneous') or *have* + Past Participle ('preceding'). The superscript in S° stands for an untensed S and corresponds with the selection of a lexical predicate followed by such argument terms as are allowed or prescribed in the lexicon for each predicate (and restricted by any features; see below).

As has been said, S″, S′ and S° have subtypes. In particular, S″, S′ and S° allow for one or more adverbials above them. (The term *adverbial* is used for adverbs and Prepositional Phrases. Note that prepositional predicates (like quantifying predicates; see 7.1) always have an object-NP after the subject-S.) That is, when an expansion contains the symbol S″, S′ or S°, it is sometimes possible to select an adverbial S″, S′ or S° first. When this is possible it is so recursively. A higher adverbial of class Adv_2 or $Prep_2$ is always allowed for S″; S° always allows for a higher Adv_3 or $Prep_3$. But S′ allows for a higher adverbial Adv_2 or $Prep_2$ only if it is part of an expansion of S'^M: rule (1e) allows for only a bare S′, without any higher adverbial, but rule (2a), which expands S'^M, does allow for a higher adverbial with S′.

The highest possible symbol in an SA-tree is S''^{ADVo}. Its second superscript indicates that the S″ in question contains a superadverbial (see 3.5) as its highest operator. Superadverbials are the highest possible operators and may occur even above a speech act operator (e.g. *Therefore, go home and take a rest*). The next highest choice is either a speech act operator such as Que for questions, or the focusing predicate *Foc*. Next comes the class of V_{Adv1} or sentence adverbials, which includes adverbs like *admittedly, secondly*, as well as Prepositional Phrases like *to my knowledge, in my opinion*, etc. Rule (1d) introduces class 2 adverbials, i.e. V_{Adv2} or V_{Prep2}. When an adverbial is selected above S″ or S′ in the complementation system it must belong to this class. When an adverbial is selected above S^o it must be of class 3, i.e. it must belong to the class V_{Adv3} or V_{Prep3}.

When S" or S' allow for a higher adverbial of class 2 the adverbial may also be a quantifying predicate (V_Q) like *all, every, a, some, many, few, most, exactly half*, etc. Since the class of V_{Adv2} contains logical scope-bearing adverbs like *not*, quantifiers can occur, in SA-structures, in exactly the positions that the negation and other logical scope-bearing adverbs can occur in, thus varying their scope relations with respect to each other.

S^o can have, besides an ADV$_3$ superscript, also the superscripts PROGR, PASS, DEX and MAUX. PROGR produces a sentence in the progressive form, with *be + V-ing*. PASS produces a passive sentence. DEX produces a sentence with an external dative (*She gave the book to John*). MAUX ('middle auxiliary') produces a sentence of the form *be + to-V* or *be going + to-V*, as in *He is to leave* or *He is going to leave*, respectively. Note that V_{Maux} acts as a second tense, i.e. as a substitute for V_{t_2}, since the option S^oMAUX in rule (1e) is part of the S"-expansion and is itself expanded by rule (3a), thus skipping S' with its second tense predicate V_{t_2} (see 3.7.3.1 for further comment).

The subscripts to L (LOWERING) in the lexicon define the possible landing sites for the element lowered (see 3.1.3): 'S' and 'V' mean ADOPTION (2.7.1.1) by the argument-S and the lower V, respectively. Since English syntax is right-branching, ADOPTION here means LEFT ADOPTION (2.8). The subscript in L_{right} moves the element to be lowered to the far right of the argument-S, but not across an embedded S and optionally across an embedded /S. Adverbs lowered by L_{right} may halt before a PrepPhrase lowered earlier by L_{right}. Disjunctive subscripts, as in $L_{S/V}$ or $L_{S/right}$, imply a choice, but $L_{S/right}$ has the additional condition that the first option, LEFT ADOPTION by S, applies only if the operator to be lowered is at the top of the tree.

SR (SUBJECT RAISING) is sometimes subscripted 'subj' and sometimes 'obj', indicating that SR applies only in subject or object position, respectively. When there is no subscript the rule applies without restriction. This helps to avoid the marked *I thought you to be in Paris* but allows for the unmarked *You were thought to be in Paris*. It avoids *You are preferred to be in Paris* but allows for *I prefer you to be in Paris*, etc.

The subscript *act* in [-to$_{act}$], with *make, see* and *hear*, suppresses the particle *to* in the active , but not in the passive. Thus we have *That made her cry* as against *She was made to cry*, or *I saw you leave* versus *You were seen to leave*.

3.1.6.2 Passive and external dative

When S^oPASS is selected in rule (2c), (3a) or (3b), rule, (3d), expands S^oPASS into the passive auxiliary *be* plus $S^oPASSPrep$ or $S^o{}^{DEX}_{[PASS]}$ or $S^o{}_{[PASS]}$, leading to an Agent Phrase, an external dative, and bare S^o, respectively. (Other passive auxiliaries, like *get*, have not been taken into account.) Rule (3e) expands the first option of rule (3d), $S^oPASSPrep$, into the Agent Phrase preposition *by* plus $S^o{}^{DEX}_{[PASS]}$ or $S^o{}_{[PASS]}$ and the *by*-object NP$_{[SUVLEX]}$. Then rule (3f) expands $S^o{}^{DEX}_{[PASS]}$

into the dative preposition *to* plus $S^o_{[PASS,DEX]}$ and the *to*-object $NP_{[IOV_{LEX}]}$. Rule (3g) expands bare $S^o_{[PASS]}$, with or without the subscript feature [DEX].

Here we see the appearance of the subscript features [PASS] and [DEX]. [PASS] is assigned to most S-options in the expansion of S^{oPASS} and then passed on in subsequent expansions in certain defined ways. The other feature is [DEX], for sentences with an external dative. The status and function of the features [PASS] and [DEX] will now be explained.

A subscript feature [a] is passed on to subsequent Ss until bare $S^o_{[a]}$ is reached. Then the feature [a] is passed on to the lexical verb selected, where it first ensures that a lexical verb is selected from the appropriate class of verbs and then makes for an appropriate gap in the lexical argument frame selection. That is, if the feature is [PASS] a verb is to be selected from the class of verbs that allow for passivization, and the argument frame selection is made without the subject term. If the feature is [DEX] a verb is to be selected from the class of verbs that allow for an indirect object, and the lexical argument frame selection is made without the indirect object term. Then, the object-NP of passive *by* is assigned the feature $[SU_{V_{LEX}}]$, i.e. selection is to be made as if it were the subject of the lexical verb, and the object-NP of dative *to* inherits the feature $[IO_{V_{LEX}}]$, i.e. selection is to be made as if it were the indirect object of the lexical verb.

It is important to note that features that have been created by the Formation Rules do not affect the application of the rules: the Formation Rules are not sensitive to features. Thus, for example, an $S^o_{[PASS]}$ is treated by rule (3g) as if it were just S^o. The feature [PASS] is disregarded. Features acquired in the course of the generation process accumulate (cf. (37) in section 3.7.2 below).

Let us recapitulate. The expansion of rule (3d) selects the passive auxiliary verb V_{Pass}, i.e. *be* + Past Participle, followed by one of four S^o-structures, three of which acquire the subscripted feature [PASS]. This feature is passed on downward until bare $S^o_{[PASS]}$ is reached, at which point the feature is passed down to the lexical main verb. There it ensures the selection of a transitive (passivizable) verb and an argument frame selection without the subject-NP. If the option that leads to an agent *by*-phrase is chosen the prepositional object-NP acquires the feature $[SU_{V_{LEX}}]$. This ensures that the NP in question will be selected as if it were the subject-NP of the lexical verb to be introduced in S^o.

When S^{oDEX} is selected in one of the rules (2c) or (3a–e), rule (3f) is activated to expand S^{oDEX} or $S^{oDEX}_{[PASS]}$. The expansion consists of the dative prepositional predicate *to*, followed by $S^o_{[DEX]}$ (with or without the feature [PASS]), and an object-$NP_{[IOV_{LEX}]}$, selected as if it were the indirect object of the main verb to be selected in S^o. The subscript feature [DEX] of S^o ensures that the lexical verb to be selected under rule (1g) allows for an indirect object and that its argument frame is filled without the indirect object. The rules of the Cycle will then ensure that the *to*-predicate together with its object-NP appear as a PP in the matrix-S^o.

Progressive, external dative, passive and manner adverbial can be combined into one sentence, as in *The letter is being written by Tom to Harry with accuracy*. Note the order: *by*-phrase, dative phrase, manner PrepPhrase. This follows from the far right LOWERING of the adverbials involved: the rightmost adverbial was lowered last. The process is demonstrated in the example sentence (37) in section 3.7.2 below.

3.2 Further preliminary remarks

The machinery presented in the preceding section contains the basic rules of English syntax and some lexicon. The rules reveal most of the central regularities of both the auxiliary system and the complementation system of English, but they do so mostly without the backing of a general theory providing the universal, or areal, parameters with the values filled in for English. Such a theory is not realistic at the moment. It will become more realistic when a sufficient number of sufficiently different languages have been investigated. The rules also incorporate the essentials of the syntax of quantification. However, in order not to overburden the presentation, a more detailed (but still incomplete) discussion of the quantification machinery is delayed until section 7.1. In this chapter only non-quantified, i.e. definite, NPs are considered.

A few gaps have been left. First, little is said about the internal structure of NPs, though some tentative NP-grammar is presented in 7.2.1. The rules given here only pay lip service to internal NP-syntax. Formation Rule (4a) allows for four NP-expansions, $:x + S^{NOM}$, $^\wedge x + S^{NOM}$, just x, and any question morpheme X_{WH} leading to a WH-question. The single variable x is either anaphoric with regard to a controlling NP or acts as a bound variable. Rule (4b), assigns two expansions to S^{NOM}. First as a surface noun with a bound variable as NP-term. A structure like (1a) is read as 'the x such that x is a cat' which becomes *the cat* in surface structure. S^{NOM} may also expand as an adjectival predicate with an S^{NOM} as subject term, as in (1b), which comes out as *the ginger cat* after NP-internal LOWERING of $_V$[ginger] onto $_V$[cat]. A structure like (1c) stands for 'the set of all cats'. (For further comment see section 7.2.1.)

Skeletal structure of NPs

Model-theoretically, the subtree dominated by the highest S^{NOM} denotes the set of all (ginger) cats. The colon operator ':' binds x and selects one specific individual from the set of all (ginger) cats — a process that normally requires information from the speech situation or from preceding discourse. The cap operator in (1c) is model-theoretically vacuous, as the top-NP denotes what S^{NOM} denotes. Its function is purely syntactic: it turns an S-structure into an NP-structure of the same type. The neglect of NP-syntax leaves the syntax of quantifiers (section 7.1) incomplete as well, as these tend to be lowered onto NPs, which carry the main load of quantificational expression.[2] In the lexicon of 3.1.2 only predicative adjectives are taken into account.

Secondly, no attempt has been made to integrate counterfactual ('irrealis') moods into the rule system. This gap is less quickly noticed for languages where the irrealis mood 'borrows' already available auxiliary means, such as the simple past tense or the past tense of the futuricity operator. But some languages have subjunctives to express counterfactuality. German does so standardly, and English occasionally, as in *If I were you I wouldn't do that*. Specific phenomena connected with counterfactuality have not been taken into account here (but see 6.6 for a partial analysis).

Thirdly, speech act operators are almost totally neglected. After Ross's well-known paper (1970) on the representation of speech act operators and Fraser's reply (1974), a stalemate arose and nothing much has been heard about them since in the theory of grammar. A separate study would be needed to account for speech act operators, and this book does not seem the right place for that. We have limited ourselves to the introduction of an abstract question morpheme, making it trigger the syntactic phenomena that go with questions. For a discussion of question formation see section 3.2.1 below.

Finally, as the reader will have noticed, the rules overgenerate in that semantic dependencies among adverbial and tense operators have been neglected. The system fails to block incorrect sentences like *Yesterday the cat may eat the mouse* or *The cat ate the mouse tomorrow*. In living speech, such dependencies are controlled by the cognitive machinery directing the generation process. But in the simplified set-up of isolated syntactic rules, with no cognitive machinery attached, they can, in principle, be regulated by a system of percolating features or co-occurrence restrictions, but such a system has not been formulated here.

---

[2] In higher order logics, predicates are normally quantified over in their predicate position by means of higher order quantifiers and variables. Not so in natural language, which restricts the quantification machinery to NPs and adverbs. If one wants to say, in natural language, that some properties possessed by dogs are also possessed by humans this cannot be expressed other than by reifying properties and referring to them in an NP-position, whether as (part of an) argument term or as predicate nominal in a copula-construction. To my knowledge, no natural language allows for expressions corresponding to something like 'this man everythings to everybody' with recognizable verb morphology. Even Turkish, which conjugates nouns, stops short of such drastic measures. (For a first Semantic Syntax analysis of Turkish see section 7.6.)

The lexicon contains a small number of lexical predicates of different surface categories, with their corresponding argument structure frames. The format in which the items are presented is still primitive: a well-organized lexicon will have a great deal of internal structure. In particular it will have a system of well-defined and hierarchically ordered semantic categorizers for predicates, such as 'action', 'process', 'state', 'movement', etc., with the necessary default properties. No attempt has been made to set up such a system here. This means that the rule system has not been formalized, or only on an ad hoc basis, for those cases where rules are sensitive to such semantic categorizers.

Special attention has been paid, in the lexicon, to complement-taking predicates (mainly verbs). Their selection is sufficiently representative to ensure a non-trivial coverage of English complementation phenomena (but not of gerunds and 'small clauses'). Extrapolation to other complement-taking predicates should be unproblematic.

The auxiliary system is, by its very nature, highly restricted lexically. It depends largely on a finely tuned interaction between the Formation Rules, some rules of the Cycle, and the postcyclic rules. Some lexical categories of the auxiliary system, such as the tenses and specific auxiliary verbs, are so restricted that they could be given in full. Others, such as the adverbial and prepositional predicates at the various levels, are much larger and could not be specified exhaustively. Yet an attempt has been made at a reasonably representative selection.

It must be pointed out, in this context, that a complete specification and grammatical integration of even a restricted word class such as, for example, prepositions, is no mean undertaking. The least demanding part is the compilation of a complete list. Then, however, comes the task of specifying at what level in the Formation Rules each preposition can be inserted, i.e. of specifying their level in the auxiliary hierarchy, corresponding with different syntactic properties. It appears that this can be done only if the prepositions are considered in conjunction with their prepositional objects. A PP made from *to + surprise*, for example, as in *to his surprise*, etc..., is usable as a sentence adverbial, introduced by rule (1c). But, judging by its only possible position in the sentence, at the far right, a PP like *to the village* with a movement verb like *go* must be of a lower level, introduced by rule (3c), closest to but still outside the matrix clause S°. The PPs most intimately connected with the matrix clause are the so-called prepositional objects, as in *write about, care for, listen to*. They behave as if they are part of the argument frame of the main verb in the matrix S. Whether they are best described as part of the lexical argument frame or as low level PPs that are optionally or obligatorily incorporated into the argument frame is a question we have had to leave undecided. For more discussion see section 3.5 below.

In the machinery provided, no account has been taken of a possible Precycle, following the Formation Rules. A Precycle component is probably useful for certain language-specific adjustments in SA-trees. For example, some languages, including English, follow a so-called 'sequence of tenses', so that the tense of complement clauses is adjusted according to that of the higher or main clause. In English one says *I knew you lived here*, rather than *I knew you live here*, as in the numerous languages that have no sequence of tenses. A precyclic tree-adjustment seems the obvious answer in such cases. Likewise for counterfactual constructions, which also imply a tense shift, for NEGATIVE RAISING phenomena (see note 4), and perhaps a few more.

It will be noted that what, in 1.4.1, 2.11 and 3.1 was referred to as the 'skeletal frame' for the auxiliary system in any language is clearly there. It is recognized in the Formation Rules (1e), (2a), (2c), (3a) and (3g). As was said, in 2.11, adverbial and prepositional elements, and often other elements as well, have to be woven into this skeletal structure in language-specific ways. The Formation Rules represent an attempt at doing so, on a limited scale, for English. Integrating the various levels at which adverbial, prepositional and quantificational activity takes place into the rule system inevitably makes the rules look less transparent than just the skeletal rules of (22) in 2.11. But it also makes them very much more powerful (to say nothing of the fact that quantification phenomena can now be incorporated at no extra cost; see 7.1).

Some theoretical linguists may baulk at the complexity of the rule system. They should realize that neater rule systems achieve their neatness only at the expense of descriptive adequacy, that is, of the facts. No generative rule system has so far been able to provide anything resembling an adequate coverage of the data of English adverbial and prepositional selection and placement (and the same can be said of many other categories of data). The only serious attempts at describing these facts are found in the traditional taxonomic literature (descriptive grammars, appendices to the better dictionaries, and the like), where categories and positions are listed and examples are given. But even these attempts, serious as they are, lack full coverage. In other words, the hard truth must be faced that no exhaustive description of the facts under discussion exists anywhere in the literature. Against this background the Formation Rules presented here score well as regards coverage of facts, compactness and neatness of organization. It is useful to remember that any machine that actually works is likely to need a great deal of wiring, even when it is based on one or two simple principles.

3.2.1 QUESTION FORMATION and FRONTING in English

English QUESTION FORMATION and FRONTING are very similar. We attempt to account for their similarity in terms of an attraction mechanism adhering to certain elements like Q_{ue} and *Foc*.

The first question to consider is the categorial status of the fillers Q_{ue} and *Foc*. Let us consider them to be elements that occur in front position in S-structures and have the property of attracting certain marked elements in their scope to satisfy their status, as part of the postcyclic rules QUESTION FORMATION and FRONTING, respectively. We call these elements *incomplete constituents*. In main sentences the SA-labelling is V_{Attr}. The surface category is of the form X/Y, meaning 'takes an X to become a Y'. Note that the notation '/S' that has been used throughout for VP, is to be read analogously: but for a subject it would be an S. If /S-constituents attracted subjects they would be written '[SU]/S'.

In *embedded* questions the surface category of Q_{ue} is $_C[WH]/_C[WH]$: it takes a WH-constituent to become one. This accounts for the attraction of WH-constituents in dependent questions like *I wonder **what** John will eat.* If there is no WH-constituent the filler *if* or *whether* labelled 'y-n' ('yes-no') is attracted, as in: *I don't know **if/whether** John has eaten.*

Attraction takes the form of ADOPTION, with the special feature that the new node's label is made up of what is at the right of the first slash in the adopting node's label. Note that 'C' in '$_C[WH]$' is a variable ranging over NP, Adj, Adv, PP. Thus, if $_C[WH]/_C[WH]$ takes an $_{NP}[WH]$ it becomes an $_{NP}[WH]$, as demonstrated in (2).

In *main* questions the category of Q_{ue} depends on whether $_C[WH]$ is the main clause subject. If it is, the labelling is identical to that for dependent questions: '$_C[WH]/_C[WH]$' (perhaps due to a constraint preventing AUX from unilaterally C-commanding its subject). If it is not the main clause subject, the labelling is $_C[WH]/AUX//S$: it takes a $_C[WH]$ to become AUX//S, which again takes AUX to become /S. This is illustrated in (3). Again, if there is no $_C[WH]$ an element labelled 'y-n', now with the filler 'Ø', is attracted. Thus, in dependent questions Q_{ue} just right-adopts any WH-constituent in the sentence[3], but in main questions Q_{ue} first does this and then RIGHT-ADOPTS the AUX-area, except if the fronted constituent is the main clause subject. (If the attracted $_C[WH]$ is the subject or predicate nominal of a complement non-NP S, $_{Comp}[that]$ is obligatorily deleted.)

(2)

(3)

---

[3] Sentences may have more than one WH-element, as in *Who sold what to whom?* The strategy followed in English seems to be to front the element that is highest in the constituent hierarchy (Keenan & Comrie 1977), in this case the subject term, and leave the others in position.

The Formation Rules allow the filler Q_{ue} to occur only in main clauses. Its occurrence in subordinate clauses is a form of complementation. Some verbs, such as *tell, doubt, know, ask,* may take a dependent question as object clause, specifiable as $_{NP}[Q_{ue}+S'']$ (see 3.1.2 for the verbs *tell* and *know*). This sends the S'' back into Formation Rules (1d) or (1e), as it should do. It also ensures that this is the only way the element Q_{ue} can occur in a subordinate clause.

The rule of QUESTION FORMATION as formulated in 3.1.5 allows for attraction of a $_C$[WH] by Q_{ue} from a complement *that*-clause but preferably not if it is dominated by NP. This explains why one can say, for example, *Who does it seem that John invited?* but hardly *?Who is it likely that John invited?*, since *likely*, but not *seem*, requires NP over S'' (see 3.1.2 and 3.8; cf. also 5.2.6)). Or why *Who do you think he invited?* is all right but **What did he wash the dishes while singing?* is not.

FRONTING is largely analogous. However, *Foc* does not normally occur in subordinate clauses, only in main clauses. There it has the label $_C$[+Foc]/ $_C$[+Foc], except when the fronted constituent contains a negative element (or seminegative, like *hardly*). In that case AUX is fronted as well, and *Foc* takes the label $_C$[+Foc]/AUX//S — except again when the fronted $_C$[+Foc] is subject. English thus has *In that way I can help*, against *In no way can I help*.

Typically, with negative fronted constituents AUX is not attracted when the constituent fronted earlier is subject: *NOBODY left* is the correct form, with focus accent on *nobody*, not **NOBODY did leave*, as for **Who did leave?* and *Who left?*

If we accept as a principle that subject combined with AUX gives S, not /S, which seems reasonable, we may have a principled reason for the otherwise curious fact that AUX-attraction is cancelled when the element attracted earlier is subject. For the result of the attraction must be /S, not S. Therefore, if a constituent labelled 'AUX//S' already contains an NP this cannot be a subject-NP. Apparently, when AUX-attraction is impossible, the element in question, Q_{ue} or *Foc*, falls back on the simpler status of $_C$[WH]/$_C$[WH] and $_C$[+Foc]/$_C$[+Foc], respectively.

Clearly, this bit of universalizing theory requires further elaboration, which cannot be given in the present context. We return to this issue in 5.2.6, when Dutch QUESTION FORMATION and FRONTING are discussed.

3.3 The generation of a few simple English sentences

Let us now demonstrate the rule system by generating a few simple English sentences. Consider the SA-tree (4a), which is generated by the application of the Formation Rules (1e), (2c) and (3g), and an appropriate choice from the Lexicon. The cyclic rules induced by each predicate are mentioned between angled brackets just beneath the predicates concerned. NP-trees are simplified to their surface form. For (4a) this means that we write *the cat* and *the mouse*, respectively. Structure (4a) will end up as *The cat ate the mouse*.

(4)a.

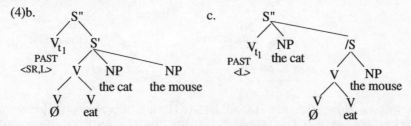

This structure now enters the next stage of the syntax, the Cycle. Here the lexically induced rules, the category-induced rules and the structure-induced rules must be applied, in that order, on each successive S-cyle, starting from the most deeply embedded S until the highest S has been processed.

The cyclic rules involved in this structure are all lexically induced and are thus all indicated between angled brackets with each inducing predicate until the rule has been carried out. When more than one rule is required or allowed for by the same predicate on the same cycle, as for example the rule pair <SR,L> (SUBJECT RAISING and LOWERING) for PRES or PAST, they are *intrinsically ordered* with respect to each other: application of one rule must not destroy the structural conditions for application of the other. Here this means that SR is to apply before L.

The first S-node up whose V has a rule feature associated with it is S': its V requires LOWERING (L). In this case, as can be seen from the lexicon, L involves the DETACHMENT of $_V$[Ø] and its LEFT ADOPTION by the lower V. The result is given in (4b). Now the S"-cycle is activated, with SUBJECT RAISING (SR) followed by (L), both induced by the predicate PAST. SUBJECT RAISING selects the first NP to the right of V in the S' of (4b). This NP, $_{NP}$[the cat], is then placed in the position of its own S, which is demoted to /S and shifted to the right. The result is as in (4c).

(4)b.   c.

Note that the combined rule features of $_V$[PAST], SR and L form the TENSE ROUTINE described in 2.7.4.2.1 of the preceding chapter and responsible for the change from a VSO format to an NP-/S format. Due to SR, S" in (4c) has a structure already containing the NP-/S structure required for the surface structure of this sentence. The metamorphosis from VSO to NP-/S is half-way. The S"-expansion now needs to get rid of the t_1-verb PAST still dangling on the left. This is achieved by the LOWERING of $_V$[PAST], which is left-adopted by the lower V-island and changes category to Affix. (4d) is thus the shallow structure of (4a).

(4)d.

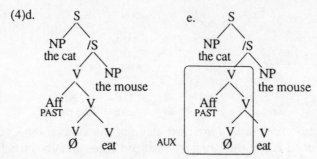

This structure is now input to the Postcyclic Rules.

AUX-FORMATION is a preliminary to the Postcycle, setting off the AUX-area as a part of any V-cluster containing an $_{Aff}[t_1]$-node and giving it the name of AUX, as a prerequisite to some of the rules of the Postcycle. AUX is formed by taking the parent V-node of $_{Aff}[t_1]$, in this case the V-node dominating the whole V-cluster. Since the right brother of $_{Aff}[t_1]$ is a branching node its rightmost dependent $_V[eat]$ is subtracted from the V-cluster. The remaining area is AUX. Application of AUX-FORMATION to (4d) gives (4e), where the AUX-area is boxed in.

The first postcyclic rule to apply is (5), *Do*-SUPPORT. The rules (1)-(4) do not apply. Since $_V[\varnothing]$ is directly followed by a lexically filled V-node, $_V[eat]$, $_V[\varnothing]$ is not replaced by the dummy verb $_V[do]$ but is, instead, deleted, as shown in (4f). Note that there is still an AUX-area, but due to the deletion of $_V[\varnothing]$ it had to be redefined, according to rule (5), so that it now also covers $_V[eat]$. The AUX-area now coincides with the whole V-cluster, as in (4f).

(4)f.

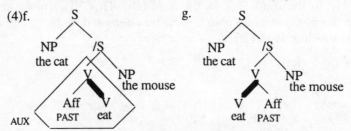

Now follows rule (6), AFFIX HANDLING (AH), which makes $_V[eat]$ right-adopt $_{Aff}[PAST]$ and relabels the V-constituent FV ('finite verb'). Together with the general Pruning Conventions this yields (4g). One sees that $_V[eat]$ and $_{Aff}[PAST]$ have, in effect, swopped places. No further treatment follows, since the last rule, MINCE, does not apply: it is not allowed to cut into AUX. (4g) is thus the surface structure corresponding to (4a).

Note that the right-branching structure of the syntactic V-cluster has now given way to left-branching, even though the simple binary structure of the V-node does not show that. To make the new branching directionality visible we have shown the spine in the V-clusters of (4f) and (4g) (see 2.8). This change of directionality marks a transition from a syntactic to a morphological structure: the V-cluster of (4g) will become one morphological word *ate*.

The generative process of *The cat ate the mouse* does not show why the AUX-area is useful in English grammar. This will be clearer when we generate the interrogative version of this sentence, starting with (5a), which is identical with (4a) but for the top of the tree.

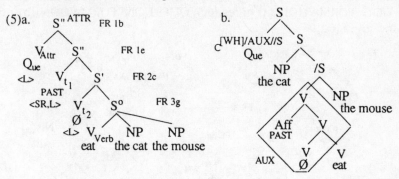

The cycle takes (5a) to the shallow structure (5b), with AUX as indicated. Now the postcyclic rule QUESTION FORMATION applies, leading to right-adoption first of the quasi WH-constituent $_{y-n}[\varnothing]$, then of AUX, as in (5c). Note that the surface category of Q_{ue} is $_C[\text{WH}]/\text{AUX}//S$, which takes $_C[\text{WH}]$ to become AUX//S, which takes AUX to become /S (see section 3.2.1 above):

(5)c.

(5)d.

At this moment the rule *Do*-SUPPORT must apply. The difference with (4e) is now apparent: $_V[\varnothing]$ is not deleted, as in (4e), but $\varnothing$ is replaced by the dummy verb *do*, since $\varnothing$ is now no longer followed directly by a lexically filled V-node. Together with AH the result is as in (5d). MINCE does not apply, since

/S$_o$ is not a C-cluster. Therefore, (5d) is the surface structure, corresponding to *Did the cat eat the mouse?*

Yes/no-questions thus illustrate one use of the AUX-constituent. Likewise for WH-questions. Take the sentence *What did the cat eat?* This corresponds to the SA in (6a) (note that the formal introduction of *what* has not been accounted for by the Formation Rules). The shallow structure is (6b). QUESTION FORMATION (a) gives (6c); QUESTION FORMATION (b) attracts AUX and gives (6d).

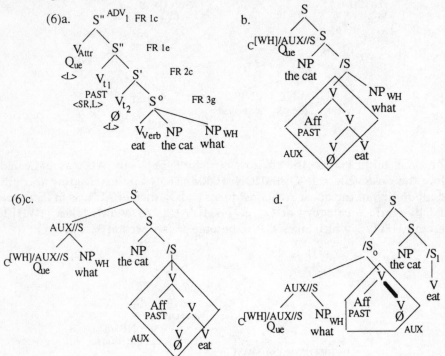

Do-SUPPORT and AFFIX HANDLING yield (6e), which is the surface structure since MINCE does not apply. We thus recognize the sentence *What did the cat eat?* Note that the /S$_1$-constituent does not take the particle *to*, since it does not begin to lack its AUX area until well after the end of the Cycle.

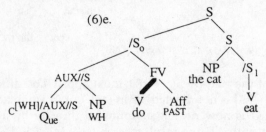

When WH fills the subject position and not, as in the preceding example, the object position, then QUESTION FORMATION (b) does not apply but QUESTION FORMATION (a) does, as shown in (7):

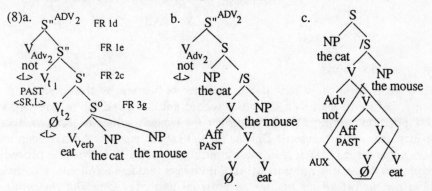

which, if $_{NP}$[WH] is provided with the necessary features, corresponds to *Who ate the mouse?*

3.4 Negation, the modals and EMPH

Negation and the modals provide further support for the notion of AUX-area. A simple case is the negation of (4a): *The cat did not eat the mouse*, which, of course, has the SA-structure (8a). The cyclic treatment of (8a) is identical with that of (4a), up to and including S'', as in (8b).

Only the top-cycle now remains to be gone through. This involves LOWERING of $_V$[not], which is to be left-adopted by the V of /S. With AUX-FORMATION this leads to (8c). Now postcyclic ADVERB PLACEMENT must be applied. Since the adverb area above AUX contains $_{Adv}$[not] option (a) is required. It detaches $_{Adv}$[not] from its V-cluster and re-inserts it at the exit of AUX. At this stage, English allows a choice (see 2.10): $_{Adv}$[not], in its new position, may become part of AUX, but it may also stay outside AUX. The choice is determined, or heavily influenced, by sociolinguistic register. In informal, colloquial English unstressed $_{Adv}$[not] normally becomes part of AUX and is then normally reduced to *n't*. But in more formal varieties of English it stays outside AUX and must keep its full form. Let us pursue both options. Thus, ADVERB PLACEMENT-(a)

leads to the two structures (8d') and (8d"). Further postcyclic treatment leads
to the surface structures (8e') and (8e").

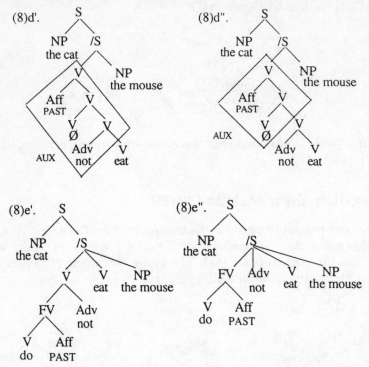

(8)d'.

(8)d".

(8)e'.

(8)e".

It is easily seen now that if the sentence is headed by the question morpheme, (8d') will lead to a structure where *not* is moved along with AUX to
front position, giving *Didn't the cat eat the mouse?*, whereas (8d") will keep
not in place, with the result *Did the cat not eat the mouse?* As has been said,
when *not* is inside AUX it is normally reduced to *n't* attached to the preceding
verb form. When it is not part of AUX it always remains a full *not*. This marks
(*)*Did not the cat eat the mouse?* as unusual and prevents **Did the catn't eat
the mouse?* from occurring.

Now consider *The cat may not have eaten the mouse*, with the SA (9a):

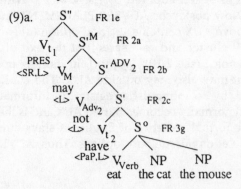

(9)a.

It is important to note that the negation is in the scope of *may* and not vice versa, since the sentence means 'it is possible that the cat has not eaten the mouse', and not 'it is not possible that the cat has eaten the mouse'. This is expressed in the SA-structure (9a) by the fact that *may* commands *not*, and not the other way around. Note that Formation Rule (2a) allows for the expansion of S'^M into a modal verb followed by S'^{ADV_2}. Rule (2b) shows the superscript ADV_2 over S', so that rule (2b) may apply after rule (2a). Rule (2b) allows for the selection of the class 2 adverb *not*, followed by an S'. This selection is shown in (9a).

The cyclic treatment gives the shallow structure (9b), with AUX defined.

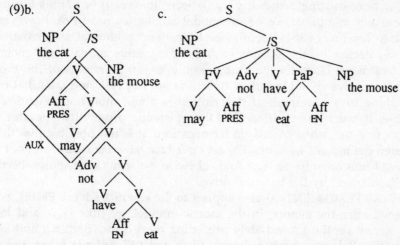

(9)b.

c.

Since ADVERB PLACEMENT does not apply (there are no adverbs above AUX) $_{Adv}$[not] cannot now become part of AUX. This explains why, in this sentence, *not* cannot be reduced to *n't*: **The cat mayn't have eaten the mouse* is ungrammatical in modern standard English and on this reading. It also explains why the question form of this sentence is *May the cat not have eaten the mouse?* The form *?May not the cat have eaten the mouse?*, though acceptable in certain dialects, does not seem to be part of modern standard British English, which is the variety approximated here. The dialects that accept it have a different corollary for AUX-formation. Of the postcyclic rules only AH (2x) and MINCE (3x) apply. The surface structure is (9c).

The English modals lack participles, infinitives and perfective tenses and occur only in the simple present and past tenses. But they do allow for perfective infinitives, as in the example given (*have eaten*). Their treatment as fillers of the optional intermediate t_m-position between t_1 and t_2 leads automatically to this defective paradigm, which is thus explained without any extra cost. They come directly under t_1 and are thus subject to t_1-tensing (simple present or past). But they can never occur under t_2 and can therefore never undergo t_2-tensing (the perfective tenses). Moreover, an S^M can never occur as an infinitive or as a participle since these forms always result from clausal (sentential) embedding, and, as shown in 2.12, sentential complements are always either S" or S' or S°, but never S'M.

Modal verbs can have many functions, as is well known (cf. Palmer 1979). The principal distinction is between *epistemic* and *agentive* modals (other terms are in use as well). The semantic functions of the epistemic modals are, in main outline, the following. Epistemic *will* expresses, for the most part, prediction in the present tense and counterfactuality in the past tense. Epistemic *may* and *must* express, respectively, compatibility with and inevitable consequence of available knowledge. The agentive modals are a great deal more complex. The general principle is that they involve a tacitly understood agent or force causing possibility (*can*), necessity (*must*) or permission (*may*). The semantic complications of the modal auxiliaries need not, however, be gone into here, since they seem to be lexical and prelexical rather than syntactic. Syntactically, the epistemic and the agentive modals are given the same treatment. Once the various possible lexical meanings of the modals have been analysed and specified (which is not our task here), all that needs to be done in a grammatical description is some morphophonemics. For example, it must be specified that the epistemic possibility operator *may* changes into *can* when placed under negation: 'it is not possible that the cat has eaten the mouse' becomes *The cat can't have eaten the mouse*, and not **The cat mayn't have eaten the mouse.*[4] And, likewise, *must* under negation becomes *needn't*, followed by the bare infinitive.[5]

ADVERB PLACEMENT-(a) also applies to the abstract adverb EMPH, which is deleted after the syntax, in the morphophonology (like Q_{ue}), and leaves heavy accent on the immediately preceding morpheme. Both *not* and *EMPH* are Positive Polarity Items: a default filter, the **PPI default filter**, prevents them from standing immediately under the adverbial predicate *not* in the SA of any sentence. The PPI-filter can be overridden when the negation is used metalinguistically, in particular when it cancels presuppositions (the radical negation; see note 8 below). The defeasibility conditions of the filter are not worked out here: it is treated as if it were categorical. The precise semantics of *EMPH* remains to be specified. Note that this excludes double negation in the classical logical sense, i.e. with the negations cancelling each other out. *EMPH* is, moreover, subject to the categorical **EMPH-filter** which stipulates that once

---

[4] Colloquial English has *mustn't*, meaning either 'not be allowed' or 'not be possible', the latter in, e.g. *It mustn't be very nice over there* (cf. the French equivalent *Ça ne doit pas être gai là-bas*). In both cases the input structure to the rule system is considered to have the negation as the highest operator, so that the postcyclic rule ADVERB PLACEMENT has to move *not* to below AUX. This is probably due to a precyclic rule of NEGATIVE RAISING (cf. Seuren (1974), where NEGATIVE RAISING is still assumed to be a cyclic rule, which is probably incorrect). To say, simply, that *mustn't* reflects an underlying NECESSARY-NOT would be semantically inadequate, and would make it impossible to account for the phonological reduction of *not* to *n't*.

[5] Besides the modal auxiliary verb *need*, which is followed by the bare infinitive as befits a regular modal auxiliary, English also has the Main Verb *need*, which is followed by a *to*-infinitival. This verb is probably best assigned the argument frame [need + S°] and the cyclic rule SUBJECT RAISING (see the Lexicon in 3.1.2).

EMPH is chosen the rules (1d) and (2b) are no longer recursive: the expansion must then contain simple S" or S'.

EMPH accounts for sentences like (10a-c), which differ from their non-emphatic counterparts (10d-f):

(10)a. He always DOES laugh
    b. He just WILL go
    c. He never HAS understood

    d. He always laughs
    e. He will just go
    f. He has never understood

Consider (10a), with the SA (10a') and the Shallow Structure (10a"):

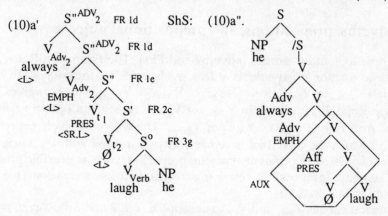

Now ADVERB PLACEMENT-(a) applies, moving $_{Adv}$[EMPH] to the exit of AUX. ADVERB PLACEMENT-(b) does not apply because AUX ends in $_V$[Ø]. Therefore, $_{Adv}$[always] stays where it is. *Do*-SUPPORT now applies, as EMPH is not a surface lexical verb, replacing $_V$[Ø] with $_V$[do]. The result is (10a'''). After AH and MINCE we have the surface structure (10a''''):

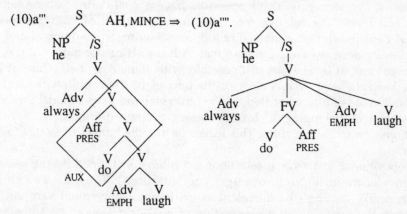

The morphophonology deletes $_{Adv}$[EMPH] and places heavy accent on the preceding *does*.

The reader will be able to generate (10b) and (10c): (10b) from *just - EMPH - PRES - will - Ø - go* and (10c) from *never - EMPH - PRES - have - understand*.

The sequence *not - EMPH* is blocked by the PPI default filter (see above). When this filter is overridden this whole sequence *not - EMPH* is subjected to ADVERB PLACEMENT-(a), and the sentence will contain a heavily emphasized *NOT*. This emphatic *NOT* can be used as the presupposition-cancelling radical negation (see note 8). Note that the order *EMPH - never - PRES - have - understand* is excluded by the EMPH-filter (see above): after the selection of EMPH as a V_{Adv2} the rules (1d) and (2b) are no longer recursive and no other members of the class V_{Adv2} may be selected.

3.5 Adverbs, prepositions, and prepositional objects

Let us now look at adverbials (adverbs and PPs). The Formation Rules allow for the introduction of adverbials at five levels: rule (1a) introduces the super-adverbials V_{Adv0} or V_{Prep0}. Rule (1c) gives V_{Adv1} or V_{Prep1}. Rule (1d) gives V_{Adv2} or V_{Prep2}. Rule (2b) gives again V_{Adv2} or V_{Prep2}, now as an option under the modals. And rule (3c) gives V_{Adv3} or V_{Prep3}. The different levels express the degree to which the adverbial is semantically connected with the nuclear S^o. They are expressed in different syntactic properties, such as possible positions in the sentence or possible relative extraction or passivization (see fig.2 further on in this section).

The lexical classes V_{Adv} and V_{Prep} subscripted 0, 1, 2 and 3, however, show a great deal of overlap, which suggests that the scale of syntactic positions as defined by the rules is the basic grid and that the fillers are chosen according to the level accorded them in the cognitive and semantic decision-taking process leading to the actual sentence. The decision as to their level will then depend largely on background or world knowledge. Strictly logical operators, such as the negation operator and the quantifiers, leave less room for such decisions. Consequently, these operators have a well-defined class-membership and level. The relative freedom, in this respect, of many adverbials would explain why grammaticality judgments as regards adverbial and prepositional placement are often marginal. Adverbials can be more natural, in a given context, at level x but still possible, with some cognitive effort, at level y. To keep the rule system clear of the tangles of the cognitive, logical and semantic roots of uttered sentences, the adverbial and prepositional predicates are staged as belonging to lexical classes corresponding to the syntactic positions defined in the rules. This leaves us just the tangles of syntax to cope with.

Prepositional and adverb selections are often constrained by the semantic category of the main verb (or larger configurations). Thus, the French verb *nager*, unlike its English equivalent *swim*, is not a movement verb and can therefore not stand under a preposition of goal or direction: *He swam across the canal* translates as *Il a traversé le canal à la nage (en nageant)* ('he crossed the canal at swimstroke (swimming)'). No account is given of such constraints here.

Besides the five levels mentioned, there is a lower, sixth level, but only for PPs. At this level PPs function as part of the lexical specification of a verb that takes a prepositional object, such as *rely on, listen to, wait on, dwell upon, abide by, look for,* or *sleep in/on* if the following NP is the object used for sleeping. Pending a fuller treatment, such verbs are perhaps best listed in the lexicon as compound verbs with the structure $_V[_V[X]_{Prep}[Y]]$. Somewhere along the line the preposition is united into a PP with the last NP in the argument frame. Since they function as direct objects of lexical verbs such prepositional objects can become the subject of a passive clause and also the antecedent of a relative clause, leaving the preposition stranded in both cases.

Some verbs have a particle as a separable part. They may be transitive, like *take up,* or intransitive, like *go out.* In either case they may combine with a prepositional object, as in *take up on* or *go out of.* The verb *take up on* is probably best listed as $_V[_V[_V[take]_{Prt}[up]]_{Prep}[on]]$, with the argument frame $+NP_1+NP_2+NP_3$. In case of passivization the first NP after the subject, i.e. NP_2, becomes the new subject: *I was never taken up on it.* A construction like **It was never taken me up on* is clearly ungrammatical. Yet relative extraction is possible for both objects: *I am the one whom you took up on it,* and *That is what you took me up on.* Other particle verbs, such as $_V[_V[_V[put]_{Prt}[up]]_{Prep}[with]]$, have the argument frame $+NP_1+NP_2$, i.e. with only a prepositional object. Here, the prepositional object allows for both passivization and relative extraction: *This cannot be put up with,* and *This is an insolence I shall not put up with.*

Normally, the PP in a collocation like *sleep in/on this bed* will count as being of level 6, as part of the lexical argument frame. This is not so, however, if instead of *this bed* an NP is selected that can hardly be interpreted as the object used for the sleeping, as with *the terrace* or *the town.* Now passivization is quaint: *!The town has been slept in* or *!The terrace has been slept on* are hardly acceptable. Consequently, a speaker will prefer rule (3c), i.e. level 5, for the introduction of *on the terrace* and rule (1d), i.e. level 3, for *in the town* (a terrace comes closer to being a sleeping place than a town, which is more remote from the action of sleeping). Note that *!The town has been slept in* is not ungrammatical, only incongruous, given standard world knowledge and normal expectations regarding what sleeping amounts to. If it is understood that the sleeping was done by an army of soldiers one may well say *The town has been slept in,* but then an image is evoked of streets littered with tents, mattresses and other military paraphernalia.

Relative extraction of a preposition object is likewise sensitive to level differences: it is allowed only from level 5 down. Thus *This is the terrace the man [has/may have] slept on* or *This is the house the man [has/may have] slept in* are normal, whereas *!This is the town the man [has/may have] slept in* sounds odd. The reason is that in the sentences with *terrace* or *house* the PP will normally have been introduced at level 5. But in the sentence with *town* the PP is introduced by rule (1d), i.e. at level 3, since the relation between sleeping and towns is distant. The PP is then too high for relative extraction.

(Some prepositions, such as *during, near, beside, before*, resist stranding, probably for phonological reasons: **This is the house I used to play near.*)

Movement verbs normally position their PPs at level 5. Sentences like *He travelled to London* or *He went over the bridge* admit relative extraction: *London is the place he travelled to, This is the bridge he went over.* But such sentences lack a passive counterpart **London was travelled to by him, *The bridge was gone over by him.* Now, when these verbs are used metaphorically the PP shifts to the lexical level 6, as appears from the correct passives in e.g. *The matter was gone over in five minutes,* or *This question has never been gone into properly.* Lexicalization and re-analysis processes are seen to be busily at work here.

Place adverbials are normally placed at level 3, 4 (with modal) or 5. At level 3 they admit LEFT-ADOPTION by their argument-S, resulting in an initial PP followed by an intonational break, as in (11a). They may also go to the far right of their argument-S, in which case they are weakly stressed and the main sentence accent falls on the /S-constituent, as in (11b). At level 5 they go to the far right of the argument-S and take sentence accent, as shown in (11c). At this level they modify S⁰, which is why the PP *in his office* takes sentence nuclear accent. In (11a,b), on the contrary, the PP *in his office* functions as a high operator over S".

(11)a. In his office, John sleeps
  b. John slééps$_{(,)}$ in his office
  c. John sleeps in his óffice

It is interesting to note that there are clear truth-conditional differences between (11a,b) on the one hand and (11c) on the other: in (11a,b) John does not do what he is supposed to do in his office and cannot be called a hard worker, but in (11c) John is such a hard worker that he even spends the night in his office. In Functional Sentence Perspective theories (see 1.3.2) this difference will be interpreted as a difference in topic-comment structure. Following the suggestion made in Seuren (1985:297) and elaborated in Van Kuppevelt (1991), this interpretation is seen as essentially correct: (11a,b) are possible answers to the question 'What does John do in his office?', with *in his office* at level 3, whereas (11c) is a possible answer to the question 'Where does John sleep?', with *where* at level 5. Note also that Steinthal's sentence, quoted in 1.3.2, *Coffee grows in Africa*, with, obviously, nuclear accent on pp[in Africa], is now seen as involving a level 5 PP, modifying S⁰ and therefore the highest lexical predicate, just as Steinthal intuited. Negation will affect precisely this highest lexical predicate.

Under the same criteria passive *by*-phrases, external dative PPs under *to* and benefactive PPs under *for* are seen to be of level 5, as appears from the ungrammatical passives (for *to* and *for*) but the grammatical relativizations. In French, the replacement of the middle NP by a PP under the preposition *à* has become standardized, with the result that internal datives have disappeared (except as clitics), and indirect objects are obligatorily cast into a PP-mould.

The rule system is such that adverbials originating at levels 4, 5 and 6 automatically become /S-constituents. An adverbial of level 3 will become an /S-constituent only if it has been lowered onto the lower V (for adverbs) or moved to the far right of the argument-S (for PPs), but not when it has been left-adopted by the argument-S, in which case it will be an initial S-constituent, followed by an intonational break, just like an adverbial of level 2. PPs of level 1 to 4 disallow relative extraction and passivization. Those of level 5 allow for relative extraction but disallow passivization. PPs of level 6 allow for both relative extraction and passivization. This distribution of grammatical properties is shown in fig. 2 below.[6]

level	Passivization	Relative Extr.	/S-constituent
1 superadverbial	-	-	-
2 sentence adverbial	-	-	-
3 just above S''	-	-	+/-
4 between modal and S'	-	-	+
5 just above bare S°	-	+	+
6 lexical argument frame	+	+	+

Figure 2   Matrix of syntactic properties of PPs of different SA-levels

Application of rule (1a) produces an SA with an item of the class Adv_0 or $Prep_0$ as the highest V-node. The superadverbials are strictly outside the sentence structure and may precede speech act operators, as in *Moreover, why did you leave?* If (1c) is the first rule to be applied the highest V-node is an item of the class Adv_1 or $Prep_1$, which contains sentence adverbs like *fortunately, admittedly,* etc.

Superadverbials and sentence adverbials induce LOWERING onto their own argument-S, by LEFT-ADOPTION, resulting in a sentence-initial phrase, separated from the main body of the sentence by an intonational break, optionally rendered as a comma in orthography: *Allegedly, he works.* LOWERING onto S by LEFT-ADOPTION is generally constrained in that it is allowed only at the top of the SA-tree: no higher structure must be present.

[6] Similar level distinctions for adverbials are recognizable in other languages as well. For example, Modern Greek often has adverb incorporation into the verb form. This is possible (for certain lexical items) for manner and direction adverbs and adverbs of 'Aktionsart'. When the adverb is incorporated the resulting complex verb suggests that the process or property denoted is of a well-known kind:

  (i)   O Yánis férete kalá   or: O Yánis kaloférete   ('John behaves well')
  (ii)   I María éfage kalá   or: I María kaloéfage   ('Mary ate well')
  (iii) O Yánis pátise píso   or: O Yánis pisopátise   ('John stepped back')
  (iv)   O Yánis píni sichná   or: O Yánis sichnopíni   ('John drinks often')
But such incorporation is never possible for time or other high adverbials:
  (v)   O Yánis tha fígi ávrio   *O Yánis tha avriofígi   ('John will leave tomorrow')
  (vi)   O Yánis míluse akómi   *O Yánis akomimíluse   ('John was still speaking')
These data suggest that lexical adverb incorporation in Modern Greek is restricted not only by lexical idiosyncrasies but also by the rank of the adverb concerned.

Sentence adverbs, but not superadverbials, may also be positioned as parenthetical additions to or interruptions of the sentence, as in:

(12) a.   She has never fallen for his charms, fortunately
    b.   John, moreover, always gets what he wants
    c.   This has never been discussed, to my knowledge
    d.   I have, regrettably, to make these words my own

These positions have not been taken into account.

Note that superadverbials, V_{Attr}, *Foc* and sentence adverbials allow only one take per sentence. For this reason, Formation Rules (1a), (1b) and (1c) have been formulated as non-recursive rules. Moreover, superadverbials combine with either V_{Attr} and *Foc*, or with sentence adverbials but not with both, and V_{Attr} and *Foc* do not combine with sentence adverbials: *So, has he left?*, *So, he has admittedly left*, but **Then, has he left, admittedly? *Admittedly, he allegedly works*. For this reason, Formation Rule (1a) allows either S"^{ATTR} or S"^{ADV_1} or bare S" in its expansion, and the rules (1b) and (1c) allow only S"^{ADV_2} or bare S".

As has been said, the superadverbials occur in the highest possible position. They express a comment on the speech act, the very act of uttering the sentence in question. They are, therefore, strictly speaking metalinguistic material, though integrated into the grammatical system of the language (as all metalinguistic elements are).[7] Examples are:

(13) a.   *Moreover,* ⟨I ask you⟩ why don't you just leave?
    b.   *Since you are here,* ⟨I ask you⟩ could you tell Ann we're off?
    c.   *If you're hungry,* ⟨I inform you⟩ there is some cheese in the kitchen
    d.   *Therefore,* ⟨I advise you⟩ don't blame me
    e.   *In that case,* ⟨I ask you⟩ what is your argument?
    f.   *Quickly,* ⟨I ask you⟩ how much did you pay?

It is not to be excluded that an adequate grammatical analysis of speech act operators will show that the superadverbials do not really form a separate class. Once a motivated rule system is provided to account for the apparently

---

[7] In saying this we mean that sentences often parade as the expression of a proposition deducible more or less compositionally from their constituent parts, while in effect they are metalinguistic statements, usually about a previously uttered sentence or word. This fact has not been given sufficient recognition in the literature. Horn (1985), for example, in attempting to analyse metalinguistic uses of negation, fails to recognize the obvious fact that a sentence like

    (i)   Miss Debenham is not a WOMAN, she is a LADY

(Agatha Christie, *Murder on the Orient Express*) is not a statement about Miss Debenham's no doubt undoubted womanhood but about the choice of the word *woman* by the previous speaker, the cabin steward on the train, who had just issued the direction *Women this way, please!* Sentence (i) thus parades as an inconsistent statement about the gender of a person but is, in fact, a corrective statement about the use of a word. I argue that the SA of this sentence must reflect this fact and must, therefore, show the real semantic status of the sentence explicitly. This requires a 'grammar of quotes', which, unfortunately, has not been written yet. Such a grammar would demystify the mysterious vanishing act performed by such metalinguistic SA-material.

mysterious disappearance of the speech act operators in surface structures it may become clear that the Adv_o-class is nothing but the class of adverbials that are then predictably licenced to occur with the speech act operators overtly present in the SA-representations. That would explain the occurrence of even low level manner adverbs like *quickly* in this position, as in (13f): 'I am asking quickly, how much did you pay?' We cannot, however, go into this question here.

The adverbial predicates of class 2 fall into at least three subclasses, according to the rule options induced by them. The subclass {*occasional, normal, often, usual, clever, stupid,...*} optionally takes the treatment of class 1 adverbs, LOWERING onto their own argument-S by LEFT ADOPTION (only at the top of the SA-tree). If they do they end up in surface structure in a position that is indistinguishable from that of the class 1 adverbs: *Occasionally, he works.* But they may also, in this position, take LOWERING onto the lower V, again by LEFT ADOPTION: *He moreover works hard.* If there is higher structure the latter treatment is obligatory: *Allegedly, he occasionally works.* Class 1 adverbs occur less felicitously as part of the verbal cluster: *He allegedly works hard* is only acceptable with intonational breaks around the adverb, as in (12b,d). A second subclass {*not, always, just, never,...*} only allows for LOWERING onto the lower V (by LEFT-ADOPTION, of course). Sentences like **Not, I love you* or **Always, I am late*, with LEFT-ADOPTION by argument-S, or **I love you not* or **I am late always*, with LOWERING to the far right of the argument-S, are definitely foreign to present-day English. And a third subclass {*today, yesterday, tomorrow, recently, soon,...*} leaves the choice between LOWERING onto the argument-S by either LEFT-ADOPTION (unless there is higher structure) or movement to the far right: *Tomorrow, I'll sort things out* besides *I'll sort things out tomorrow*, but not the ponderous **I will tomorrow sort things out.*

Note that LOWERING or MOVEMENT of an adverbial element, whether adverb or PP, to the far right of an S-structure is normally constrained by embedded Ss: the element in question will stop short of crossing an embedded S-constituent, as shown in (14a,b). With embedded /S-structures the adverbial is free to stop before /S or to cross it, as shown in (14c,d):

(14)a.   I maintain today that you were right
    b.   *?I maintain that you were right today
    c.   I have wanted for a long time to do that
    d.   I have wanted to do that for a long time

The three subclasses of class 2 form one superordinate class because they share the positions afforded by the Formation Rules to the class of predicates V_{Adv2} and V_{Prep2} (and the quantifiers; see section 7.1). Since these predicates are allowed to occur recursively one gets sentence pairs differing only in the order of class 2 adverbs.[8] Sometimes, if both operators are sensitive to logical

---

[8] But note that independent filters may block certain combinations, e.g. the PPI default filter (see section 3.4), preventing *not* just above *not* or EMPH. If immediate repetitions of *not*

scope (in the sense that the surface order reflects their scope relation), there is a semantic difference due to surface order variation, as in:

(15)a. She just never laughs
   b. She never just laughs
   c. She doesn't usually laugh
   d. Usually, she doesn't laugh
   e. She usually doesn't laugh

The difference between (15a) and (15b) is due to the different scopes of *just* and *never*, which corresponds with the left-to-right order in which these words occur in the surface sentences. Likewise for (15c) on the one hand and (15d,e) on the other, where *usually* and *not* have swapped scopes and positions. The modalities of LOWERING ensure that the logical scope of the operators concerned corresponds with their surface structure order of appearance.

The class 2 prepositions induce OBJECT INCORPORATION and LOWERING, the standard routine for all prepositional predicates. The LOWERING is either by LEFT-ADOPTION or by movement to the far right, just like the third subclass of the class 2 adverbs just mentioned. These, too, mingle freely with each other and with the class 2 adverbs, sometimes, again with scope differences, depending on the logico-semantic quality of the operators involved:

(16)a. He always snores during some arias
   b. During some arias, he always snores
   c. He always snores during the service
   d. During the service, he always snores

(16a) and (16b) differ again semantically due to logical scope differences between the quantified elements *always* and *some arias*. More precisely, (16a) is ambiguous between a reading where at every opera performance there are some arias during which he snores (represented in (17a)), and one in which there are specific arias during which he always snores (as in (17b)). (16b) only seems to have the latter reading.[9]

---

occur in grammatical sentences the default has been overridden and a marked interpretation arises. For example, the sentence *She did* NOT *not stop in time*, with heavy accent on the first *not*, allows for an interpretation under which it is fully grammatical, involving an 'echo': it suggests that somebody has just said *She didn't stop in time*, and the speaker wants to express the proposition that the previously uttered sentence is inappropriate in the present discourse, due to presupposition failure. This inappropriateness is expressed by the presupposition-cancelling radical negation NOT (see Seuren 1985:228-234), which can only occur in construction with the finite verb form, excluding all other positions that can be filled by the 'normal' *minimal negation*. This radical negation consists of *not-EMPH*, where the violation of the PPI default filter signals a marked use (in this case the radical use) of the negation operator. This also explains without extra cost why the radical negation can only occur with the finite verb: EMPH can only be lowered onto the lower V and does not share the other possibilities afforded to *not* (as in *not all, no-one*, etc.) (which are due to the SCOPE ORDERING CONSTRAINT; see section 7.1 for further discussion).

[9] In the late '60s and early '70s there was a great deal of controversy about possible scope readings of quantifiers and negation, fanned by the fact that Montague grammar predicts that all scope readings are always possible in all sentences with multiple scope-bearing operators. Although one may accept, as indeed one should, that Montague

The two readings of (16a,b) are represented in (17a,b). (The quantifier *some* has not been factorized out (see 7.1), but this makes no difference here.)

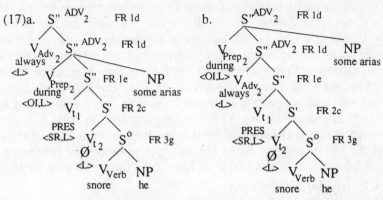

In (17b) the V_{Prep_2} predicate *during* induces first OBJECT INCORPORATION, giving the V-cluster $_V[_V[during]_{NP}[some\ arias]]$, and then LOWERING of the whole V-cluster. As specified by the rules, V_{Prep_2} predicates take LOWERING either as LEFT-ADOPTION by the argument-S or to its far right. In the case of (17a), however, only one option exists, since LEFT-ADOPTION by the argument-S is possible only when the operator in question is at the very top of the tree. On the highest cycle, *always* must be lowered, which can only take the form of LEFT-ADOPTION by the lower V. (17a) thus leads to only one structure, (16a). But in (17b), *during* is the highest predicate and can therefore be lowered in two different ways, either to the far right, as in (16a), or to the top left, as in (16b). (17b) is thus represented by both (16a) and (16b), but only (16a) represents, in addition, (17a).

(16c,d) are treated analogously, but with *the service* for *during some arias*. Here, however, there is no semantic difference, despite different possible hierarchical positions of the operators involved: it does not matter which of the two operators, *always* or *during the service*, takes larger scope. The reason for this semantic neutrality lies in the fact that, other than (16a,b), (16c,d) only contain one logical scope-bearing operator: *always*. The other operator, *during the service*, is not quantified but definite, so that there is no room for logical or semantic scope differences. For comprehension (and therefore also for translation) processes this means that the semantic representation corresponding to (16c) or (16d) may remain underdetermined.

Finally, a few words must be said about class 3 adverbials. They all take LOWERING to the far right of the argument-S, at least as the most preferred option, whether they are surface adverbs or prepositions.[10] The adverbs of

---

grammar is simply observationally wrong on this issue, scope intuitions with regard to surface sentences often remain shaky. The cases (16a) and (16b), however, seem clear enough. See 7.1 for further discussion.

[10] Note that, according to the formulation of LOWERING in 3.1.3, manner adverbs may stop before PPs of any level, as in *She looked carefully into the matter*, which is at least as good

this class are commonly known as manner adverbs. In Formal Semantics, these are usually taken to denote functions from verbs to verbs, but Semantic Syntax is more sparing with its formal means and has no category for such a function at SA-level. Semantic Syntax has no choice but to assign manner adverbs the category V taking an S^o as the subject argument term and introduced by Formation Rule (3c), thus making them close associates of the lexical predicate (usually a Verb) selected in Formation Rule (3g). Like the level 5 (class 3) PPs, they carry nuclear sentence accent. The difference between a manner adverb such as *cleverly* or *stupidly*, i.e. Adv_3, on the one hand and the same adverb but now of class Adv_2, is demonstrated in (18). The sentences (18a,b) mean that it was clever of John to do the job, while (18c,d,e) say that John did the job in a clever way. The two positions can be combined, as in (18d,e), which say that it was stupid of John to do the job in a clever way:

(18) a. Cleverly, John did the job
    b. John cleverly did the job
    c. John did the job cleverly
    d. Stupidly, John did the job cleverly
    e. John stupidly did the job cleverly

Cleverly in (18a,b) and *stupidly* in (18d,e) belong to the class Adv_2, introduced by Formation Rule (1d) and inducing LOWERING onto the top-S, as in (18a,d) or onto the lower V, as in (18b,e) (in which case it is handled postcyclically by ADVERB PLACEMENT-(b)). But *cleverly* in (18c,d,e) cannot be regarded as having the origin it has in (18a,b), due to its position at the far right. Here it can only be an adverb of class 3, i.e. a manner adverb.

The LOWERING of manner adverbials is to the far right. Sometimes there will be a class 3 PP over a class 3 adverb. In such a case the PP will automatically end up to the right of the adverb, as in *He wrote interestingly about Napoleon*, which is better than *He wrote about Napoleon interestingly*. This is explained if it is assumed that in this sentence the PP *about Napoleon* is a level 5 (class 3) adverbial, but that, though of the same level and class as *interestingly*, it is in a higher SA-position. Likewise for PPs with the dative preposition *to*: *He sold the car profitably to the man* seems better than *?He sold the car to the man profitably*, since the PP with *to* is more distant from S^o than the manner adverb *profitably*.

The system accounts for the semantic difference between (19a) and (19b):

(19) a. At six, the secretary had left
    b. The secretary had left at six

(19a) can only mean that at six the situation was such that the secretary had left. This sentence therefore entails that the secretary's leaving took place before six o'clock. But (19b) is ambiguous between this reading and the reading where the leaving took place at six o'clock. This observation was made in Hornstein (1977:529), but at that time it was still impossible to account

---

as *She looked into the matter carefully*. Here *into the matter* is a lexically induced prepositional object, and the manner adverb *carefully* may precede it or come after it.

syntactically for this obvious semantic difference. Now we say that in (19a) and in one reading of (19b) the PP *at six* is of class 2, introduced by Formation Rule (1d) and therefore above the highest tense, as in the corresponding SA-structure (20a). In this position it determines the moment in the past at which the V_{t_1}-tense PAST is to be located. Being a V_{Prep2} and at the top of the tree, it can end up either sentence-initially, as in (19a) or sentence-finally, as in (19b). In the other reading of (19b), however, the reading implying that the leaving took place at six o'clock, the PP *at six* contains a class 3 preposition, of level 5, introduced by Formation Rule (3c) and therefore below the tenses and just above S, thus taking the lexical verb *leave* in its immediate scope, as shown in (20b). From this position it can only go to the far right. After OI at the top cycle, (20a) looks as in (21a). Subsequent LOWERING then leads to either (21b=19a)) or (21c=19b). In (20b) there is only one choice, LOWERING to the far right of the argument-S, as shown in (22=19b). Note that the PP *at six* is now part of /S, and not, as in (21c), part of S".[11]

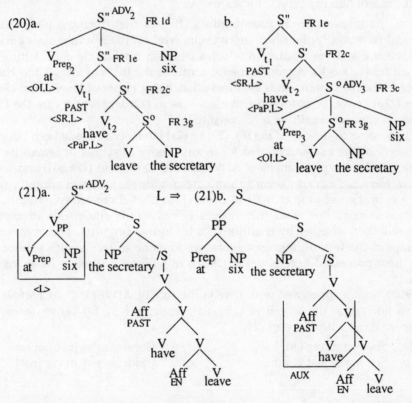

[11] This is reminiscent of the analysis of the ambiguous *He decided on the boat* given in Chomsky (1965:101).

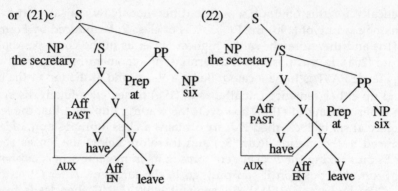

In similar fashion we account for the semantic difference between, for example:

(23)a.   For six weeks I lent him my bicycle
     b.   I lent him my bicycle for six weeks

Again, the (a)-sentence is unambiguous. It says that during a period of six weeks I (repeatedly) lent him my bicycle, while (21b) is ambiguous between this reading and the reading in which I lent him my bicycle once, letting him have it for six weeks. Again, in the (a)-sentence the PP is of level 3 and class 2, while in the (b)-sentence it is best treated as being either of level 3 and class 2, as in (22a) above, or of level 5 and class 3, as in (22b), in which case the PP *for six weeks* ends up, again, as a /S-constituent.[12]

Phenomena as described in (16), (19) or (23) have occasionally been observed but never before been accounted for in any theory of syntax or semantics. The same goes for the phenomena of ADVERB PLACEMENT in (15a,b,d) and (24a-e) below. Here, the adverbs seem to jump around the sentences in arbitrary ways. Yet, the bracketed ungrammatical cases show that there are constraints, and hence a system. But what this system is has so far eluded all attempts at unravelling it, whether by traditional or by formal linguists. The only serious attempt in the formal linguistic literature to come to terms with phenomena like those presented here is Baker (1991), to which this section owes inspiration.

What we are concerned with here is the rule of ADVERB PLACEMENT-(b). Let us take again the sentences (15a,b,d), repeated here for convenience, and compare these with those of (24):

(15)a.   She just never laughs   (*She laughs just never)
     b.   She never just laughs   (*She laughs never just)

---

[12] The verb *lend*, with a class 3 and level 5 PP *for* + [period of time], is interesting from the point of view of prelexical syntax. It can be analysed as 'let have' (with further lexical semantic specialization). The PP *for* + [period of time] goes with *have* and though it would normally be of level 3 and class 2 the lexical unification process ties it in more closely with *have*, turning it into a level 4 and class 3 adverbial modifying the whole composite new verb [let-have] → *lend*. (A level 3 and class 2 status for the *for*-PP would be impossible since *let* takes an S⁰-complement.)

   d. She usually doesn't laugh

(24)a. She will just never laugh   (*She just never will laugh)
   b. She will never just laugh   (*She never just will laugh)
   c. She just never will/does   (*She will/does just never)
   d. She never just will/does   (*She will/does never just)
   e. She doesn't usually laugh

All the adverbs concerned are class 2 adverbs, introduced by the Formation
Rules (1d) or (2b). *Just* and *never* only take LOWERING onto the lower V,
usually also allows for LOWERING onto the argument-S (see 3.1.2). (All
LOWERINGS onto V are, of course, by LEFT-ADOPTION.) In the cases at hand,
only LOWERING onto V is at issue. It will now become clear that the rule system presented in 3.1 accounts for the grammaticality and the ungrammaticality of the cases presented at least in principle (not entirely, as ellipsis has not
been taken into account). Moreover, the scope differences between (15a and b),
(24a and b), (24c and d), and between (15d) and (24e) are also accounted for.

   Let us, by way of example, illustrate how (24a) is generated. A possible SA-
structure is as in (25a) (though SAs with *just* and *never*, or only *never*, below
will will also do). (25a) is cycled down to the shallow structure (25b). Now
ADVERB PLACEMENT-(b) applies. It detaches the area of the V-cluster above
AUX and re-attaches it at the exit of AUX, as in (25c). Further treatment then
gives the surface structure (25d).

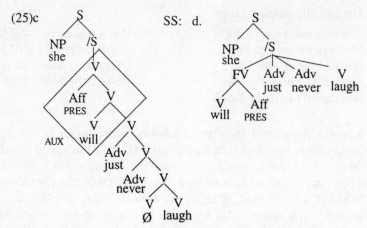

Clearly, if there had been an $_{Adv}$[not] or $_{Adv}$[EMPH] in (25a) between *never* and PRES, the sentence would have been *She just never won't laugh* or *She just never WILL laugh*, with ADVERB PLACEMENT-(a). Note that in (24e) *usually* comes under *not*, so that it is moved along with *not* to the exit of AUX by ADVERB PLACEMENT-(a).

In (24d) ADVERB PLACEMENT-(b) is blocked because AUX is V-cluster final, due to ellipsis of the main verb. In (15a,b) ADVERB PLACEMENT-(b) is blocked because AUX ends in $_V$[Ø]. In (15c) AUX ends in $_{Adv}$[not], which means that ADVERB PLACEMENT-(a) has applied.

3.6 Internal and external datives

Let us now consider one specific type of PP, the external datives, and their relation with internal datives. An example of the former is (26a), whereas (26b) is an instance of an internal dative:

(26)a. Tom sold the car to Harry
    b. Tom sold Harry the car

It used to be widely believed that both kinds of dative are freely inter-changeable, but since Green (1974) it has been known that this is not so. The following pairs differ semantically and hence in their conditions of use, some even to the point where one of the two is considered unacceptable:

(27)a. !Give a kiss to me
    b. Give me a kiss

(28)a. He offered his services to the king
    b. ≠He offered the king his services

(29)a. He paid a visit to his native country
    b. !He paid his native country a visit

The external dative seems to bestow more importance and status on the refer-ent of the prepositional object than the internal dative. (28a), for example, expresses a perfectly honourable state of affairs, but (28b) borders on the shady. But other conditions are at work as well. In this respect, the situation is comparable with the semantic differences between the active and the passive voice (see 3.7.1): the Agent Phrase places greater importance on the referent of the prepositional object than a regular subject term does, and other conditions are also at work.

Our immediate problem here, however, is more the syntactic analysis of the two kinds of dative than their semantic properties. The internal dative is part of the lexical argument frame assigned to certain verbs. For example, the verbs *give* and *sell* are listed in the lexicon of 3.1.2 as taking an optional internal dative, in accordance with the General SA-Format specified in 1.3.2 and 2.2. No provision is made in the lexicon, however, for external datives. These are taken to originate as expansions of S^{oDEX}, according to Formation Rule (3f). Through standard OBJECT INCORPORATION and subsequent LOWERING they end up at the far right of the matrix-S^o. The different origins of the internal and the external datives are thus made to correspond to their different meanings.

There is a formal parallel with the passive voice. Just as the selection of the passive Agent Phrase preposition *by* is allowed only if the lexical matrix-S contains a transitive main verb and then forces the matrix-S to leave out the normal lexical subject term, the selection of the external dative preposition *to* requires the selection of a dative-taking verb and subsequently prohibits the filling in of the dative (indirect object) term. In the passive case there is a feature [PASS] that signals the conditions mentioned. For the external dative there is a feature [DEX] ('dative extraction') that does the same.

The feature [DEX] is assigned to the S^o in the expansion of S^{oDEX} (FR 3f). It is then passed down to the lexical main verb in $S^o_{[DEX]}$, so that the lexical argument frame is filled without the indirect object term, which reappears as the object-NP of the dative preposition *to*.

The process is demonstrated in (30a), the SA underlying (26a). OBJECT INCORPORATION and LOWERING on the *to*-cycle give (30b). The cyclic TENSE ROUTINE then gives the shallow structure (30c). Application of the postcyclic rules finally yields the surface structure (30d):

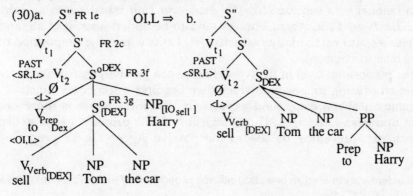

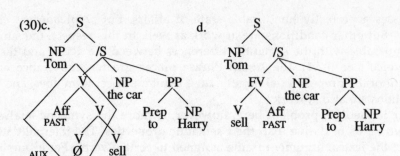

Some external datives have become lexicalized. Their prepositional objects no longer function as external datives but as prepositional objects to the main verb, which is composed of an original verb and a fixed direct object forming one V with it, as in $_V[_V[_V[pay]\ _N[attention]]\ _{Prep}[to]]$ followed by an object-NP. This process is well-known and found in cases like *take care of, keep tabs on* and other widely known instances. The single V status of the original V with the object noun appears from passives like *She was taken care of*, discussed in the following section.

3.7 Passives, Progressives and other *be*-sentences

3.7.1 Passives

Passivization is not a simple syntactic process. It is still poorly understood although a great deal is known about it. Modern theories of syntax have added surprisingly little to what was already known from traditional grammar. In the present context there is little we can do but point at some phenomena and some of the difficulties encountered in passivization theory.

Not all languages have passives. The passive voice develops gradually in a language, if at all. Young languages, such as the Creoles, tend to lack passive or, if they are in the process of developing one, it is lexically restricted, without morphological marking and without an Agent Phrase. Typically, in such languages, a sentence like *The house was built* translates as an intransitive: *The house built*. Agent Phrases tend to be added later, if at all, and are sometimes also categorially restricted (cf. Latin where the preposition object must refer to a person).

The preposition used in the Agent Phrase of a passive construction is always either an existing preposition which then acquires a secondary function, or a regrammaticalized compound expression. The former case is illustrated by most European languages. Thus, English *by* has a primary meaning, like the French *par*, preceding its use as the passive Agent Phrase preposition.[13]

---

[13] In older forms of English one also finds the preposition *of* in this function: *"This sacred bond instituted of God..."*.

German *von* is the equivalent of English *of*. Dutch *door* has the primary meaning 'through', etc. (In older Dutch *van* was used, the equivalent of German *von*.) The other case is illustrated by Turkish, where the postposition (Turkish is an SOV-language) of the Agent Phrase is *tarafından*, literally, i.e. primarily, 'from its/his/her side'. The Agent Phrase 'by Mehmet' translates as *Mehmet tarafından*. Yet, if one wants to say in Turkish 'from the side of Mehmet' the genitive suffix *-in* must be added to *Mehmet*: *Mehmedin tarafından*, 'of Mehmet from his side'. It thus appears that the Agent Phrase postposition *tarafından* has been regrammaticalized from a semantically transparent complex expression to a single postposition.

This shows that the category 'passive' is, though part of the universal linguistic charter known as 'universal grammar', not part of what a language has to have in order to be a natural human language.[14] Passive is a secondary category in the sense of Stassen (1985), along with the comparative, concessive clauses, conditionals (especially *unless*-conditionals), indicators of measure or degree, reflexives, possessive or *have*-constructions, expressions for the notions underlying words like *only* or *even*, etc. In an ideal pristine language (and Creoles often seem to come close to that) none of these categories exist as part of their grammar book. The corresponding notions are expressed in semantically transparent and sometimes ad hoc ways. In some languages, for example, a sentence like *A buffalo is stronger than a goat* translates as 'a buffalo is strong, a goat is not,' or as 'a buffalo is strong from a goat', or any of a number of further alternatives. Only some of these possible renderings, however, will make it as regrammaticalized categories (Stassen 1985).

English has made its own specific choice from the possibilities apparently afforded by Universal Grammar. Unlike German and Dutch, English lacks impersonal passives. Its passive formation is relatively straightforward: lexical selection is made without the subject-NP and the next term to its right, provided it is an NP, is assigned the feature [SU]. If the next term to the right is not an NP, no passive is possible. Unlike other European languages, the new subject may be an internal IO, a DO, or a surface prepositional object, as in (31d,e) (see fig. 2 above).[15] This explains the wellformedness of, for example, (31a-e) and the ungrammaticality of (31g). (31f) is grammatical on account of the fact that *pay attention to* has the status of a lexical verb, with the NP

[14] It is naive to think that UG looks like the grammar of a natural language stripped down to the barest minimum, as is proposed by Bickerton (1981), implying that Creole grammars come as close to UG as is possible for a human language. Apart from the lack of empirical support, the position is naive and highly implausible, as it would entail that all secondary phenomena that languages develop beyond the bare minimum are unconstrained by UG. The development of passives in the languages of the world provides strong evidence that secondary phenomena are as much constrained as the primary phenomena.

[15] It seems advantageous to represent verbs that take a prepositional object as complex verbs with the preposition incorporated into the verbal complex, as described in 3.5 above. The prepositional object then functions as a normal direct object. At some appropriately late stage, when all the cyclic work has been done, the direct object of such a complex $_V[_V[X]_{Prep}[Y]]$ will be placed under $_{Prep}[Y]$.

following *to* as the prepositional object, as discussed at the end of the preceding section 3.6:

(31)a. The man was punished
    b. Your car was sold to Mr. Harris
    c. Mr. Harris was sold your car
    d. My cousin can be relied on
    e. This sofa has been slept on
    f. He must not be paid any attention to
    g. *Mr. Harris was sold your car to

But this analysis fails to explain why passivization is blocked in many cases, like those in (32):

(32)a. He will make a good prof   *A good prof will be made (by him)
    b. It was raining manna   *Manna was being rained
    c. He lost his bearings   *His bearings were lost (by him)
    d He broke his leg   ≠His leg was broken (by him)
    e. He walked two miles   *Two miles were walked (by him)
    f. It weighs two pounds   *Two pounds are weighed (by it)
    g. He has two children   *Two children are had (by him)
    h. He met his wife   ≠His wife was met (by him)
    i. He has lived a good life   *A good life was lived (by him)
    j. I want an apple   ≠An apple is wanted (by me)
    k. This rings a bell   ≠A bell is rung (by this)
    l. This never happens to me   *I am never happened to (by this)
    m. She was married to Olaf   *Olaf was married to (by her)
    n. This amounts to murder   *Murder is amounted to by this

Often the diagnosis, but not the explanation, is clear. Thus, reflexive objects (32c,d), measure phrase objects (32e), measure copulas (32f), symmetrical predicates (32h,m), and verbs like *have* (32g), *want* (32j), *happen* (32l) apparently block passivization. But why? Whatever universal constraints may be at work here must be mitigated by language-particular factors, since, for example, the English verb *own* does passivize (*The boat is owned by John*), while its Dutch, German, French, etc. counterparts do not.

There is no known answer to these questions, and no attempt is made here to find one. This area of syntax and semantics is still relatively obscure. All we do here is demonstrate the syntactic machinery of English passives, specifying only the necessary conditions for passive to occur. In terms of the lexicon given, any verb with an NP direct or indirect object is allowed to occur in the passive.

Let us take first the simple sentence *The mouse was eaten by the cat*. Its SA is (33a), generated by application of the Formation Rules (1e), (2c) with the option S^oPASS, (3d) with the first option (i.e. the *by*-phrase), therefore (3e), and, finally, (3g). Rule (3d) assigns the subscript feature [PASS] to the S^o in its expansion, and rule (3e) the feature [SU$_{eat}$] to its object-NP. The subscript feature [PASS] is passed on to the lexical main verb *eat* in the expansion of rule (3g), ensuring a lexical frame selection without the subject term. The lexical direct object becomes grammatical subject: [DO]→[SU]. On the SᵒPASSPrep-cycle, *by* first takes OI and then LOWERING, as in (33b). Then, on the SᵒPASS-cycle, the rule PAST PARTICIPLE (PaP) applies, leading to (33c). After LOWERING we have (33d). TENSE ROUTINE gives (33e), with AUX. Note that Passive marks the first NP as [SU], to be raised by SR. Then Ø-*be*-DELETION gives (33f), with revised AUX. AH (twice) gives (33g), and, finally, MINCE yields the surface structure (33h).

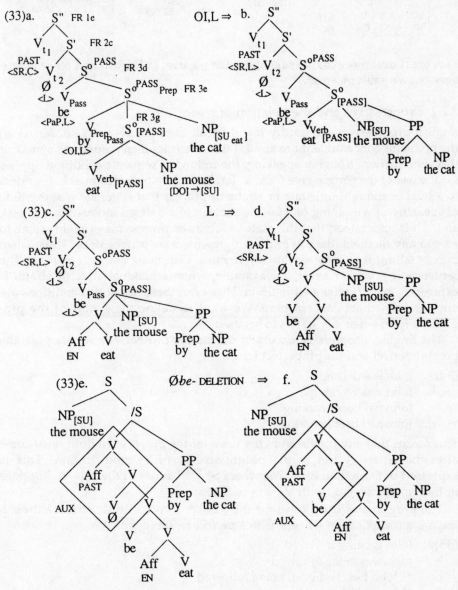

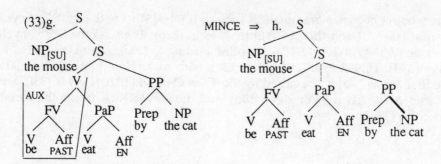

A great deal more can be said about the passive, in English and other languages, but we must move on.

3.7.2 Progressives and the deletion of *being*

English progressives are hardly less difficult than passives. Again, however, the problems concentrate more around the semantics than around the syntax of this construction. Roughly speaking, the following semantic condition applies for the use of the progressive form in English: if the proposition at hand refers to a (real or thought up) state of affairs or process that is going on at the time of speaking or was going on at some contextually defined moment in the past, and if it is understood that this state of affairs or process may (might) come to an end any moment, the use of the progressive form is obligatory. Thus, when rain is falling it is incorrect to say *It rains*. One must say *It is raining*. The sentence *It rains* is correct, for example, when a habitual state of affairs is expressed, as in *It rains a lot in Spain*. However, these semantic conditions are not our immediate concern here. We want to define the syntax of the progressive form when it is, or has to be, used.

The English progressive occurs in the simple present, the simple past, the present perfect and the pluperfect tenses:

(34)a.　John is working
 b.　John was working
 c.　John has been working
 d.　John had been working

This means that any provision in the rules for the progressive form must come after the tenses t_1 and t_2: the progressive is an S^o modification. This is expressed in Formation Rule (2c), where S^{oPROGR} is one of the subject-S options in the expansion of S', with V_{t_2} as predicate.

The progressive also allows for the passive to occur in its scope, although there is a complication when it is in a perfect tense:

(35)a.　John is being followed
 b.　　John was being followed
 c.　　*? John has/had been being followed
 d.　　*? John is likely to be being followed

The doubtful status of sentences like (35c,d) has puzzled many linguists: no other cases are known where a verb can occur in all four tenses when followed by a Present Participle of any verb but the verb *be*, in which case it occurs only in the simple present or past tense. One way out would be to remodel the Formation Rules in such a way that the unwanted combination is ruled out. This is feasible but inelegant as it would mess up an otherwise well-constrained set of rules. Another solution is to put in a late deletion rule, deleting $_{PrP}$[being] under certain conditions. Such a rule would be semantically correct: a sentence like *I have been for some time* functions equally well as an answer to *You're being foolish* as it does to *You're foolish*. The latter solution is clearly preferable. It is realized by a morphophonological rule like the following, to be placed after the Postcycle and before any other morphophonological rule:

Being-DELETION:
> Inside /S $_{PrP}$[being] is deleted in all cases except when /S-initial or preceded by FV.

This rule deletes $_{PrP}$[being] in (35c,d), turning them into fully grammatical sentences which retain their progressive reading.

Formation Rule (3b) rewrites S^oPROGR as V_{Progr} plus a class 3 adverbial, passive, external dative or active S^o. The class of V_{Progr}-predicates is limited to the verb *be*, which takes the cyclic rules PRESENT PARTICIPLE and LOWERING onto the lower V. An example is the SA (36a), which corresponds to *John is being followed*. Cyclic treatment leads to the shallow structure (36b), with AUX in place. The rule Ø-*be*-DELETION gives (36c), with revised AUX. AH (three times) and MINCE (twice) lead to the surface structure (36d).

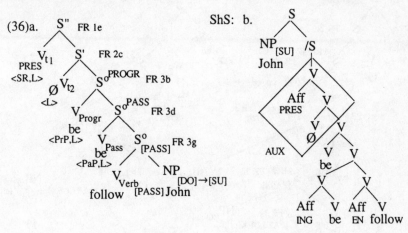

(36)c. ... SS: d. ...

Note that sentences like *He is to be leaving*, i.e. with progressive under the MAUX-verb *be to*, are ruled out by the Formation Rules, as rule (3a) does not lead to S⁰PROGR. Note, moreover, that PrP[being] is not deleted, as it is immediately preceded by FV.

Let us now consider a sentence that combines progressive, passive and external dative:

(37)a.   The car is being sold to Harry by Tom

Its SA is (37b). Note that the argument frame of the verb *sell* has been rather mutilated, due to the features [PASS] and [DEX], which have taken away the subject and the indirect object terms, respectively. The cyclic treatment is as follows. OI and L on the S⁰DEX[PASS]-cycle gives (37c). OI and L on the S⁰PASSPrep-cycle gives (37d). The Shallow Structure with AUX is (37e). The usual post-cyclic treatment gives the Surface Structure (37f).

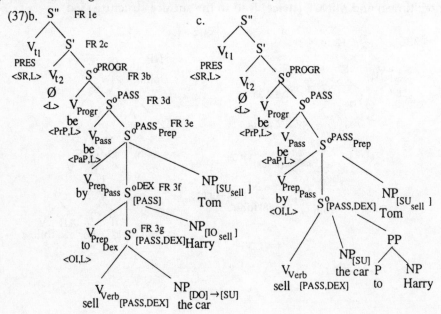

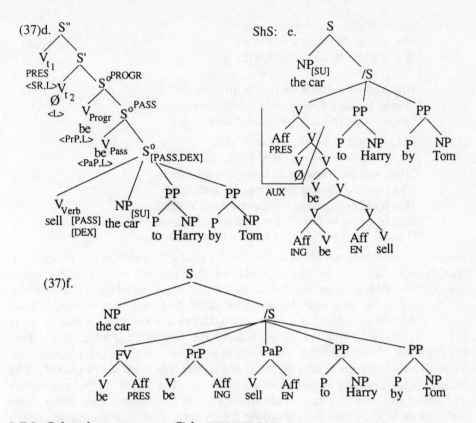

3.7.3 Other *be*-sentences: Ø-*be* DELETION

In English, *be*-sentences are subject to the special postcyclic rule of Ø-*be*-DELETION, already invoked a few times in the preceding sections. This rule deletes the Ø-tense when it is directly followed by the verb *be*. When Ø is part of AUX the AUX-area has to be redelimited and will incorporate v[be]. This explains why v[be] is fronted in questions and does not require *Do*-SUPPORT under negation. In certain dialects and sociolects the same applies to the verb of possession *have*. There one finds sentences like *Have you a book?* or *I haven't a book*, but modern Standard English no longer treats possessive *have* in this way, though, of course, the perfect tense auxiliary verb *have* moves along with AUX as predicted by the rules. Interestingly, certain English dialects, especially in Scotland, lack the postcyclic rule of Ø-*be*-DELETION altogether. There the verb *be* is treated as a main verb, so that one gets sentences like *I do not be your friend*, or *I didna be drunk*, or *Did you be drunk?*[16]

3.7.3.1 The MAUX-verbs *be to* and *be going to*

Let us now consider two types of sentences, exemplified in (38) and (39):

---

[16] In Standard English Ø-*be*-DELETION does not operate with imperatives: *Don't be silly* versus **Be not silly*.

(38)a. This is to be treated with care
  b. This was to be treated with care
  c. *This will be to be treated with care
  d. *This has been to be treated with care
  e. *This had been to be treated with care
  f. *This is to have been treated with care
  g. *I expect this to be to be treated with care

(39)a. This is going to be treated with care
  b. This was going to be treated with care
  c. ?*This will be going to be treated with care
  d. *This has been going to be treated with care
  e. *This had been going to be treated with care
  f. *This is going to have been treated with care
  g. ?*I expect this to be going to be treated with care

These two constructions show a defective paradigm which is reminiscent of, though not identical to, the modals. In this respect they differ from a construction like *be about to*, which has a complete paradigm. The two are clearly of a kind, although the restrictions on *be-to* are more clearcut than those on *be going to*. Neither construction allows for the perfect tenses, as is shown by the (d) and (e) cases, which are clearly ungrammatical. This suggests that these auxiliary verbs are alternatives to the modal auxiliaries, to be placed between t_1 and t_2, the more so because they do not want to be placed under a modal, as shown in the (c) cases. (The fact that (39c) seems less bad than (38c) will be commented upon shortly.) However, they differ from the modals in that they do not allow for perfective complement infinitivals, as shown in the (f) cases. For the modals this is, of course, perfectly normal: *This will have been treated with care.*[17]

The conclusion can only be that these, and perhaps a few more, auxiliary verbs are to be placed, in the Formation Rules, directly under S" and are to go straight for S°, bypassing S' and the modals. This is expressed in the rules by introducing the option S°MAUX in rule (1e), which rewrites S", and providing rule (3a) which rewrites S°MAUX as V_{Maux} plus any type of S°. The category V_{Maux} is defined as containing the verb $_V$[be] and the complex verb $[_V[be]_{Prt}[going]]$, where the second element is labelled 'Particle' as it is assumed that the original status of Present Participle has been lost. They have been assigned the rule SUBJECT RAISING not only because this accounts automatically for the introduction of the particle *to* but also because the alternative rule, LOWERING, fails to work, as the reader will be able to check.

An example is given in (40), which shows the generation of (38a). (40f) is the surface structure, which can be fed into the morphological component.

---

[17] There is also a more strongly deontic *be to* which behaves like the modals: *You are not to have done that.*

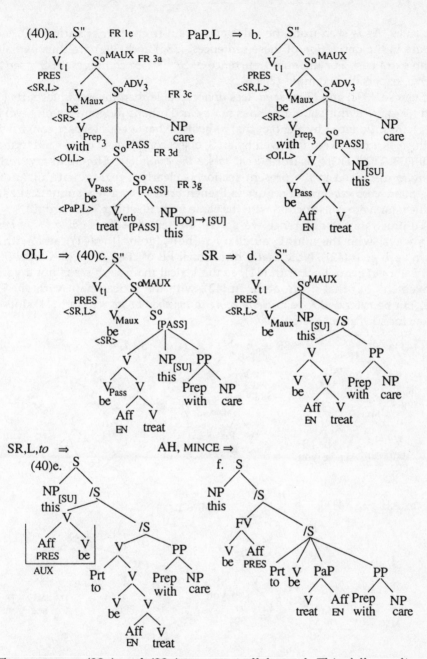

The sentences (38g) and (39g) are not well-formed. This follows directly from the fact that they must involve an S' complement clause under *expect* (see the argument frame for *expect* in 3.1.2): in no other way could the offending infinitivals *to be to be treated with care* and *to be going to be treated with care* have come about. But an S'-origin is precisely what is blocked by the rules. As is seen from the rules and again from the derivation (40), no S′ occurs in the derivation of these sentences. (38g) and (39g) are thus explained at no extra cost. For the non-occurrence of S⁰MᴬUX in complement-S⁰s see 2.12 above, especially example (26a,b).

Even so, (39c) and (39g) seem less unacceptable than their counterparts (38c) and (38g). Why this should be so is not clear. Perhaps judgements on (39c) and (39g) are influenced by the fact that *be going to* has a counterpart construction with *go* as a main verb followed by an S'_0 object complement clause and inducing SUBJECT DELETION, as in *He went to see the exhibition.* The auxiliary verb *be going to* discussed in the present section is clearly a regrammaticalization of this main verb construction (just as French *venir de* is a regrammaticalization of the main verb construction with the same verb, meaning 'come from').

To illustrate the difference we derive the sentence *He is going to see you* in two ways, with the middle auxiliary [ᵥ[be]ₚᵣₜ[going]] (=(41)) and with the main verb *go* (=(42)). Note that a directional PP of class Prep₃ (i.e. level 5; see fig. 2 above) cannot occur in (41), as the lexical main verb *see* is not a verb of movement, but that it can occur in (42), with the lexical main verb *go*. Thus (42) can be extended to, e.g. *He is going to the shop to see you*, but (41) does not allow for such an extension.

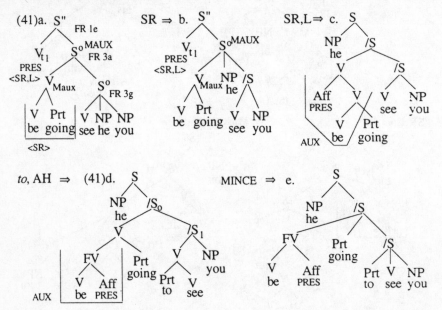

(42)a. S_0'' FR 1e   ShS + *to* : b. S_0 Ø- *be* -DELETION ⇒
                                                Do -SUPPORT

(The following are syntactic tree diagrams (42)a, b, (42)c, d containing node labels:)

(42)a.: S_0'' FR 1e; V_{t1} PRES <SR.L>; S_0' FR 2c; Ø V_{t2} <L>; S_0^o PROGR FR 3b; V Progr *be* <PrP.L>; S_0^o FR 3g; V_{Verb} *go* <SD>; NP$_x$ *he*; S_1' FR 2c; V_t Ø^2 <L>; S_1^o FR 3g; V NP NP *see* x *you*

(42)b.: S_0; NP *he*; /S$_0$; V Aff PRES; V V Ø; V V *be* AUX; Aff V ING *go*; /S$_1$; V *to* Prt V; V Ø V *see*; NP *you*

(42)c. S_0'' AH, MINCE ⇒ d. S_0''

(42)c.: S_0''; NP *he*; /S$_0$; V; Aff PRES V; V V *be* AUX; Aff V ING *go*; /S$_1$; V *you* NP; Prt V *to see*

(42)d.: S_0''; NP *he*; /S$_0$; FV; V Aff *be* PRES; PrP; V Aff *go* ING; /S$_1$; Prt V NP *to see you*

Due to the rule MINCE the surface structures (41e) and (42d) are similar, in spite of the rather different·derivations. The only difference is that *going* is labelled 'Particle' in (41e) but 'Present Participle' in (42d). In principle, this analysis provides the basis for the colloquial contracted form *gonna* for *going to* in (41e). Linear successions of small unaccented words, such as $_{Prt}$[going] directly followed by $_{Prt}$[to] in (41e), tend to contract and amalgamate, even if they belong to different constituents. The classical example is, of course, the contraction and amalgamation of a pronominal subject and the finite forms of *be, have, will*, etc. in English sentences. The Present Participle in (42d) cannot undergo phonological contraction as it is the accentual focus of the matrix clause.

3.7.3.2 COPULA INSERTION

The Formation Rules generate SA-structures not only with verbs as V_{LEX} in S^o but also with V_{Adj} predicates, as in (44a), and with V_{NP} predicates, as in (45a) below. As regards the latter, Formation Rule (3g) contains an alternative expansion of S^o: V_{NP} + NP. This expansion covers all sentences whose predicate is formed by an NP, such as:

(43)a.   He is the one

   b.   That's it
   c.   The man in the white hat is the captain
   d.   The men in the white hats are the captains
   e.   That man is a spy
   f.   Those men are spies
   g.   He is all the things I am not
   h.   The temperature is 20 degrees

As we do not go into the internal structure of NPs the NP-predicates are left unanalysed. Yet we observe that NP-predicates are subject to number agreement: the singular subject in (43c) and (43e) corresponds with the singular form in the predicate nominal, and likewise for the plural in (43d) and (43f). With a definite predicate nominal, as in (43a-d), the sentence is often an identity statement. With an indefinite one, as in (43e,f), the sentence expresses class attribution (cf. the computer language 'isa'). (43g) contains universal quantification over properties and is of a higher order (see note 2 above). (43h) assigns a value to a parameter. The Formation Rules give (44a) and (45a), the latter with V_{NP} unanalysed (V_{NP} is merely a category of convenience; see 3.2).

(44)a.

$$
\begin{array}{l}
S'' \quad \text{FR 1e} \\
\quad V_{t1} \quad S' \quad \text{FR 2c} \\
\text{PAST} \\
\text{<SR,L>} \quad V_{t2} \quad S \quad \text{o FR 3g} \\
\quad\quad \emptyset \\
\quad\quad \text{<1>} \quad V_{Adj} \quad NP \\
\quad\quad\quad \text{small} \quad \text{the child}
\end{array}
$$

(45)a.

$$
\begin{array}{l}
S'' \quad \text{FR 1e} \\
\quad V_{t1} \quad S' \quad \text{FR 2c} \\
\text{PAST} \\
\text{<SR,L>} \quad V_{t2} \quad S^o \quad \text{FR 3g} \\
\quad\quad \text{have} \\
\quad\quad \text{<PaP,L>} \quad V_{NP} \quad NP \\
\quad\quad\quad\quad\quad \text{the man} \\
\quad\quad\quad \text{a good pilot}
\end{array}
$$

In such cases, a copula verb *be* must be inserted. The proper way to do this appears to be by means of a category-induced cyclic rule which, being category-induced (2.7.3), applies after the lexically induced rules. The rule is (see 2.7.3.2 and 3.1.3):

COPULA INSERTION (CI):
S^o directly above V_{Adj}, Adj or V_{NP} left-adopts V_{Cop}[be].

The lexicon contains the copula verb *be*, Verb in surface structure. In view of SURFACE CATEGORY ASSIGNMENT, by which the adjectival and nominal predicate are to be relabelled Adjective and NP, respectively, it seemed best to let the copula verb *be* induce PREDICATE RAISING, rather than LOWERING. The LOWERING would affect the element lowered, i.e. $_V$[be], whereas the element to be affected is the adjectival or nominal predicate in question. If these are raised, as is the case with PR, SCA affects the right elements.

It is true that this case of PR stands out conspicuously in the grammar of English, which otherwise prefers SR to PR (only *let go* induces PR in the English complementation system (see 2.7.1.1), which standardly works with SR). Yet highly standardized and widespread routine procedures, such as COPULA INSERTION or TENSE ROUTINE, do sometimes involve rules that are otherwise avoided in the language. TENSE ROUTINE involves SR, even in otherwise exclusively PR-languages like Dutch. Auxiliary and complementation systems do not seem to have to obey the same language-specific constraints. Alternative treatments are anyway possible. Thus, CI could be formulated as consisting of LEFT ADOPTION of $_V$[be] not by the parent S but by the V_{Adj} or V_{NP} in question. But this possibility has not been further explored here. Nor have other copula verbs than *be* been taken into account. Copula verbs clearly deserve extensive specialized study, which cannot be carried out here.[18]

The application of CI to (44a) and (45a) results in (44b) and (45b), respectively. Now the tenses have a proper verb to attach themselves to.

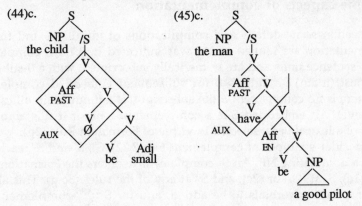

The reader will have no difficulty, by now, deriving the shallow structures (with AUX). The postcyclic rules Ø-*be*-DELETION and AH (for (44b)), and AH and MINCE (for (45b)) give the surface structures (44d) and (45d), respectively.

---

[18] A related hard question is the status of locative *be* in e.g. *The cat is in the house*. It could be treated as a copula verb, introduced by CI, as with adjectival and nominal predicates, or as a separate intransitive Main Verb *be* as a lexical choice in the subject-S^o under S^{o}ADV3 (but also independently, as in *I think, therefore I am*). Which is the better treatment is a question that is left open for the time being. Considerations of crosslinguistic simplicity will eventually help to find the optimal choice (cf. 7.6 on Turkish S^o prepositional predicates).

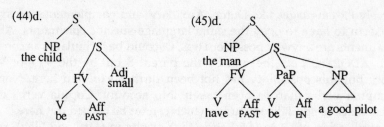

Although the predicate NP of (43g) contains quantification it does not follow that the forms *a spy* and *spies* in (43e) and (43f), respectively, also reflect a form of quantification. Montague (1970) analysed *John is an American* as 'there is at least one American x such that John is identical with x'. Linguists have been quick to reject this. Yet, if Montague's analysis is accepted some generalizations are captured. For if the predicate NPs in (43e,f) are analysed as first order quantified NPs the predicate in these cases is the identity predicate, just as in (43c,d). The difference between the identity predicate and the classifying 'isa' predicate thus disappears: 'isa' is then replaced by the identity predicate, generalized over all admissible values for the bound variable. It would, moreover, explain why predicate nominals as in (43e,f) have the grammatical form of quantified phrases, which was Montague's motivation in the first place.[19]

3.8 Some aspects of complementation

In this section some details and complications of infinitival and full clause complementation are looked at. As was indicated in 3.1.6.1, complement-Ss count as sentence units and are numerically subscripted, with a 0-subscript for the highest (main) S, and $n > 0$ for subsequent embedded complement-Ss. When there is no complement-S the subscript 0 is left out (as in all cases dealt with above). An embedded S is a complement-S only if it fills an argument position of a lexical verb, selected in virtue of Formation Rule (3g).

We consider six types of complement (see 2.12): S", S' and S°, each with or without a dominating NP. An S"-complement re-enters the Formation Rules at (1d) or (1e), S' at (2b) or (2c), and S° at any of the rules (3c-g). This allows for the appropriate adverbials to be added, and for S°PASS-complements (*I saw him be punished*), but it excludes S°MAUX and S°PROGR-complements (**I saw him be working*). A complement-S[PASS] (whether S" or S' or S°), as with *easy, hard, tough* (see 3.1.2), is not allowed to enter any Formation Rule that assigns the subscript feature [PASS] to an argument-S, thus excluding FR (3d) and (3e) (see 3.8.3).

---

[19] But note that in many languages the indefinite article is dropped for professions or official functions. These languages distinguish between "John is a spy" (quality) and "John is spy" (profession).

3.8.1 NP-over-S" and bare S"

In this section we look at a particular problem in the grammar of English sentential complementation that has so far remained unsolved in any of the existing theories of grammar, but turns out to have a natural solution in terms of Semantic Syntax. Consider the following observations:

(46)a. Tom is likely to be ill   (47)a. Tom seems to be ill
   b. It is likely that Tom is ill   b. It seems that Tom is ill
   c. That Tom is ill is likely   c. *That Tom is ill seems

(48)a. Tom tends to be ill   (49)a. *Tom follows to be ill
   b. *It tends that Tom is ill   b. It follows that Tom is ill
   c. *That Tom is ill tends   c. That Tom is ill follows

The question is why (46a-c) are grammatical while the c-sentences in (47) and (48), and (48b) and (49a), are ungrammatical. The solution is straightforward: it depends on a proper assignment of lexical argument frames to the lexical predicates concerned. The predicates are:

SA-cat	Fillers	Argument frame	Surface cat	Cyclic rules
V_{Adj}	(un)likely	$+ NP/S'/_{NP}[S'']$	Adj	SR
V_{Verb}	seem, appear, ...	$+ S'/S''$	Verb	SR
V_{Verb}	tend, ...	$+ S'$	Verb	SR
V_{Verb}	$follow_2$, make sense, ...	$+ NP/_{NP}[S'']$	Verb	— —

The infinitival in (46a) shows that this sentence is derived from an SA with S' for subject with *likely*. SR is obligatory. (50a) is thus the SA of (46a). Cyclic CI on S_1^o gives (50b). PREDICATE RAISING on the higher S_1^o-cycle, LOWERING on the S_1'-cycle, and SR on the S_0^o-cycle give (50c). Then CI applies again on the S_0^o-cycle, introducing a second copula verb *be*. PREDICATE RAISING on the new S_0^o-cycle and TENSE ROUTINE give the ShS (50d), with AUX and $_{Prt}[to]$. Further postcyclic treatment yields the surface structure (50e).

(50)a. [tree diagram with root S_0'' (FR 1e), branching to V_{t1} PRES <SR,L> and S_0' (FR 2c); S_0' branches to V_{t2} Ø <I> and S_0^o (FR 3g); S_0^o branches to V_{Adj} likely <SR> and S_1' (FR 2c); S_1' branches to V_{t2} Ø <I> and S_1^o (FR 3g); S_1^o branches to V_{Adj} ill and NP Tom]

CI ⇒ b. [tree diagram with root S_0'', branching to V_{t1} PRES <SR,L> and S_0'; S_0' branches to V_{t2} Ø <I> and S_0^o; S_0^o branches to V_{Adj} likely <SR> and S_1'; S_1' branches to V_{t2} Ø <I> and S_1^o; S_1^o branches to V_{Cop} be <PR> and S_1^o; which branches to V_{Adj} ill and NP Tom]

(50)c. S_0''

V PRES t_1 S_0' <SR,L>

$\emptyset$ $V t_2$ <L> S_0^o

V be ^{Cop} S_0^o <PR>

V_{Adj} likely   NP Tom $/S_1$ | V

V $\emptyset$ V

V be   Adj ill

d. S_0

NP Tom $/S_0$

V $/S_1$

Aff PRES V

V $\emptyset$ V

AUX V be   Adj likely

e. S_0

NP Tom $/S_0$

FV   Adj likely $/S_1$

V be   Aff PRES V

Prt to V

V $\emptyset$ V

V be   Adj ill

Prt to V be   Adj ill

The derivations of (47a) and (48a) are analogous, with the verbs *seem* and *tend*, respectively, both with S' (*tend* leaves no choice). (49a) is ruled out because the verb *follow* does not have the S'-option in subject position.

Now to the (b)-sentences. We start with the *likely*-case (46b). The presence of the *that*-clause indicates that an S"-option has been chosen for the subject position of *likely*. The argument frame of *likely* shows that this is possible only with NP-over-S". The rule feature of *likely*, SUBJECT RAISING, remains inactive, as SR can only apply to an argument-S' or S^o (see 3.1.4 above). Consequently, the SA-structure of (46b) is as in (51a). COPULA INSERTION on the S_1^o-cycle gives (51b). S_1'' is simple and leads to *Tom is ill*. At the S_0^o-cycle, the rule IT (cyclic rule (5), also known as EXTRAPOSITION), applies since the subject term of *likely* is $_{NP}[S'']$. SR, lexically induced by *likely*, does not apply: SR applies only with argument-S' or S^o. Therefore, the instruction <SR> remains vacuous. But COPULA INSERTION must apply again, giving rise to (51c). PREDICATE RAISING on the new S_0^o-cycle and the normal TENSE ROUTINE, followed by the postcyclic rules, give the surface structure (51d), with the default complementizer *that* (LEFT-ADOPTION by S_1'' in virtue of corollary (4)).

(51)a. ... FR 1e   CI ⇒   b. ...

(51)c. ...   d. ...

For the (b)-sentences in (47)-(49), again, the possibility of an analogous treatment depends on the options afforded by the lexical argument frames of the predicates concerned. The verb *seem* allows for an S" subject clause, making the application of IT obligatory. The verb *tend*, however, only allows for an S' subject clause, which immediately rules out anything like a fully tensed *that*-clause. *Follow*, finally, again does allow for a fully tensed subject clause, which, as with *likely*, must be dominated by an NP-node. A proper selection of the various lexical argument frames, combined with a proper rule system, thus explains the grammaticality phenomena of the (b)-sentences.

The (c)-sentences, finally, are likewise explained at no further cost. Here, the grammaticality or ungrammaticality depends on whether the fully tensed subject clause S", if allowed by the lexical argument frame, is or is not dominated by an NP-node. If it is, the NP-constituent over the *that*-clause can be fronted, provided it is marked [+Foc], by the postcyclic rule FRONTING. (It will be remembered that we do not have a formal structural account of the origin of the feature [+Foc]. It is assumed that external factors, to do with discourse and situation, are responsible for the feature.) FRONTING leads to the right-adoption of the constituent marked [+Foc] by the sentence-initial constituent *Foc*, as described in section 3.2.1 above. Moreover, FRONTING of an $_{NP}$[S"] leads to the deletion of the dummy subject $_{NP}$[it] introduced by the cyclic rule IT. This leads to sentences of the form (46c) or (49c), where $_{NP}$[S"] figures in the argument frame of the main predicate.

If, however, the subject clause is not dominated by an NP-node, as with *seem* or *tend*, IT applies as well, but no focus-driven FRONTING is possible, as the FRONTING rule excludes bare Ss. Hence the ungrammaticality of (47c) and (48c), but the grammaticality of (46c) and (49c). Let us demonstrate the process for (46c). FRONTING of $_{NP}$[S"], followed by AH, gives (52), which is the surface structure of (46c).

(52)

The ungrammaticality of (47c) and (48c), as against the grammaticality of (46c) and (49c), is thus explained by the difference in lexical argument frame options between *seem* and *tend* on the one hand and *follow* and *likely* on the other: the former take no NP over the subject S", whereas the latter do. This explanation would be a little thin if cases like (46)-(49) were the only evidence for such lexical frame assignings. There is, however, more, as was pointed out earlier in 2.12. Typically, in English, NP-over-S" pronominalizes as *it*, while bare S" pronominalizes as *so*. Indeed, we find the following pattern:

(53)a. It is likely d. So it seems
   b. *So (it) is likely e. *So it tends
   c. *It seems f. It follows

Note that (53e) is ungrammatical because *tend* does not have an S"-option.[20]

Further evidence comes from other verbs, such as *believe* which takes both NP-over-S" and bare S" (see 3.1.2). And both forms of pronominalization are possible, though with a subtle semantic difference (Lindholm 1969):

(54)a. Do you believe that John is at home? — Yes I believe so (!it).
   b. Do you believe that God exists? — Yes I believe it (!so).

Apparently, *believe* with NP-over S" is used for articles of faith, whereas *believe* with bare S" is appropriate for casual beliefs. *Expect* allows for SD; otherwise it behaves like *believe*, using both *it* and *so* as pronominalizations.

(55)a. I expect to be in Rome next week
   b. *I believed to be in Rome

Think, on the other hand, is classified as taking only bare S" as a possible object term. And indeed, *I think so* is good normal English but *I think it* is not. Nowadays less current forms of English have sentences like:

(56)a. I never thought that true
   b. I thought you in Rome

These require an S'-complement clause for *think*, with *be*-DELETION, but this option has not been incorporated into the lexicon of 3.1.2.

As is seen from the lexical argument frames of the predicates concerned, *(un)likely*, *follow*, *make sense*, etc. also take simple NP as an option for the subject term, whereas *seem*, *appear*, *tend*, etc. do not. This corresponds with the fact that one can say *That is likely* or *That follows* or *That makes sense*, but not *That seems* or *That appears* (unless, of course, the intransitive main verb *appear* is used) or *That tends*.

3.8.2 Helping Jim

Note the difference, never observed in the literature, between the following two sentences:

(57)a. I helped Jim go bankrupt
   b. I helped Jim to go bankrupt

The former is ambiguous between the reading 'I collaborated with others to bring about Jim's bankruptcy' and the reading 'I collaborated with Jim to bring about his bankruptcy'. (57b) can only have the latter meaning. This can be accounted for by specifying the following two alternative argument frames for

---

[20] The adjectival predicate *rumoured* functions in a way almost identical to *likely*: replacement in (46a-c) of *likely* by *rumoured* yields identical grammaticality judgements. There is, however, a small difference. Whereas (53b) is ungrammatical, the sentence *So it is rumoured* is not (observation made by Bart Diels). This is accounted for by assigning to *rumoured* an argument frame identical to that of *likely*, except that the NP over S" is obligatory for *likely* but optional for *rumoured*, as shown in the lexicon 3.1.2.

help, the first implying collaboration with others in bringing about what is said in S^o, the second implying assistance to the NP_x-object in doing what is said in S^o. The first obligatorily drops *to* over the embedded /S_1, the second optionally drops *to*:

V_{Verb} help$_1$	+ NP + S^o	Verb	SR_{obj},[-to]
V_{Verb} help$_2$	+ NP + $NP_{x[DO]}$ + (S^o)	Verb	SD,([-to])

This enables the setting up of two different SA-structures, (58) and (59).

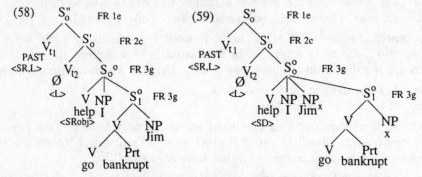

(58) reflects *help$_1$* and (59) *help$_2$*. It is now easily seen that (59) leads to both (57a), without the particle *to*, and (57b), with the particle *to*. But (58) can only lead to (57a), as *help$_1$* obligatorily drops *to*.

Interestingly, the same semantic difference is found in the Dutch pair (Seuren 1986):

(60)a. Ik heb Jim helpen failliet gaan
     I have Jim help bankrupt go

   b. Ik heb Jim geholpen failliet te gaan
     I have Jim helped bankrupt to go

(60a) is ambiguous in precisely the way (57a) is, and (60b) only has the reading implying that the speaker assisted Jim in bringing about Jim's own bankruptcy. Dutch does have SD but no SR at all in its complementation system. Instead of SR Dutch systematically has PREDICATE RAISING (PR; see 2.7.4.1). Dutch also has a default particle *te* ('to'), which is, however, not sensitive to embedded /S-constituents but to embedded infinitivals. As in English, *te* can be dropped by an explicit overriding of the default. Moreover, Dutch V-clusters resulting from PREDICATE RAISING prohibit the formation of Past Participles: the PaP-rule remains inoperative when the verb to be affected is part of a V-cluster.

The corresponding two alternative argument frames for *helpen* ('help') are:

V_{Verb} helpen$_1$	+ NP + S^o	Verb	[-te], PR
V_{Verb} helpen$_2$	+ NP + $NP_{x[DO]}$ + (S^o)	Verb	SD/SD,[-te],PR

In the first reading, which implies collaboration with others, PR (without *te*) is obligatory, whereas in the second reading, which implies assistance-to-

NP_x, SD (with *te*) is obligatory and PR (without *te*) is optional. The two corresponding SAs are as in (61) and (62).

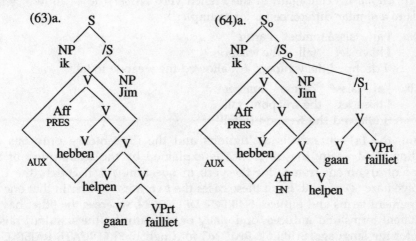

With PR, both (61) and (62) result in the shallow structure (63a), without Past Participle. Without PR, (62) results in (64a), with Past Participle (with AUX in place).

Note that, due to PR, there is no depth of sentence unit embedding left in (63a). In (64a), however, only SUBJECT DELETION has applied on *helpen*, so that there is an embedded $/S_1$.

Dutch has a postcyclic rule V-FINAL, which, in main clauses, moves the non-AUX part of the V-cluster to the far right under the same /S (not across embedded S or /S). This, together with the treatment of *te* and AFFIX HANDLING, leads to the corresponding near-surface structures (63b) and (64b).

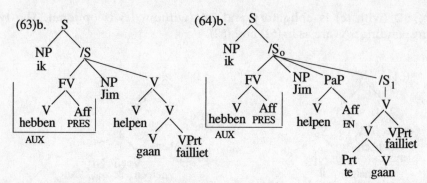

A late rule of END CLUSTER ARRANGEMENT places *failliet* before *(te) gaan*. MINCE does not apply. This shows how (61) results in both (63b) (=(60a)) and (64b) (=(60b)), whereas (62) results only in (63b) (=(60a)), and, therefore, how (60a) is ambiguous in a way (60b) is not. More about Dutch complementation, in particular about the two verbs *helpen*, is said in 5.4.2.

The grammars of at least the European languages turn out to be remarkably similar. French complementation provides a further example of this analogy: the kind of alternation between the two argument frames for English *help* and Dutch *helpen* is seen again in the French verb *laisser* ('let', 'allow'), which leads to a similar difference in, for example:[21]

(65)a. J'ai laissé tomber l'arme
      I have let fall the weapon
      'I dropped the weapon' / 'I allowed the weapon to fall'

   b. J'ai laissé l'arme tomber
      I have let the weapon fall
      'I allowed the weapon to fall'

Again, the (a)-sentence is ambiguous and the (b)-sentence only has one reading. And again, the difference is explained by the assumption of two different argument frames for the verb in question. As in Dutch, the rules involved are SD and PR. In all these cases the two frames differ in that one has *n* argument terms and induces SUBJECT DELETION, whereas the other has *n*-1 argument terms and induces (optionally or obligatorily) the standard raising rule for the language, SUBJECT RAISING for English, PREDICATE RAISING for Dutch and French. We may speak of the RAISING and the CONTROL frames, respectively (Ruwet 1991:56-81).[22]

---

[21] The example is due to Nicolas Ruwet. See also the following chapter, section 4.4.3.

[22] A further instance of RAISING versus CONTROL is found in (i) and (ii) (cf. ch. 2, note 9):
    (i)   I saw Jim tame the horse
    (ii)   I saw Jim taming the horse
The former is best derived from a RAISING analysis: $_V$[see] + NP + S⁰, with SR (and [-to]). The semantics of this construction implies that the speaker saw the process of Jim's taming the horse completed: if (i) is true then it follows that the horse was tamed. (ii), on the other hand, carries no such implication. All it says is that the speaker saw Jim in the process of taming the horse. This is probably best derived from a lexical CONTROL frame $_V$[see] + NP +

For the two verbs *laisser* the argument frames are as follows (see also section 4.2.2):

V_{Verb} laisser$_1$ $+ NP + S^o$ Verb   PR
V_{Verb} laisser$_2$ $+ NP + NP_{x[DO]} + (S^o)$ Verb   SD,(PR)

One notes the similarity with Dutch *helpen* and English *help*. The first argument frame is realized in (66), the second in (67). With PR, both (66) and (67) result in the shallow structure (68). Without PR, (67) results in (69) (with AUX in place).

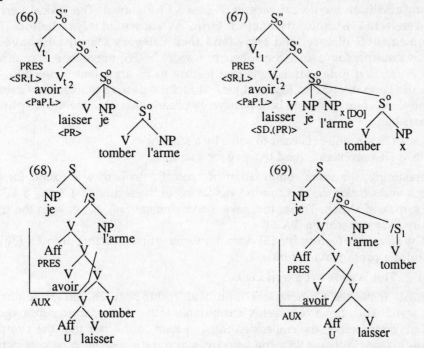

It is easy to see now that (68) corresponds with (65a) and (69) with (65b). (68) thus goes back to both (66) and (67), whereas (69) is derivable only from (67).

3.8.3 Eager and easy to please

The same machinery provides a simple and direct solution to the widely quoted cases:

(70)a. John is eager to please
   b.   John is easy to please

The adjectives in question and the verb *please* are listed as follows in the lexicon:

V_{Adj} eager, ... $+ NP_x + S'_o$ Adj   SD

$NP_{x[DO]} + {}_{NP}[S^o]$ with SD. The NP-over-S^o leads to the gerund *taming* instead of the infinitive *tame* (7.4).

V_{Adj} $easy_1$, $hard_1$, $tough_1$, ... $+ NP/S'_{\emptyset[PASS]}$ Adj   SR
V_{Adj} $easy_2$, $hard_2$, $tough_2$, ... $+ NP_x + S'_{\emptyset[PASS]}$ Adj   SD
V_{Verb} please $+ NP + NP_{x[DO]} + {}_{NP}[S'']$ Verb   — —

Note that the argument frames for $easy_1$ and $easy_2$ (and their category mates) differ again in that the former conforms to a RAISING pattern while the latter shows a CONTROL pattern.

Note also that both $easy_1$ and $easy_2$ (and their category mates) take a complement-$S'_{\emptyset[PASS]}$. The subscript feature [PASS] is passed on to the Ss below it, and finally to the lexical verb in S^o (see 3.1.6.2 above). The lexical verb is then selected without its subject term, as shown in (74a) below. The complement-S of $easy_1$ and $easy_2$ (and their category mates) will have no passive morphology, since the subscript feature [PASS] prevents entrance into any Formation Rule that assigns that feature to its argument-S (see 3.8), i.e. into the Formation Rules (3d) and (3e). Therefore, passive morphology cannot come about. Nor can there be a passive *by*-phrase, though a level 2 *for*-phrase is possible:

(71)a.   *This problem is hard to solve by a student
    b.   This problem is hard to solve for a student

Interestingly, the same combination of syntactic properties is found for the Dutch verbs *vallen (te)* and *zijn (te)*, discussed in the sections 5.1.3 and 5.4.3 on the syntax of Dutch. These, too, take a complement-$S_{[PASS]}$, i.e. with the obligatory subscript feature [PASS].

The subscript feature [PASS] does, however, allow entrance into FR (3b) to produce a progressive infinitival:

(72)   This is good to be working at

In many instances a progressive infinitival in this position will strike one as awkward. This, however, seems attributable rather to semantic subcategorization conditions on the embedded $S'_{\emptyset[PASS]}$ than to the fact that the complement-S is single-tensed (S'): the adjectives in question seem to require action verbs rather than stative verbs in their complement-S. The alternative is to assign to the *easy*-class of adjectives a complement $S^o_{[PASS]}$, which automatically skips the S^{oPROGR} option (FR (3b)). But then one must also declare sentences like:

(73)   This pie is difficult not to eat

out of bounds, which does not seem right. In any case, the discussion on which of these two alternatives is preferable is open.

(74a-d) will thus be the derivation for (70a).

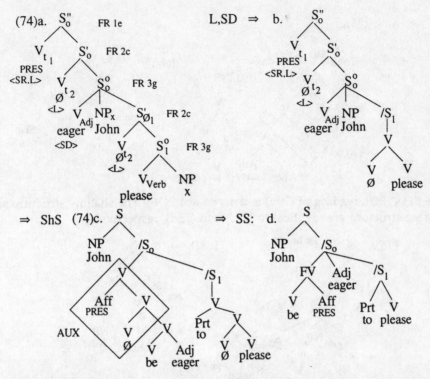

(70b) is sometimes considered to have two readings, a RAISING reading and a CONTROL reading. Both are easy to accommodate. The RAISING reading is derived in (75a–d):

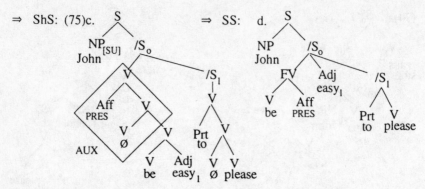

The CONTROL reading of (70b) is derived as in (76). The shallow structure and surface structure are identical to (75c) and (75d), respectively:

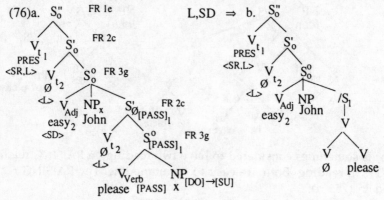

The surface structures of (70a) and (70b) are thus identical, despite their different derivations.

CHAPTER 4

The French auxiliary and complementation system

4.1 Preliminary comparative observations

The French auxiliary system is very similar to its English counterpart. Yet there are a few significant differences. The main new problems for the French auxiliary system are the syntactic treatment of datives and clitic pronouns, the modals and the tenses and aspects, in particular the aorist aspect, and defective paradigm verbs such as the middle auxiliary (MAUX) verbs *aller* and *venir de*.

Datives and clitics are discussed in section 4.3.1. To account for them it is necessary to insert an extra routine for the Cycle, assigning the feature [+Clitic] under certain conditions to weak pronouns and to the negation particle *ne*, and a filter that deals with successive datives resulting from cyclic predicate raising. These are given with the corollaries (4.2.4).

The basis for the syntactic treatment of modals and tenses (and aspects), as well as the MAUX-verbs *aller* and *venir* (*de*), is laid in the Formation Rules (4.2.1) and the Lexicon (4.2.2). No further provisions are necessary as all phenomena follow directly from the way the Formation Rules and the Lexicon are organized.

Besides these main differences, obvious to anyone familiar with both English and French, there are smaller differences, which are dealt with by changing minor rule parameters or by different orderings of the postcyclic rules. Furthermore, French has no grammatical category corresponding to the English Progressive Form, which simplifies the Formation Rules system. Apart from these differences, however, the similarities with the rules for English are striking. The rules of the Cycle are identical, but for the extra cyclic rule of DATIVE EXTRACTION needed for French. The Corollaries that apply between the Cycle and the Postcycle are also largely identical, as becomes apparent in 4.2.4. The postcyclic rules are very similar, so much so that some of them need not be repeated but can be taken over directly from English. (The postcyclic rules for French question formation are not given here, since the facts are, though manageable, too complex for a fully elaborated treatment in this context.)

One would, of course, wish to exploit these similarities further and reduce them to, possibly systematically, different values on universal parameters. More inductive work, however, is needed before such generalizations can be presented to any degree of reliability. For the moment we will restrict ourselves to referring to English for those rules and corollaries that are identical.

4.1.1 The French tenses and S"-complementation

The Formation Rules for French specify three classes of tense predicates: the finite tense operator V_{t_1} (PRES or PAST), the optional future tense operator V_{FUT}, which occurs in the position below V_{t_1} and, therefore, comes in two varieties, the present future and the past future, and the non-finite tense operator V_{t_2}, which indicates either simultaneity with or precedence to the temporal value resulting from the previous tense operator.

The precedence relation is symbolized by the perfective auxiliary followed by a past participle. The perfective auxiliary is either *avoir* ('have') or *être* ('be'), depending on the verb concerned. Which verbs take *avoir* and which take *être* is a question we shall not try to answer in a principled way, though certain semantic generalizations can no doubt be made (see also section 5.1.1 for a discussion of the analogous problem in Dutch). Here, we prefer to leave the semantics alone and will have the lexicon specify which verb takes which: those that take *être* are marked with an asterisk in the lexicon.[1]

Simultaneity is, in principle, symbolized by Ø. PRES + Ø is realized as the simple present tense, while PAST + Ø, normally speaking, appears as the simple past tense. French does, however, have the possibility of expressing aorist aspect for past events. The aorist aspect presents the information contained in the S^0-clause as a *point event*, i.e. one single momentary past event which cannot be, or is not to be, regarded as a duration containing component time extensions or moments. As is well-known from studies on the semantics of tenses, the aorist aspect is impossible for the simple present, since the present tense refers to the time of speaking, which is necessarily a time span, not a point event. In English, for example, one cannot say felicitously, reporting on a horse race, *At this very moment Fortuna wins the race.* One uses either the progressive or the present perfect: *is winning* or *has won.* This explains why, in languages expressing the aorist aspect, it is connected mainly with past tenses (and in some languages, such as Modern Greek, also with the future). Modern French links the aorist only with the past tense: it has a separate morphological category only for the aorist simple past.

The morphological tense that expresses this aspect is the so-called *passé défini* or definite past tense. This passé défini is not a feature of all varieties of French. It belongs only to the more cultivated or literary forms of the language, and is not part of colloquial or familiar style registers (unlike some other Romance languages or dialects). In order to capture the phenomena associated with the passé défini, an operator PE, i.e. 'point event', is introduced as a possible filler of V_{t_2}, but only if directly under PAST. The combination PAST + PE leads to the morphological passé défini and not to the *imparfait* or simple past, which expresses PAST + Ø. In the grammar of

---

[1] Ruwet (1991:143-170) discusses the 'unaccusative hypothesis', according to which 'unaccusative' intransitive verbs (see 1.3.3) take *être* and 'unergative' intransitive verbs take *avoir*. He shows, with a wealth of examples, that this hypothesis is massively falsified by the facts of French. Since no reply has come forth from the quarters where the 'unaccusative hypothesis' was developed we may take it that Ruwet is right.

colloquial French the PE-operator does not occur, and Ø takes over all of its grammatical and semantic functions. The rules given below reflect the more formal registers of French, and thus contain PE as an alternative under V_{t_2}.

French V_{FUT} occupies the position of English V_{MOD}, i.e. optional between V_{t_1} and V_{t_2}. As in English, full sentences with a finite verb form thus have obligatory S" (finite tense clause), obligatory (except with MAUX-verbs) S' (perfective tense clause), and obligatory tenseless S°. S'^{FUT} is an option between S" and S'. Complement S-embeddings are of type S", i.e. fully tensed embedded clauses, or of type S', i.e. tensed infinitivals, or of type S°, i.e. tenseless infinitivals. No predicate is lexically specified for a complement-S'^{FUT}: all future tense clauses are necessarily finite tense clauses and therefore of type S". This is different in languages which have a morphological future infinitive, such as Classical Greek or Latin.

For some verbs the lexically specified embedded S" is subscripted '[subj]'. This subscript prescribes the use of the subjunctive mood, a feature not further elaborated here. It does, however, entail the impossibility of the use of the future tense as well as of any MAUX-verb (see 4.1.3). (To account for this formally, one might consider treating the subjunctive as an alternative to the future tense (V_{FUT}) in the Formation Rules.)

Furthermore, there is a special feature which we did not encounter in English but do in French, the obligatory copying of the first tense, t_1, in the embedded S". This is indicated by the subscript 'co-t_1'. In the lexicon of 4.2.2 this subscript is found for the object-S" of the verbs *vouloir* ("want") and *préférer* ("prefer").

Finally, with the subject-S' of the verb *falloir*$_2$ ("must, be necessary") we find the subscript '[SU:pro]'. This is an instruction that the subject term of this S' must be pronominal, allowing e.g. *il lui faut partir* ("he has to leave") but preventing **il faut partir à Jean* ("Jean has to leave"). (See 4.4.2 for further commentary.)

4.1.2 The French modals

The French modal predicates are full verbs, with the full verbal paradigm. They take all the normal tenses, and their semantic arguments are treated syntactically as part of the sentential complementation system of the language, i.e. as embedded subject-Ss forming new S-units. They do not, therefore, as they do in English, occupy the position between the finite tense operator for PRES and PAST on the one hand, and the perfective tense operator (PE, or Ø or *avoir/être*) on the other. Their position in the Formation Rules is that of a lexical verb in S°. In English, the position in the Formation Rules directly under V_{t_1} is occupied by the modals and the MAUX-verbs *be to* and *be going to*, which explains their defective paradigm. In French, only the future tense operator FUT and MAUX-verbs like *aller* and *venir (de)* occupy this position. We shall see in chapter 6 that this position is filled in German exclusively by the future tense modal verb *werden*. Dutch (chapter 5) is like French in that Dutch modals are also full lexical verbs.

As in English, no syntactic distinction is made between various kinds of modals, such as epistemic modals ('it is possible/necessary/probable/etc. that ...') and agentive modals (expressing ability, duty, etc.). That is, the widely accepted view that modals have a RAISING and a CONTROL variant is not taken over here. Semantically there is a wealth of subtle distinctions, but the syntax is the same for all, at least at this level of description. *Devoir* ('must') and *pouvoir* ('can','may') are subcategorized for a subject-S', with SR. Besides these, there are also the (syntactically reflexive) epistemic modal *se pouvoir* ('be possible') and the two verbs *falloir* ('must'). *Se pouvoir* and *falloir₁* take a subject-S" in the subjunctive mood (and the structure-induced cyclic rule IL to create a dummy subject-NP). *Falloir₂* is idiosyncratic in that it takes a subject-S' (which must have a pronominal subject) and the cyclic rules IL and SR. After IL and SR the pronoun automatically becomes a pronominal dative NP, to be cliticized postcyclically (the impersonal *on* ('one'), is deleted in non-nominative cases). For details see section 4.4.2.

4.1.3 The MAUX-verbs *aller* and *venir (de)*

French has at least two verbs with a defective paradigm, the middle auxiliary (MAUX) verbs *aller* ('go') and *venir (de)*, literally 'come from' The former places the proposition as an event in the immediate future, the latter as an event in the immediate past. Both require an event-verb in the embedded proposition. *Aller* corresponds roughly to the English MAUX-verb *be going to*. The English translation of *venir (de)* requires a temporal adverb like *just* or *only just*, together with a perfective tense. Since *venir (de)* is the more interesting of the two, the examples will concentrate on this verb, rather than on *aller*, but they display identical syntactic behaviour. The following sentences illustrate the meaning and the defective paradigm of *venir (de)*.

(1)a. Robert vient de partir   b. Robert venait de partir
     Robert comes from leave   Robert came from leave
     'Robert has (only) just left'   'Robert had (only) just left'

The paradigm of *venir (de)* is defective: it does not take the future (2a), nor the perfect (2b), nor the passé défini (2c). Its argument-S can only be a tenseless infinitival, i.e. S⁰ (2d). And it does not occur as an infinitival complement (2e):

(2)a. *Robert viendra de partir   d. *Robert vient d'être parti
     Robert will come from leave   Robert comes from having left
     'Robert will just have left'   ??

   b. *Robert était venu de partir   e. *Robert me semble de venir de partir
     Robert had come from leave   Robert me seems to come from leave
     ??   'Robert seems to me to have just left'

   c. *Robert vint   de partir
     Robert came (passé défini) from leave
     ??

These facts are naturally captured in the Formation Rules by letting the MAUX-verbs *aller* and *venir (de)* occupy the position just below V_{t_1}, as an alternative to V_{FUT}, while specifying that they must take an S⁰-argument, thus letting it skip the V_{t_2} tenses. In this respect they behave precisely like the English MAUX-verbs *be to* and *be going to*. *Aller* and *venir (de)* induce SUBJECT RAISING (SR), as appears unambiguously from the behaviour of clitics: *Je viens de le lui donner*, and not **Je le lui viens de donner*. SUBJECT RAISING automatically accounts for this, since it creates a subordinate /S (=VP), and French CLITIC MOVEMENT stays within the nearest /S (=VP) (see the postcyclic rule of CLITIC MOVEMENT). We thus account for the facts without any extra provisions outside the normal rule format. The defective paradigm of *aller* and *venir (de)* is automatically captured by the position assigned to these verbs in the Formation Rules, just as in the case of the English modals and the MAUX-verbs *be to* and *be going to*.

The case of *venir (de)* is interesting for a variety of reasons. There is the question of the formal translation procedure between sentences containing *venir (de)* and their equivalents in other languages. We shall see in section 7.5 how Semantic Syntax is able to provide a principled solution to this formal translation problem. But what interests us more at this point is the status of *venir (de)* in the Formation Rules, and the process of re-analysis or regrammaticalization, whereby a verb which must originally have been an ordinary full lexical verb gradually became an auxiliary verb moving up the rules of the French auxiliary system. The historical picture that suggests itself shows *venir (de)* first as a full lexical verb, selected in S⁰, then as an alternative to Ø, PE and *avoir/être* in S', and finally as an alternative to FUT, skipping the S'-stage, giving the normal modern usage.[2] If this picture is correct it invites the inductive inference, vague as it will have to remain for the time being, that the position just below V_{t_1} apparently has a certain attraction for auxiliary elements that interact with the tenses.

An interesting complication, observed in Grevisse (1986:1237), is presented by:

(3) Mettez-vous à la place d'une jeune femme à qui vous *viendriez* de faire
une déclaration
'Put yourself in the place of a young woman to whom you have just
made a declaration'

This sentence (which belongs to an elevated style register: in ordinary French one would rather use the present: *à qui vous venez de faire une déclaration*) contains the past future form *viendriez* ('you would come'), which is excluded by the rule system given here, as it treats FUT and *venir (de)* as alternatives under V_{t_1}. It is to be noted in any case that sentence (3) becomes ungrammatical if the future past tense is replaced by the future present: *viendrez* ('you will

---

[2] The development of *venir (de)* is closely matched by *sortir (de)*, literally 'go/come out from'. *Sortir (de)*, however, has penetrated only into colloquial spoken French (Grevisse 1986:1237).

come'). The acceptability of the relative clause in (3) is best taken as resulting from its being a counterfactual clause. If this is correct, special provisions must be made in the Formation Rules for the expression of counterfactuality. One may think of an *irrealis* (or *counterfactuality*) operator, to be inserted somewhere high up in the rules and taking the combined forms of PAST and FUT as its morphological expression. The form *viendriez* would then be accounted for by such secondary use of the past and future tense operators. This complication will, however, be ignored in the rule system (as it was ignored for English: see 3.2).[3]

4.1.4 The Cycle

But for DATIVE EXTRACTION (4.3.1), the routine of [+Clitic] feature assignment and the filter for successive datives, the Cycle is without complications. Most auxiliary predicates take LOWERING, whereby they are left-adopted by the lower V, which thus grows into a V-cluster, just as in English. As in English, sentence adverbials are left-adopted by the argument-S. Intermediate adverbials are left-adopted by the lower V, but they are introduced at different levels from their English counterparts. The MAUX-verbs *aller* and *venir de* take SUBJECT RAISING.

The French complementation system differs from its English counterpart mainly in that the rule of PREDICATE RAISING plays a much more prominent role in the former than in the latter, where it is virtually absent. As regards the complementation system, English is a SUBJECT RAISING (SR) language. German and Dutch are exclusively PREDICATE RAISING (PR) languages. French is mixed in that it has PR as the dominant rule for object complement clauses that follow the RAISING pattern (and SUBJECT DELETION for object-clauses that follow the CONTROL pattern), and SR for all RAISING subject complement clauses. It is probably correct to say that, in French, SR occurs only from subject clauses, never from object position. PR does occur from object position and is, moreover, restricted to a small class of inducing verbs, mainly *faire* ('do', 'make'), *laisser* ('let','allow'), *voir* ('see'), *entendre* ('hear'), *envoyer* ('send'), and *donner à* ('give something to someone to [V]'), often with further structural restrictions. When PR, and not SR or SD, is the correct rule this appears most clearly from the behaviour of clitics: in *Je le lui ferai voir* ('I will get him to see it'), with PR, the clitics cluster *le lui* precedes the finite verb *ferai voir*. But in *Je veux le lui donner* ('I want to give it to him'), with SD, the same cluster precedes the infinitive *donner* ('give'), which forms a separate embedded /S *le lui donner*. In the sections 4.4.1, 4.4.2 and 4.4.3, and in section 4.7, the RAISING and the CONTROL constructions are dealt with in some further detail.

---

[3] Another interesting complication, likewise ignored here, is the fact that *venir (de)*, just like its (usually adverbial) translation equivalents in other languages, is a Positive Polarity Item. This means that it provokes a so-called 'echo-effect' when placed directly under negation: the negative sentence echoes the non-negative sentence and the negation implies a correction (Baker 1970; Seuren 1985:233-234).

4.2 Some basic machinery

4.2.1 The main Formation Rules

(1)a. $S''^{ADV_0} \rightarrow V_{Adv_0} + S''^{ATTR}/S''^{ADV1}/S''^{ADV2}/S''$

     or: $V_{Prep_0} + S''^{ATTR}/S''^{ADV1}/S''^{ADV2}/S'' + NP$

or b. $S''^{ATTR} \rightarrow V_{Attr} + S''^{ADV2}/S''$

or c. $S''^{ADV1} \rightarrow V_{Adv1} + S''^{ADV2}/S''$

     or: $V_{Prep1} + S''^{ADV2}/S'' + NP$

or d. $S''^{ADV2} \rightarrow V_{Adv2} + S''^{ADV2}/S''$

     or: $V_{Prep2} + S''^{ADV2}/S'' + NP$

     or: $V_Q + NP[^{\wedge}x + S''^{ADV2}/S''] + NP$

or e. $S'' \rightarrow V_{t_1} + S'^{FUT}/S'^{ADV2}/S^o{}^{MAUX}/S'$

(2)a. $S'^{FUT} \rightarrow V_{FUT} + S'^{ADV2}/S'$

   b. $S'^{ADV2} \rightarrow V_{Adv_2} + S'^{ADV2}/S'$

     or: $V_{Prep_2} + S'^{ADV2}/S' + NP$

     or: $V_Q + NP[^{\wedge}x + S'^{ADV2}/S'] + NP$

   c. $S' \rightarrow V_{t_2} + S^o{}^{PASS}/S^o{}^{ADV3}/S^o$

(3)a. $S^o{}^{MAUX} \rightarrow V_{Maux} + S^o{}^{PASS}/S^o{}^{ADV3}/S^o$

   b. $S^o{}^{PASS} \rightarrow V_{Pass} + S^o{}^{PASS}Prep/S^o{}^{ADV3}_{[PASS]}/S^o_{[PASS]}$

   c. $S^o{}^{PASS}Prep \rightarrow V_{PrepPass} + S^o{}^{ADV3}_{[PASS]}/S^o_{[PASS]} + NP_{[SU_{V_{LEX}}]}$

   d. $S^o{}^{ADV3} \rightarrow V_{Adv3} + S^o{}^{ADV3}/S^o$ **or:** $V_{Prep3} + S^o{}^{ADV3}/S^o + NP$

   e. $S^o \rightarrow V_{LEX} + \langle lex.arg.frame \rangle$ **or:** $V_{NP} + NP$

(4)a. $NP \rightarrow :x/^{\wedge}x + S^{NOM}$ **or:** x **or:** X_{WH}

   b. $S^{NOM} \rightarrow V_{Nom} + NP[x]$ **or:** $V_{Adj} + S^{NOM}$

4.2.2 Some lexicon

SA-cat	Fillers	Surface cat	Cyclic rules
V_{Adv_0}	en outre, premier, aussi, donc, ...	Adverb	L_S
V_{Attr}	$Q_{ue,}$	X: see 3.2.1	L_S
V_{Adv1}	en outre, premier, ...	Adverb	L_S
	(mal)heureux, peut-être, ...	Adverb	$L_{S/V}$
V_{Adv2}	$[_V[ne]_V[pas]]$, $[_V[ne]_V[jamais]]$, souvent, toujours, absolu, presque, ...	Adverb	L_V
V_{Adv3}	volontiers, vite, un peu, bon, mauvais, soigneux, beaucoup, ...	Adverb	L_{right}

V_{Prep0}	quant à, ...	Prep	OI,L_S
V_{Prep1}	à(Loc), dans, avec, pour, pendant, ...	Prep	$OI,L_{S/right}$
V_{Prep2}	à(Loc), dans, avec, pour, pendant, vers, ...	Prep	OI,L_{right}
	en, sans, pour, ...	Prep	$OI,SD,L_{S/right}$
V_{Prep3}	à(Loc), dans, avec, ...	Prep	OI,L_{right}
$V_{PrepPass}$	par	Prep	OI,L_{right}
V_{t1}	PRES, PAST	Affix (AH → FV)[4]	SR,L_V
V_{FUT}	FUT	Affix	L_V
V_{t2}	Ø	Verb	L_V
	PE ('point event'; only if directly under PAST)	Affix	L_V
	avoir/être	Verb	PaP,L_V
V_{Maux}	venir	Verb	SR [+de]
	aller	Verb	SR
V_{Pass}	être	Verb	PaP,L_V
V_{Cop}	être	Verb	PR
V_Q	chaque, tout, un, quelque, ...	Det(erminer)	OI,L_{var}

V_{LEX}:

SA-cat	Fillers	Argument frame	Surface cat	Cyclic rules
V_{Nom}	maison, chat, enfant, souris, livre, ...	+ NP	Noun	— —
V_{Adj}	petit, rouge, vieux, rond, ...	+ NP	Adj	— —
V_{Adj}	fidèle, ...	+ NP (+ $NP_{[IO]}$)	Adj	— —
V_{Adj}	probable, possible, vrai, ...	+ $NP/_{NP}[S'']$	Adj	— —
V_{Verb}	rire, dormir, courir, *mourir...	+ NP	Verb	— —
V_{Verb}	lire, manger, boire, ...	+ NP (+ NP)	Verb	— —
V_{Verb}	donner, vendre, laisser$_3$, ...	+ NP (+ NP) + NP	Verb	— —
V_{Verb}	présenter, ...	+ NP +NP +NP	Verb	— —
V_{Verb}	*partir, *arriver, ...	+ NP	Verb	——
V_{Verb}	sembler, paraître, ...	+ S'/S''	Verb	SR
V_{Verb}	continuer$_1$, commencer$_1$, ...	+ $NP/S'_\emptyset$	Verb	SR [+à]
V_{Verb}	continuer$_2$, commencer$_2$, ...	+ NP_x + $S'_\emptyset$	Verb	SD [+à]
V_{Verb}	promettre$_1$, ...	+ NP_x + (NP) + $S'_\emptyset$	Verb	SD [+de]

[4] With the postcyclic rule of AFFIX HANDLING the V-node directly above Aff is relabelled FV ('finite verb').

V_{Verb} promettre$_2$, ...	+ S$'_\emptyset$	Verb	SR [+de]
V_{Verb} croire, ...	+ NP + NP/S$'$/$_{(NP)}$[S'']	Verb	SD
V_{Verb} penser, ...	+ NP + (NP/S$'$/S'')	Verb	SD
V_{Verb} savoir (-Pass), ...	+ NP + NP/S$'_\emptyset$/$_{NP}$[S'']	Verb	SD
V_{Verb} vouloir(-Pass), ...	+ NP$_x$ + NP/S^o/S''$_{[subj;co-t_1]}$	Verb	SD
V_{Verb} préférer, ...	+ NP$_x$ + NP/S$'$/S''$_{[subj;co-t_1]}$	Verb	SD
V_{Verb} obliger, ...	+ NP + NP$_{x\ [DO]}$ + S^o	Verb	SD [+à/de]^5
V_{Verb} tenter, ...	+ NP$_x$ + NP/S$'_\emptyset$	Verb	SD [+de]
V_{Verb} aimer, ...	+ NP$_x$ + NP/S$'_\emptyset$	Verb	SD([+à])
V_{Verb} devoir, pouvoir, ...	+ S$'$	Verb	SR
V_{Verb} se pouvoir, falloir$_1$	+ S$'_{[subj]}$	Verb	— —
V_{Verb} falloir$_2$	+ S$'_{[SU:pro]}$	Verb	SR,IL
V_{Verb} dire, ...	+ NP + NP$_x$ + NP/S$'_\emptyset$/S''	Verb	SD [+de]
V_{Verb} faire, laisser$_1$, ...	+ NP + S^o	Verb	PR
V_{Verb} laisser$_2$, ...	+ NP + NP$_{x\ [DO]}$ + (S^o)	Verb	SD,(PR)
V_{Verb} voir, entendre, ...	+ NP + NP/$_{(NP)}$[S'']/S^o	Verb	PR

4.2.3 Cyclic rules

The rules of the Cycle are identical to those of 3.1.3, except for lexical differences: (a) The rule IT is now called IL, and $_{NP}$[il] is inserted. (b) For COPULA INSERTION V_{Cop}[être] is inserted. (c) For PAST PARTICIPLE $_{Aff}$[U] is inserted. (d) For PRESENT PARTICIPLE $_{Aff}$[ANT] is inserted. The only extra rule needed is:

DATIVE EXTRACTION (DE): The rightmost NP in an S^o marked [IO] and not marked [+Cl] is right-adopted by S^o. At the same time S^o left-adopts V_{Prep}[à].

4.2.4 Corollaries

The corollaries are identical to those of 3.1.4, except for FEATURE ASSIGNMENT and FILTER, and some lexical differences:

FEATURE ASSIGNMENT: On completion of each S-Cycle: If S dominates a weak non-subject pronoun assign the feature [+Cl], except for a pronominal NP — fe=[IO] flanked on the right by an accusative 1st or 2nd ps, or 3rd ps reflexive, pronoun. If the V-cluster contains $_{Adv}$[ne] and $_{Aff}$[PRES/PAST] assign the feature [+Cl] to $_{Adv}$[ne].

FILTER: If the Cycle leads to two successive occurrences of NP$_{[IO]}$ the derivation is blocked, except with NP$_{[IO,+Cl]}$ + NP$_{[IO,+Cl]}$: then the second NP$_{[IO,+Cl]}$ loses the feature [+Cl] and undergoes DATIVE EXTRACTION.

For *that*-INSERTION $_{Comp}$[que] is inserted. *To*-INSERTION is now split up into *de*-INSERTION and *à*-INSERTION, in the following way:

***De*-INSERTION and *à*-INSERTION** are corollaries at the end of the Cycle of /S-constituents not containing AUX provided the V-constituent under the parent of /S is marked [+de] or [+à]: /S left-adopts the particle $_{Prt}$[de] or $_{Prt}$[à], respectively.[5]

4.2.5 Some postcyclic rules (to be applied in the order given)

(1) Ø-DELETION: Delete $_V$[Ø]. Redefine AUX according to the Corollary.

(2) ADVERB PLACEMENT (AP): Insert all Adverbs above AUX in the V-cluster just below AUX, in the same order. (Insertion at the end of the V-cluster: right-adoption by the bottom $_V$[a].)

(3) CLITIC MOVEMENT (CM):
a. Assign weight features to the [+Cl]-nodes:

3 ps (non-reflexive) pronouns	→	[0]
Accusative [DO] pronouns	→	[0]
1,2 ps, 3 ps reflexive pronouns	→	[1]
Dative [IO] pronouns	→	[1]
ne	→	[3]

b. Accumulate the feature-values for each [+Cl]-node.
c. The highest V of AUX under the nearest /S left-adopts the [+Cl]-nodes. If there is no AUX the leftmost highest V-node under the nearest /S left-adopts the [+Cl]-nodes. CM is applied as many times as there are [+Cl]-nodes to the right of V. The order of application is [1]-[0]-[2]-[3] for the accumulated values. The cliticized nodes are relabelled 'CL'. CL-nodes adopted by AUX become part of AUX.

(4) AFFIX HANDLING (AH): As in 3.1.5 (lexical differences as in 4.2.3).

(5) MINCE: As in 3.1.5.

4.3 Some example sentences

4.3.1 Datives, clitics and DATIVE EXTRACTION

The phenomenon of preverbal pronominal cliticisation is something French has in common with the other Romance languages, the Slavonic languages, Modern Greek and many non-European languages: unaccented oblique pronouns end up just in front of the finite verb form or the infinitive or participle (sometimes, as in imperatives and Italian or Spanish infinitives and participles, attached to the right of the verb form). Such prefixed (or suffixed) weak pronouns are called clitics. The order in which the clitics appear in clitic clusters is strictly defined. Weak pronouns are sometimes not cliticized,

---

[5] The choice between *de* or *à* is not entirely idiosyncratic. Most verbs that take a direct object select *à* (e.g. *engager, contraindre, inviter,* but not e.g. *décourager, prier, empêcher*). Occasionally, their passive form takes *de* (e.g. *obliger, contraindre, encourager*). Intransitive verbs or verbs that take an indirect object always take *de* (*conseiller, promettre*). These phenomena are left to a subroutine to be developed later. (Atanas Tchobanov called my attention to these facts.)

under conditions which are clear enough to allow for listing but have so far resisted any principled description in terms of a rule system without exceptions, despite the existence of a sizable body of literature.[6] It seems that clitic clusters tend to occur in languages with obligatorily external datives.

In French, as in the other Romance languages fully lexical indirect objects (datives) are generally external, i.e. ordered after the direct object (accusative) and preceded by the dative preposition, which in French is *à*. These external datives are considered to be extracted by means of the structure-driven cyclic rule DATIVE EXTRACTION (DE). However, weak pronominal datives almost always occur as preverbal clitic pronouns. In the present rule system clitic dative pronouns are taken to originate as non-extracted, internal datives (see 2.7.2.2).[7]

This behaviour of datives differs from English, which, on the whole, allows for both internal and external datives. It has been observed, however, by many linguists (e.g. Green 1974) that in English there are semantic differences between the two kinds of dative. For that reason, Semantic Syntax has different sources for English external and internal datives. In English, the external dative is derived from an S^o with V_{Prep3}[to], a matrix S^o-subject containing the lexical verb, and an NP object containing the prepositional object. The English external dative is thus derived from a PP introduced at level 5, as specified in fig.2 of section 3.5 (see also (30a) in section 3.6). For English and other languages, such as Dutch, which allow for both internal and external datives, though often with slight semantic differences, Semantic Syntax requires no DATIVE EXTRACTION rule. In these languages the external dative is base-generated.

In French, however, the external variant has become generalized for all datives. Even so, the French external dative is not base-generated in Semantic Syntax. Instead, the seemingly circuitous route is followed of base-generating only internal datives and then, in the Cycle, raising the internal dative out of the S^o and fitting it out with the preposition *à*.

One reason for this apparently roundabout way of accounting for French external datives is the fact that the general format of SA-structures, as

---

[6] For the transformational literature, see in particular Perlmutter (1971), Seuren (1976). The bibliographical references in Kayne (1991) give a partial idea of the amount of literature produced in this area.

[7] It must be noted that not all middle NPs are datives. There are cases where a verb takes three arguments but assigns accusative case to the middle NP. This occurs in particular with verbs that take an object-S whose subject term is deleted under condition of referential identity with a higher controlling middle NP. The verbs laisser₂ ('let, allow') or *persuader de* + inf. ('persuade to') assign accusative case to their middle NP. On the other hand, verbs like *dire de* + inf. ('tell to') or *conseiller de* + inf. ('advise to') assign dative case to their middle NPs. Which verbs of this class assign dative and which accusative case is a question to which, so far, no principled answer has been found. Yet, remarkably, foreign learners of French generally have no difficulty in deciding, for each particular verb of this class, which case is assigned. This shows that the knowledge that is available at present about the proper analysis of lexical meanings is still badly inadequate.

specified in section 1.3 above, does not allow for prepositional phrases, whereas it does allow for internal or middle NPs. But further empirical support comes from the cyclic rule of PREDICATE RAISING, from the pronominal system and also from a typical property of certain triadic verbs. When all these facts are taken into account a system whereby datives are generated internally to be 'externalized' cyclically would seem much more efficient. We shall first have a look at PR and the lexical facts. The pronominal phenomena are discussed below.

As was said in chapter 2, PR destroys the lower S and the remaining material is re-attached higher up. The two Vs form a new V-island, for example $_V[_V[\text{faire}]_V[\text{avoir}]]$ ('cause-have') as in (4b) (see fig.2 in section 2.4):

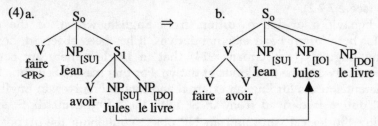

In surface structure, however, the internal dative $_{NP}[\text{Jules}]$ is externalized: *Jean fera avoir le livre à Jules* ('Jean will let Jules have the book'). Syntactically generated external datives therefore originate as internal datives. The assumption of an internal origin for all datives is thus preferable.

Moreover, the internal dative is recognized in the behaviour of a number of verbs taking either two or three arguments. One such verb is *servir* ('serve'). As in its English equivalent, both the dative and the accusative are optional, but if the dative occurs alone it automatically becomes accusative: *servir le potage au client* ('serve the soup to the client'), *servir le potage* ('serve the soup'), *servir le client* ('serve the client'). Other examples are:

(5) fournir de la marchandise au magasin ('stock the shop with goods')
     fournir de la marchandise   ('provide goods')
     fournir le magasin   ('stock the shop')

     conseiller du repos au malade   ('advise rest to the patient')
     conseiller du repos   ('advise rest')
     conseiller le malade   ('advise the patient')

     payer mille francs au médecin   ('pay the doctor 1000 francs')
     payer mille francs   ('pay 1000 francs')
     payer le médecin   ('pay the doctor')

     voler de l'argent à une dame   ('steal money from a lady')
     voler de l'argent   ('steal money')
     voler une dame   ('rob a lady')

déléguer une tâche à l'élève	('delegate a task to the pupil)
déléguer une tâche	('delegate a task')
déléguer l'élève	('delegate the pupil)
souffler le texte à l'acteur	('give the actor his cue')
souffler le texte	('prompt the text')
souffler l'acteur	('prompt the actor')
encourager le garçon au travail	('encourage the boy to work')
encourager le garçon	('encourage the boy')
encourager le travail	('encourage the work')

All such verbs are causatives. A prelexical analysis in terms of PREDICATE RAISING produces a V-island like the one in (4b), and the original subject of the embedded S_1, NP_2, has now become the internal indirect object of the higher S_o, while the original direct object of S_1 has become the direct object of S_o. Replacement of the V-island by a new lexical item, with further lexico-semantic specifications, provides the internal dative structure that fits the theory (Seuren 1972b). Clearly, when S_1 has only one argument term, this term becomes the direct object of S_o. In the light of this analysis, the switch from dative to accusative in the examples of (5) is natural and to be expected. Considerations of this nature make a treatment as given here preferable.

As regards clitic pronouns, the first attempt to account for their behaviour in the context of Transformational Grammar was Perlmutter (1971), which, however, failed to come to terms with the more difficult cases. One well-known stubborn difficulty for French is the fact that accusative clitics precede dative clitics when both are 3rd person, but follow datives when the accusative is 3rd person and the dative is a 1st or 2nd person or 3rd person reflexive pronoun, whereas weak dative pronouns remain uncliticised when they co-occur with a 1st or 2nd person or 3rd person reflexive accusative weak pronoun. This problem has never been solved in terms of a non-ad-hoc rule system in any existing analysis of French clitics. In Seuren (1976) a system was proposed that assigned weight values to weak pronouns in French, Italian and Modern Greek. This system provided a principled solution, i.e. in terms of a rule system, for most of the problems connected with clitic clusters, but it left the dative-accusative ordering problem in French unsolved: an ad hoc exception was still needed to get the facts right. The system presented here is an improvement in that it gets all the facts right, without having to resort to exceptions. The price to pay is an unorthodox system involving value assignments. Without that price, however, it is simply unclear what the solution could be.

Let us inspect some representative data from French ('1', '2', '3', '3^{refl}' stand for 1st, 2nd, 3rd person and 3rd person reflexive, respectively, 'A' for accusative, and 'D' for dative):

(6)a.   Il le comprend   A3
         he it understand
         'he understands it'

b.   Il me le donnera   **D1 - A3**
     he me it give-FUT
     'he will give it to me'

c.   Il ne se trompe pas   **ne - A3^{refl}**
     he NEG1 himself mistake NEG2
     'he is mistaken'

d.   Il se l' est promis   **D3^{refl} - A3**
     he himself it be promise-PaP
     'he has promised it to himself'

e.   Je ne le lui donnerai pas   **ne - A3 - D3**
     I NEG1 it him give-FUT NEG2
     'I will give it to him'

f.   *Je vous lui présenterai   **A2 - D3**
     I you him introduce-FUT

g.   Je vous présenterai à lui   **A2**
     I you introduce-FUT to him
     'I will introduce you to him'

h.   Je ne vous le présenterai pas   **ne - D2 - A3**
     I NEG1 you him introduce-FUT NEG2
     'I will introduce him to you'

i.   * Il vous se présentera   **D2 - A3^{refl}**
     he you himself introduce-FUT

j.   Il se présentera à vous   **A3^{refl}**
     he himself introduce-FUT to you
     'he will introduce himself to you'

Though still incomplete, these facts already look uncomfortable. Yet they allow for the following generalizations:

(i)   In preverbal position, **D** precedes **A**. This generalization holds generally for the Romance languages, for Modern Greek, and for the cliticizing Slavonic languages. The only exception is found in French with the order **A3-D3** which is required when **A3** and **D3** are combined. This exception is troublesome and it has so far never been captured in a rule system.

(ii) **A3**-clitics can be combined with all other pronominal clitics.

(iii) **A1/A2/A3^{refl}**-clitics can be combined with no other pronominal clitic.

(iv) The negative clitic *ne* precedes all other clitics.

Thus only the following pronominal preverbal clitic clusters (with or without *ne*) are allowed:

     (a)   **D1/D2/D3^{refl} + A3**   (b)   **A3 + D3**

The question now is: how can we get the rule system to operate in such a way that the facts that have been observed are generated with a minimum of extra apparatus? That some extra machinery will be needed is something one has to accept. Since Perlmutter (1971) it has been clear that clitic phenomena escape the more or less familiar boundaries of standard rule systems as developed in transformational syntactic analyses of any style.

Part of the problem has been solved already, at least in principle, due to the conditions imposed on DATIVE EXTRACTION. Since CM does not apply to NPs in a dative prepositional phrase, we have, in principle, accounted for the generalizations (ii) and (iii), and hence for the impossibility of the combinations found in (6f), i.e. **A2-D3**, and (6i), i.e. **D2-A3^{refl}**, above. What remains is a question of ensuring the correct ordering of the clitics in their preverbal clusters. To that end weight features are assigned to all [+Cl]-nodes in the following way (whereby it is taken for granted that the pronouns in question are marked for the features concerned):

non-reflexive 3rd person pronouns:	**3**	→ [0]
accusative (i.e. [DO]) pronouns:	**A**	→ [0]
1st, 2nd and reflexive 3rd ps pronouns	**1,2,3^{refl}**	→ [1]
dative (i.e. [IO]) pronouns	**D**	→ [1]
ne		→ [3]

These features are cumulative. That is, an **A3** clitic, for example, will have the feature value [0+0] = [0], a **D2** clitic will have [1+1] = [2], and **D3** will have [1+0] = [1]. CM now moves postverbal clitics to a preverbal position by letting the highest V of AUX under the nearest /S left-adopt them in the order [1]-[0]-[2]-[3]. If there is no AUX under the nearest /S (as in infinitivals or participials) the highest V-node left-adopts the clitics in the same order. Clitics left-adopted by AUX become part of AUX. CM thus first selects clitics with the cumulative feature value [1]; after that it selects clitics with the total value [0]; then it takes clitics valued [2]; and finally *ne* is cliticized. In general, other cliticizing languages differ from French in that they start with the lowest accumulated value, climbing up regularly to the highest value.

French has a split negation, consisting of two parts, *ne* (NEG1) and (NEG2). For ordinary negation NEG2 is *pas* (for more emphatic negation also *point*).[8] Other NEG2 elements are *jamais* ('never'), *personne* ('nobody') or *rien* ('nothing'). But for *point*, these can all be preceded by prenegative adverbs, such as *toujours* ('still'), *absolument* ('absolutely') or *presque* ('almost'). *Jamais, rien* and *personne* represent negative existential quantification. *Jamais* and *rien* can, in principle, be lowered into two positions, either to the far right or onto the V-cluster. *Personne*, on the other hand, can only be lowered to the far right. Moreover, in perfective infinitivals all NEG2 elements except *pas* are moved (postcyclically) to a position after the perfective auxiliary *avoir* or *être*. Some relevant facts are given in (7a-l):

---

[8] The original negation was just *ne*. From an historical point of view, the addition of *pas* ('footstep') or *point* ('dot') is secondary. *Pas* and *point* were originally idiomatic Negative Polarity Items in direct object position: 'not a step', 'not a dot'. They were, however, regrammaticalized, and now it is these secondary elements that carry the main semantic load of negation.

(7)a. Je n'ai jamais / rien volé
    I NEG1 have never / nothing stolen

   b. Je n'ai volé jamais / rien
      I NEG1 have stolen never / nothing

   c. *Je n'ai   personne vu
     I NEG1 have nobody seen

   d. Je n'ai vu personne
     I NEG1 have seen nobody

   e. ... pour ne pas avoir répondu
     ... for NEG1 NEG2 have answered

   f. *... pour n'avoir pas répondu
     ... for NEG1 have NEG2 answered

   g. *... pour ne jamais avoir répondu
     ... for NEG1 never have answered

   h. ... pour n'avoir jamais répondu
     ... for NEG1 have never answered

   i. ... pour n'avoir répondu jamais
     ... for NEG1 have answered never

   j. ... pour n'avoir vu personne
     ... for NEG1 have seen nobody

   k. *... pour ne personne avoir vu
     ... for NEG1 nobody have seen

   l. *... pour n'avoir personne vu
     ... for NEG1 have nobody seen

No rule system exists that accounts for such facts, and no attempt is made here to make one. All that can be said is that the syntactic behaviour of NEG2 elements like *jamais, rien, personne* is very much like that of adverbs (see 4.5). The system given here is limited to just *ne...pas*. Other NEG2 elements like *que* ('only') or *guère* ('hardly') are also left out of account.

To illustrate the machinery, let us consider first (8a) with the SA (8b).

(8)a. Il ne vous l'   aurait   pas donné[9]
      he NEG1 you it would have NEG2 given
      'he wouldn't have given it to you'

   b.

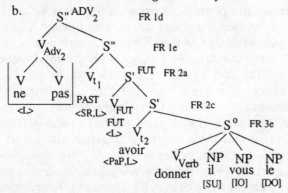

NP[vous] is marked [IO] because it is flanked by two NP constituents. On the S°-cycle it is also marked [+Cl] since it is a pronoun and not flanked on the right by a 1st or 2nd person or a 3rd person reflexive pronoun. (The formal marking of person of these pronouns has been omitted here: the reader is invited to make the necessary inferences.) The direct object NP[le] is also marked [+Cl] on the S°-cycle, because it is a non-subject pronoun. The negation particle Adv[ne] is also marked [+Cl], as specified by the corollary of FEATURE ASSIGNMENT. Since NP[vous] is marked [+Cl] DATIVE EXTRACTION (DE) does not apply on the S°-cycle: NP[vous] is not extracted by DE, and will therefore not become the prepositional phrase *à vous*.

---

[9] 'NEG2' is used to render *pas*, not any other NEG2 element.

The Cycle yields the shallow structure (8c), with AUX. The effect of the postcyclic rule ADVERB PLACEMENT is shown in (8d). Now CLITIC MOVE-MENT applies. This requires the assignment of weight values to the NPs marked [+Cl]. NP[vous] is 2nd person, which earns it [1]. It is also [IO], which earns it another [1]. NP[vous] thus has the accumulated value [2]. The accusative pronoun NP[le] gets the accumulated weight value [0], since it is accusative and 3rd person. The NEG1 Adv[ne] gets the value [3]. The accum-ulated clitic values are shown in (8d), just before CLITIC MOVEMENT.

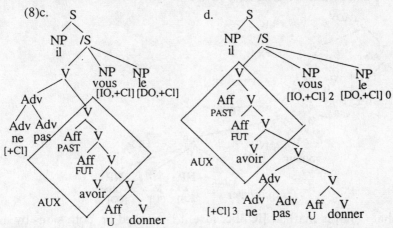

The [+Cl] constituents are now left-adopted by AUX, in virtue of CLITIC MOVE-MENT, in the order [0]-[2]-[3]. The first clitic to be treated, *le* (value [0]), comes closest to AUX. Since a clitic pronoun, once cliticised, becomes part of AUX, the next clitic, *vous* (value [2]), ends up on the left of *le*. The last clitic is *ne* (value [3]). This ends up on the left of *vous*. The NP-labels over the pronouns are replaced by 'CL', which makes the [+Cl] markings superfluous. The result is (8e). AFFIX HANDLING and MINCE result in (8f) and (8g), respectively.

(8)e.

f.

g.

Note that the question form of (8a), *Ne vous l'aurait-il pas donné?*, is easily generated by a postcyclic rule preposing AUX, to be ordered after CM. But as has been said (section 4.1), French question formation is subject to too many idiosyncrasies for us to venture a formal treatment here.

Now consider (9a) with the SA (9b):

(9)a.　Je ne　veux　pas　vous présenter à lui
　　　　I NEG1 want　NEG2 you introduce to him
　　　　'I don't want to introduce you to him'

b.

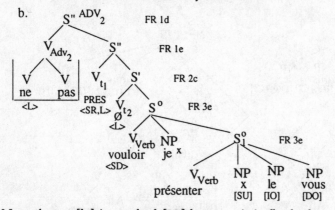

Note that $_{NP}$[le] is marked [IO] because it is flanked on both sides by an NP. But it will not be marked [+Cl] due to the 2nd person pronoun *vous* on the right. Therefore, the structure-induced cyclic rule of DATIVE EXTRACTION (DE) must be applied on the S_1^o-cycle. In virtue of DE, $_{NP}$[le] is right-adopted by S_1^o, and at the same time S_1^o left-adopts V_{Prep}[à], which induces OBJECT INCORPORATION (OI) and LOWERING (L) to the far right. This is shown in (9c). Then the new S_1^o-cycle undergoes its cyclic treatment, consisting, as has been said, of OBJECT INCORPORATION and LOWERING and resulting in $_{PP}$[$_{Prep}$[à]$_{NP}$[le]] in the original S_1^o, and eliminating the S_1^o newly created by the rule of DATIVE EXTRACTION. S_1^o is the object clause of S^o, which has *vouloir*, inducing SUBJECT DELETION (SD), as its main verb. Now SD can apply on the S^o-cycle: the subject of S_1^o, $_{NP}$[x], is deleted and S_1^o is downgraded to /S_1, as shown in (9d). Further cyclic treatment leads to the shallow structure (9e), with AUX. Note that there are now two /S-constituents. Ø-DELETION and ADVERB PLACEMENT first give (9f), with the [+Cl] markings and the accumulated values needed for CLITIC MOVEMENT. CM then results in (9g), where $_{NP}$[ne] has been left-adopted by AUX, i.e. under its own /S, and $_{NP}$[vous] by the V-constituent under its own /S. AH and MINCE give the surface structure (9h).

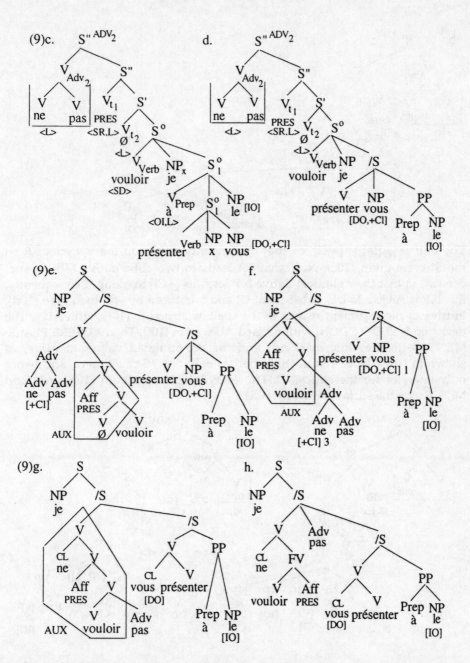

Contrast this with (10a), where not SD but PREDICATE RAISING (PR) has applied (for a discussion of French PREDICATE RAISING see section 4.4.3):

(10)a. Je ne   te le laisserai pas donner à elle
       I NEG1 you it will let NEG2 give to her
       'I won't let you give it to her'

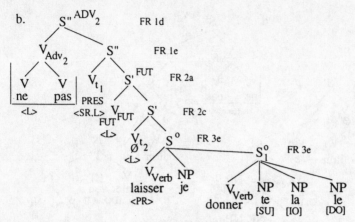

The dative $_{NP}[la]$ is [+Cl], so that DE does not apply on the S_1^o-cycle. PR on the S^o-cycle gives (10c). Note that PR leads to two clitic dative NPs in succession, so that the rightmost dative NP loses its [+Cl] marking. Consequently, this NP is subject to DE. Subsequent OI and L induced by $_V[à]$ then give (10d). Further cyclic treatment results in the shallow structure (10e), with AUX. The next step is Ø-DELETION, with revised AUX, as in (10f). Then ADVERB PLACE-MENT, with the clitic markings and the accumulated values in place, as shown in (10g). Note that in (10g) there is only one /S-constituent, and hence only one slot for the clitics. CLITIC MOVEMENT results in (10h). AH and MINCE give the surface structure (10i).

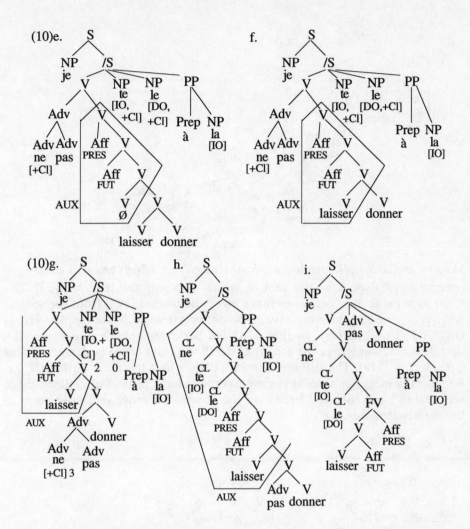

Now suppose the pronoun distribution in (10b) is different, so that we get (11a), meaning 'I won't let her give it to you':

(11)a. Je ne le lui laisserai pas donner à toi
      I NEG1 it her will let   NEG2 give   to you
      'I won't let her give it to you'

b.

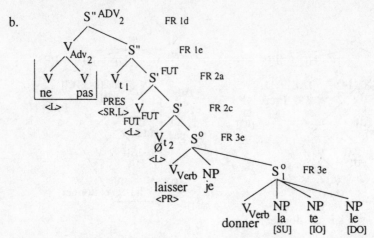

Now PR on the S_1'-cycle produces the structure (11c), which has two successive pronominal dative NPs, the first of which also gets the feature [+Cl]. The Filter given with the corollaries takes away the feature [+Cl] from the second $NP_{[+Dat,+Cl]}$, so that this will have to be dative-extracted.[10] The application of DATIVE EXTRACTION is shown in (11d). Further treatment is analogous to (10), up to the moment where the accumulated clitic values are to be assigned. This is shown in (11e). The difference with (10g) is that the clitic dative (*la*, i.e. *lui* after the morphophonology) now has the value 1 instead of 2. Since clitics with value 1 are cliticised before all the others, the order will now be as in the surface structure (11f).

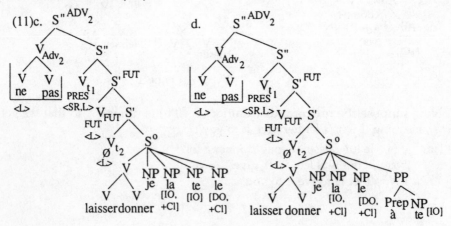

(11)c.

d.

---

[10] Note that the Filter blocks sentences like **Je ferai donner le livre à Jean à Marie* ('I'll get Marie to give the book to Jean'). The usual strategy followed by French speakers is to passivize the lowest S, leading to the correct *Je ferai donner le livre à Jean par Marie* ('I'll get the book to be given to Jean by Marie').

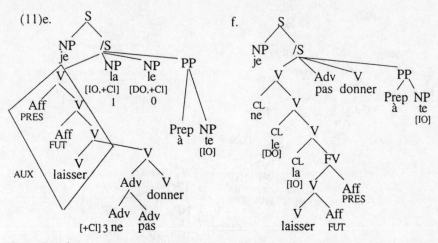

Note that *laisser* occurs twice in the lexicon. It also allows for an argument frame with an object-NP[+DO] followed by an object-S. This *laisser₂* induces obligatory SD, controlled by the object-NP, and optional PR. This is shown in (12a), which has a subtle semantic difference with (10a).[11] Note that the middle term of *laisser* in (12b) is not marked [IO] (see note 7 above). One will observe the remarkable difference in the treatment of the clitics between (10a) and (12a), despite their lexical similarity. It may be noted that no existing grammar of French even remotely accounts for these facts.

(12)a. Je ne   te laisserai pas le lui donner
    I NEG1 you will let NEG2 it her give
    'I won't allow you to give it to her'

---

[11] The semantic difference is brought out clearly by the sentence pair *Laissez tomber l'arme* ('drop the weapon' or 'allow the weapon to fall'), with PR, and *Laissez l'arme tomber* ('allow the weapon to fall'), with an extra accusative NP and SD but no PR (see (64) in section 3.8.2 and below, section 4.4.3.). The first sentence is ambiguous, the second is not (observation attributed to Nicolas Ruwet). In (10a) and (11a) the difference is hardly expressible in English.

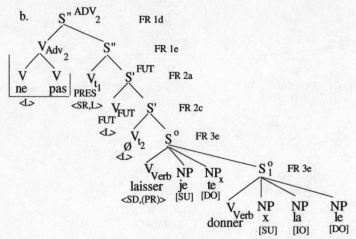

Since, with this argument frame, *laisser*$_2$ induces obligatory SD, and optional PR, the grammar is free not to apply PR. If PR is not applied the shallow structure has two /S-constituents, and hence two slots for the clitics. Interestingly, the dative $_{NP}$[la] is now cliticized in the normal way, since nothing now takes away its [+Cl] marking. The shallow structure is as in (12c) (with AUX). Ø-DELETION and ADVERB PLACEMENT give (12d), with the CLITIC MOVEMENT markings. CLITIC MOVEMENT then gives (12e). AFFIX HANDLING and MINCE lead to the surface structure (12f). Note that with PR the derivation is as from (10c) onward.

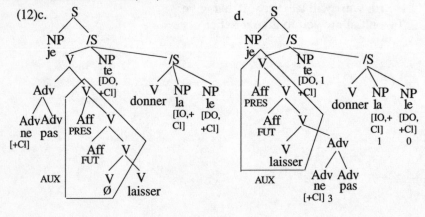

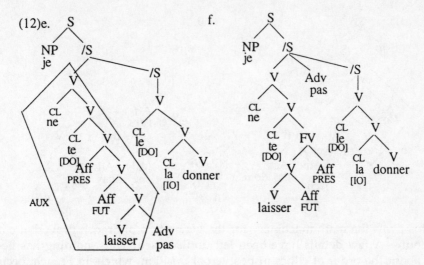

Now consider the sentence:

(13)a. Je préfère ne   pas   te le donner
        I prefer NEG1 NEG2 you it give
        'I prefer not to give it to you

b.

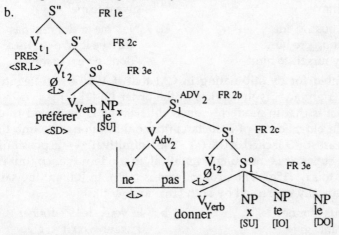

The Shallow Structure is (13c). Ø-DELETION, CLITIC MOVEMENT and AFFIX HANDLING give the Surface Structure (13d). The rule of ADVERB PLACEMENT applies only to the extent that $_{Adv}$[ne] loses its [+Cl] marking, since, due to the absence of AUX in this /S-constituent, the adverbial cluster [[ne][pas]] is not moved by this rule (see postcyclic rule (2)). MINCE does not apply.

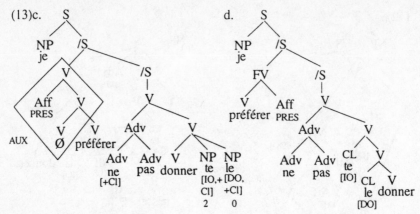

This gives the main machinery for the generation of French preverbal clitic pronouns. A few details have been left undiscussed. Thus, nothing has been said about the order of clitics in postverbal position, which, in French, occurs only with non-negative imperatives. The combinations are exactly as in preverbal position, but the order is always: **A-D**:

(14)a. Donnez-le-lui
      give-IMP it him
      'give it to him'

    b. Donnez-le-moi
       give-IMP it me
       'give it to me'

    c. Présentez-vous à lui
      introduce you$_{\text{refl}}$ to him
      'introduce yourself to him'

    d. Ne me le donnez pas
       NEG1 me it give-IMP NEG2
       'don't give it to me'

This can be accounted for by stipulating in CM that if V is a non-negative imperative, then V right-adopts the clitics, in the order [0]-[1]-[2].[12]

An important fact is that in modern French cliticization is restricted to the nearest /S (=VP). In older forms of French, clitics could optionally climb to a higher /S if the nearest /S lacked AUX (i.e. was infinitival), — a possibility still open to Italian clitics. It is thus ungrammatical, in modern French (but not in 17th C. French), to say (15a). The proper form is (15b). In Italian, the same meaning is grammatically expressed by both (16a) and (16b):

(15)a. *Je te le veux donner
      I you it want give
      'I want to give it to you'

    b. Je veux te le donner
       I want you it give

(16)a. (Io) te lo voglio dare
      I you it want give

    b. (Io) voglio dartelo
       I want give-you-it

But Italian does not allow the clitic cluster to be broken up:

(17)a *(Io) ti voglio darlo   b. *(Io) lo voglio darti

---

[12] Italian clitics are, on the whole, obligatorily postverbal with imperatives, participles and infinitives. Their order is always identical to that found with preverbal clitics: **D-A**.

All French grammar books tell the user that clitics originating with embedded infinitives stay with their infinitives, as in (15b), except with a small class of verbs, including *faire* (make, do), which obligatorily attract the clitics of their infinitives:

(18)a. Je te le ferai   voir
       I you it make-FUT   see
       'I will make you see it' 'I will show it to you'

   b. *Je ferai te le voir

   c. *Je te ferai le voir

As has been shown repeatedly above, and is shown again in section 4.4.3, this is not a complication at all. On the contrary, it provides immediate support for the analysis given here, since verbs like *faire* induce cyclic PREDICATE RAISING, which results in a lexical V-node $_V[_V[faire]_V[voir]]$, and hence in the emergence of only one /S, whose AUX obligatorily left-adopts the clitics. This analysis receives further support from the analogous facts associated with the verbs *laisser$_1$* and *laisser$_2$*.[13]

(19)a. Je te le laisserai voir
       I you it   let-FUT see
       'I will let you see it'

   b. *Je laisserai te le voir

   c. Je te laisserai le voir
      'I will allow you to see it'

Unlike (18c), (19c) is grammatical, though, as has been said (note 11 above), there is a subtle semantic difference with (19a). The reader will have no difficulty now in deriving the grammatical sentences of (18) and (19) and explaining the ungrammaticality of the remaining ones.

4.3.2 A sentence with a high PrepPhrase

Consider the simple sentence (20a) with the SA (20b) and the almost shallow structure (20c):

(20)a. Je viendrai   avec plaisir
       I come-FUT with pleasure
       'I will be happy to come'

---

[13] Cf. (10) and (11) above. This argument was already presented in Seuren (1972b).

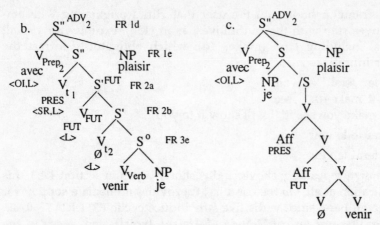

Up to the highest cycle nothing special is to be noted. At the top cycle, OBJECT INCORPORATION (OI) takes place first, leading to (20d). LOWERING to the far right of the argument-S gives the shallow structure(20e), with AUX. Ø-DELETION gives (20f), and AFFIX HANDLING gives the surface structure (20g).

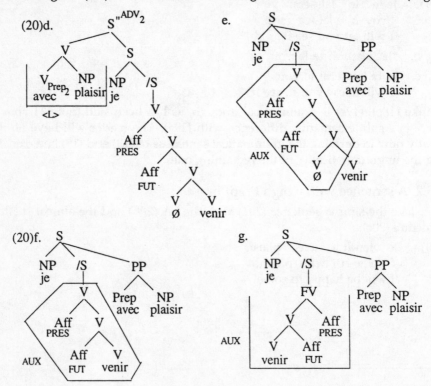

4.4 The complementation system: SR, SD, PR

As English, French has six types of sentential complement: S", S' and S°, each with or without a dominating NP. An S"-complement re-enters the Formation Rules at (1b) or (1c), an S'-complement at rule (2b) or (2c), and an S°-complement at any of the rules (3c-e). Unless otherwise specified in the lexicon, possible subscript features of S°, e.g. [PASS], may be selected for an S°-complement (as in (50) below).

4.4.1 SUBJECT RAISING and the case of *venir (de)*

As in all SVO-languages, SUBJECT RAISING is induced by PRES or PAST, as part of the TENSE ROUTINE (see 2.7.4.2.1). Note that SR (if not induced by PRES or PAST), like SD and PR, typically produces infinitival complement embeddings. Languages that lack a morphological infinitive, such as the Balkan languages (where it is an areal feature), therefore tend not to have these rules (but see section 2.7.4.1, especially note 5).

SUBJECT RAISING occurs mostly, in French, with verbs with a sentential subject term. That is, French mostly has SUBJECT-to-SUBJECT RAISING, and hardly any SUBJECT-to-OBJECT RAISING.[14] In the Lexicon of 4.2.2 the verbs with SR are the MAUX-verbs *venir (de)* and *aller*, and the lexical verbs *sembler* and *paraître*, both meaning 'appear', $continuer_1$ and $commencer_1$, meaning 'go on, keep' and 'begin', respectively, *devoir* (must) and *pouvoir* (can).

As in English (see 3.1.2), the verbs *continuer* and *commencer* occur in a RAISING and a CONTROL argument frame (Perlmutter 1970). In the former they take only one term ($continuer_1$ and $commencer_1$) and induce SR. This frame is recognized in sentences like *Il a commencé à pleuvoir* ('it started to rain'). In the CONTROL frame they occur with two terms ($continuer_2$ and $commencer_2$) and induce SD, exactly as in English. The latter argument frame is preferred in sentences like *Il a continué à manger* ('he continued to eat'). One notes the parallel with the two verbs *help* (3.8.2). $Help_1$, with two arguments (RAIS-ING), takes SR, meaning 'contribute to', but with three arguments (CONTROL) it means 'assist' and takes SD, controlled by the higher object-NP. The difference with *continue* or *start* consists merely in the addition of one argument. The French verb *laisser* (let, allow) shows the same parallel, as will be shown below (4.4.3).[15]

The result of SR is an embedded /S-constituent. As was shown in the previous section, the behaviour of clitic pronouns is an infallible test for em-

[14] See, for example, Ruwet (1972:48-86).

[15] It would be interesting to see if there is some system in this interplay of rules. It could be, for example, that the group of languages to which English and French belong have a tendency to remove the subject from embedded S's and S°s, in order to create infinitivals. The first rule in line would be SD. If SD cannot apply (usually this would be because there is no anaphoric reference identity relation of the right kind) then SR or PR come up, according to the type of the language concerned: English would normally take SD, Dutch and German would take PR, French would be mixed (see the end of section 2.12).

bedded /Ss in French. Let us illustrate this with the MAUX-verb *venir (de)*, rendered in English by means of *just* plus present or past perfect. Consider (21a), with the SA (21b). Note that the MAUX-verb *venir* is an idiosyncratic tense incorporating the second and third tenses. SR on the S°MAUX-cycle results in (21c). SR and L on the highest cycle give the shallow structure (with *de*-INSERTION and AUX) (21d).

(21)a. Il vient de le faire
       he comes from it do
       'he has just done it'

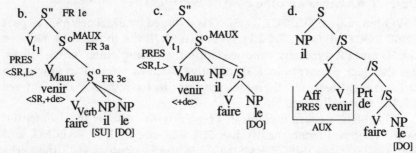

CM results in (21e). AH gives the surface structure (21f). (MINCE does not apply.) Note that CM attaches the accusative pronoun *le* to *faire*, and not to AUX: the clitic *le* must stay within its own nearest /S. This rules out *Il vient le de faire* and *Il le vient de faire*.

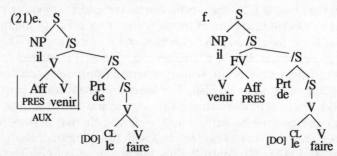

It will be interesting, of course, to see what the formal translation relation is between the French sentence (20a) and its English equivalent *He has just done it*. Although formal translation relations are not discussed until section 7.5 a few observations can be made here. It will be necessary to introduce a language-independent level of semantic representation, with elements like 'shortly before' and specifications as to how different languages express such elements at SA-level. The semantic element 'shortly before' can then be said to be expressed in English by the combination V_{Adv2}[just] and V_{t2}[have], while French has the special MAUX-verb *venir (de)* available for that purpose. Given that information, a procedure is easily devised that looks for V_{Adv2}[just] and V_{t2}[have] in the English lexicon (if the translation is from French into English) and finds the Formation Rules that allow for their introduction, thus enabling the setting up of the relevant parts of the SA-tree. Analogously for a translation from English into French.

4.4.2 SUBJECT DELETION, SUBJECT RAISING and the case of *falloir*

SUBJECT DELETION occurs in two forms, vertical and horizontal SD. The vertical form is, or was, generally known under the name of EQUI-NP DELE-TION, a clumsy name which is better replaced by a less extravagant label. The horizontal form is not or hardly known. It occurs in sentences like (22a) with the partial SA (22b). (For more comment see 2.7.4.3 and 7.4.)

(22)a. Il est mort en chantant
      he is died   in singing
      'he died while singing'

b.

Horizontal SD, however, will not be discussed here. The discussion is limited to vertical SD.

As in all European languages that have an infinitive (see 2.7.4.1), vertical SUBJECT DELETION is frequent and is normally induced by verbs taking object-complements and requiring or allowing anaphoric referential identity between a controlling NP (often the subject) in the main clause and the subject-NP of the complement clause. But note that the mere possibility of referential identity between a controller and the lower subject is not enough to guarantee SD. The English verb *believe*, for example, does not take SD, even when the two subjects are referentially identical: **I believed to be in Rome*. Its French counterpart, however, *Je croyais être à Rome*, is fully grammatical, which shows that SD is not automatic but, to some extent, item-specific.

Vertical SD is unproblematic in the standard cases. Consider the sentence:

(23)a. Il a voulu partir
      he has wanted   leave
      'he wanted to leave'

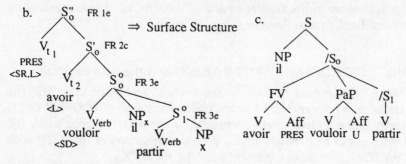

SD has resulted in an embedded /S consisting just of the verb *partir*.

A special case of SD is presented by the idiosyncratic verbs *falloir₁* ('be necessary, must') and the intrinsically reflexive *se pouvoir* ('be possible'). We have the following items, including *falloir₂*, which takes SUBJECT RAISING besides obligatory lexicon-driven IL (4.2.2):

V_{Verb} se pouvoir, falloir₁   + $S''_{[subj]}$ Verb   — —
V_{Verb} falloir₂   + $S'_{[SU:pro]}$ Verb   SR,IL

We shall look first at *falloir₁*. Consider (24) (the subscript 'subj' is an instruction to use the subjunctive mood):

(24)a. Il   faut   que tu   partes
        it is necessary that you leave-SUBJ
        'you must leave'

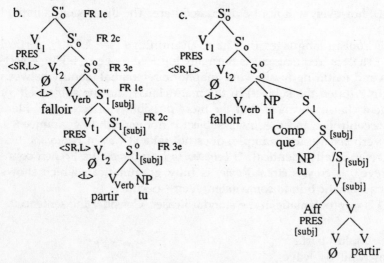

On the S^o_0-cycle the cyclic rule IL applies, structure-driven. This gives (24c), assuming that the feature [subj] is passed on to $_{Aff}$[PRES]. The rule IL is presented here, for convenience, as applied to French (see 3.1.3 and 4.2.3):

IL: (structure-driven when V of S° has subject S" or $_{NP}$[S"]; otherwise lexically induced): Create new constituent $_{NP}$[il]. Attach $_{NP}$[il] to the immediate right of V. The S"or ₙₚ[S"] to the immediate right of $_{NP}$[il] is moved to direct object position if not already there, still marked [SU]. The shallow structure is (24d), and the surface structure is (24e):

(24)d.

```
              S
           ／  ＼
         NP    /S
         il
        ／＼
       V      S₁
    ／＼     ／＼
  Aff  V  Comp   S [subj]
  PRES  ／＼  que   ／＼
      V  V      NP   /S[subj]
      Ø  falloir tu    │
  AUX                V[subj]
                    ／＼
                  Aff   V
                  PRES ／＼
                 [subj] V  V
                        Ø  partir
```

e.

```
              S
           ／  ＼
         NP    /S
         il
        ／  ＼
      FV      S₁
    ／｜＼    ／＼
   V  Aff Comp  S [subj]
falloir PRES que  ／＼
                NP   /S[subj]
                tu    │
                    FV[subj]
                    ／＼
                   V   Aff
                 partir PRES
                       [subj]
```

Besides this construction, however, there is *falloir₂*, which takes an S' as its subject-complement, whose subject term has to be pronominal. This *falloir₂* induces SR and obligatory lexicon-driven IL. Thus one has sentence (25a), with *falloir₂* as main verb, which means exactly what (24a) means.

(25)a.   Il   te   faut   partir
       it   you   must   leave
       'you must leave'

(25)b.

```
        S"₀   FR 1e          IL, SR  ⇒
      ／  ＼
     V      S'₀   FR 2c
   t₁ ／  ＼
 PRES  V      S₀°   FR 3e
<SR,L> t₂  ／  ＼
     Ø   V      S'₁  FR 2c
    <l>  Verb ／  ＼
       falloir V      S₁°  FR 3e
      <IL,SR> t₂ ／  ＼
            Ø   V      NP
           <l>  Verb   pro
              partir   tu
```

c.

```
        S"₀
      ／  ＼
     V      S'₀
   t₁ ／  ＼
 PRES  V      S₀°
<SR,L> t₂ ／｜  ＼
     Ø   V   NP  NP      /S₁
    <l>  Verb il  te       │
       falloir    pro      V
              [IO,+Cl]   ／＼
                        V   V
                        Ø  partir
```

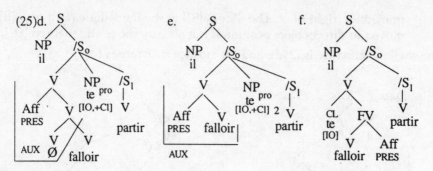

(25b) is the SA. On the S_0^0-cycle the rules SR and IL apply. The result is (25c). Note that, due to IL, the raised subject *tu* of S_1^0 finds itself in the regular position of indirect object, which is precisely what it is in surface structure. Further cyclic treatment results in the shallow structure (25d). Ø-DELETION gives (25e), with the accumulated clitic weight 2 for the dative pronoun *te*. CLITIC MOVEMENT plus AFFIX HANDLING gives (25f). MINCE has no effect.

To see that the *falloir₂*-construction really has a surface structure embedded $/S_1$ consider (26), where the clitic pronoun *le* goes with the infinitive *faire*:

(26)a. Il   te   faudra   le faire
      it   you   must-FUT   it do
      'you will have to do it'

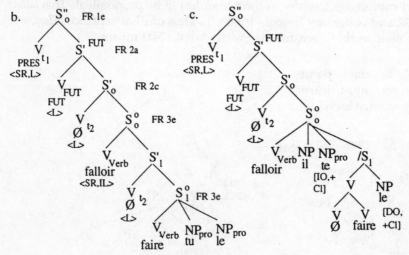

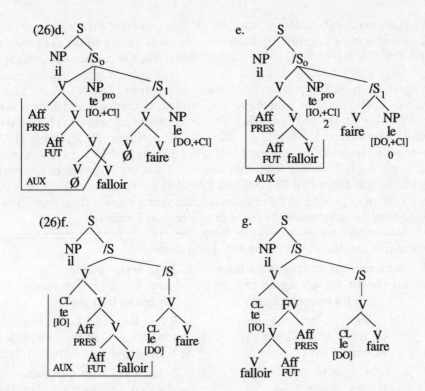

(26b) and (26c) are the exact parallels of (25b) and (25c), respectively. The shallow structure is (26d). Ø-DELETION and clitic weight assignments give (26e). Now CLITIC MOVEMENT gives (26f). AFFIX HANDLING gives (26g). MINCE is not operative. Clearly, the clitic *le* would not end up in front of *faire* if there had not been a separate embedded /S₁. It would, therefore, be wrong to assign the rule PREDICATE RAISING to *falloir₂*, as this would unite *falloir* and *faire* into one V-island and no embedded /S₁ would occur.

The two verbs *falloir* represent a somewhat idiosyncratic instance of the Raising-Control alternation discussed in section 4.7 below.[16]

4.4.3 PREDICATE RAISING and the case of *faire* and *laisser*

The rule of Predicate Raising (PR) was first proposed by McCawley (1968; also in McCawley 1973:155-166) in connection with tentative ideas concerning internal or 'prelexical' syntactic structure in certain verbs. His prime example was

---

[16] Note, in this connection, that a sentence like *Il faut partir* ("one must leave") is generated by giving the embedded subject clause of *falloir₂* the impersonal pronominal subject *on* ("one"), which, in French, can occur only as a subject. The grammar will have to posit a morphophonemic rule reducing *on* to Ø whenever it is bereft of its subject status. We have assigned an S' as subject term to *falloir₂*, and not S⁰, given the occurrence of sentences like *Il faut avoir fini le ménage avant trois heures* ("one must have finished the house-cleaning before three o'clock"). I am indebted to Marianne Desmets and Atanas Tchobanov for these observations.

the English verb *kill*, analysed as CAUSE-BECOME-DEAD. Although this analysis met with a barrage of objections, its main strong point was the fact that PREDICATE RAISING, invoked by McCawley for the purpose of prelexical syntax, is in fact a major cyclic rule in the complementation system of many languages, i.e. in ordinary 'open', not-prelexical, syntax. English, is not one of them, but most Romance languages are, as well as German and Dutch (and many other languages in the world). This was shown in Seuren (1972b), with material drawn from Kayne (1969) (elaborated in Kayne 1975), Evers (1971) (elaborated in Evers 1975), Langacker (1973) (then available in prepublication form), Starosta (1971) and a few other sources. Thus the criticism in Chomsky (1972:142) to the effect that PREDICATE RAISING is an 'otherwise quite unnecessary rule' was proved to be unfounded. It sprang merely from insufficient knowledge of the grammars of languages other than English.

The motivation comes primarily from the French *faire*-construction. Its main features are illustrated in the following sentences:

(27)a. Je ferai manger une pomme à Jules
     I make-FUT eat an apple to Jules
     'I'll get Jules to eat an apple'

   b. Je la lui ferai manger
     I it-ACC him-DAT make-FUT eat
     'I'll get him to eat it'

   c. Je ferai partir Jules
     I make-FUT leave Jules
     'I'll get Jules to leave'

   d. Je le ferai partir
     I him-ACC make-FUT leave
     'I'll make him leave'

   e. Il fera tuer les rats par Jean
     he make-FUT kill the rats by Jean
     'he'll have the rats killed by Jean'

   f. Il les fera tuer par Jean
     he them-ACC make-FUT kill by Jean
     'he'll have them killed by Jean'

Three observations are to be made. First, if the object-S is intransitive, as in (27c,d), its subject becomes accusative, but if it is transitive two things may happen, depending on the thematic function assigned by the lexical verb of the embedded S to the subject term (see section 2.4). Since, as was said in 1.3.3, lexical classification on the basis of thematic functions is still too shaky to be incorporated in an adequate syntactic theory, our formulation must remain tentative. With this proviso we can say that when the lower verb is of the recipient type (i.e. it assigns the thematic function 'recipient' to the subject term), as in (27a,b), the embedded verb normally stays in the active voice and the underlying subject becomes dative while the semantic object remains accusative. But if the lower verb is actor-oriented (i.e. it assigns the thematic function 'actor' to the subject term), as in (27e,f), the embedded S must be passivized (though without passive morphology) and the original subject is either left out or expressed under the preposition *par*. (Given the uncertainty regarding thematic functions, no account is taken of them in the rule system.)

Secondly, the position of the clitic pronouns in (27b,d,f) shows that the lower verb is not part of a separate embedded /S: (28a,b,c) are ungrammatical:

(28)a. *Je ferai la lui manger
   b. *Je ferai le partir
   c. *Il fera les tuer par les soldats

Then, tensed infinitives are excluded, and negation is forced (cf. (25) in 2.12):

(29)a. *Je   lui   ferai   avoir mangé la pomme
       I him-DAT make-FUT have eaten   the apple

   b. ?*Je   lui   ferai   ne pas   manger la pomme
       I him-DAT make-FUT NEG1 NEG2   eat   the apple
       'I'll get him not to eat the apple'

We therefore posit that the object complement-S of *faire* is of the type S^o.

Kayne (1969) is opposed to PR as a rule of syntax and proposes the rule of *faire*-ATTRACTION (FA), slightly modified as *faire*-INFINITIVE (FI) in Kayne (1975). FI may be taken to transform (30a) into (30b).[17]

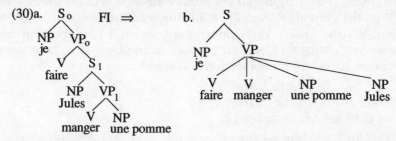

A rule of *à*-INSERTION will then turn $_{NP}$[Jules] into a dative PrepPhrase. Note that Kayne expressly argues (1975:217-220) that the lower V is brother-adjoined to the higher V under VP_o. It was shown in Seuren (1972b) that this must be incorrect in view of cases of double application of PR, as in (31a). FI would produce (31b-d), Note that (31d) contains an embedded VP. Kayne (1975) does not mention this, but Kayne (1969) requires the embedded VP. It would anyway go against all principles of grammar to delete VP over V + NP.

(31)a. Je ferai   faire   entrer   le monsieur
       I make-FUT make come in   the gentleman
       'I'll have the gentleman shown in'

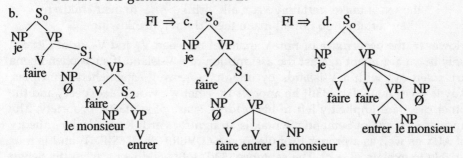

---

[17] Strangely, Kayne (1975), almost 450 printed pages of French syntax, contains no tree structures, and the text heavily underspecifies derived structure. On the basis of Kayne (1969), however, which does contain tree structures, one may take it that the structures as given represent Kayne's intentions.

However, (31d) must be incorrect, since if $_{NP}$[le monsieur] is pronominalized as $_{NP}$[le] the resulting sentence would be the ungrammatical (32a) and not the grammatical (32b):

(32)a. *Je ferai faire l'entrer
   b. Je le ferai faire entrer

If one wants to eliminate the embedded VP of (31d) a second application of FI on the same cycle would be required, so as to rescue $_V$[entrer]. This, however, would be grossly ad hoc. The correct solution is, obviously, to unite $_V$[faire] with the lower V into one V-island, as is done by PR.[18] This yields a doubly layered V-island on the second application of PR, and no embedded VP.

Kayne (1975:217-220) argues for the brother-adjunction of the lower V to the higher V on the grounds that in the following sentences the succession of V_1 (*faire*) and V_2 (the raised V) is interrupted, either by intervening non-V material or by CONJUNCTION REDUCTION, as in (33d). This, he maintains, shows that the two verbs cannot form one V-island:

(33)a. Fera-t-il   partir Marie?
     make-FUT-he leave Marie
     'will he get Marie to leave?'

   b. Fais-lui   lire ce livre
     make-him-DAT read this book
     'make him read this book'

   c. On ne   fera   pas partir Jean
     one NEG1 make-FUT NEG2 leave Jean
     'one will not make Jean leave'

   d. Il   a   fait boire et danser la sœur de Jean-Jacques
     he has made drink and dance the sister of Jean-Jacques
     'he made Jean-Jacques' sister drink and dance'

   e. Ils ne font sûrement pas tous boire du vin à leurs enfants
     they NEG1 make certainly NEG2 all drink wine to their children
     'they certainly do not all make their childen drink wine'

However, the occurrence of non-V material between V_1 and V_2, or of CR, can only be an argument against the assumption of a V-island if such phenomena are ruled out within V-islands by one or more well-established principles. Kayne gives none. For (33d) he appeals to 'what we would ... expect', and the other cases are implicitly left to his readers' sense of syntactic propriety. The answer in terms of Semantic Syntax is straightforward: Kayne lacks a theory of AUX as well as a proper formulation of ADVERB PLACEMENT, and is thus unable to explain (33a-c). The sentence (33d) follows directly from the SeSyn theory of CONJUNCTION REDUCTION (see section 7.3). (33e) contains the

---

[18] Although this argument was presented in great detail in Seuren (1972b) and although Seuren (1972b) was repeatedly brought to the attention of Kayne, no answer ever came forth. Kayne (1975) contains no reference. It is difficult not to interpret Kayne's apparent refusal to react as an implicit admission of defeat.

'floating' quantifier *tous* ('all'), which is probably best treated as an adverbial of class 2, and hence belongs with *sûrement* ('certainly') and *pas* (NEG2) in the same cluster. Generally speaking, it is the incompleteness and the lack of formal precision in Kayne's treatment of French syntax that have led to his rash and evidently incorrect treatment of the French *faire*-construction. There is no substance to his arguments in this respect.

To illustrate the working of PR in the theory of Semantic Syntax we shall now generate the sentences (33a), (33c) and (33e), the latter, however, without the floating quantifier *tous*, as quantifiers have not been discussed so far. Instead of *tous* we shall insert the time adverb *souvent* ('often'), so as not to appear to have too easy a ride. It will then become clear that the sentences produced by Kayne in favour of his treatment of the *faire*-construction in fact show the oppositie: these sentences cannot be generated unless PR is taken to lead to a unified V-island under a V-node. Later rules, such as QUESTION FORMATION or MINCE, will then be responsible for the cutting up of a V-island under certain conditions.

Let (33a) be derived from (34a). The shallow structure, with AUX, is (34b):

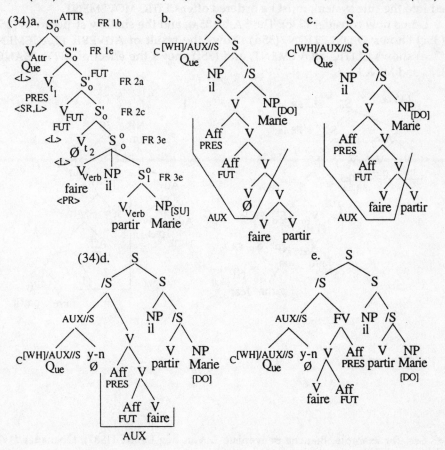

Ø-DELETION applies, eliminating $_V[Ø]$ in AUX. AUX is redefined, according to the corollary, as shown in (34c). The postcyclic rules do not contain a provision for the question morpheme Q_{ue}, since, as was said in 4.1 above, the facts of French question formation are too complex to be treated here.[19] Yet, as was indicated in connection with (8) above, one type of question is straightforward: it is generated by letting Q_{ue} right-adopt first $_{y\text{-}n}[Ø]$, then AUX, as in English QUESTION FORMATION (see 3.2.1). (This is, on the whole, allowed when the subject is pronominal, as is the case here.) The movement of AUX due to QUES-TION FORMATION would have to be placed after CLITIC MOVEMENT, as illustrated above with the question form of (8). This results in the structure (34d). AFFIX HANDLING (no MINCE) then gives the surface structure (34e).

After PR the original subject term of *partir*, $_{NP}[Marie]$, becomes the direct object of the complex verb $_V[faire\text{-}partir]$, according to the definitions in section 2.4. Ironically, in surface structure $_{NP}[Marie]$ is now the direct object of the same verb to which it is the subject term in SA. Yet, if $_{NP}[Marie]$ had been pronominal the sentence would not have been *Fera-t-il la partir* but *La fera-t-il partir*, which shows that French QUESTION FORMATION, when introduced into the rule system, must be ordered after CLITIC MOVEMENT.

Let us now consider (33c). The SA is (35a), and the shallow structure is (35b). (35c) shows Ø-DELETION. (35d) shows the result of ADVERB PLACEMENT. (35e) shows CLITIC MOVEMENT, and (35f) shows the effect of AFFIX HANDL-ING and MINCE.

(35)a. / b.

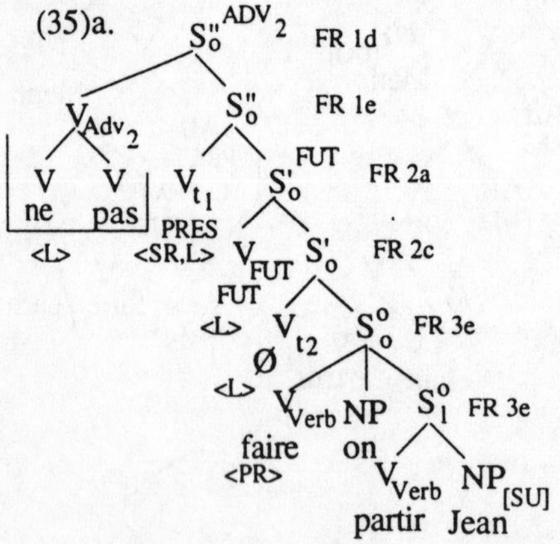

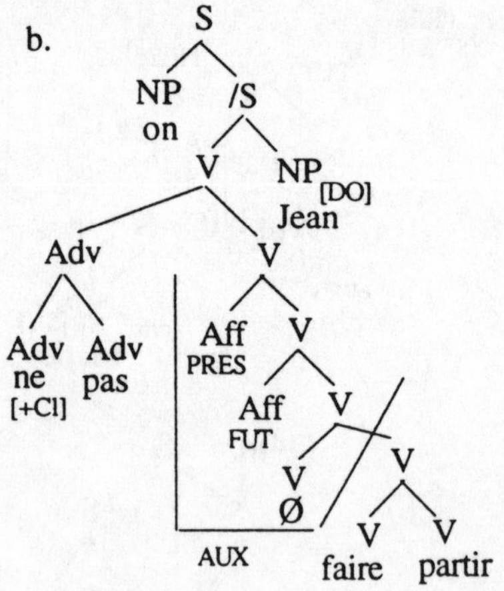

---

[19] See, for example, Blanche-Benveniste & van den Eynde (1987), Obenauer (1976), Renchon (1969).

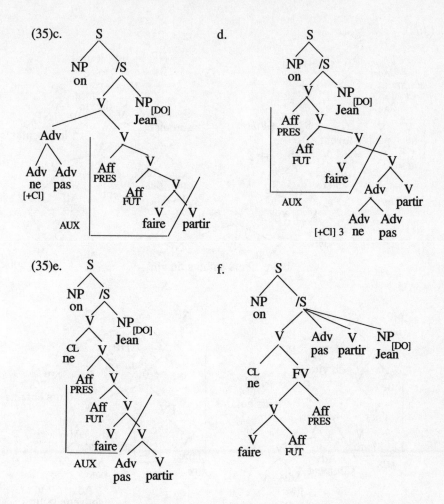

Now we consider (36a), with its SA (36b) and its shallow structure (36c):

(36)a. Ils ne font sûrement pas souvent boire du vin à leurs enfants
        they NEG1 make certainly NEG2 often drink wine to their children
        'they certainly do not make their children drink wine often'

The high adverb *sûrement* is taken to belong to the class Adv₁, specifically to the subclass that takes LOWERING either onto S (i.e. left-adoption by S) or onto the V-cluster. The latter option has been taken in (36c). Under the former option the sentence would have been *Sûrement ils ne font pas souvent boire du vin à leurs enfants*. Ø-DELETION, ADVERB PLACEMENT and CLITIC MOVEMENT give (36d). AFFIX HANDLING gives (36e). MINCE gives (36f).

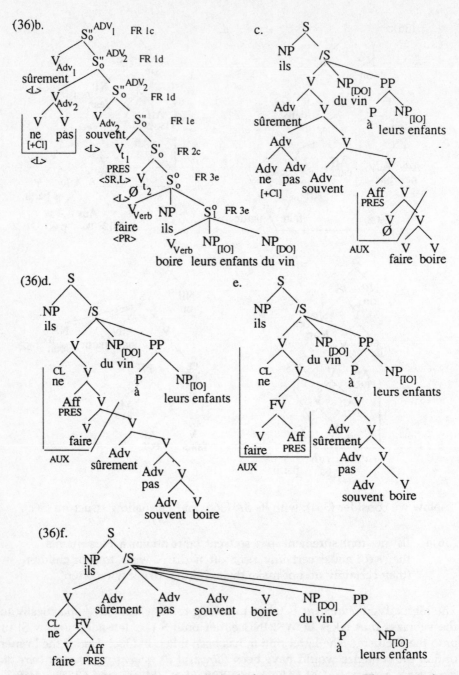

This gives the essentials of the French *faire*-construction. There are, how-ever, complications and exceptions, the most important of which we shall now discuss. First, as was observed in 2.4 note 3, the dative resulting from PR must allow for the thematic role of beneficiary. If this is not so PR is blocked: *Il*

fera atteindre son but à l'article is ungrammatical as an article is not interpretable as a beneficiary. A better expression is *Il fera de sorte que l'article
atteigne son but* ('he'll make sure that the article achieves its purpose').

Then, the 3rd person reflexive clitic pronoun *se* is often found between *faire*
and the raised V:

(37)a. Voilà ce qui a fait   se   tuer votre ami
       here is what has made himself kill your friend
       'that's what made your friend kill himself'

   b. Je l'   ai fait   s' enfuir
       I him-ACC have made himself   flee
       'I made him flee'

   c. Nous les   ferons   se   retirer   d' ici
       we them-ACC make-FUT themselves withdraw from here
       'we will get them to withdraw from here'

This is irregular, since CLITIC MOVEMENT places clitics before, not after AUX.
Kayne (1969:181) suggests that CLITIC MOVEMENT for *se* might be cyclic,
whereas the other clitic pronouns are moved postcyclically. Under this
assumption the problem seems indeed solved. But French grammarians are
unanimous in condemning sentences like (37a-c), although they admit that
they do occur. In old-fashioned, formal French reflexive *se* is often deleted
under *faire*: instead of (37b) one then finds *Je l'ai fait enfuir* ('I made him
flee'), even though the verb is *s'enfuir* ('flee, escape'). Martinon (1927:302)
regrets the modern development, with *se* between *faire* and the raised verb,
calling sentences like those in (37) 'bien peu élégants et qu'on ferait mieux
d'éviter ... qui autrefois auraient paru barbares' (quite unelegant and better
avoided ... that would have appeared barbarian in the old days).

A further interesting complication is the fact that, exceptionally, *faire*
appears to induce SR and not PR. Grevisse (1986:1317-§873) notes that one finds,
though rarely, an accusative where a dative is expected. He cites, a.o.:

(38)a. ... ces quelques mots qu' il fait NISUS adresser à son Euryale ...[20]
       ... those few words that-ACC he makes Nisus-ACC address to his Euryalus
       '... those few words that he(=Virgil) lets Nisus say to his Euryalus ...'

   b. Des nouvelles un peu moins bonnes LES firent précipiter leur départ[21]
      news a little less good them-ACC made precipitate their departure
      'slightly less good news made them hasten their departure'

These sentences are syntactically deviant, or else Grevisse would not have
quoted them. Yet they are considered good French, or else Gide would not have
been a celebrated writer. What has happened is that SR has applied instead
of PR. The question is why. Now note what (38a,b) would have been if they
had been constructed according to the book, with PR. (38a) would be either
(39a) or (39b), and (38b) would become (40):

[20] André Gide, *Journal 1942-1949*, p.306.
[21] André Gide, *La porte étroite*, p.129.

(39)a.　... ces quelques mots qu'il fait adresser à Nisus à son Euryale ...

　　b.　... ces quelques mots qu'il fait adresser à son Euryale à Nisus ...

(40)　　Des nouvelles un peu moins bonnes leur firent précipiter leur départ

In (39) one has a succession of two PPs with *à*, which is stylistically awkward and, moreover, semantically ambiguous as it is no longer clear who spoke to whom. In (40) the word *leur* occurs twice in close succession. Now *leur* is relatively heavy from the phonological point of view but light in semantic content.[22] Apparently, the French language keeps open the possibility to vary on PR for reasons of clarity or stylistic elegance. Considerations of clarity, euphony, rhythm or balance may, apparently, not only influence choices within the grammar but also outside it. This is interesting in the light of what has been said (section 2.12) about the rules of SR and PR as alternatives in complementation systems. Apparently, speakers occasionally, in order to solve certain dilemmas of expression, atavistically fall back on a universal linguistic competence.[23] (For the relatively rare cases where French uses SR for object clauses see 4.7.)

Faire is not the only verb that takes PR, though it is the best known among them. There is also *laisser* ('let, allow'), which takes PR optionally and about which more in a moment. Then there are the perception verbs *voir* ('see') and *entendre* ('hear'). Their use of PR is subject to more or less idiosyncratic restrictions. They do take PR but do not seem to like full nominal datives. With pronominal datives they are a great deal happier. Passive raised verbs are all right:

(41)a.　Je　lui　ai　vu　écrire　la lettre
　　　　I him-DAT have　seen　write　the letter
　　　　'I saw him write the letter'

　　b.　??J'　ai　vu　écrire　la lettre　à Jean
　　　　I have seen　write　the letter　to Jean
　　　　'I saw Jean write the letter'

　　c.　Je　lui　ai　entendu　chanter　la chanson
　　　　I him-DAT have　heard　sing　the song
　　　　'I heard him sing the song'

　　d.　??J'　ai　entendu　chanter　la chanson　à Jean
　　　　I have heard　sing　the song　to Jean
　　　　'I heard Jean sing the song'

---

[22] Historically it derives from the Latin genitive plural *illorum*, like the Italian *loro*. Their disproportionate phonological heaviness is no doubt the reason why *leur* and *loro* behave exceptionally in some respects.

[23] In Seuren (1990, 1995) it is shown how (French-based) Mauritian Creole more or less freely chooses between SR and PR, according to precisely the kind of considerations reflected in (38a,b): when PR would lead to NP-crowding or otherwise improperly balanced or even ambiguous constructions, SR takes over.

e. J' ai entendu chanter la chanson par Jean
   I have heard   sing   the song by Jean
   'I heard the song being sung by Jean'

A further case often mentioned in traditional grammars is the verb *envoyer* ('send'). However, whether this is a genuine case of a lexical verb inducing PR is doubtful, as it never produces datives. It does occur in more or less fixed collocations, with specialized meanings, as in *envoyer chercher* ('send for', lit. 'send seek'), or *envoyer (se) coucher* (lit. 'send sleep', in practice 'send to hell'), or *envoyer (se) promener* (lit. 'send walk', in practice, again, 'send to hell'). One thus gets sentences like:

(42)   Je l'   ai envoyé chercher
        I him-ACC have   sent seek
        'I sent for him'

Such collocations no doubt once originated as PR-constructions, but they have become semi-lexicalized, a process which is facilitated by the fact that PR gives rise to a V-island. A comparable case in English is the collocation *let go*, as in *I let go (of) the rope*, which is also clearly derived from an original PR-construction.

Not usually mentioned is *donner à* ('give to'), with the particle *à*, as in:

(43)a. J' ai donné à boire ce vin   à Pierre
       I have given to drink this wine to Pierre
       'I gave Pierre this wine to drink'

   b. Je le   lui ai donné à boire
      I it-ACC him-DAT have given to drink
      'I gave it him to drink'

In (43b) the position of the clitics shows that there is no embedded /S. SD controlled by the higher indirect object is ruled out by (43a), as this would have given the hardly felicitous *?*J'ai donné ce vin à Pierre à boire*. Note that SD in *à* + infinitival constructions is normal, as in (44a,b), where the position of the clitics reveals the presence of an embedded /S:

(44)a. Je tiens à l' écrire
       I wish to it-ACC write
       'I wish to write it'

   b. Il procéda à l' écrire
      he proceeded to it-ACC write
      'he proceeded to write it'

More cases of PR in French could perhaps be unearthed,[24] but let us now concentrate on the verb *laisser*, already briefly touched on in section 3.8.2, and

---

[24] An interesting case is (Ruwet 1991:255):
    (i)   Quelle théorie trouves-tu valoir mieux que la mienne?
            which theory find-you be-worth better than the mine
            'Which theory do you find is better than mine?'

also in 4.3.1 and 4.4.1. The entries for *laisser₁* and *laisser₂* were given in 4.2.2 as follows:

V$_{Verb}$ laisser$_1$, ...	+ NP + S°	Verb	PR
V$_{Verb}$ laisser$_2$, ...	+ NP + NP$_{x\ [DO]}$ + (S°)	Verb	SD,(PR)

It was pointed out in 3.8.2 that *laisser* follows either a RAISING or a CONTROL pattern, a pair of alternatives regularly found in other cases as well, such as English *help* and its Dutch equivalent *helpen*, as well as in verbs of beginning and continuing, and often also stopping, in a variety of languages. The pattern is for such verbs to occur with two argument frames that differ in that one (the CONTROL frame) has an NP-term more than the other, which then controls SUBJECT DELETION. Semantically they differ in that with the CONTROL frame the verb assigns a more prominent role to the extra NP-term. Both frames have a complement S° or S'. In some cases the complement-S is the subject term in the RAISING frame which contains nothing else. The CONTROL frame then adds a subject-NP, so that the embedded S becomes the object term. This is found in cases like the English verb *begin* (Perlmutter 1970), or the French verbs *continuer* and *commencer*. Note that *falloir* is exceptional in that it embeds an S" in the RAISING frame (which, therefore, does not raise) but an S° in the CONTROL frame (4.4.2). With other verbs there is an NP-subject anyway, but the RAISING frame simply has an object S° or S', whereas the CONTROL frame adds a controlling NP middle term, which then functions as direct object, not as indirect object. This is what is found in the case of French *laisser*, German *lassen*, English *help* and Dutch *helpen*. In all cases the RAISING frame induces the standard raising rule of the language, SR for English, PR for German and Dutch, PR or SR for French. The CONTROL frame induces SD, controlled by the extra NP-term, and sometimes also, optionally or obligatorily, the standard raising rule of the language.

For the generation of the sentences (65a,b) of chapter 3, repeated here as (45a,b), the reader is referred to section 3.8.2 (see also note 11 above).

(45)a. J' ai laissé tomber l'arme
      I have let fall the weapon
      'I dropped the weapon' or: 'I allowed the weapon to fall'

Unfortunately, Ruwet does not comment further on this case, which is peculiar, first, because native speakers accept it only with a grudge, and secondly because its non-WH-forms are mostly unacceptable. Both Alain Peyraube and Bernard Bichakjian inform me that neither of the non-WH-forms (ii) or (iii) of (i) is acceptable, nor are (iv) or (v) with the pronominal clitic *la*. But (vi), with the negation, seems much better (due, in Peyraube's view, to the fact that the V-cluster *trouve(s)-valoir* is interrupted by a non-V element, *pas* in (vi), the subject pronoun *tu* in (i)):

    (ii)   *Il trouve ta théorie valoir mieux que la mienne
    (iii)   *Il trouve valoir ta théorie mieux que la mienne
    (iv)   *Il trouve la valoir mieux que la mienne
    (v)   *Il la trouve valoir mieux que la mienne
    (vi)   Il ne la trouve pas valoir mieux que la mienne

Note that the position of the clitic *la* in (vi) shows that this is a PR construction, but it must be one that is subject to heavy, possibly idiosyncratic, constraints.

b. J' ai laissé l'arme   tomber
  I have let   the weapon fall
  'I allowed the weapon to fall'

4.5 Negative and other adverbs

The correct positioning of adverbs in French sentences is hard to describe, harder even than for English sentences. An attempt has been made in the lexicon of 4.2.2 to assign rule features in such a way that a decent result is obtained. The postcyclic rule of ADVERB PLACEMENT in 4.2.5 is also an attempt at getting some of the facts straight. But although the system seems to work well as far as it goes, it is still far removed from a complete and adequate coverage of the data.

For just manner adverbs, consider the following cases (the manner adverbs are in italics):

(46)a. Je mange *bien*   b. Je mange toujours *bien*
     I   eat   well

   c. J'ai *bien*   mangé   d. J'ai mangé *bien*
     I have well   eaten

   e. J'ai toujours *bien* mangé   f. J'ai toujours mangé *bien*
     I have always well   eaten

   g. Il n' a pas *bien* nourri son chat   h. Il n' a pas nourri *bien* son chat
     he NEG1 have NEG2 well fed his cat

   i. ?*Il n' a pas nourri son chat *bien* j. ?*Il n' a pas *vite* nourri son chat
     he NEG1 have NEG2 fed his cat well

   k. ?*Il n' a pas nourri *vite* son chat l. Il n' a pas nourri son chat *vite*
     he NEG1 have NEG2 fed quickly his cat

   m. Il ne   veut pas *bien* manger   n. Il ne veut pas manger *bien*
     he NEG1 want NEG2 well eat

   o. ?*Il ne veut pas *vite* manger   p. Il ne veut pas manger *vite*
     he NEG1 want NEG2 quickly eat

   q. Il ne   veut pas le faire *bien*   r. *Il ne veut pas le *bien* faire
     he NEG1 want NEG2 it do well

   s. *Il ne veut pas *bien* le faire   t. J'espère ne pas te revoir *vite*
     he NEG1 want NEG2 well it do

These facts look troublesome, and it is not difficult to complicate the picture further by providing more observations. Some manner adverbs, like *vite*, prefer being lowered to the far right of the argument-S, whereas others, like *bien*, have a preference for adoption by the V-cluster. But if *bien* is modified by, for example, *trop*, as in *trop bien* ('too well'), the preference is reversed: *Il n'a pas nourri son chat trop bien* ('he hasn't fed his cat too well') is more acceptable than (46i). Yet, phonological weight of the manner adverb does not seem a decisive factor since the phonologically light adverb *vite* usually prefers final position, whereas, e.g., *soigneusement* ('carefully') is happy in the position immediately following AUX: *Il a soigneusement préparé le repas* ('he has prepaired the meal carefully'). On the other hand, in a sentence like *Il a vite laissé tout à sa fille* ('he quickly left everything to his daughter') the adverb *vite* is hardly free to occupy any other than the post-AUX position. The whole matter is still rather opaque.

What is remarkable, in this context, is that there seems to be a correspondence with NEG2 elements like *jamais*, *rien* or *personne* (see the examples in (7) in section 4.3.1 above). There too, some, like *personne*, need to go to the far right whereas others prefer the V-cluster but also allow the far right position. It would, however, take us too far to go into these and related questions any further at this stage. The matter must be allowed to rest.

Yet despite these problems we are now in a position, in principle at least, to generate sophisticated French auxiliary constructions containing adverbs. As an example consider the sentence (47a) with the SA (47b):

(47)a. Il   n'   aurait   toujours pas dû   te   dénoncer à moi   si vite

he NEG1 have-PAST-FUT still NEG2 must-PaP you-ACC denounce to me so quickly

'he should still not have denounced you to me so quickly'

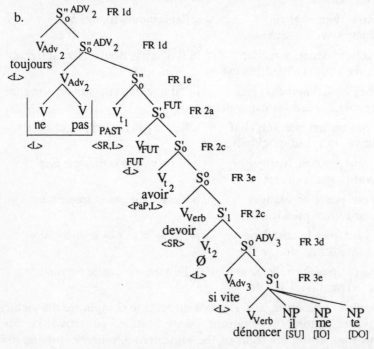

In the Cycle, DATIVE EXTRACTION applies, since the pronominal middle NP $_{NP}$[me] has a right brother which is an **A2**-pronoun: *te*. With LOWERING of *si vite*, the result is the reshaped S_1^o (47e). After SR on S_0^o its structure is as in (47f). PaP and LOWERING on S_0', and again LOWERING on $S_0'^{FUT}$ result in (47g)

for S_o''. Further cyclic treatment gives the shallow structure (47h). Ø-DELETION, AP and CM yield (47i). AH gives (47j). Mince gives (47k).

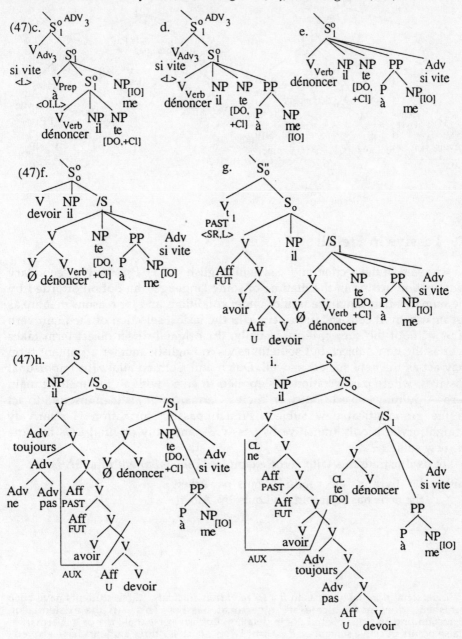

(47)j.

S — NP il — /S$_0$
V — CL ne, V
FV
V Aff PAST
V avoir, Aff FUT
AUX
/S$_1$
V — CL te [DO], V dénoncer — Adv si vite
V — Adv toujours, V
Adv pas, PaP
V devoir, Aff U
PP — P à, NP [IO] me

k.

S — NP il — /S$_0$
V — CL ne, FV — Adv toujours — Adv pas — PaP — /S$_1$
V Aff, V avoir Aff FUT, PAST
V devoir, Aff U
V Aff
V — CL te dénoncer [DO], V — Adv si vite
PP — P à, NP [IO] me

4.6 Passive in French

As was said in the section on Passive in English (3.7.1), Passive is a secondary construction arising in the lifetime of some languages, an option afforded by the human innate language faculty under conditions and for reasons that are as yet unknown. It consists, in principle, in the lexical selection of the main verb of S^0 without the subject term. Usually, the original direct object term takes over as the new subject, but sometimes, as in English, another argument term may act as the new subject as well. Dutch and German allow for impersonal passives, where passivization has applied to an S^0 with an intransitive main verb. A dummy subject (Dutch *er* 'there', German *es* 'it') is then inserted to act as the grammatical new subject. French passive formation is relatively straightforward: only transitive Ss passivize, and only original DOs become the new subject.[25]

Let us illustrate this with some examples. Take (48a) with the SA (48b):

(48)a. Le livre a   été vendu à Louis par Albert
        the book has been sold to Louis by Albert

---

[25] Impersonal *il* in passives, as in *Il a été puni trois étudiants*, 'three students have been punished', does not indicate an impersonal passive. This *il* is the existential *il*, corresponding, in principle but not in detail, to English existential *there* or to German *es*. It also occurs in active sentences: *Il est arrivé trois étudiants*, 'three students have arrived'. Whether the impersonal passive of Dutch and German actually represents higher order existential quantification over events is an interesting question which, however, we shall not take up here. Here it suffices to note that French lacks the true impersonal passive constructions of German and Dutch. French has no impersonal passive sentences of the type **Il a été dansé* ('there has been dancing').

b.

```
          S"        FR 1e
         /\
      V_t1   S'      FR 2c
     PRES   /\
    <SR.L>  V   S^o PASS   FR 3b
     avoir^t2 /\
    <PaP.L>  V   S^oPASS Prep   FR 3c
     être^Pass /\
    <PaP.L>  V   S^o  FR 3e        NP
     Prep^Pass  [PASS]          [SU_vendre]
     par                          Albert
    <OI.L>  V   NP    NP
         [Pass] [IO]  [DO]→[SU]
         vendre Louis le livre
```

In section 2.4 above definitions were given for the argument functions of 'subject' (SU), 'direct object' (DO) and 'indirect object' (IO) in terms of node connections, and it was specified that the corresponding features [SU], [DO] and [IO] are assigned automatically, as a default procedure, to argument terms of lexical verbs not already provided with an AF feature for special (lexical) reasons. The features then stick to their arguments throughout the derivation unless they are modified by some rule or procedure, such as the Passive procedure, which changes the original direct object into a grammatical subject: [DO] → [SU].

Let the verb *vendre* have the following lexical argument structure, with the regular AF features [SU], [IO], and [DO]:

$$V_{verb} \text{ vendre} \qquad\qquad + NP_{[SU]} + NP_{[IO]} + NP_{[DO]}$$

Passive selection cuts out the subject term, which recurs, in this case, as object term under the Agent Phrase preposition *par*. As was specified in section 3.1.6.2, the prepositional object (in this case: NP[Albert]) inherits the feature [SU] with respect to the verb *vendre*. This is indicated as $[SU_{vendre}]$. The features [IO] and [DO] → [SU] are attached to *Louis* and *le livre*, respectively.

Note that the feature change from from [DO] to [SU] cannot be made to depend on the position of the new subject term, i.e. to the immediate right of V. For (48) this would incorrectly have made NP[Louis] the passive subject. Even if DATIVE EXTRACTION is taken into account the result is still wrong for cases where the pronominal indirect object is not dative-extracted, as in (49). The feature change has to reach across the [IO]-term and select the original [DO]-term. This is one of the reasons why AF features are needed in the rule system.

The first cyclic rule to apply in (48b) is DATIVE EXTRACTION on NP[Louis], resulting in (48c). Then, on the S^oPASSPrep-cycle, the cyclic rules OBJECT INCORPORATION and LOWERING (to the far right) are to be applied, leading to (48d). Now PaP and LOWERING, first on the S^oPASS-cycle, then on the S'-cycle, giving (48e) and (48f), respectively. Ordinary TENSE ROUTINE then gives the shallow structure (48g). The surface structure is (48h).

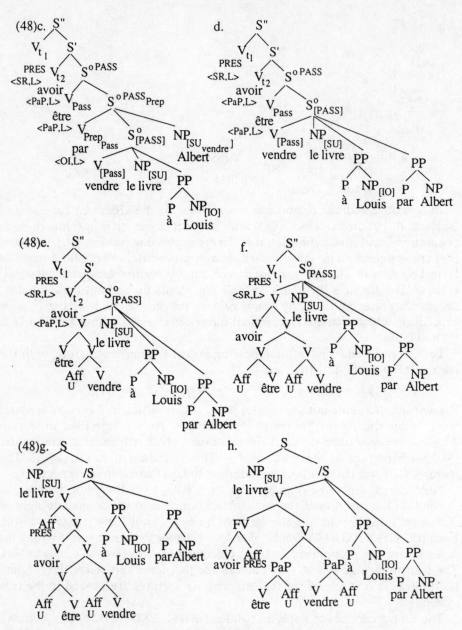

(49) runs parallel to (48), but for the treatment of the indirect object:

(49)a. Le livre   lui   a été vendu
      the book him-DAT has been sold
      'the book has been sold to him'

b.

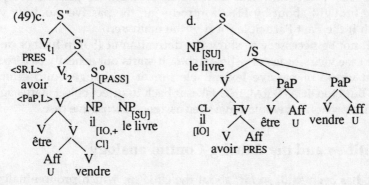

Now DATIVE EXTRACTION does not apply, so that after PaP and LOWERING on the S⁰ᴾᴬˢˢ-cycle the tree looks as in (49c). Further treatment then gives the surface structure (49d):

(49)c.   d.

Finally, we look at a case of passive embedding under *faire*. Consider the sentence:

(50)a. Il a   fait tuer le garçon par le soldat
       he has made kill the boy by the soldier
       'he had the boy killed by the soldier'

b.   ShS: c.

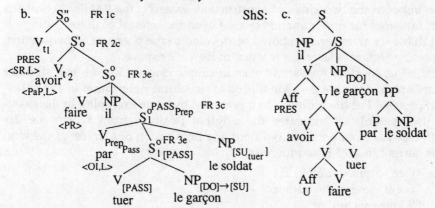

Note that, as has been said before, the verb *faire* takes an S^o-complement clause, which means, as was said in section 4.4, that the S^o-complement re-enters the Formation Rules at any of the rules (3c-e). This allows for the standard optional adverbial and/or prepositional additions of the appropriate level to be added. It also allows for the selection of the subscript feature [PASS] under the complement-S^o. In (50) this feature [PASS] results from Formation Rule (3c), but even it the Formation Rules are entered at (3e) this feature may be selected. Here FR (3c) has been activated, introducing the Agent Phrase specific for passive Ss, with the preposition *par*. This creates an $S^o_{[PASS]}$ leading to FR 3e, but with passive lexical selection, as shown.

The fact that *faire* selects for an S^o-complement clause is crucial in ensuring the lack of passive morphology in the infinitival under *faire*, since now the embedded S^o_1 enters the Formation Rules at FR 3c or 3d or 3e, but not at FR 3a or 3b, as has been said. This automatically excludes passive morphology, which is brought about by FR 3b introducing the passive auxiliary verb *être* and with it the Past Participle form of the main verb.

It will not be necessary to show the derivation of (50) in further detail. But note the case vicissitudes of $_{NP}$[le garçon]. It starts out lexically as direct object. Then, in virtue of passive lexical selection it is changed into grammatical subject. But PREDICATE RAISING takes it back to direct object status again. If it had been a pronoun it would have been assigned accusative case.

4.7 Clitic *en* and the Raising-Control analogy

Nothing has been said, so far, about the clitic *en*, which pronominalizes a PP under the preposition *de* ('of'). Ruwet (1991:56-81) has shown that *en*, cliticized from a subject head, can sometimes be used as a test to decide whether a sentence contains a RAISING or a CONTROL construction, and he finds that there are many more RAISING cases than is usually thought. He finds in particular that there is a systematic, though not fully predictable, alternation between the two kinds of construction, whereby the RAISING construction is favoured for non-human subjects. Given the interest of these findings, it is felt that a separate section should be devoted to the phenomena in question. The present section is largely a reaction to Ruwet's exposé.

First let us consider the syntax of *en* in simple clauses. Ruwet, like all other authors on *en*, does not provide a precise structural description of the cliticization process. The discussion is best preceded by some examples. In the examples the symbol 'Ø' indicates the original position from which the *de*-PrepPhrase has been removed (without any implication of a 'trace' of the kind that is current in MIT-based linguistics):

(51)a.   J' en connais l'auteur Ø
          I of-it know the author
          'I know its author'

b. L'auteur Ø en est connu
   the author of-it is known
   'its author is known'

c. J'en suis [content Ø / coupable Ø / l'auteur Ø]
   I of-it am [happy   / guilty   / the author]
   'I am [happy about it / guilty of it / its author]

d. Max lui   en a   parlé Ø
   Max to-him of-it has spoken
   'Max has spoken to him about it'

e. Max en a   donné la clef Ø au   portier
   Max of-it has given the key   to the porter
   'Max has given its key to the porter'

f. Max (*en) a   donné la clef au   portier Ø
   Max (of-it) has given the key to the porter
   'Max has given the key to porter (of it)'

g. L'auteur Ø (*en) a   ri
   the author (of-it) has laughed
   'its author has laughed'

h. La cheminée Ø (*en) penche   (Ruwet 1991:57)
   the chimney   (of-it) leans
   'its chimney leans'

i. La préface Ø (*en) intéresse Max   (Ruwet 1991:57)
   the preface   (of-it) interests Max
   'its preface interests Max'

Facts like these are to some extent puzzling. They can be formally treated in terms of Semantic Syntax only up to a point. The main difficulty lies in the delimitation of the class of predicates that allow cliticization of *en* from a subject head: it is all right in (51b), with the predicate *être connu* ('be known'), but not in (51g,h), with the predicates *rire* ('laugh') or *pencher* ('lean'). This particular problem will be taken up below. For the moment, we can state the following principles:

(i)   A PP under a head noun or a head predicate with $_{Prep}$[de] and a non-human pronominal object NP is replaced, during the cycle at which the PP is formed, with $_{Pro}$[en].

(ii) If $_{Pro}$[en] stands under a head noun it is detached from its head noun and forms a separate constituent $_{Pro}$[en] to the immediate right of its head and marked [+Cl]. If the NP is RAISED by SR or otherwise moved $_{Pro}$[en] stays behind.

(iii) $_{Pro}$[en] is cliticized postcyclically before the other clitics if its original head is the main predicate or the head noun of the direct object to the main predicate. If the original head is the head noun of the subject to the main predicate cliticization of $_{Pro}$[en] is possible only if the predicate is intransitive. In that case it is, moreover, subject to heavy restrictions regarding the main predicate (about which more below). When $_{Pro}$[en] is not cliticized it is deleted.

The procedure is illustrated as follows. Consider (52), which derives (51a):

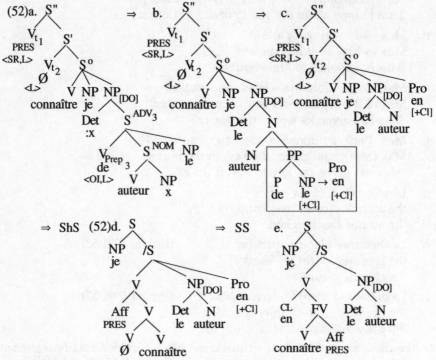

(51b) is derived as in (53) (the predicate *être connu* is of the right category):

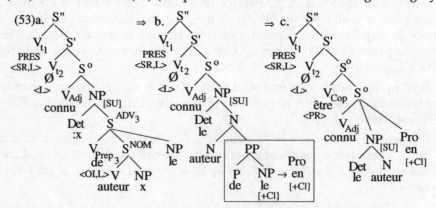

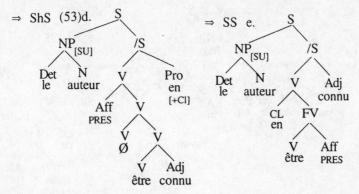

(51c) goes as in (54):

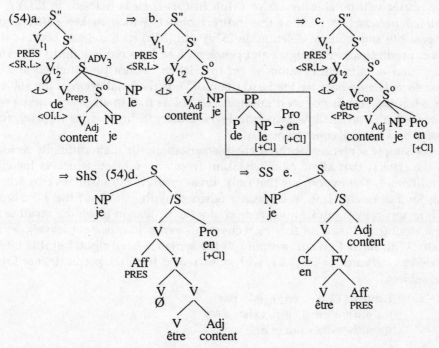

Then, (51d) is derived in (55):

⇒ (55)c. S'' ⇒ ShS d. S ⇒ SS e. S

(syntactic tree diagrams)

⇒ (55)c. S''
  V$_{t_1}$ — S'
  PRES
  ⟨SR,L⟩ V$_{t_2}$ — S⁰
  avoir
  ⟨L⟩ V — NP NP Pro
  parler Max le en
  [IO, [+Cl]
  +Cl]

⇒ ShS d. S
  NP — /S
  Max
  V NP Pro
  le [IO, en
  +Cl] [+Cl]
  Aff V
  PRES
  V V
  avoir
  Aff V
  U parler

⇒ SS e. S
  NP — /S
  Max
  V PaP
  CL V V Aff
  le parler U
  [IO]
  CL FV
  en
  V Aff
  avoir PRES

After this demonstration of the cliticization process of *en* in simple cases the reader will be able to derive (51e). In (51f-i) *en* is deleted. In (51f) it is deleted because its head is the indirect object, which makes cliticization impossible and leads to deletion. In (51g) and (51h) *en* is deleted because the main predicates *rire* ('laugh') and *pencher* ('lean') do not belong to the category that admits cliticisation of *en*. In (51i) *en* cannot be cliticized and is therefore deleted because the head noun of *en* is the head noun of the subject term but the verb is not used intransitively. Note that in all cases where *en* is cliticized it is, at shallow structure level, either /S-final or, as in (51e), followed by a non-NP constituent.

For simple sentences, without complementation, the main difficulty resides in the criteria that allow *en*-cliticization from the subject, which is heavily conditioned. The hypothesis that only 'unaccusative' intransitive verbs admit this kind of *en*-cliticization is quickly falsified: with just about the most typical 'unaccusative' intransitive verb *exister* ('exist'), as in (56a), the result is at best doubtful. Likewise for 'unaccusative' verbs like *partir* ('leave'), as in (56b). With *sortir* ('go out, get out of') the sentence is all right, but it is interpreted as indicated in (56c), i.e. with *en* extracted from the predicate, not from the subject:

(56)a.   *?L'auteur Ø n' en existe pas
     the author NEG1 of-it exist NEG2
     'its author does not exist'

   b.   *?L'auteur Ø en est parti
     the author of-it is left
     'its author has left'

   c.   L'auteur (*Ø) en est sorti Ø
     the author of-it is gone out
     'the author has got out of it'

The successful cases mostly involve adjectives, but not all adjectives will do, and some only in some positions. For example, *riche* in (57a) seems infelicitous. Yet in (57b) it is all right:

(57)a. *?L'auteur   en est riche
          the author of-it is rich
          'its author is rich'

  b.   L'auteur   en est devenu riche
          the author of-it is become rich
          'its author has become rich'

It is hard to give the right answer to this question. Perhaps the following tentative principle will turn out to stand further scrutiny. The assumption would be that *en*-cliticization from the subject *is allowed only when the predicate bears on the function of the referent expressed by the subject term*, and is not just an extraneous contingent property. Thus, (51b) is understood as implying that the author is well-known *as the author of the work in question*, not for other, unrelated reasons. Likewise, (57b) implies that the author has become rich *from the proceeds of the work he wrote*, not because of other, unrelated windfalls. Where *en* is better left out it is felt that the predicate has no functional relation to the quality expressed in the subject term, as in (51g) and (51h). If there is indeed such a principle determining the admissibility of *en*-cliticization from the subject term we have a clear case of external, cognitive conditioning of a rule of grammar. This would mean that the grammatical machinery will be able to reflect native judgements only if it encompasses a formal treatment of the cognitive factors involved, a requirement that is unrealistic given the present state of the art.

Leaving this problem aside, we can now proceed to complementation cases. Consider the following sentences:

(58)a. L'auteur Ø semble en être génial   (Ruwet 1991:57)
          the author seems of-it be a genius
          'its author seems to be a genius'

  b.   La préface Ø menace de ne jamais en être publiée   (ibidem:61)
          the preface threatens to not ever of-it be published
          'its preface threatens never to be published'

  c.   La solution Ø commence à en être connue   (ibidem:62)
          the solution   begins to of-it be known
          'its solutions begins to be known'

  d.   Je soupçonne la solution Ø d'en être fausse   (ibidem:64)
          I suspect the solution to of-it be false
          'I suspect its solution to be incorrect'

  e.   La seconde partie n' est pas digne d' en être publiée   (ibidem:65)
          the second part NEG1 is NEG2 worthy to of-it be published
          'its second part is not worthy of publication'

(59)a. J'en soupçonne le chef Ø de ne pas être intègre   (ibidem:64)
          I of-it suspect the head to NEG1 NEG2 be honest
          'I suspect the head (of it) of not being honest'

    b. Le fondateur Ø en est digne d'être statufié de son vivant (ibidem:65)
       the founder   of-it is worthy to be sculpted at his living
       'its founder is worthy of being sculpted while still alive'

    c. L'intérieur Ø en est difficile à améliorer
       the interior of-it is difficult to improve
       'its interior is hard to improve'

The sentences of (58) and (59) differ systematically in that the former place *en* with the embedded /S while the latter place it with the main /S. As was shown in 4.3.1 and 4.4.1-4.4.3, clitics in modern French are left-adopted by the V of their own /S. Since *en* in (58a-e) is extracted from the surface main subject term its position with the embedded /S can be accounted for only if it is assumed that the main surface subject originates as the subject of an embedded S and has been raised through SR. That is, (58a) is derived as in (60):

(60)c. — ⇒ d. — ⇒ e. — ⇒

[syntactic tree diagrams for (60)c, d, e with nodes including S''_0, V_{t_1} PRES <SR,L>, $\emptyset_{t_2}$ <L>, sembler <SR>, être <PR>, V_{Adj} génial, NP[SU], Det le N auteur, Pro en [+Cl], V_{Cop}, être génial]

ShS (60)f. — ⇒ SS g.

[syntactic tree diagrams for (60)f and (60)g with nodes including S, NP[SU] Det le N auteur, $/S_0$, $/S_1$, Aff PRES, sembler, Pro en [+Cl], être génial, FV, CL en]

The other sentences of (58) are derived in analogous ways, always with SR induced by the main verb. Note that (58d) must be a case of SR from an object clause. It cannot be a CONTROL construction, since that requires *en* to be placed with the main verb, as in (59a). Moreover, the semantics that goes with CONTROL constructions is inappropriate for (58d): there is no implication that the solution is suspected of anything evil, in the way that the chef in (59a) is suspected of something evil. The raising in (58d) cannot be PREDICATE RAISING, as that would again land *en* with the main verb, not in the subordinate /S. Only SR gives the correct structure. Besides *soupçonner* ('suspect'), Ruwet mentions (1991:268) *empêcher* ('prevent') as a verb inducing SR, besides SD, from its object clause. SD is present in (61a), SR in (61b):

(61)a. La censure en a empêché l'éditeur Ø de publier ce livre
the censorship of-it has prevented the publisher to publish this book
'censorship has prevented its publisher to publish this book'

b. La censure a empêché la préface Ø d'en être publiée
the censorship has prevented the preface to of-it be published
'censorship has prevented its preface from being published'

In (61a) *l'éditeur* is the direct object of *empêcher*, controlling SUBJECT DELETION in the complement clause. There is thus no reason for *en* to appear in the lower /S. This is, likewise, the reason why *en* in (59a) appears with the main verb and not in the lower /S. In (61b) *la préface* is the grammatical subject of the passive embedded object clause, raised into the main clause by SR but leaving ₚᵣₒ[en] behind to be cliticised in the lower /S.

In (59b) *en* is cliticised in the main clause, again because it has been detached from the controlling main clause subject, whose predicate *digne* induces SD. (59b) contrasts with (58e), where SR from the embedded subject clause must have taken place. This shows that the adjective *digne* ('worthy') occurs with both a CONTROL and a RAISING frame, with SR as the RAISING rule. Ruwet lists quite a number of adjectives and verbs that show this double patterning, though, admittedly, native judgements vary a good deal. Apart from the common *continuer (à)* ('continue') and *commencer (à)* ('begin'), he mentions e.g. *prêt (à)* ('ready'), *foutu (de)* ('doomed'), *risquer (de)* ('risk'), *promettre (de)* ('promise'), *prétendre* ('claim'), *s'avérer* ('turn out'), *donner l'impression (de)* ('give the impression'), *attendre (de)* ('wait'), *admettre (de)* ('admit, allow'), *exiger (de)* ('demand'), *réussir (à)* ('manage'). The list is surprising in that many of these predicate seem to require a human or at least an animate subject. In fact, when the subject is human (animate), the CONTROL version is preferred or even mandatory, which suggests that the CONTROL reading is the default.

Surprisingly, the adjectives *facile* ('easy') and *difficile* ('difficult'), not discussed by Ruwet, do not seem to allow for a RAISING frame: any occurrence of *en* with the embedded /S is rejected by native speakers. The only correct form for a sentence like (59c) is (59c), i.e. with a CONTROL frame. (62), which results from a RAISING analysis, is rejected by all informants:

(62)   *L'intérieur Ø est difficile à en améliorer

In this respect, French differs from English, Dutch, German and other languages, assuming that the RAISING analysis standardly proposed for the corresponding adjectives in those languages is indeed correct.

The modals *pouvoir* ('can') and *devoir* ('must'), on the other hand, seem to allow only for a RAISING analysis. Ruwet (1991:81) accepts only (63a), not (63b), no matter whether the interpretation is epistemic or agentive:

(63)a.   Les responsables Ø doivent en   être compétents
         the executives   must of-it be competent
         'its executives must be competent'

   b.   *Les responsables Ø en doivent être compétents

This confirms the treatment given to the modals in this book: although the difference between epistemic and agentive modals (and possibly further varieties) is fully recognized the syntax appears to be the same.

Quite a few questions still remain to be answered. Yet it seems that the central elements of the machinery are there now. Ruwet's worries about cognitive factors ('human experience') (co)determining the applicability of syntactic rules appear entirely justified, but a closer, more formal analysis has hopefully taken away some of the anxiety and provided a greater insight.

CHAPTER 5

The Dutch auxiliary and complementation system

5.1 Preliminary comparative observations

The syntax of Dutch, as of English and French, is unambiguously right-branching: LOWERING always takes LEFT ADOPTION and PREDICATE RAISING takes RIGHT ADOPTION. The morphological structures are, as in the other two languages, predominantly left-branching.

In SAs the middle position between the two tenses is not filled: all modal verbs function as full main verbs. Passive differs in that intransitive action verbs are also passivizable. Moreover, unlike English, only original direct objects can become subjects of passive sentences (though colloquial Dutch allows prepositional objects as passive subjects, complete with preposition stranding).

No adverbial is lowered onto the lower V. They all go to the far right, but for the Adv_0-class, which takes left-adoption by S. Dutch and German far-right LOWERING differs from English and French in that an adverbial lowered earlier to the far right may not be crossed (this restriction guarantees the mapping of scope onto left-to-right ordering — see section 7.1). As in English and French, no LOWERING is admitted across an embedded S or /S.

In the complementation system, Dutch is an exclusively PR-language: SR only occurs with the highest tense operator in the auxiliary system.

As regards the Postcycle, main clause constituent FRONTING is common, as in German. FRONTING is topic-sensitive but less marked for non-/S constituents than for /S-constituents, where it implies contrast. All FRONTING brings along subject-AUX inversion, which leads to the famous V-second constraint for Dutch and Geman. A distinction exists between the Adv_0-class, which are left-adopted by S, and the lower adverbial classes, which take far-right LOWERING. The latter are easily fronted, always with subject-AUX inversion. The former always occur initially, without inversion.

Then, in both German and Dutch, the non-AUX (non-finite) part of the V-cluster is moved to the far right in main clauses, and the whole V-cluster in subordinate clauses, with some restrictions. This is taken care of by the post-cyclic rule of V-FINAL. Finally, Dutch has a special postcyclic rule, END CLUSTER ARRANGEMENT (ECA), for verbal end-clusters.

It has been claimed (Koster 1975) that Dutch and German are underlyingly SOV (see 1.3.2). While certain elements in Dutch and German seem to be vestiges of an old SOV stage (all Indo-European languages were once SOV), it appears counterproductive to assume underlying SOV order for modern Dutch and German. This point is taken up in section 5.8 of this chapter.

Most other syntactic differences are due to the lexicon or to minor details in the rules.

5.1.1 The tenses

The grammatical composition of the Dutch tenses is that of all European languages: the double tense system, with the rough semantics as explained in section 2.11. We shall not go into the fine semantics, as it is the grammar that counts here, not the semantics (but see section 7.5).

In Dutch, the PaP-rule does not operate when, at the cycle where the perfective auxiliary is lowered, the main verb is part of a V-cluster and has a right brother in the V-cluster labelled 'V'. In that case it stays infinitival, the well-known 'infinitivus pro participio' from traditional grammar. German has a similar phenomenon, discussed in section 6.2.

Like French and German, Dutch has two perfective auxiliaries, *hebben* ('have') and *zijn* ('be'). The choice depends largely on the main verb. A rough but far from adequate principle is that state or process verbs (including verbs of movement) take *zijn* and action verbs (including causatives) take *hebben*.[1] Sometimes the same verb can be used with either, but with a semantic difference. Thus, (1a) and (b) are both good Dutch, but their meanings differ. In (1a) the main verb *klimmen* ('climb') is used as a verb of movement, and thus expresses a process, whereas in (1b) it is used as an action verb:

(1)a. Ik ben in de boom geklommen   b.   Ik heb in de boom geklommen
     I am in the tree climbed   I have in the tree climbed
     'I (have) climbed into the tree'   'I (have) climbed in the tree'

It has so far proved impossible to present a general principle determining the correct perfective auxiliary choice. One of the reasons for this is the fact that the languages that distinguish between a *have*-type and a *be*-type perfective auxiliary do so in similar but far from identical ways. In German for example, the auxiliary *sein* ('be') is sometimes used where Dutch has *hebben* ('have'), as is shown in the semantically equivalent sentences (1c) and (1d):

(1)c. Ik heb hard gereden   d.   Ich bin schnell gefahren
     I have fast driven   I am fast driven
     'I have driven fast'   'I have driven fast'

In any case, therefore, if there is a general principle it cannot be the same for all languages concerned. Yet to deny the existence of a general principle would go too far. Native speakers of each of the languages in question have a 'feel' for the right choice, and foreign learners quickly develop one, which suggests that there is a general principle, with room for variation. In other words, the data suggest a parametrized general principle. Yet neither the parameters nor the precise values have so far been discovered. Possibly, a fine analysis of the data together with an adequate theory of lexical meaning will show the parameters and the values. But no such lexical meaning theory is available as yet. We therefore have to leave the issue open. For the moment we will, as we did

---

[1] It has been said that true intransitive verbs, the 'unaccusatives' (see 1.3.3) take *zijn* and quasi-intransitives or 'unergatives' take *hebben*. This is, however, easily shown to be inaccurate. See Ruwet (1991:143-170) for a falsification of a similar claim for French (see also section 4.1.1).

for French and German, simply mark those verbs that (normally) take *zijn* (or its equivalent) in the lexicon with an asterisk.

5.1.2 The modals and futuricity

Unlike English, the Dutch modal predicates do not occupy the position of a middle tense but are full lexical verbs. Unlike French, there is no morphological middle tense to express the future. Unlike German, there is no special modal for the future tense, occupying the middle tense position. Dutch has settled for the simplest way of expressing modalities, including futuricity: they are all expressed by means of lexical main verbs. These take a subject-S' and induce the cyclic rule of PREDICATE RAISING. Futuricity in particular is expressed (if at all) by means of the lexical main verb *zullen* accompanied by an embedded S' as subject term and inducing PR.

5.1.3 The MAUX-verb *vallen (te)* and the full verb *zijn (te)*

So far, only one middle auxiliary or MAUX-verb (see 2.11) has come to light in Dutch, the verb *vallen (te)*, meaning 'be humanly possible' or 'be feasible' (lit. 'fall'). It has the features of a MAUX-verb: it only occurs in the simple present or past, never in the perfective tenses and never as an infinitival embedding, and it takes an S⁰-complement. It contrasts with the synonymous verb *zijn (te)* whose paradigm is complete:

(2)a. Dit valt te doen   Dit is te doen
     this falls to do   this is to do
           'it is humanly possible to do this'

   b. Dit viel niet te doen   Dit was niet te doen
     this fell not to do   this was not to do
           'it was not humanly possible to do this'

   c. Dit viel vlug te doen   Dit was vlug te doen
     this fell quickly to do   this was quickly to do
          'it was humanly possible to do this quickly'

   d. *Dit is nooit te doen gevallen   Dit is nooit te doen geweest
     this is never to do fallen   this is never to do been
          'it has never been humanly possible to do this'

   e. *Dit moet te doen vallen   Dit moet te doen zijn
     this must to do fall   this must to do be
          'it must be humanly possible to do this'

   f. *Dit valt gedaan te hebben   *Dit is gedaan te hebben
     this falls done to have   this is done to have
          'it is humanly possible for this to have been done'

   g. *Dit moet te doen gevallen zijn   Dit moet te doen geweest zijn
     this must to do fallen   be   this must to do been be
          'it must have been humanly possible to do this'

Both *vallen (te)* and *zijn (te)* subcategorize for a passive tenseless embedded S^o, i.e. $S^o_{[PASS]}$. The embedded S cannot be tensed: both forms of (2f) are ungrammatical. Negation, as in (2b), is to be construed with the main verb, *viel* or *was*, not with the infinitival. Yet the manner adverb *vlug* ('quickly'), as in (2c), is naturally construed with the infinitival. This shows that the embedded S is S^o, not S'. The ungrammaticality of (2e) and (2g) for *vallen (te)*, but not for *zijn (te)*, is due to the fact that *moeten* ('must') subcategorizes for an S'-embedding. As the Formation Rules show, there is no way of getting from S' to S^oMAUX. This confirms the MAUX-status of *vallen (te)*.

The fact that the embedded S is S^o explains the absence of passive morphology: S^o-complements re-enter the Formation Rules at any of (3c-f), not at (3b), which produces passive morphology (see 4.6 for an analogue in the French *faire*-construction).

Moreover, *vallen (te)* and *zijn (te)* disallow a passive Agent Phrase under the preposition *door* ('by') in the embedded S, as shown in (3a). Instead, the semantic subject of the embedded S can be expressed by means of a level 2 PrepPhrase under the preposition *voor* ('for'), as in (3b), but this PP modifies the main verb, *vallen (te)* or *zijn (te)*, not the embedded passive S^o. In this respect they behave exactly like the *easy*-class in English (see 3.8.3). In S^o-embeddings not lexically specified for the feature [PASS] but allowing for this feature to be added the Agent Phrase is not blocked, as shown in (3c):

(3)a. *Dit valt niet te doen door een kind *Dit is niet te doen door een kind
  this falls not to do by a child   this is not to do by a child
   'it is not humanly possible for this to be done by a child

 b. Dit valt niet te doen voor een kind Dit is niet te doen voor een kind
  this falls not to do for a child   this is not to do for a child
   'it is not humanly possible for a child to do this'

 c. Ik zal mijn wagen door Jan laten repareren
  I will my car by Jan make repair
  'I will have my car repaired by Jan'

For *zijn (te)* this is explained by the fact that the embedded S^o carries the subscript feature [PASS] as part of its lexical specification. As stipulated in 3.8, a complement-$S^o_{[PASS]}$ is not allowed to enter any Formation Rule that assigns the subscript feature [PASS] to an argument-S. This means that a complement-$S^o_{[PASS]}$ cannot enter FR (3c) (nor, of course, rule (3b)), but it can still enter (3d-f). For *vallen (te)*, which is a MAUX-verb, this restriction is expressed in FR (3a). See section 5.6 below for further discussion of *zijn (te)*.

Let us now pass on to the actual rule system.

5.2 Some basic machinery

5.2.1 The main Formation Rules

(1)a. $S''ADV_0 \rightarrow V_{Adv_0} + S''ATTR / S''ADV_1 / S''$

or: $V_{Prep_0} + S''ATTR / S''ADV_1 / S'' + NP$

or b. $S''ATTR \rightarrow V_{Attr} + S''ADV_1 / S''$

or c. $S''ADV_1 \rightarrow V_{Adv_1} + S''ADV_1 / S''$

or: $V_{Prep_1} + S''ADV_1 / S'' + NP$

or: $V_Q + _{NP}[\hat{}x + S''ADV_1 / S''] + NP$

or d. $S'' \qquad \rightarrow V_{t_1} + S'ADV_2 / S' / S^oMAUX$

(2)a. $S'ADV_2 \rightarrow V_{Adv_2} + S'ADV_2 / S'$

or: $V_{Prep_2} + S'ADV_2 / S' + NP$

or: $V_Q + _{NP}[\hat{}x + S'ADV_2 / S'] + NP$

b. $S' \qquad \rightarrow V_{t_2} + S^oPASS / S^oADV_3 / S^oDEX / S^o$

(3)a. $S^oMAUX \rightarrow V_{Maux} + S^{oADV_3}_{[PASS]} / S^{oDEX}_{[PASS]} / S^o_{[PASS]}$

b. $S^oPASS \rightarrow V_{Pass} + S^oPASSPrep / S^{oADV_3}_{[PASS]} / S^{oDEX}_{[PASS]} / S^o_{[PASS]}$

c. $S^oPASSPrep \rightarrow V_{PrepPass} + S^{oADV_3}_{[PASS]} / S^{oDEX}_{[PASS]} / S^o_{[PASS]} + NP_{[SU_{V_{LEX}}]}$

d. $S^oADV_3 \rightarrow V_{Adv_3} + S^oADV_3 / S^oDEX / S^o$

or: $V_{Prep_3} + S^oADV_3 / S^oDEX / S^o + NP$

e. $S^oDEX \rightarrow V_{PrepDex} + S^o_{[DEX]} + NP_{[IO_{V_{LEX}}]}$

f. $S^o \qquad \rightarrow V_{LEX} + <\text{lex.arg.frame}>$ or: $V_{NP} + NP$

(4)a. $NP \rightarrow :x / \hat{}x + S^{NOM}$ or: x or: X_{QU}

b. $S^{NOM} \rightarrow V_{Nom} + NP[x]$ or: $V_{Adj} + S^{NOM}$

5.2.2 Some lexicon

SA-cat	Fillers	Surface cat	Cyclic rules
V_{Adv_0}	en, want, maar, dus, bovendien, daarom, ...	Adverb	L_S
V_{Attr}	Q_{ue}, Foc, ...	X: see 3.2.1; 5.2.6	L_S
V_{Adv_1}	dus, gelukkig, morgen, gisteren,	Adverb	L_{right}
V_{Adv_2}	dus, gelukkig, morgen, gisteren, bovendien, misschien, vaak, daarom, altijd, bijna, nooit, reeds, †niet, †al, ...[2]	Adverb	L_{right}

[2] For the meaning of † see LOWERING and FRONTING in 5.2.3 and 5.2.5, respectively.

V_{Adv3}	vlug, goed, slecht, zorgvuldig, daar, hier, ...	Adverb	L_{right}
V_{Prep0}	wat betreft, ...	Prep	OI, L_S
V_{Prep1}	wat betreft, in, met, tijdens, naar, ...	Prep	OI, L_{right}
V_{Prep2}	in, met, voor, tijdens, naar, zonder, ...	Prep	OI, L_{right}
V_{Prep3}	in, met, op, voor, aan,...	Prep	OI, L_{right}
$V_{PrepPass}$	door	Prep	OI, L_{right}
V_{t1}	PRES, PAST	Affix $(AH \rightarrow FV)^3$	SR, L_V
V_{t2}	Ø	Verb	L_V
	hebben/zijn	Verb	PaP, L_V
V_{Maux}	vallen	Verb	PR
V_{Pass}	*worden	Verb	PaP, L_V
V_{Cop}	*zijn	Verb	PR, [-te]
V_Q	ieder, elk, een, sommige, de meeste, ...	Det	OI, L_{var}

V_{LEX}:

SA-cat	Fillers	Argument frame	Surface cat	Cyclic rules
V_{Nom}	huis, kat, kind, muis, boek, tafel, vrouw, man, ...	+ NP	Noun	— —
V_{Adj}	klein, rood, oud, rond, groot, ...	+ NP	Adj	— —
V_{Adj}	trouw, bekend, ...	+ NP (+ $NP_{[IO]}$)	Adj	— —
V_{Adj}	waarschijnlijk, mogelijk, waar, ...	+ $NP/_{NP}[S'']$	Adj	— —
V_{Adj}	makkelijk$_1$, moeilijk$_1$, onmogelijk$_1$, ...	+ $NP/S'_{ø[PASS]}$	Adj	PR
V_{Adj}	makkelijk$_2$, moeilijk$_2$, onmogelijk$_2$, ...	+ NP_x + $S'_{ø[PASS]}$	Adj	SD
V_{Verb}	lachen, slapen, rennen, wachten, ...	+ NP	Verb	— —
V_{Verb}	*gaan$_1$, *komen$_1$, *vertrekken, ...	+ NP	Verb	— —
V_{Verb}	eten, drinken, schrijven, ...	+ NP (+ NP)	Verb	— —
V_{Verb}	bedriegen, $_V[_V[eten]_{VPrt}[op]]$, ...	+ NP + NP	Verb	— —
V_{Verb}	geven, verkopen, ...	+ NP (+ NP) + NP	Verb	— —
V_{Verb}	$_V[_V[stellen]_{VPrt}[voor]]$, ...	+ NP + NP + NP	Verb	— —
V_{Verb}	schijnen, lijken, ...	+ S'/S''	Verb	PR
V_{Verb}	*beginnen$_1$, ...	+ $S'_ø$	Verb	PR
V_{Verb}	*beginnen$_2$, ...	+ NP_x + $S'_ø$	Verb	SD, (PR)
V_{Verb}	helpen$_1$, laten$_1$, ...	+ NP + S^o	Verb	[-te], PR

^{3} With the postcyclic rule of AFFIX HANDLING the V-node directly above Aff is relabelled FV ('finite verb').

V_{Verb}	helpen$_2$, ...	$+ NP + NP_{x[DO]} + (S^o)$	Verb	$SD/[SD,[\text{-te}],PR]$
V_{Verb}	laten$_2$, ...	$+ NP + NP_{x[DO]} + S'_\emptyset$	Verb	$SD,[\text{-te}],PR$
V_{Verb}	doen, ...	$+ NP + S'_\emptyset$	Verb	$[\text{-te}],PR$
V_{Verb}	leren$_1$ ('learn'), ...	$+ NP_x + NP/S'_\emptyset/_{NP}[S'']$	Verb	$SD/[SD,[\text{-te}],PR]$
V_{Verb}	leren$_2$ ('teach'), ...	$+ NP + NP_x + NP/S'_\emptyset/_{NP}[S'']$	Verb	$SD/[SD,[\text{-te}],PR]$
V_{Verb}	geloven, ...	$+ NP_x + NP/S'/_{(NP)}[S'']$	Verb	SD
V_{Verb}	denken, ...	$+ NP_x + (S'_\emptyset/S'')$	Verb	SD
V_{Verb}	weten (-Pass), ...	$+ NP + S^o/_{NP}[S'']/_{NP}[Q_{ue}+S'']$	Verb	PR
V_{Verb}	willen (-Pass), ...	$+ NP_x + NP/S'_\emptyset/S''$	Verb	$SD,[\text{-te}],PR$
V_{Verb}	besluiten, ...	$+ NP_x + S'_\emptyset/_{NP}[S'']$	Verb	SD
V_{Verb}	verkiezen, ...	$+ NP_x + NP/S'_\emptyset/_{NP}[S'']$	Verb	SD
V_{Verb}	verzoeken, ...	$+ NP + NP_x + S'_\emptyset$	Verb	SD
V_{Verb}	beloven, ...	$+ NP_x + NP + NP/S'_\emptyset/_{NP}[S'']$	Verb	SD
V_{Verb}	proberen, trachten (-Pass), ...	$+ NP_x + S'_\emptyset$	Verb	$SD,(PR)$
V_{Verb}	moeten, kunnen, zullen, ...	$+ S'$	Verb	$[\text{-te}],PR$
V_{Verb}	lopen, zitten, liggen, staan, ...	$+ NP_x + (S^o)$	Verb	SD,PR^4
V_{Verb}	*zijn$_1$	$+ S^o_{[PASS]}$	Verb	$PR{\rightarrow}Adj^5$
V_{Verb}	*zijn$_2$, *gaan$_2$, *komen$_2$, ...	$+ NP_x + S^o$	Verb	$SD,[\text{-te}],PR$
V_{Verb}	*komen$_3$, ...	$+ NP_x + S^o$	Verb	SD,PR
V_{Verb}	verbieden, ...	$+ NP + NP_{x[DO]} + S^o$	Verb	SD
V_{Verb}	zien$_1$, horen$_1$, ...	$+ NP + NP/S^o/_{(NP)}[S'']/_{NP}[Q_{ue}+S'']$	Verb	$[\text{-te}],PR$
V_{Verb}	zien$_2$, horen$_2$, ...	$+ NP + NP_{x[DO]} + S'_\emptyset$	Verb	$SD,[\text{-te}],PR$

5.2.3 Cyclic rules

The rules of the Cycle are identical to those of 3.1.3, except for lexical differences: (a) The rule IT is now called HET, and $_{NP}$[het] is inserted. (b) For DATIVE EXTRACTION V_{Prep}[aan] is inserted. (c) For COPULA INSERTION V_{Cop}[zijn] is inserted. LOWERING to the far right is subject to stricter conditions than those for English and French (probably as a result of the large number of cases where L_{right} applies in Dutch). The conditions are stated as follows:

L_{right} does not cross an embedded S or /S, nor an adverbial to the right of V. An Adv$_2$ not marked † and lowered by L_{right} may stop before NP$_{[DO]}$.

The rule PAST PARTICIPLE is subject to a V-cluster condition:

PAST PARTICIPLE:
The highest lexically filled non-spine V-node in the V-cluster of the argument-S right-adopts $_{Aff}$[EN]. With postcyclic AFFIX HANDLING the V-node directly above Aff is relabelled 'PaP'. If the right brother of PaP is label-

---

[4] The particle *te* is preferably deleted when the verbs *lopen, liggen, zitten, staan* fall outside AUX after the postcyclic rule of Ø-DELETION.
[5] With the application of PR, the raised element is relabelled 'Adjective'; see section 5.6 below.

led 'Prt' (verbal particle) the parent V is also relabelled 'PaP'. The rule is inoperative when the highest lexically filled non-spine V-node in the V-cluster has a spine brother node labelled 'V'.

5.2.4 Corollaries

But for *to*-INSERTION and a lexical difference, the corollaries are identical to those of 3.1.4. For *that*-INSERTION $_{Comp}$[dat] is inserted. *To*-INSERTION is replaced by *te*-INSERTION, which functions differently:

Te-INSERTION is a corollary of any cyclic S inducing SD or PR unless barred by [-te]: The highest lexically filled V-node, except $_V$[Ø], in the V-cluster of the argument-S that has undergone SD or PR left-adopts $_{Prt}$[te]. If there are two highest lexically filled V-nodes, the non-spine V left-adopts $_{Prt}$[te].

5.2.5 Some postcyclic rules (to be applied in the order given)

(1) **Ø-DELETION:** Delete $_V$[Ø]. Redefine AUX according to the Corollary.

(2) **CLITIC MOVEMENT (CM):** Move 3rd ps [-animate] DO pronoun to immediate right of V-cluster.

(3) **QUESTION FORMATION:**
   a. $_X$[Q$_{ue}$] right-adopts $_C$[QU] (any QU-constituent up to phrase level in scope of $_X$[Q$_{ue}$] but not in $_{NP}$[S] or complement question). If no $_C$[QU] is found, $_X$[Q$_{ue}$] right-adopts $_{y-n}$[Ø] in main questions and $_{y-n}$[of] in dependent questions. X is $_C$[QU]/AUX//S or $_C$[QU]/$_C$[QU] (see 3.2.1; 5.2.6).
   b. AUX//S right-adopts the nearest AUX.

(4) **FRONTING:**
   a. $_X$[Foc] right-adopts any major constituent $_C$[+Foc], except S, /S, AUX, and adverbs marked '†'. X is: $_C$[+Foc]/AUX//S or $_C$[+Foc]/$_C$[+Foc] (see 3.2.1 and 5.2.6).
   b. If the node above $_X$[Foc] is AUX//S, it right-adopts AUX.

   NB1: If $_C$[+Foc] is a PP$_3$ or a locative Adv$_3$, dummy subject $_{NP}$[er] is deleted.
   NB2: If $_C$[+Foc] is any adverbial and $_{NP}$[er] — rb = locative adverb, $_{NP}$[er] is deleted.
   NB3: If $_C$[+Foc] is a subject *dat*-clause dummy subject $_{NP}$[het] (Cyclic Rule (6)) is deleted.

(5) **AFFIX HANDLING (AH):** As in 3.1.5.

(6) **V-FINAL** (applies to the non-AUX part of the V-cluster in main clauses, and to the whole V-cluster in non-main S or /S): Move the (sub)cluster to the far right of /S, but never across an embedded S or /S. It may stop before a Prep$_2$Phrase (not Prep$_3$).

(7) **PASSIVE PaP-DELETION:** Delete $_{PaP}$[$_V$[worden]$_{Aff}$[EN]] under V with right brother PaP.

(8) END-CLUSTER ARRANGEMENT (ECA):

a. Assign FV, PaP, $_V[_{Prt}[te]_V[X]]$ and the remaining lexically filled nodes of any V-cluster a value from [0] to [3] according to the following scale:

[+V]

FV (=Finite Verb)	[3]		never raised
$_V[_{Prt}[te]_V[X]]$ or V	[2]		preferably not raised
Past Participle	[1]		preferably raised
$\begin{Bmatrix} \text{Verbal Particle} \\ \text{Adjective} \end{Bmatrix}$	[0]		obligatorily raised

[-V]

b. Pass the value on to the parent node. If two values are to be passed on to the same parent node, select the highest. Pass value on to parent node on spine if still unvalued.

c. Raise the rightmost node over higher-valued nodes on the spine. Spine nodes labelled 'Adj' or 'PaP' form a separate unit with internal ECA. They are considered rightmost nodes and raise the whole subcluster provided the raising conditions are fulfilled. Obligatory for [0]-nodes, preferred for [1]-nodes, not preferred for [2]-nodes. Maximal raising is preferred most, minimal raising comes next, intermediate raising is least preferred. A raised element is left-adopted by the node above which it is raised.

(9) MINCE: As in 3.1.5.

5.2.6 QUESTION FORMATION and FRONTING in Dutch

As for English, but not for French, the processes of question formation and fronting are relatively easy to describe in a factually correct way. The point is, however, that merely factual descriptions will fail to show up any deeper principles that are at work in language generally. This point is the more pressing as question formation and fronting are very similar, though not identical, processes in each of the two languages. Moreover, and even more significantly, English and Dutch differ only minimally from each other. The obvious surface difference of English *do*-support in questions, which is lacking in Dutch, has been taken care of by postponing the deletion of the Ø-tense for English and have it replaced by the dummy verb *do* when it is separated from its main verb. The notion of AUX made it possible to do that in an orderly way. Other than that, the only significant difference is that Dutch FRONTING brings along attraction of AUX (and hence the so-called V-2 phenomena), while English FRONTING attracts AUX only when a negative adverbial has been fronted, as in *Under no conditions will they surrender.*

In section 3.2.1 we discussed the English question formation and fronting processes from the point of view of universal linguistic theory and introduced *incomplete constituents*, defining them as typically sentence-initial elements that attract certain marked sentence constituents to satisfy their status. For main clause questions in Dutch, as in English, Q_{ue} is the lexical filler of an incomplete constituent node whose surface structure label is, for most cases, $_c$[QU]/AUX//S: it takes a QU-constituent (or $_{y-n}$[∅] if no proper QU-constituent is available) to form a constituent labelled AUX//S, which takes the nearest AUX to form /S. Only if $_c$[QU] is the main clause subject is the surface category $_c$[QU]/$_c$[QU]. (As was observed in 3.2.1, the exceptional status of the subject may be due to a constraint preventing AUX from unilaterally C-commanding its subject, which would happen if AUX were to be attracted with a QU-constituent in subject position.) In dependent questions Q_{ue} is the lexical filler of an incomplete constituent surface-labelled $_c$[QU]/$_c$[QU]: it takes a $_c$[QU] to form a $_c$[QU].

In Dutch, as in English, QU-terms can be attracted by Q_{ue} from a complement *dat*-clause but preferably not if the clause is directly dominated by NP (see 3.2.1). The German case is different (6.4). It is thus possible to generate (4a) but not (4b):

(4)a.   Wie denk je dat Jan gezien heeft?
       who think you that Jan seen   has
       'who do you think that Jan has seen?'

    b.   *Wie ging je weg omdat Jan had uitgenodigd?
       who went you away because Jan had invited
       '*who did you go away because Jan had invited?'

(Dutch *Foc* is normally taken to be the lexical filler of a node labelled $_c$[+Foc]/AUX//S: it takes a [+Foc]-constituent to form a constituent labelled AUX//S, which takes AUX to form /S. Only if $_c$[+Foc] is subject is the surface category $_c$[+Foc]/$_c$[+Foc]. In English, *Foc* is labelled $_c$[+Foc]/AUX//S only with *negative* fronted constituents like *never* or *hardly*, or PPs or NPs with a negation. Otherwise English FRONTING does not attract AUX, and *Foc* is described as $_c$[+Foc]/$_c$[+Foc], i.e. it takes a [+Foc]-constituent to become one.

The famous 'V-2 conspiracy' in Dutch and German (Weerman 1989) thus seems to be the automatic result of the fact that Dutch and German FRONTING involve attraction of AUX besides the [+Foc] constituent. The term 'V-2 conspiracy' is somewhat misleading in that adverbials of class V_{Adv_o}, such as *dus* ('so'), *en* ('and'), *want* ('for'), or *maar* ('but'), may precede fronted elements, so that AUX comes in third, not second, position, as shown in (5a). This third position of AUX follows from the rules given above. The SA-structure corresponding to (5a) is (5b), leading to the shallow structure (5c). Now the postcyclic rule FRONTING first makes $_c$[+Foc]/AUX//S right-adopt $_{NP}$[die man], as in (5d). Then AUX//S right-adopts AUX to deliver /S, as in (5e). AFFIX HANDLING and V-FINAL produce the surface structure (5f).

(5)a.   Maar die man heb ik nooit bedrogen
       but   that man have I never deceived
       'but that man I have never deceived'

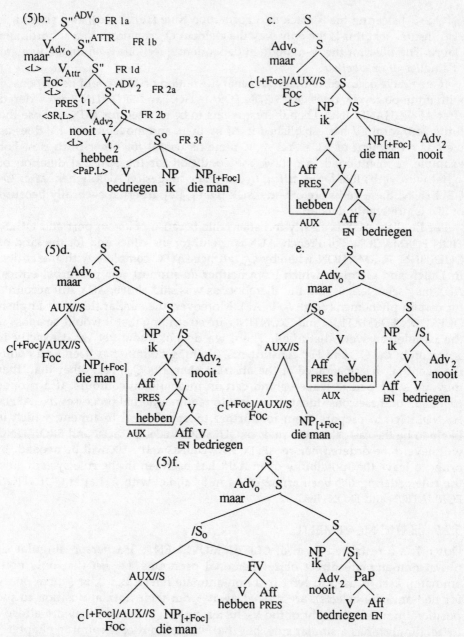

(5)b., c., (5)d., e., (5)f.

Main clause and dependent questions are now easily derived with the help of the machinery provided. Note that a verb that subcategorizes for a dependent question will automatically slip the dependent question in at the right Formation Rule. Take, for example, the verb *weten* ('know'). Besides direct object NP, S^o or $_{NP}[S'']$, as specified in the lexion of 5.2.2, it may, as in English, also take a dependent question as object complement. This is specifiable as

$_{NP}$[Q_{ue}+S"] steering the S" back into Formation Rule (1c) or (1d), as it should. It also ensures that this is the only way the element Q_{ue} can occur in a subordinate clause. The filler for the 'y-n'-node in dependent questions is *of*, the equivalent of English *if* or *whether*.

It may have occurred to the reader that the notion of AUX could be dispensed with if the postcyclic rules QUESTION FORMATION and FRONTING are ordered after AFFIX HANDLING. Then there appears to be no need for AUX because the finite verb form FV has established itself by then, and movement of FV does as well as movement of AUX. Yet AUX remains useful for other purposes. For example, as mentioned in note 4, the condition for the optional deletion of $_{Prt}$[te] with verbs like *lopen, zitten, liggen, staan* hinges on AUX: when, after Ø-DELETION, these verbs are outside AUX then $_{Prt}$[te], inserted cyclically because of SD, is preferably deleted.

For English, AUX is clearly indispensable because of *do*-support and QUESTION FORMATION. For French, AUX is useful for the clitics and for the kind of QUESTION FORMATION whereby Q_{ue} attracts AUX, complete with the clitics. In Dutch and German, which have neither *do*-support nor preverbal clitics, AUX may seem less useful. But there too, as was said above, AUX still accounts for certain phenomena (e.g. V-FINAL). Moreover, the similarities with English QUESTION FORMATION and FRONTING are so striking that it would be a loss if the parallelism were disturbed. Then, we do not know yet what exactly is going on in the Q_{ue} and *Foc* constituents. Nothing definite has been said about the eventual disappearance of the abstract elements Q_{ue}, *Foc*, other than that they are supposed to leave behind certain intonational contours. If a proper treatment of these constituents turns out to require internal processes like AFFIX HANDLING, to prepare them for further morphological treatment, which is likely to be the case, then the rules of QUESTION FORMATION and FRONTING will have to be ordered before AFFIX HANDLING and AUX will be needed. In order to leave that possibility open AUX has been left in the rule system, and the rule ordering has been arranged as in 5.2.5, i.e. with AH after QUESTION FORMATION and FRONTING.

5.2.7 CLITIC MOVEMENT

Dutch has a restricted form of CLITIC MOVEMENT: 3rd person singular or plural non-animate direct object personal pronouns, i.e. *het* ('it', only non-animate), *hem* (if used to refer to a non-animate referent: 'it'), *ze* ('them', only for non-animate objects), are moved away from their normal position to the position immediately right of the V-cluster, unless, of course, they are already there. (English has a similar rule, but that was left out of account in chapter 3 so as not to burden the presentation too much.)

This explains *Ik gaf het haar* ('I gave it her'), with the direct object *het* before the indirect object *haar*. CLITIC MOVEMENT precedes any rule moving about either the whole V-cluster (i.e. V-FINAL) or just AUX (i.e. QUESTION FORMATION or FRONTING) because the clitic, once moved to the right of the V-cluster, stays behind, as appears from, e.g. *Heb je het haar gegeven?* (lit.:

'have you it her given?', i.e. 'did you give it to her?'), which has the shallow structure [Q$_{ue}$ [je $_V$[$_{AUX}$[PRES + hebben] gegeven] haar het]]. CM first moves *het* in front of *haar*: [Q$_{ue}$ [je $_V$[$_{AUX}$[PRES + hebben] gegeven] het haar]]. Then AUX is attracted by Q_{ue} in virtue of QUESTION FORMATION: [[Q$_{ue}$ + $_{AUX}$[PRES + hebben]] [je gegeven het haar]]. Then, after AH, V-FINAL moves *gegeven* to the far right: [[Q$_{ue}$ + $_{AUX}$[hebben + PRES]] [je het haar gegeven]]. (See also (31) and (63) below.)

Likewise in subordinate clauses, where V-FINAL moves the whole V-cluster to the far right: ... *dat je het haar gegeven hebt.* From the shallow structure dat [je $_V$[$_{AUX}$[PRES + hebben] gegeven] haar het] CM produces dat [je $_V$[$_{AUX}$[PRES + hebben] gegeven] het haar]. Then, after AH, the whole V-cluster is moved to the far right, giving dat [je het haar $_V$[$_{AUX}$[hebben + PRES] gegeven]]. END CLUSTER ARRANGEMENT (postcyclic rule 8) then preferably puts *gegeven* in front of *hebben+PRES*.

5.3 Passive in Dutch

Although Passive is part of Universal Grammar, the universal charter for grammars of natural languages, not all languages have it and it is by no means identical for all languages that do. It is not known what the actual stipulations are in Universal Grammar, and therefore what room is left to individual languages for variation. In this situation all we can do is carefully scrutinize each language that we come across. This we will now start doing for Dutch.

Unlike English, only direct objects can become subjects of passive sentences, though colloquial Dutch allows for prepositional objects to be passive subjects, with the preposition stranded, as in (6). But we shall not take colloquial Dutch into account here.

(6)   Die man wordt nooit over geschreven
        that man is   never about written
        'that man is never written about'

Another point is that Dutch allows for Passive even when there is no direct object, but only for action verbs, not for verbs expressing a state or a process (cf. 5.1.1). The construction is called the 'impersonal passive'. Impersonal passives have a dummy subject *er* put in when the lexical selection is made in virtue of Formation Rule (3f). *Er* is probably best assigned NP-status (like the English dummy subject *there*). Examples are (7a-c):

(7)a.   Er   werd gelachen
        there was   laughed
        'someone laughed'

   b.   Er   wordt nooit over die man geschreven
        there is   never about that man written
        'that man is never written about'

c.   Er   wordt aan die mensen geleend
    there is   to those people borrowed
    'lending is taking place to those people'

d.   Er wordt (aan) die mensen geld geleend
    there is   (to) those people money lent
    'there is money being lent to those people'

e.   *Er wordt die mensen geleend
    there is   those people borrowed
    'borrowing is taking place to those people'

f.   !*Er   wordt hier niet gestorven
    there is   here not died
    'there will be no dying here'

(7d) is probably not to be treated as an impersonal passive, though it is a passive sentence and does have a dummy subject *er*. Yet it also has a lexical direct object, *geld* ('money'), now the subject of the passive sentence. In this case, *geld* is existentially quantified ('indefinite' in traditional grammar), and Dutch has, like English *there* but under different conditions, a dummy subject *er* also for existentially quantified subjects. Whether there is a link between passive dummy *er* and existential *er* is a moot point, which we shall not try to solve here.

(7b) is one of the standard Dutch versions of (6), together with (8b). (7e) is ungrammatical because the impersonal passive does not allow for other argument-NPs of the same main verb, only for PrepPhrases. Therefore, the internal dative *die mensen* must be DATIVE-EXTRACTED to *aan die mensen*, as in (7c). Note that with the existentially quantified *geld*, as in (7d), the sentence is grammatical. Moreover, (7f) is odd, or jocular, as the verb *sterven* ('die') is clearly not an action verb but a process verb. Its use in this construction forces the listener to construe it as an action verb, which may be jocular, depending on the situation.

When a main constituent is fronted by means of postcyclic FRONTING, the dummy subject $_{NP}$[er] is sometimes obligatorily deleted, as in (8a-c), and sometimes it has to stay, as in (8d-g). The conditions for this *er*-deletion are not entirely clear. The following is a tentative generalization. When $_{NP}$[er] is deleted a level 3 adverbial (introduced by FR (3d)), has been fronted, or $_{NP}$[er] is immediately followed by a locative adverb (*hier, daar*) after AUX-attraction by FRONTING(b). But not all level 3 adverbial frontings require *er*-deletion. As far as can be judged, only FRONTING of level 3 PPs and of locative adverbs require deletion of $_{NP}$[er]. And if $_{NP}$[er] is immediately followed by a locative adverb it is preferably deleted, no matter what element has been fronted. If this is correct *er*-deletion after FRONTING means that the fronted element is an adverbial of level 3, unless $_{NP}$[er] stands right before a locative adverb.

(8)a.   Aan die mensen wordt (*er) geleend
    to those people   is   (there) borrowed
    'borrowing is taking place to those people'

b. Over die man wordt (*er) nooit geschreven
    about that man is (there) never written
    'that man is never written about'

c. Hier wordt (*er) niet gewerkt
    here is (there) not worked
    'no work is being done here'

d. Nooit wordt (er) hier gewerkt
    never is (there) here worked
    'never is any work being done here'

e. Misschien wordt er nog gewerkt
    perhaps is there still worked
    'perhaps there is still some work being done'

f. Gisteren werd er nog gewerkt
    yesterday was there still worked
    'yesterday there was still some work being done'

g. Vlug werd er niet gewerkt
    quickly was there not worked
    'they weren't working what one might call quickly'

Then, idiosyncratically, in the perfective tenses the past participle *geworden* of the passive auxiliary *worden* is normally dropped. When it is not, the sentence is somehow marked as belonging to a different variety of the language, though it is not known what the sociolinguistic connotations of that variety are. In German, too, the passive auxiliary past participle has an idiosyncratic feature: its prefix *ge-* is dropped, so that it appears as *worden*, not as the expected *geworden*. Apparently, the immediate succession of two full past participles is felt to be awkward and some expedient is drawn in to avoid that.

A final observation is the following. There are verbs that take an NP middle term followed by an object-clause. Sometimes the NP middle term is indirect object, as with *leren₂* ('teach'), *verzoeken* ('ask'), *beloven* ('promise'). But occasionally the middle term is not indirect object, as it does not allow for DATIVE EXTRACTION, and must be considered to be direct object, even though it is followed by an object clause, as with *helpen₂* ('help') or *laten₂* ('allow, make, get to'). Such direct objects cannot become the subject of a passive sentence. Since they cannot be DATIVE-EXTRACTED either, no passive is possible for such verbs.

Let us now generate the passive sentence (9a) with the SA-structure (9b):

(9)a. De muis is de kat door het kind gegeven
       the mouse is the cat by the child given
       'the cat has been given the mouse by the child'

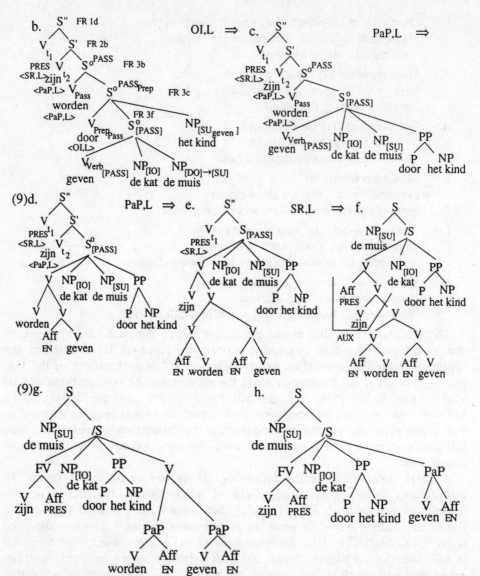

OBJECT INCORPORATION and LOWERING to the far right on the S^{oPASS}_{Prep}-cycle gives (9c). Then, PaP and LOWERING (onto lower V) on the S^{oPASS}-cycle gives (9d), followed by, again, PaP and LOWERING (onto lower V) on the S'-cycle, as shown in (9e). TENSE ROUTINE gives the shallow structure (9f), with AUX. Note that the NP[de muis], marked [DO], has been re-marked [SU] and has thus become the NP to be raised by SR. Postcyclic AFFIX HANDLING and V-FINAL give (9g). PASSIVE PaP-DELETION gives (9h), which is the surface structure. MINCE does not apply.

As was said on the previous page, there is an unpreferred variant with non-application of PASSIVE PaP-DELETION used by some speakers. In this variant, the only correct order of the two past participles is *gegeven geworden*. The alternative **geworden gegeven* is ungrammatical, though generated by the Cycle and Postcycle, and not affected by ECA. This would indicate that we have to do here with a different variety or dialect of the language, possibly with right-adoption for all LOWERINGS in the V-cluster (i.e. with a left-branching V-cluster) which would generate the correct order in the Cycle. No systematic study has been carried out so far to investigate any correlations between the use of *geworden* and other possible deviations in verbal end clusters in the speech of the speakers of this dialect.

Let us now try (7b), with its variant (8b). The input SA-structure is (10a). In (10a) the dummy subject $_{NP}$[er] has been inserted, due to passive lexical selection: when *schrijven* is selected without direct object and then loses its subject due to Passive, no NP-term remains and the dummy subject $_{NP}$[er] is inserted. (10e) is the shallow structure, with AUX in place.

Note that the LOWERING of *nooit* in (10d), though to the far right, is blocked by the PrepPhrase *over die man*, in virtue of the principle that far right LOWERING may never cross an adverbial to the right of V (see LOWERING in 5.2.3). All the rest is as in the previous chapters.

Now postcyclic Ø-DELETION incorporates $_V$[worden] into AUX. AFFIX HANDLING results in (10f). V-FINAL sends the non-AUX part of the V-cluster (we are in a main clause) to the far right of /S. The result is (10g), which is the surface structure of (7b). If $_{PP}$[over die man] is a [+Foc] constituent and is therefore FRONTED, the result is first (10h), then, after AUX-attraction, AH and V-FINAL, (10i), which is the surface structure of (8b). Since $_{PP}$[over die man] is a level 3 PrepPhrase, its FRONTING requires the deletion of $_{NP}$[er]. Note that the /S$_1$-node in (10i) is not erased by DOWNGRADING 2 (see 2.7.1.4), since /S$_1$ still dominates $_V$[schrijven].

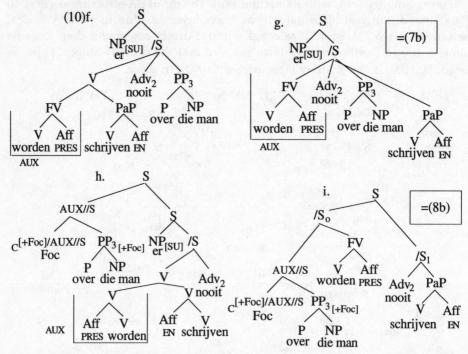

This finishes our discussion of Passive in Dutch. Readers will find it easy to construct a few passive sentences themselves .

5.4 The complementation system

Dutch has six types of sentential complement: S", S' and S°, each with or without a dominating NP. An S"-complement re-enters the Formation Rules at rule (1c) or (1d), an S'-complement at rule (2a) or (2b), and an S°-complement at any of the rules (3c-f). Unless otherwise specified in the lexicon, possible subscript features of S°, e.g. [PASS], may be selected for an S°-complement. The main lexically induced cyclic rules in the complementation system are SD and PR, both always preceded by the corollary *te*-INSERTION, except when the verb induces [-te].

5.4.1 PREDICATE RAISING

Repeated cyclic application of PR produces the so-called Dutch construction, with NPs on the left and a verbal cluster on the right, and with crossing dependencies between the verbs and the NPs. We shall now have a detailed look at a few cases. In doing so we shall, as is the habit in Dutch and German grammar, use subordinate clauses, which have the whole verbal cluster at the end, not just the non-finite part.

Consider the following synonymous subordinate clauses:

(11) ... dat Jan Marie de tekst door de student heeft proberen te leren laten corrigeren

... that Jan Marie the text by the student has try to teach make correct

'... that Jan has tried to teach Marie to have the text corrected by the student'

(12) ... dat Jan heeft geprobeerd Marie te leren de tekst door de student te laten corrigeren

... that Jan has tried Marie to teach the text by the student to have correct

(13) ... dat Jan Marie heeft proberen te leren de tekst door de student te laten corrigeren

... that Jan Marie has try to teach the text by the student to have correct

(14) ... dat Jan heeft geprobeerd Marie de tekst door de student te leren laten corrigeren

... that Jan has tried Marie the text by the student to teach make correct

They are all generated from the SA-structure (15a). The reader will have no problem following the cyclic process. First, the passive Agent Phrase is dealt with by OBJECT INCORPORATION and LOWERING. Then *laten*$_1$ induces PR, but without *te*. The result is shown in (15b), where the grammatical passive subject $_{NP}$[de tekst] has been redefined as direct object of the complex verb $_V$[laten-corrigeren]. Then the Ø-tense must be LOWERED, and SD and PR (without *te*) are induced by *leren*$_2$. Note that *leren*$_2$ also leaves the option of SD (with *te*), but here the option <SD,[-te],PR> has been selected. This result is shown in (15c). Then, again, Ø-LOWERING, followed by SD, and PR induced by *proberen* (PR is optional, but has been selected). This is (15d). Then, PaP and L on S'_0, but note that PaP remains inoperative as the verb to be affected by it is part of a V-cluster. Finally, TENSE ROUTINE. The shallow structure, with AUX, is (15e). Since we have a *dat*-clause *dat*-INSERTION applies: S" left-adopts $_{Comp}$[dat]. In the postcycle Ø-DELETION, V-FINAL (moving the whole V-cluster) and AFFIX HANDLING apply. The result is (15f).

(15)a.

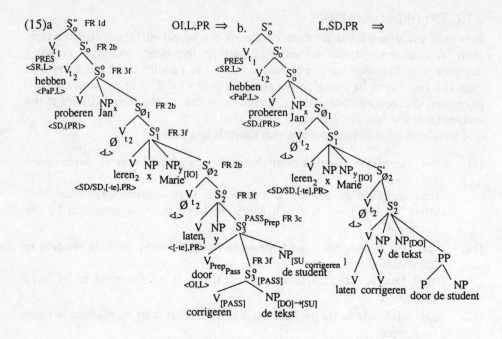

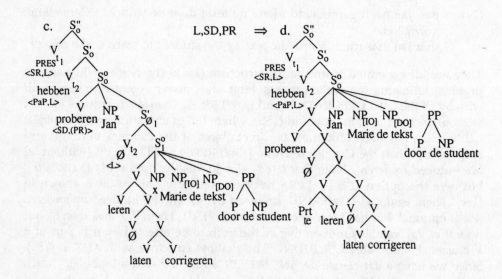

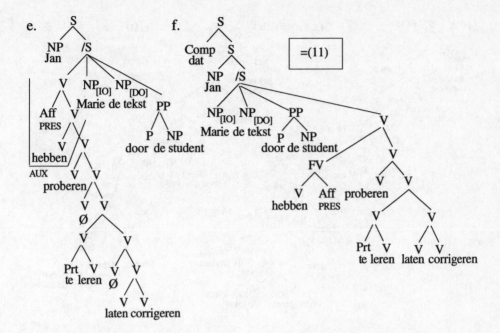

This is how (11) is generated. The variants (12)-(14) are produced analogously, but with different rule options. Sentence (12) is generated by not applying optional PR on the *leren₂*-cycle and on the *proberen*-cycle. The process is demonstrated in (16) (overleaf). Note that *leren₂* now induces SD with *te*. In the postcycle, V-FINAL applies three times over, one for every /S, though the effect is vacuous on the highest /S. The V-cluster always stops before a further embedded /S. After MINCE, the surface structure is (16g). The reader will be able to work out that (13) is generated by not applying PR on the *leren₂*-cycle, and (14) by not applying PR on the *proberen*-cycle. Note that in (16f) the highest V-cluster, i.e. the cluster under /S$_o$, allows for an application of ECA, since $_{PaP}[_V[\text{proberen}]_{Aff}[EN]]$ is valued [1] and the highest V-node [3]. This means that raising of $_{PaP}[_V[\text{proberen}]_{Aff}[EN]]$ is preferred, giving the perfectly well-formed (17):

(17) ... dat Jan geprobeerd heeft Marie te leren de tekst door de student te laten corrigeren
    ... that Jan tried has Marie to teach the text by the student to make correct

The V-clusters under /S$_1$ and /S$_2$ leave no room for ECA.

(16)a.   OI,L,PR ⇒ b.   L,SD ⇒

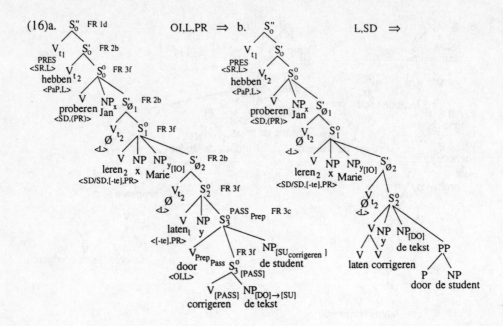

(16)c.   L,SD ⇒ d.

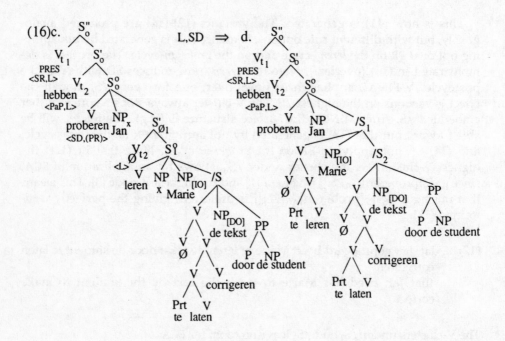

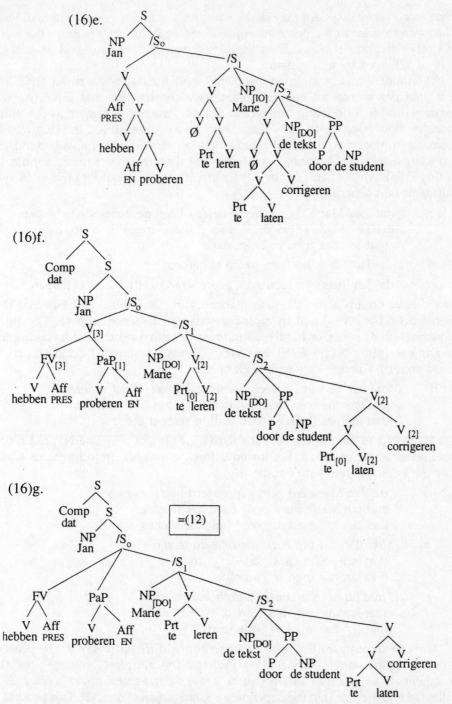

(16)e.

(16)f.

(16)g. =(12)

So far this has been successful. The Dutch construction appears to have been tamed. The fact that even subtle differences are accounted for makes one expect that whatever rule system may in the end prove to be the correct one will have the main features of the description presented here. In fact, we may claim that no other treatment available in the literature achieves the level of success that is achieved by this system.

Yet there is one remaining problem: with the verbs meaning 'try', i.e. *proberen, pogen, trachten*, speakers often use a construction that should be ungrammatical in all existing treatments. The construction is known as the 'third construction' (Den Besten & Rutten 1989) and is exemplified in (18a) where, contrary to the rules, the verbal cluster has penetrated into the embedded /S, crossing $_{NP}$[Marie]. According to all existing theories, the sentence should be either (18b), with SD and PR, or (18c), with SD and without PR (and with two different ECA orderings):

(18)a   ... dat Jan Marie [geprobeerd heeft / heeft geprobeerd] te helpen
     ... that Jan Marie   [tried   has / has   tried]   to help
     '... that Jan has tried to help Marie'

   b.   ... dat Jan Marie heeft proberen te helpen

   c.   ... dat Jan [heeft geprobeerd / geprobeerd heeft] Marie te helpen

Some have doubts about the grammaticality of (18a), but it is a fact that this construction is often used in ordinary standard Dutch discourse. The third construction does not, or hardly, seem to occur with any other verbs taking the argument frame NP_x + S'/S°, like *leren$_1$* ('learn'), *besluiten* ('decide'), *verkiezen* ('prefer'), whether they induce PR or not:

(19)   ... *dat Jan de wet [geleerd/besloten] heeft te respekteren
       ... that Jan the law [learned/decided] has   to respect
       '... that Jan has [learned/decided] to respect the law'

According to the present author's native judgement only one NP, not more, and no adjective or adverb is allowed before *geprobeerd*, but judgements about the third construction vary notoriously:

(20)a.   ... *dat Jan Marie het geld geprobeerd heeft te geven
       ... that Jan Marie the money tried has to give
       '... that Jan has tried to give Marie the money'

   b.   ... *?dat Jan beleefd heeft geprobeerd te zijn
       ... that Jan polite has   tried   to be
       '... that Jan has tried to be polite'

   c.   ... *?dat Jan rechtop heeft geprobeerd te lopen
       ... that Jan upright has   tried   to walk
       '... that Jan has tried to walk upright'

How to account for the third construction is difficult to say at the present state of grammatical knowledge. Perhaps the simplest solution, for the moment, is to say that for the verbs *proberen, trachten, pogen* V-FINAL is allowed to penetrate into the dependent /S, crossing just one NP. This process is demonstrated in (21). (21a) shows the structure of (18a) after AH, but before V-FINAL. V-FINAL should have no effect, since the V-cluster to be moved cannot cross an embedded S or /S. We assume that in (18a) V-FINAL has penetrated into $/S_1$ crossing just the first NP, as shown in (21b). TREE PRUNING 1 (section 2.7.1.3) erases one /S-node.

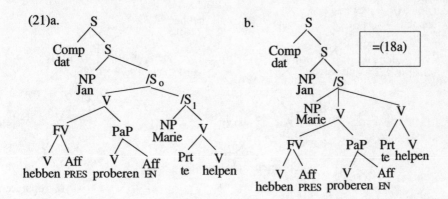

(21)a.

b. =(18a)

We have explained the absence of passive verb morphology in some PR-clusters by the assumption of S^o-embeddings under the PR-inducing verbs in question. This works well, but a complication arises with perception verbs like *zien* ('see') or *horen* ('hear') and with *laten* ('let, make'). These verbs normally leave out passive morphology, but they also, though less currently, allow for passive morphology in the infinitive:

(22)a. Ik heb de wagen [zien/laten] repareren
I have the car   [see/let]   repair
'I have seen the car be repaired / I have had the car repaired'

b. Ik heb de wagen gerepareerd [zien/laten] worden
I have the car   repaired   [see/let]   be
'I have seen the car being repaired / I have had the car repaired'

The explanation of this fact is sought in the independently motivated double argument frame of these verbs: they not only have a RAISING analysis but also a CONTROL frame, and thus fall into the category of predicates that show this systematic dichotomy. By assigning these verbs a complement-S'_θ in the CONTROL frame the possibility of passive morphology is automatically intro-duced, since S'-complements re-enter the Formation Rules at (2a) or (2b), which allows them to take the option of S^{o}PASS and thus pass through rule (3b). For the sake of completeness, we show the generation of (22b), with $zien_2$, in (23):

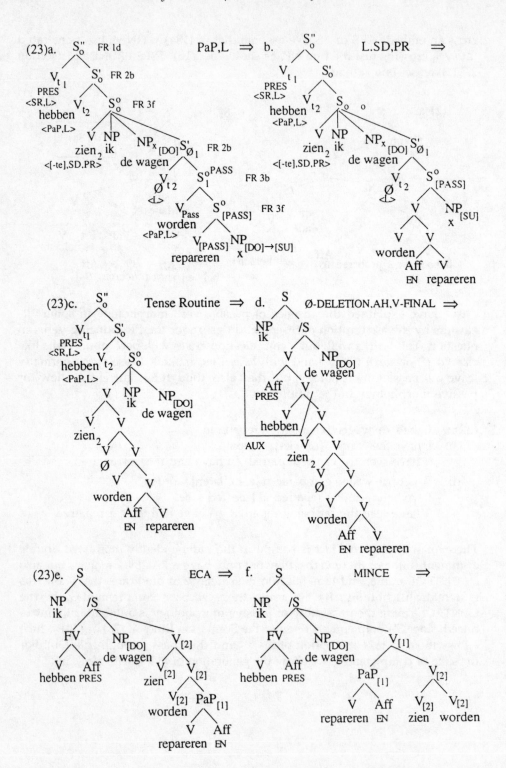

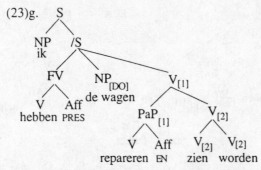

(23)g.

Note, finally, that ECA allows for two more end clusters: *zien gerepareerd worden* en *zien worden gerepareerd* (i.e. with no raising at all).

5.4.2 Two verbs *helpen*

We may now take up (60) again of section 3.8.2, repeated here for convenience:

(24)a. Ik heb Jim [helpen failliet gaan / failliet   helpen gaan]
I have Jim [help   bankrupt go / bankrupt help   go]
'I have helped Jim go bankrupt'

b. Ik heb Jim geholpen failliet   te gaan
I have Jim helped   bankrupt to go
'I have helped Jim to go bankrupt'

The former, (24a), is ambiguous in that it can mean (a) I have contributed with others to bring about Jim's bankruptcy, and (b) I have assisted Jim in bringing about his own bankruptcy. Sentence (23b) can only have the latter meaning. We must therefore derive (24a) from two different sources, and (24b) from only one source: SA_1 leads only to (24a) while SA_2 leads to both (24a) and (24b). Let us first consider (25a) and (26a), both representing SA_2, which leads to both (24a) (in two versions) and (24b):

(25)a. S''_0 FR 1d   SD,PR $\Rightarrow$ b.   S'' Tense Routine $\Rightarrow$ c.   S

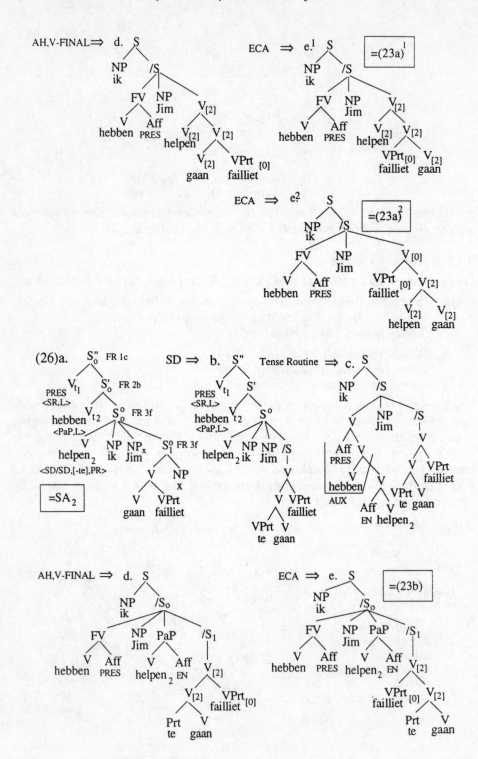

Now we will derive (24a) (in both versions) from SA₁, and it will be clear that SA₁ cannot lead to (24b):

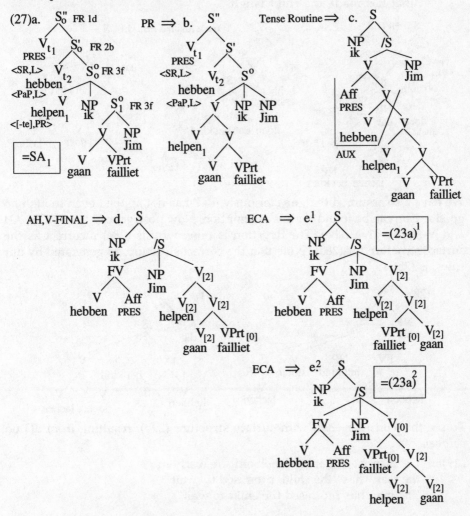

5.4.3 Why Dutch complementation has no SUBJECT RAISING

In this section we develop an argument to show that proposals to the effect that the Dutch complementation system contains SR and not PR are erroneous. It is, unfortunately, still widely believed among Dutch grammarians that SR, and not PR, is the dominant rule in Dutch syntax.

As it is not feasible, in this context, to go through all cases of possible SR we take as an example a sentence that would be a prototypical candidate for SR in the eyes of those who defend that position. We consider the sentence (28a), with the SA-structure (28b), and will assume, contrary to the specification in 5.2.2 above, that the verb *doen* induces SUBJECT RAISING.

(28)a. Dat heeft het kind doen lachen
       that has the child make laugh
       'that has made the child laugh'

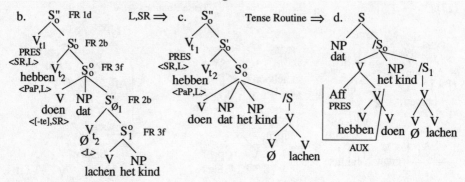

We have also assumed that, mysteriously, PaP has not applied even though no good reason can be found for this assumption. Now postcyclic Ø-DELETION, AH and V-FINAL give (28e). The question is now: why is (28e) incorrect as the surface structure for (28a)? Note that the correct structure, as generated by our rules, is (28f).

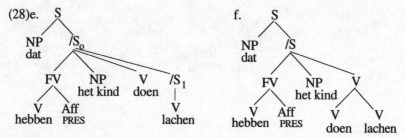

To see this consider (29a) with surface structure (29b), resulting from SD on *beloven*:

(29)a. De man heeft het kind beloofd te wachten
       the man has the child promised to wait
       'the man has promised the child to wait'

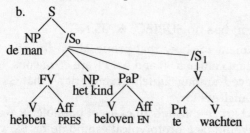

Note that, in spite of the different rules involved, (28e) and (29b) are isomorphic, except that (29a) has a past participle and the particle *te* (since *beloven* does not induce [-te], as *doen* does).

Now compare the possible FRONTINGS of main constituents:

(30)a. Beloofd heeft de man het kind te wachten
   b. Te wachten heeft de man het kind beloofd
   c. *Beloofd te wachten heeft de man het kind
   d. *Doen heeft dat het kind lachen
   e. *Lachen heeft dat het kind doen
   f. Doen lachen heeft dat het kind

FRONTING is possible for main constituents, as is generally known and accepted. The possibility of FRONTING thus constitutes a test for main constituenthood, and thus, in part, for the correctness of surface structures. It is not hard to see that (29b) is the right structure for allowing precisely the FRONTINGS shown in (30a) and (30b), and disallows (30c), whereas (28e) is the right structure for the ungrammatical FRONTINGS in (30d) and (30e), while it disallows the correct (30f). This clearly shows that (28e) is all wrong. The correct result is obtained from (28f), which gives the grammatical FRONTING (30f) and disallows (30d) and (30e).

It is now easy to derive the sentence:

(31)a. Ik heb het de man zien doen
      I have it the man see do
      'I saw the man do it'

From the SA (31b) we get the shallow structure (31c). CLITIC MOVEMENT gives (31d). Further postcyclic treatment, (AH, V-FINAL, MINCE) gives the surface structure (31e):

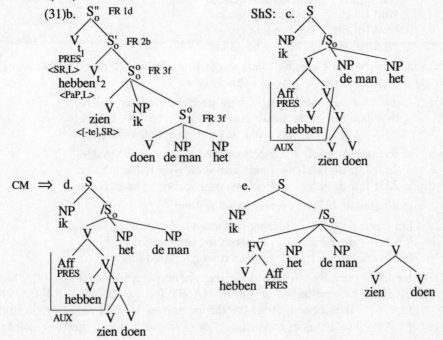

5.5 VERB-FINAL and END CLUSTER ARRANGEMENT

There is one postcyclic rule that makes Dutch stand out among the other languages discussed in this book, i.e. the rule END CLUSTER ARRANGEMENT (ECA). German has no ECA at all, despite the fact that German V-clusters appear complex and hard to grasp (we shall see in the next chapter that the German facts fall into place without exception by a few settings on the directionality parameter). ECA has to do with a curious set of phenomena in verbal end groups — phenomena that have so far escaped proper formulation in any rule system, generative or other. Matters are complicated further by the fact that there are notable dialectal differences, especially between Standard Netherlandic Dutch, Flemish Dutch and the Saxonian northern dialects. We shall restrict ourselves here to Standard Netherlandic Dutch.

To illustrate the problem we first consider some data, most of which are presented as subordinate clauses, which have the advantage of V-clusters being left intact and placed at the far right by V-FINAL. Main clauses are also considered, in order to bring out the contrast with the corresponding subordinate clauses. In (32) we have listed all six possible permutations of the verbal cluster consisting of three elements, in order of preference:

(32)a.   ... dat hij dit   gezegd kan hebben
         ... that he this   said   can have
                   '... that he may have said this'

   b.   ... dat hij dit   kan gezegd hebben
   c.   ... dat hij dit   kan hebben gezegd
   d.   ... ?dat hij dit   gezegd hebben kan
   e.   ... *dat hij dit   hebben kan gezegd
   f.   ... *dat hij dit   hebben gezegd kan

Similar observations can be made regarding the wanderings of the verbal particle *weg* in $_V[_V[halen]_{VPrt}[weg]]$ ('take away'):

(33)a.   ... dat Jan de tafel weg heeft proberen te laten halen
         ... that Jan the table away has   try   to let take
                   '... that Jan has tried to have the table taken away'

   b.   ... dat Jan de tafel   heeft proberen te laten weghalen
   c.   ... ?dat Jan de tafel   heeft proberen weg te laten halen
   d.   ... ?dat Jan de tafel   heeft weg proberen te laten halen

As a main clause, (33) has fewer possibilities:

(34)a.   Jan heeft de tafel   weg proberen te laten halen
   b.   Jan heeft de tafel   proberen te laten weghalen
   c.   Jan heeft de tafel   proberen weg te laten halen

In order to account for these and similar phenomena the local rule ECA has been devised, to be applied after AFFIX-HANDLING, V-FINAL and PASSIVE PaP-DELETION. It is based, first, on the notion of 'verbal rank' or 'verbal status' of the various types of constituents or elements found in verbal clusters.

Each element is assigned a value, ranging from [0] to [3], indicating its degree of verbalness: elements valued [3] have the highest verbal status, those valued [0] the lowest. Secondly, it is based on the principle that elements with the values [0] and [1] are subject to pressure to be raised over elements with higher values, the pressure being stronger for [0] than for [1]. Raising for [0]-elements is obligatory; for [1]-elements it is optional but preferred. Elements valued [2] may be raised over elements valued [3], but not preferably. No raising is allowed for elements of equal rank, nor, of course, of higher over lower values.

For ease of reference the postcyclic rule ECA is repeated here:

END CLUSTER ARRANGEMENT (ECA):

  a. Assign FV, PaP, $_V[_{Prt}[te]_V[X]]$ and the remaining lexically filled nodes of any V-cluster a value from [0] to [3] according to the following scale:

		[+V]	
FV (=Finite Verb)	[3]		never raised
$_V[_{Prt}[te]_V[X]]$ or V	[2]		preferably not raised
Past Participle	[1]		preferably raised
$\left\{\begin{array}{l}\text{Verbal Particle}\\ \text{Adjective}\end{array}\right\}$	[0]		obligatorily raised
		[-V]	

  b. Pass the value on to the parent node. If two values are to be passed on to the same parent node, select the highest. Pass value on to parent node on spine if still unvalued.

  c. Raise the rightmost node over higher-valued nodes on the spine. Spine nodes labelled 'Adj' or 'PaP' form a separate unit with internal ECA. They are considered rightmost nodes and raise the whole subcluster provided the raising conditions are fulfilled. Obligatory for [0]-nodes, preferred for [1]-nodes, not preferred for [2]-nodes. Maximal raising is preferred most, minimal raising comes next, intermediate raising is least preferred. A raised element is left-adopted by the node above which it is raised.

To demonstrate the working of the rule let us consider a few examples. First take the V-cluster (35a), which underlies the sentences (33) and (34). Values are assigned to the terminal elements according to the scale given in the rule, and then passed on to the spine. Of two competing values the higher one is chosen for the spine. Now $_{VPrt}[weg]$ must be raised, since raising of [0]-elements is obligatory. The most preferred raising of $_{VPrt}[weg]$ is maximal, i.e. above $V_{[3]}$, giving (35b=33a). Minimal raising, which lands $_{VPrt}[weg]$ just above *halen*, is next preferred, giving (35c=33b). Intermediate raisings are represented by (35d=33c) and (35e=33d). For the main clauses in (34), (35b) is impossible as FV is separated from the rest of the V-cluster. The most preferred option, (34a) is represented in (35e), next comes (35c=34b), and finally (35d=34c).

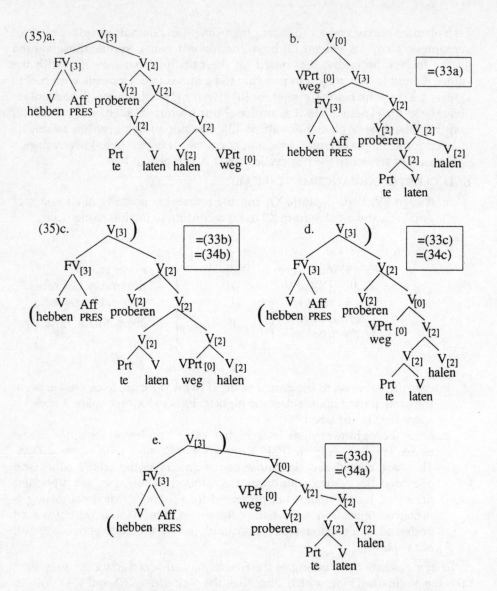

Now consider the cluster underlying (32), repeated here for convenience:

(32)a.　... dat hij dit gezegd kan hebben　d. ... ?dat hij dit gezegd hebben kan

　　b.　... dat hij dit kan gezegd hebben　e. ... *dat hij dit hebben kan gezegd

　　c.　... dat hij dit kan hebben gezegd　f. ... *dat hij dit hebben gezegd kan

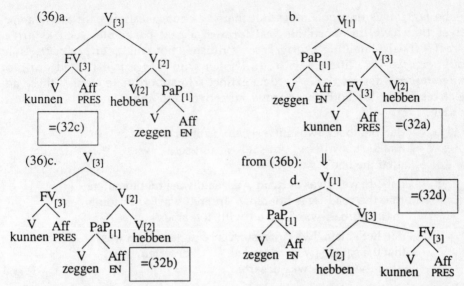

(36a) is the structure as it comes out of V-FINAL. This may remain unchanged, as there is no [0]-value that would make raising obligatory. However, the most preferred version is (36b=32a), with PaP maximally raised. Note that now ᵥ[hebben] may be raised, but not preferably, over the next V-node up on the spine, which is valued [3]. This gives the least preferred (36d=32d). Intermediate raising of PaP from (36a) gives (36c=32b). The ungrammatical (32e) and (32f) cannot be generated.

Let us now consider adjectives in the end cluster. In subordinate clauses with a non-perfective tense the adjective must precede the finite verb, clearly because the adjective is valued [0] while the finite verb is valued [3], so that raising is obligatory. For (37) this is shown in (39a), which is the structure just before ECA, obligatorily turned into (39b), and hence, by MINCE, into (39c). In (38), the main clause version of (37), ECA does not apply, as the cluster has been cut up due to V-FINAL, as shown in (40).

(37) ... dat de man [oud was / *was oud]
      ... that the man [old was / was old]
      '... that the man was old'

(38) De man was oud
      the man was old
      'the man was old'

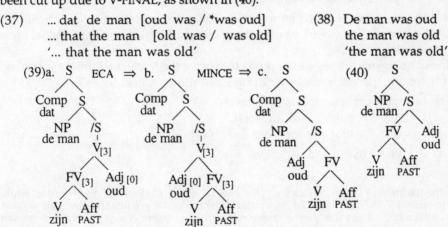

So far, this is unproblematic, but there is a complication with a few adjectives that have the morphological form of a past participle, such as *uitgepraat* ('finished talking'), *uitgekeken* ('finished looking'), *uitverkocht* ('sold out', *bezaaid met* ('littered with', lit. 'sown with'), *ingericht* ('fitted out'), or *uitgestorven* ('deserted', lit. 'become extinct'). In subordinate clauses these adjectives allow for both the normal adjectival and the past participle word order:

(41)a.   ... dat het boek [was uitverkocht / uitverkocht was]
       ... that the book [was   out-sold / out-sold   was]
       '... that the book was sold out'

   b.   ... dat de weg [was bezaaid / bezaaid was] met tomaten
       ... that the road [was littered / littered was] with tomatoes
       '...that the road was littered with tomatoes'

   c.   ... dat het plein [was uitgestorven / uitgestorven was]
       ... that the square [was   deserted   /   deserted was]
       '... that the square was deserted'

Other adjectives with the morphological form of past participles, such as *uitgeslapen* ('shrewd'), *uitgekookt* ('sly'), *verknocht* ('emotionally strongly attached'), *bezopen* ('drunk, crazy') or *geschift* ('crazy'), do not show this behaviour. They behave as normal adjectives.

The adjectives in (41) are really adjectives as they lack a verb with corresponding meaning. Despite their morphological form they cannot be construed as past participles. It is hard to make sense, even metaphorically, of 'selling out the book', or 'sowing the road with tomatoes', or of 'the square has become extinct'. In any case, the usual tests for adjectival status show these words to be adjectives. For example, they allow for durative phrases like *al een hele tijd* ('for a long time'), as in:

(42)a.   ... dat het boek   al   een hele   tijd uitverkocht was
       ... that the book already a whole time out-sold   was
       '... that the book had been sold out for a long time'

The only solution seems to be to assign these adjectives, idiosyncratically, a double categorial status of past participle and of adjective. This makes both word orderings possible.

In subordinate clauses with a perfective tense the V-cluster is more complex, and there are, therefore, more ordering possibilities. Consider (43):

(43)a.   ... dat de man   trouw geweest is[6]
       ... that the man   faithful been   is
        '... that the man has been faithful

   b.   ... dat de man   trouw is geweest

---

[6] In the tradition of Dutch dialectology, the order PaP-FV is called the 'green' order, while the inverse, FV-PaP, is called the 'red order'. The red order results from the rule system without the application of ECA. The green order, which requires ECA, is preferred in spoken Dutch, and corresponds with what is found in German.

c.   ... ?dat de man   is trouw geweest
d.   ... *dat de man   is geweest trouw
e.   ... *dat de man   geweest is trouw
f.   ... *dat de man   geweest trouw is

The structure underlying all of (43) is (44a), with the shallow structure (44b), leading to (44c=43d) after V-FINAL, with the ECA values assigned. ECA must operate, since the rightmost element on the spine has the value [0]. Maximal raising of $_{Adj}$[trouw] gives (44d=43b). From there, the past participle of *zijn* can be raised over FV, giving (44e=43a). Intermediate raising of $_{Adj}$[trouw] gives (44f=43c). The ungrammatical (43d-f) cannot be generated.

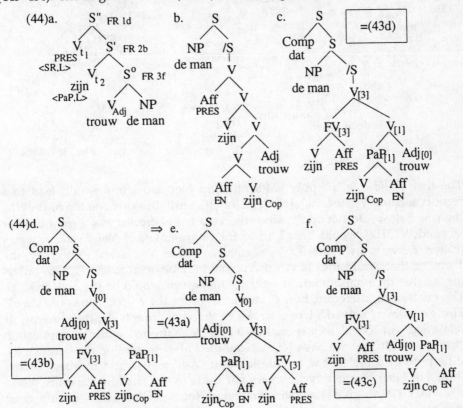

5.6 PR on *zijn$_1$* and adjectives

The verb *zijn$_1$* is in more than one way idiosyncratic. It induces PR, yet when it occurs in a perfective tense it has the past participle *geweest*, not the 'infinitivus pro participio' which is normal for PR-clusters. Moreover, in subordinate clauses *zijn$_1$* produces a word order that seems to contradict our rules. Consider (45a-c), with the SA (46a):

(45)a.   ... dat dit niet   te doen is geweest
         ... that this not   to do is been
                  '... that it has not been humanly possible to do this'

  b.   ... dat dit niet   te doen geweest is

  c.   ... dat dit niet   is te doen geweest

(46)a.

The first cyclic rule to apply is PR on *zijn₁*. Normally, this would lead to a right-branching V-cluster $_V[_V[zijn]_V[_{Prt}[te]_V[doen]]]$. But then, on the next cycle, the rule PaP would not apply, since the verb to be affected has a right brother labelled 'V'. This would then lead to the ungrammatical **dat dit niet is wezen te doen* (*wezen* is a variant of *zijn*, normally used in V-clusters). Moreover, the V-cluster that would thus have arisen would not be open to any ECA-re-ordering, so that the ungrammatical sentence just given would be the end product. The question is, therefore, how do we account for the correct forms of (45a-c)? The problem is solved at one stroke if the constituent $_V[_{Prt}[te]_V[doen]]$ is relabelled 'Adjective', as a special case of SCA connected with the application of PR. If we do that we have (46b). Now the PaP-rule does apply, because the V-node to be affected has a node labelled 'Adj' as its right brother. This is shown in (46c). Further cyclic treatment leads to the shallow structure (46d). AH and V-FINAL give (46e), with the values for ECA. Some ECA-raising must take place now, since the rightmost node is valued [0]. Maximal raising of $_{Adj}$[te doen] gives (46f=45a). (46f) allows for the raising of PaP over FV, which gives (46g=45b). Intermediate raising of $_{Adj}$[te doen] from (46e) gives the least preferred (46h=45c).

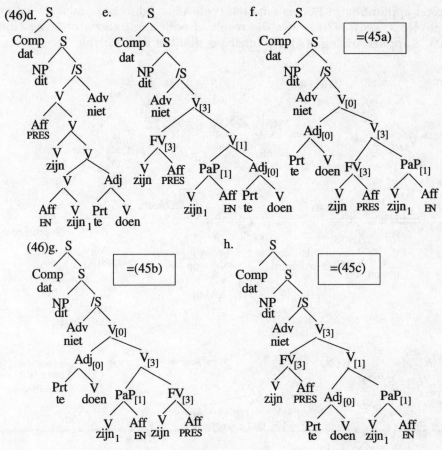

Let us now pass on to the case where PR is induced by adjectives. The lexicon in 5.2.2 contains a class of adjectives inducing PR on an embedded $S'_{\emptyset[PASS]}$. The adjectives specified are *makkelijk* ('easy'), *moeilijk* ('difficult'), *onmogelijk* ('impossible'). The construction at hand is the Dutch equivalent of what is found in the English *This is hard to explain* (see 3.8.3). Besides a single $S'_{\emptyset[PASS]}$-complement with PR (the RAISING frame) they also allow for $NP_x + S'_{\emptyset[PASS]}$, with SD (the CONTROL frame). Other constructions they may enter into are not discussed here. First we consider the RAISING construction. Consider the subordinate clause (47a) with the SA (47b). The main verb used is $_V[_V[lossen]_{VPrt}[op]]$ ('solve', lit. 'loosen up'):

(47)a. ... dat dit probleem niet makkelijk op te lossen is
      ... that this problem not   easy   up to loosen is
      '... that this problem is not easy to solve'

The shallow structure is (47g). After V-FINAL the structure is (47h). Now ECA applies. The Adj-node on the spine counts as a separate unit with internal ECA-raising. Thus, the subcluster $_{Adj}[_{Adj}[makkelijk]_V[_V[_{Prt}[te]_V[lossen]]_{VPrt}[op]]]$ is valued [0] and obligatorily raised as a whole over the FV-subconstituent. A second application of ECA is required within the Adj-cluster, raising $_{VPrt}$[op] over $_V$[te lossen]. (47i) shows the result of both applications of ECA. Now MINCE applies, giving (47j). No other possibilities are available.

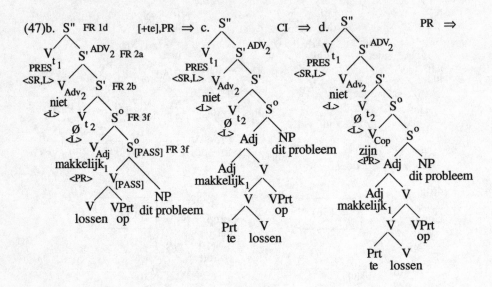

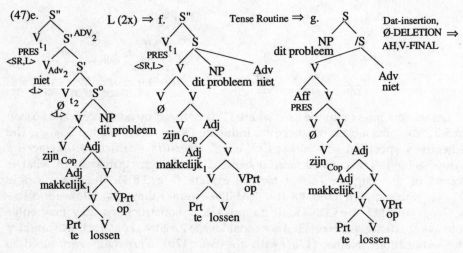

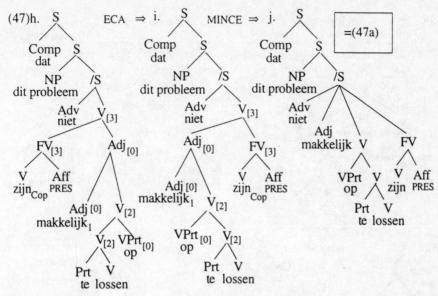

However, (48a) is also acceptable, with or without a semantically empty
Prt[om] (used by many speakers and avoided by many others). It is insertable in
virtue of a corollary, which is not taken into account in the present rule system.
(48a) is derivable from the CONTROL frame associated with the adjectives
concerned. The associated SA-structure is (48b), and the shallow structure is
(48g). After V-FINAL the structure is as in (48h). Double application of ECA,
once in /S_1 and once in /S_2, followed by MINCE, leads to (48j=48a).

(48)a.   ... dat dit probleem niet makkelijk is (om) op te lossen

(48)e. [tree diagram]   L (2x) ⇒ f. [tree diagram]   Tense Routine ⇒ g. [tree diagram]   Dat-insertion. Ø-DELETION ⇒ AH.V-FINAL

(48)h. [tree diagram]   ECA (2x) ⇒ i. [tree diagram]   MINCE ⇒ j. [tree diagram]   =(48a)

This terminates our discussion of the verbal end groups in Dutch subordinate clauses. We will now pass on to the syntax of adverbs and negation.

5.7 The syntax of adverbs and negation; the Queuing Principle

In Dutch, as in the other languages considered, the syntax of adverbs and negation is complex. One complicating factor in Dutch is that all except the sentence adverbials are LOWERED to the far right of their argument-S, which may cause adverbial crowding at the far right of the receiving S. This, together with the V-clusters resulting from PR and moved to the far right by V-FINAL, makes the middle and end sections of a Dutch sentence potentially very heavy. Traditional Dutch grammarians speak of the 'middle field' and the 'end field' of Dutch sentences, the former being the 'field' for Noun Phrases, adverbs and the like, the latter for verbal clusters.

As said in 5.2.3, Dutch far right LOWERING forbids the crossing of adverbials to the right of V. As a result, the left-to-right order of subsequently lowered adverbials in surface structure mirrors their hierarchical position in the

SA-structure. Thus, in an SA of the form (49a) the adverbials Adv^1, Adv^2 and Adv^3 will appear in the surface structure (49b) in that order:

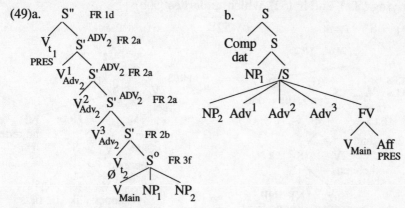

This property of LOWERING in Dutch and German we call the *Queuing Principle* (QP). The reality of QP appears from the fact that a sentence that breaches QP runs the risk of not meaning what its SA means. Take the example:

(50)a. ... dat ik de fiets   om die reden   niet heb verkocht
     ... that I the bicycle for that reason   not have   sold
     '... that for that reason I did not sell the bicycle'

  b. ... dat ik de fiets   niet om die reden   heb verkocht
     ... that I the bicycle not for that reason   have   sold
     '... that I did not sell the bicycle for that reason'

If clause (50a) is true the bicycle has not been sold, while (50b) implies that the bicycle has been sold, though not for that reason.

We have to do here with *scope differences*. Any SA-predicate, whether 'abstract' or lexical, that takes an S-structure as argument (subject or object) has scope. Scope-bearing elements we call *operators*. The scope of an operator is the whole S-constituent that forms its argument. Successive scope-bearing elements in an SA-structure thus create a scope hierarchy. Among the scope-bearing operators we count the tenses, modalities, MAUX-verbs, adverbials and quantifiers (discussed in section 7.1).

From a semantic point of view operators set a frame in terms of which their scope is to be interpreted. For some configurations of operators, the semantic differences between different scope assignments are crucial, for others the scope hierarchy matters less, depending on which operators are involved. Some operators are scope-sensitive, for others the scope they have matters less. Roughly speaking, the scope-sensitive operators are the quantifiers, those that contain negation and those that induce a presupposition. Time and place indicators tend not to care so much about their scope. QP ensures that, in any case, scope relations are respected.

Returning now to (50a,b) we see that the semantic difference between them is expressible in terms of the scope of the operators *niet* ('not') and *om die reden* ('for that reason'). In (50a) *om die reden* has wider scope than *niet*, and in (50b) it is the other way round. This is shown in (51), which is the SA-structure underlying (50a), and in (52), which underlies (50b):

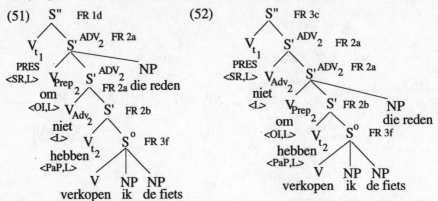

Far right LOWERING of the adverbials mirrors their SA-status in the surface structure left-to-right order: the higher operator comes first.

This is important for the following reason. All natural languages have certain provisions built into their grammars to ensure that, within definable limits, the left-to-right order of the scope-sensitive operators in surface structure mirrors their scope, i.e. their hierarchical status in SA-structure. This is the *Scope Ordering Constraint* (SOC), noted first in Seuren (1967), then discussed in Seuren (1984, 1985:141-166) and in Lakoff (1971), and again in section 7.1 of this book. When SOC is not observed there is a risk, depending on a variety of grammatical factors, that the sentence will be construed in a way that does not correspond to its SA-structure. A great deal has been written since 1970 about this intriguing relation between semantic structure and syntax, but no consensus has arisen as to the status of SOC, mostly due to the fact that intonational features and, occasionally, lexical selection may override SOC. We shall not digress on this question any further here. The reader is referred to section 7.1 for further discussion. We simply accept here the obvious fact that scope differences can be crucial and that they are are expressed mainly by means of the left-to-right ordering of the elements concerned.

In Dutch and German, but not in English and French, the rule of LOWERING is subject to QP, which ensures that the scope hierarchy is automatically reflected in the surface left-to-right ordering of the operators concerned, regardless of whether the operators are or are not scope-sensitive. QP is, therefore, stricter than SOC. Yet it is also weaker, since not all scope-sensitive operators are adverbial. A special device is, therefore, needed to ensure observance of SOC (in 7.1 scope-sensitive operators are 'flagged', which keeps them from crossing other flagged operators lowered earlier).

While in English and French, typically, place indicators precede time indicators (*He has lived in London for five years*, and not **He has lived for five years in London*), in Dutch the order is inverted: first time then place.

Given that time and tense operators are generally higher (have larger scope) than place operators, the English order follows from far-right LOWERING as formulated for English: lowered elements cross adverbials already to the right of V, unless checked by a flag, which unquantified time and place operators are not. The Dutch order follows from QP: higher elements do not, when lowered, cross adverbials already to the right of V. We note, incidentally, that in English and French, which have a great deal of adverbial LOWERING onto the V-cluster, LOWERING onto V again automatically ensures a regular correspondence between scope hierarchy and left-to-right ordering, though postcyclic ADVERB PLACEMENT may again disturb the regular picture.

Back to (50a,b). In this case, as has been said, the semantic difference is crucial. This is explained by the fact that the prepositional phrase *om die reden* is *factive*, in the sense of Kiparsky & Kiparsky (1971): it presupposes the truth of its argument-S.[7] In (50a) the S embedded under *om die reden* is the equivalent of 'I did not sell the bicycle', whereas in (50b) it has the meaning of 'I sold the bicycle', as is easily seen from (51) and (52), respectively. Hence, (50a) entails that I did not sell the bicycle, and from (50b) it is naturally inferred (by default, unless the inference is cancelled by context) that I did.

A similar case where left-to-right ordering of the operators is semantically crucial, owing to the negation and two quantifiers, is (53a,b):

(53)a. Nobody here speaks two languages
   b. Two languages are spoken by nobody here

In most academic contexts, (53a) is false, but (53b) true. (53a) corresponds to an SA where the operators *not*, *somebody*, and *two languages* are arranged in such a way that *not* is higher than *somebody*, and *somebody* higher than *two languages*. We shall not go into the question of how this works for quantifiers like *somebody* or *two languages*: that question is discussed in section 7.1. Here it suffices to point out that the scope relations expressed in SA-structure in terms of tree hierarchy are reflected in left-to-right order in surface structure.

---

[7] The usual tests for presuppositional status (see Seuren 1994) yield positive results: (1) The argument-S (scope) of *om die reden* is semantically entailed (if the whole sentence is true then, necessarily and without escape clauses, the S under *om die reden* is true). (2) The argument-S (scope) of *om die reden* is normally projected (Karttunen 1970, 1973, 1974) (i.e. default-inferred, overridden when the inference is cancelled by contextual factors) when the whole sentence is embedded in a non-entailing context. (3) A text composed of the presupposition followed by the presupposition-carrying sentence, with the connective *and* or *but*, is judged natural and well-ordered. Thus, both (i) and (ii) are well-ordered little texts, the one entailing that I sold the bicycle, the other that I did not:
   (i) I did not sell the bicycle, and I did not sell it for the reason you mentioned
   (ii) I sold the bicycle, but I did not sell it for the reason you mentioned
In (i) the operator *for the reason you mentioned* has larger scope than *not*, so that the S-structure containing the negation is presupposed to be true. The second conjunct can be read as: *and it is for the reason you mentioned that I did not sell it*. In (ii) *not* takes scope over *for the reason you mentioned*, so that the presupposition is expressed by the S-structure without negation. Here the second conjunct can be reformulated as: *but it is not for the reason you mentioned that I sold it*. Note that English grammar allows the violation of SOC in this case, making up for it by intonational means.

Not always is the semantic difference between different operator orderings as clear as in this case. It makes little difference, for example, whether one says (54a) or (54b), despite the different scopes of *niet* and *morgen*, though (54a) sounds more natural:

(54)a. ... dat Dirk morgen niet zal vertrekken
     ... that Dirk tomorrow not will   leave
     '... that Dirk will not leave tomorrow'

    b. ... dat Dirk niet morgen   zal vertrekken
     ... that Dirk not tomorrow will   leave
     '... that Dirk will not leave tomorrow'

The greater naturalness of (54a) seems due to the fact that Dutch prefers to place its sentence negation under deictic tense or time operators, like t_1 or *morgen*, and not above them, as is done in some other languages. Semantically, it makes little difference whether one does it one way or the other. Note that in (54a,b) both operators, *morgen* and *niet*, are Adv_2 and introduced by Formation Rule (2a). It is also possible for *morgen*, but not for *niet*, to be introduced by FR (1c), as *morgen*, but not *niet*, also belongs to the class Adv_1 and can thus enter the SA-structure at rule (1c). In that case, however, its far-right LOWERING keeps it outside the /S-constituent, and V-FINAL keeps the V-cluster to the left of *morgen*, as in (55a). Its counterpart (55b) is grossly ungrammatical:

(55)a. ... dat Dirk niet zal vertrekken, morgen
    b. ... *dat Dirk morgen zal vertrekken, niet

Here, the left-to-right ordering of *niet* and *morgen* does not reflect their mutual scope relation. This type of violation of strict SOC is well-known and is due to the fact that *morgen* is not a /S-constituent but is directly attached to the main S-node. Its hierarchical status in the surface tree allows it to cross over the scope-sensitive operator *niet* that has been lowered earlier. Again, see section 7.1 for further discussion.

Apart from class 1 adverbials, therefore, the mechanism of far right LOWERING ensures the observance of SOC. There is, however, another problem, of a purely syntactic nature. Consider the following sentences, with and without the negation:

(56)a. ... dat ik morgen   de fiets (niet) zal verkopen
     ... that I tomorrow the bicycle (not) will   sell
     '... that I will (not) sell the bicycle tomorrow'

    b. ... dat ik om die reden   de fiets   (niet) zal verkopen
     ... that I for that reason the bicycle (not) will   sell
     '... that for that reason I will not sell the bicycle'

What is to be noted about (56a) and (56b) is the position of the adverbials *morgen* and *om die reden*, respectively. LOWERING to the far right of *niet* places it properly right after *de fiets*, as in the sentences shown. But subsequent far right LOWERING of *morgen* or *om die reden* should place these operators just before *niet*, giving the fully grammatical (57a) and (57b):

(57)a.   ... dat ik de fiets morgen (niet) zal verkopen
　　b.   ... dat ik de fiets om die reden (niet) zal verkopen

These two sentences are entirely synonymous with (56a) and (56b), respectively. The difficulty is that (56a,b) are also fully grammatical. The Queuing Principle does not account for this. Therefore, an extra provision is needed, given in the formulation of LOWERING in 5.2.3. The provision is:

An Adv_2 not marked † and lowered by L_{right} may stop before $NP_{[DO]}$.

Since *niet* is marked †, it is not allowed to stop before $NP_{[DO]}$. Therefore, if *niet* is the highest operator and therefore precedes *morgen* or *om die reden*, it is not allowed to precede the direct object *de fiets*, as shown in (58a,b):

(58)a.   ... *dat ik niet de fiets morgen zal verkopen
　　b.   ... *dat ik niet de fiets om die reden zal verkopen

Moreover, QP ensures that in (59a) both adverbials, *niet* and *morgen*, precede the direct object *de fiets*, just like *niet* and *om die reden* precede it, in that order, in (59b):

(59)a.   ... dat ik niet morgen de fiets zal verkopen
　　b.   ... dat ik niet om die reden de fiets zal verkopen

There are thus two subclasses among the class 2 adverbials, one whose members behave like *niet*, and one whose members behave like *om die reden* or *morgen*. Further investigation shows that the former subclass is closed and limited, while the latter is open-ended, and therefore the default class. In the lexicon of 5.2.2 the members of the small closed class are marked †. They are: *niet* ('not'), *reeds* en *al* (both: 'already'). The exact size of this class will appear on further investigation.

Note that a single indirect object-NP is not, or only marginally, allowed to intrude into an adverbial cluster: (60a) is much less acceptable than the canonical (60b). More than one NP in that position seems awkward, as is shown by (60c) and the correct (60d) and (60e):

(60)a.   ... *?dat ik morgen Dirk zal schrijven
　　　　　... that I tomorrow Dirk will write
　　　　　'... that I will write to Dirk tomorrow'

　　b.   ... dat ik Dirk morgen zal schrijven

　　c.   ... ?*dat ik morgen Dirk de brief zal schrijven
　　　　　... that I tomorrow Dirk the letter will write
　　　　　'... that I will write Dirk the letter tomorrow'

　　d.   ... dat ik Dirk morgen de brief zal schrijven

　　e.   ... dat ik Dirk de brief morgen zal schrijven

As a final observation we note that the extra clause needed for the LOWERING rule is somehow reminiscent of the 'third construction' discussed at the end of section 5.4.1 above. There, too, a rule, V-FINAL, is disturbed by one single NP. Although there is not, or not yet, sufficient justification for a more general formulation, the similarity is striking.

5.8   Dutch an SOV-language?

Largely on the basis of V-final phenomena it has been proposed (Koster 1975) that Dutch, and German likewise, should be treated as an underlying SOV-language, and the proposal has since gained wide acceptance. No matter what the advantages may be in other theories of grammar, in Semantic Syntax the SOV-hypothesis does not pay for Dutch. Whether it pays for German is another matter, to be discussed in the following chapter.

In terms of Semantic Syntax, the SOV-hypothesis can be presented in different forms or degrees. There is a strong and a weak version. But in all forms the general format SU-IO-DO-V is used, as in the SA-structure (61b), which would underlie the sentence (61a):

(61)a. Schijnt het kind de melk te willen drinken?
        seems the child the milk to want   drink
        'does the child appear to want to drink the milk?'

(61)b.

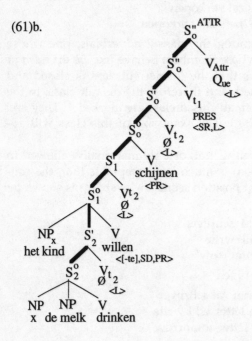

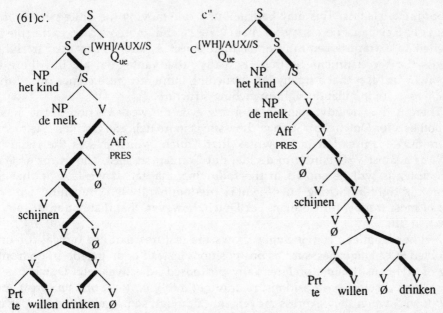

The question now is: will the LOWERING rule left-adopt, as in the rule system of 5.2 above, or is it right-adopting? Note that the SA-structure (61b) is, as a whole, left-branching, which would make right-adoption for LOWERING the regular choice (see section 2.8). This is what is found in unambiguous SOV-languages like Turkish. But PR has to be right-adopting, given Dutch surface word order. It must, therefore, create right-branching structures, or else the surface word order will come out all wrong. If we combine right-branching PR with left-branching LOWERING, the shallow structure will be like in (61c'), which has a mixture of left-branching and right-branching constituents. If, on the other hand, we make LOWERING left-adopting and thus right-branching, the shallow structure is as in (61c''), which is right-branching throughout, but for the fact that the V-cluster under /S is on the right, and not on the left, as in proper right-branching structures.

(61c') is a stronger version of SOV than (61c''). And it is awkward because of the mixing of directionality, but also because, after Ø-DELETION, $_{Aff}$[PRES] will have difficulty finding its main verb, which is on the other side of the V-cluster. It is formally possible to get it right, but then the AUX-area has to go, and the whole process becomes needlessly complex. Also, the Q_{ue}-element is on the wrong side of the V-cluster and would attract the WH-constituent to sentence-final position. To repair this is possible but would complicate the system.

Plainly, the weak version of (61c'') is preferable on all counts. But (61c'') is identical to what our own rule system produces, but for the final position of the V-cluster under /S. And (61c'') is entirely right-branching, but for, again, the position of the V-cluster. It has been claimed that structures with /S-final V-constituents have the advantage of making the rule V-FINAL superfluous for subordinate clauses. This may be true but a rule moving the finite verb to the front of /S remains necessary for main clauses, and, moreover, an extra rule is needed to extrapose centrally embedded object Ss and /Ss to the far right, across the V-constituent. So there is really no advantage at all. But there is the awkward fact that a totally left-branching input structure comes out of the Cycle as a predominantly right-branching structure.

There is thus no advantage in adopting even the weak version of the SOV-hypothesis for Dutch. For German the issue is more delicate. German has many more SOV-features left in its syntax than Dutch, which makes the issue of SOV as against VSO harder to decide. But German, at least, allows for a clear principle, as will be shown in the following chapter: if we take it that S-syntax is right-branching but V-syntax predominantly left-branching we are out of most trouble for German. For Dutch, however, that distinction does not work at all.

Neither language convincingly shows the features that are typical for un-doubted SOV-languages, such as postpositions instead of prepositions, no front-ing of WH-constituents, preferentially postposed adjectives, etc. Dutch has a very limited set of postpositions, mainly *in* ('into'), *uit* ('out of'), *op* ('up') and *af* ('down') when they express movement (although some grammarians prefer to treat them as verbal particles). German has its own small set of postposi-tions, as in *dem Gesetze gemäß* ('according to the law'). In ancient epic Greek prepositions alternate with postpositions, as in:

(62) Steíchō   pròs Moúsās kaì Kastalíēs ápo pī́nō
      ascend-1SG towards Muses-ACC and Kastalia-GEN from drink-1SG
      'I am ascending towards the Muses and am now drinking from Kastalia'

(The author is saying that his ascent to the pinnacle of arts, Mount Parnassus, where the Muses live, is only beginning, the spring Kastalia being at the foot of the mountain.) Here *pròs* is a preposition and *ápo* a postposition, though *ápo* might also have been a preposition (with change of accent into *apó*). It is no doubt legitimate to regard such phenomena as traces of an older stage of the languages concerned where they were all indeed SOV. But a language does not have to be SOV to be able to live with SOV-relics.[8]

It has been proposed that the predominantly far right position of adverb-ials in Dutch and German points to SOV-status, as this would help the gen-eralization that V-constituents attract adverbials. But there is no indication at all that far right adverbials cluster with the V-constituent. On the con-trary, they clearly do not cluster. If they did, the difficulties connected with end clusters would be compounded.

It is often said, in this context, that the far right position of the negation word *niet* is due historically to its association with sentence-final V. But as it

---

[8] It is interesting to note that Chinese has been undergoing a gradual change from surface SVO to surface SOV word order, with SVO more dominant in the South and SOV more in the northern dialects, each dialect carrying features of both word order schemes (Li & Thompson 1974; Hashimoto 1976).

happens, the etymology of *niet* is well-known and identical to that of its counterparts *not* in English and *nicht* in German. These words are composed of the
original negation word *ne* plus a word *iet* (English *ought*, German *icht*) meaning 'something' (see also note 7 in section 2.7.4.2). Just like the French NEG2-
element *pas* (originally 'footstep'), the additional element served to reinforce
the negation *ne* which was felt to be too weak to carry its heavy semantic load.
The development in English, Dutch and German, recent enough to be well
documented, has been as follows. The original structure [ne+V - X] became
[ne+V - X - ought/iet/icht] by strengthening of the negation. Then there was
negation copying, well-known in hundreds of languages and dialects: [ne+V - X
- ne+ought/iet/icht]. Then the original negation before V was dropped: [V - X -
ne+ought/iet/icht]. German and Dutch have so far left it at that, integrating
the negation into the wider class of Adv_2.[9] English has, over the past four
centuries, brought [ne+ought] back to the V-cluster (no doubt under the influence
of Norman French), as shown in the rule system of chapter 3. There is thus no
reason at all to regard the far right position of the negation in Dutch, German,
and Middle and Early Modern English as an SOV-feature.

In general, it does not pay to treat Dutch as an underlying SOV-language.
Besides the difficulties that have been pointed out there are others as well.
For example, the postcyclic rule of CLITIC MOVEMENT moves non-animate
third person direct object personal pronouns to the position just to the right of
the V-cluster, as shown in 5.2.7 and in (31) above, and in (63):

(63)a. Ik heb het [haar / het meisje] gegeven
     I have it [her / the girl] given
     'I have given it [her / to the girl]'

   b. ... dat ik het [haar / het meisje] gegeven heb
     ... that I it [her / the girl] given have
     '... that I have given it [her / to the girl]'

The pronoun does not cluster with the V-constituent but just stays close to it.
The cliticization rule is to be ordered before V-FINAL, as V-final in subordinate
clauses moves the entire V-cluster to the far right, leaving the clitic stranded,
as in (63b). In all European languages that have a well-developed clitics system cliticization involves attraction of weak pronouns by the V-constituent. In
an SOV-treatment this phenomenon could not be accounted for in terms of
attraction to the V-constituent and subsequent stranding in subordinate clauses.
The weak pronoun would have to be moved to the leftmost position of /S, to be
accompanied later, but only in main clauses, by the finite verb form. This
would disturb the picture of cliticisation in all European languages.

The upshot is that, even if it is formally possible to describe Dutch as an
SOV-language, it is counterproductive to do so, as it brings along a series of
unnecessary complications and crosslinguistic irregularities.

---

[9] The Scandinavian languages went through essentially the same process, with [ne+V - X -
ikke], except that no negation copying took place (Jespersen 1924:335).

CHAPTER 6

The German auxiliary and complementation system

6.1 Preliminary comparative observations

The foremost problem in German syntax stems from the fact that German syntax is not uniformly right-branching, as is the syntax of English, French and Dutch. There is no way German syntax can be described other than by allowing a mixture of left and right branching. Even if the basic underlying word order is taken to be SOV, which is not preferable, and in all default cases lowering of elements onto the V-cluster is given a left-branching turn, which is preferable, there is still the fact that question words and focused elements are attracted to sentence-initial position, which requires right-branching. German PREDICATE RAISING, in any case, is left-branching, as surface word order leaves no room for any other interpretation. Historically speaking one may say that German is a great deal more conservative than Dutch and English.

On balance, the most efficient solution appears to be to keep basic VSO-order, but with predominantly left-branching V-clusters. As will be shown below, right-branching is found in V-clusters only with a small class of verbs and only when these verbs are clustered and non-spine, and stand directly under the perfective auxiliary. This is a clear principle and avoids messiness in the rule system: *S-syntax is right-branching but V-syntax is, in principle, left-branching.* It allows for whatever valid generalizations can be made with regard to underlying and/or surface verb-initial languages, such as predominance of prepositions as against postpositions, fronting of question words and focused elements, preferentially preposed adjectives, etc. It avoids, moreover, the necessity of postcyclic adjustments in verbal end clusters. Whether it also means that German V-clusters are more prone than their counterparts in the other languages discussed to become morphological structures (as happened in Turkish) is a question that must be left open.

PREDICATE RAISING is less frequent in German than in Dutch. As in Dutch, SUBJECT RAISING need not be assumed at all in the complementation system, and is taken to occur only with the highest tense operator in the auxiliary system. As opposed to Dutch, verbal end clusters are, in the rule system presented below, entirely tame and need no re-adjustment.

The middle position between the two tenses is filled exclusively by the future modal verb *werden*, which also acts as the passive auxiliary and as the verb for 'become'. In the latter two meanings it can occur as an infinitive: *Ich hoffe, nicht entlassen zu werden* ('I hope not to be fired'), and *Ich hoffe, Lehrer zu werden* ('I hope to become a teacher'), but as the future modal it lacks an infinitive: **Ich hoffe, es schaffen zu werden* ('I hope I will manage it'). Note that the Dutch equivalent of the last sentence: *Ik hoop het te zullen klaar-*

spelen, is perfectly grammatical, which corresponds to the middle position between the tenses being empty in Dutch.

Some further differences with the other languages discussed will appear in the text below. Other differences have been left undiscussed. No MAUX-verbs have so far been detected.

6.2 Branching directionality in V-clusters: the R-condition

The main problem with regard to a proper formulation of the rule system has proved to be the question of when V-clusters deviate from their standard left-branching orientation and become right-branching. In order to bring about order in what seemed to be a messy database we have formulated the principle that German V-clusters are standardly left-branching, but switch over to right-branching when a member of a small class of verbs is clustered and non-spine (i.e. has a left brother labelled 'V'), and stands directly under the perfective auxiliary (*haben* or *sein*). In that position the same verbs block the application of the cyclic rule PAST PARTICIPLE. (The reader will remember that the rule PAST PARTICIPLE is blocked in Dutch under the same condition, though for all verbs and, of course, with inverted directionality.) Moreover, the post-cyclic rule V-FINAL has to be extended with the option (for loftier style registers) of allowing the V-cluster to be moved across an embedded /S. Under these two principles all phenomena appear to fall into place. The phenomena in question have been observed in the literature (see note 1), but no principled solution is offered. With the help of the general principle of directionality and of the technique of V-clustering, Semantic Syntax can account for the seemingly irregular data in a straightforward and principled way.

Let us have look at the details. In clause (1a) the standard left-branching principle has applied in the V-cluster. The shallow structure is as in (1c), derived from the SA (1b), formally specified by the Formation Rules in 6.3.1.

(1) a.   ... daß ich tanzen gegangen bin
    ... that I   dance   gone   am
    '... that I have gone dancing'

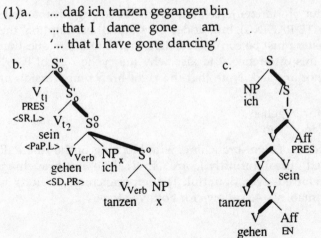

We assume that German syntax is right-branching, as in the other languages concerned, but that the V-cluster is, in principle, left-branching, as shown in (1c). If one applies the rules that form the V-cluster, i.e. PREDICATE RAISING and LOWERING, in the left-branching fashion, i.e. PR with left-adoption and LOWERING with right-adoption (see 2.8), one gets the shallow structure (1c) (the spine is indicated by heavy lines).

An analogous V-cluster underlies the clause (2a). The clauses (1a) and (2a) cause no trouble, since the V-clusters are left-branching throughout. However, (2a) is considered to be good German only (roughly speaking) in the Southern dialects. In standard German (2a), with the shallow structure (2b), is not liked, and (3a) is preferred, with the shallow structure (3b).

(2)a.   ... daß ich dich tanzen gesehen habe
         ... that I you   dance seen   have
         '... that I have seen you dance'

(3)a.   ... daß ich dich habe tanzen sehen
         ... that I you have dance see
         '... that I have seen you dance'

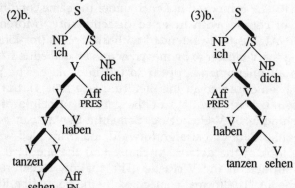

In (3b) only the subcluster $_V[_V[tanzen]_V[sehen]]$ is left-branching (due to left-adoption under PREDICATE RAISING), but, under the simplest assumption, the two top layers of the cluster must be considered right-branching. The question is why there should be this difference, and also why the cyclic rule of PAST PARTICIPLE (PaP) has not applied. Note that the right-branching version of (1a) is ungrammatical:

(1)c.   *... daß ich bin tanzen gehen
         ... that I am dance   go

Further cases of this form of right-branching, with blocking of the rule PaP (leading to the so-called 'Ersatzinfinitiv'), are (4a-d). The left-branching version in (4a) is less preferred, even doubtful. The left-branching versions in (4b,c) are clearly ungrammatical. (4d) allows for both versions:

(4)a.   ... daß ich dich habe tanzen gehen lassen
                              (?... tanzen gehen gelassen habe)
        ... that I you have dance go   allow
        '... that I let you go dancing'

   b.   ... daß ich habe tanzen wollen
                              (*... tanzen gewollt habe)
        ... that I have dance want
        '... that I have wanted to dance'

   c.   ... daß er das wird haben hören können
                              (*... hören gekonnt haben wird)
        ... that he that FUT have hear   be able
        '... that he will have been able to hear that'

   d.   ... daß er das wird hören können   (... hören können wird)
        ... that he that FUT hear be able
        '... that he will be able to hear that'

Close inspection of the data reveals that the right-branching variety is controlled by a small class of verbs, which we call the *R-class*. The R-class contains at least the following verbs, with *sehen, hören, fühlen* and, though to a
much lesser extent, *lassen* (cp. (4a)), as optional members:

sehen ('see') (optional)	*können* ('be able')	*mögen*('like','perhaps')
hören ('hear') (optional)	*müssen* ('must')	*dürfen* ('be allowed')
fühlen ('feel') (optional)	*sollen* ('must')	
lassen ('let, allow, make')	*wollen* ('want')	

All R-verbs induce PREDICATE RAISING (in the left-branching mode, i.e. with
left-adoption of the lower V). They induce a switch-over to right-branching in
the construction of the remaining higher parts of the V-cluster under certain
conditions, jointly labelled the *R-condition*. The R-condition runs as follows:

R-condition:
When an R-verb V_R is the higest V_{LEX} in S^o and is clustered but not on the
spine, (i.e. has a left-brother labelled V), then all subsequent lowerings in
the auxiliary system are right-branching (i.e. with left-adoption):

(a) **obligatorily** when V_R stands directly under a perfective auxiliary (i.e.
     haben or *sein*), and

(b) **optionally** when V_R stands directly under the V_{FUT} *werden*.

NB1: When the R-condition applies the cyclic rule PaP for *haben/sein*
          does not apply.

NB2: When the R-condition applies the auxiliary system must be fully
          tensed, i.e. contain a t_1 (PRES or PAST): non-finite V-clusters (i.e.
          without AUX) must be uniquely left-branching. Non-finite V-clusters
          with mixed directionality are filtered out and rejected.

The R-class consists of verbs of perception, a causative (*lassen*), and a number of
verbs with a modal flavour. Although the members of the R-class share

certain grammatical features, these features are not sufficient to determine class membership: the verbs *gehen₂* and *kommen₂*, in particular, have the same grammatical features as *wollen* and *lassen₂* (see 6.3.2 below), yet do not belong to the R-class, as is illustrated by the ungrammaticality of (1c) above.[1]

Under this assumption, (5a) is the SA and (5b) the shallow structure of (4c):

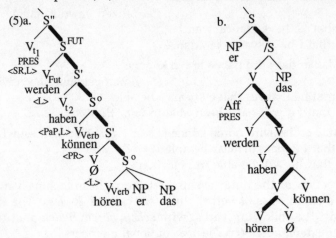

[1] The facts have been noted in the literature. Heidolph et al. (1981:724) notes the directionality switch but has no solution. Among the observations made are the following:
(i)a. ... daß er die Lieder wird haben singen lernen können
    ... that he the songs FUT have sing learn be able
    '... that he will have been able to learn to sing the songs'
  b. *... daß er die Lieder wird singen lernen können haben
Abraham (1995:382) quotes:
(ii)a. Er meinte, daß er ein UFO hat sehen können
    he thought that he a UFO has see be able
    'He thought that he has been able to see a UFO
  b. Er meinte ein UFO sehen können zu haben
  c. Er meinte ein UFO haben sehen zu können
and comments: 'It is undeniably the case that ... the order of the elements of the [verbal P.S.] complex is prima facie not very transparent', referring the reader to p. 498, where he discusses right and left branching phenomena, without, however, coming to a firm conclusion. It must be observed, however, that (iib) and (iic) send shivers down the spines of competent and authoritative German native speakers, who consider them grossly ungrammatical (...*gesehen haben zu können* is, of course, correct, though with a different meaning). They are not generated by the present rule system, as applicability of the R-condition blocks the formation of infinitivals (NB2 in the R-condition).
    Eisenberg et al. (1995), i.e. the Duden Grammar, and especially Bech (1983), give many data and provide some taxonomic ordering principles. Both use numerals to indicate the hierarchical order of the verb forms. The Duden data (pp. 786-7) include the following:
(iii) ... obwohl er die Arbeit nicht *hat (1) erledigen (3) können (2)*
    ... although he the work not has carry out be able
    '... although he has not been able to carry out the work'
(iv)a. ... weil er sich das Paket *wird (1) schicken (3) lassen (2)*
    ... because he himself the parcel FUT send let
    '... because he will have the parcel sent to him'
  b. ... weil er sich das Paket *schicken (3) lassen (2) wird (1)*
Neither Duden nor Bech mention branching directionality, though the numerical order is strongly suggestive of that.

One must keep in mind that all LOWERING and RAISING operations that lead to V-clustering are applied in such a way that the V-cluster is left-branching, unless the R-condition is fulfilled. That is, LOWERING normally leads to right-adoption, except when the R-condition applies, and RAISING always leads to left-adoption, since the R-condition cannot apply with RAISING. As regards (5a) one sees that until the stage in the derivation where the subcluster $_V[_V[_V[essen]_V[\varnothing]]_V[können]]$ comes about all clustering is left-branching. Then, however, the R-condition applies, because *können* belongs to the R-class, is clustered but not on the spine (has a left-brother labelled V), and stands directly under a perfective auxiliary. Now the rule PaP, which is regularly induced by perfective auxiliaries, does not apply (is blocked), and all further LOWERING affecting this V-cluster changes over to right-branching. (One notes, incidentally, that the correct result can be obtained only if the future auxiliary verb *werden* is indeed treated as a V_{FUT} and is made to stand in the inter-tense position.)

The reader will now be able to explain the difference between (6a) and (6b):

(6)a. ... daß er es getan haben muß   b. ... daß er es hat tun müssen
     ... that he it done have must   ... that he it has do must
     '... that he must have done it'   '... that he has had to do it'

The difference is one of scope relations. In (6a) *muß* is the highest verb (in the simple present), which has an embedded S' with the perfective auxiliary *haben*. Consequently, the V-cluster in (6a) is uniformly left-branching. In (6b) the highest verb is the perfective auxiliary *haben*, over the main verb *müssen*, which has an embedded S' with $\varnothing$ for t_2. The V-cluster in (6b) has mixed directionality, as it satisfies the R-Condition. Theoretically one could have:

(6)c. ... daß er es hat getan haben müssen
     ... that he it has done have must
     '... that he has had to have done it'

But one quickly reaches the limits of human processing capacity.

In German, the class of PR-inducing verbs is much smaller than in Dutch. Besides the R-verbs, one counts also the non-R-verbs *kommen* ('come'), *gehen* ('go'), both with the perfective auxiliary *sein*, *scheinen* ('seem'), *wagen* ('dare'), and perhaps a few others. There are, moreover, RAISING adjectives like *leicht* ('easy'), *schwierig* ('difficult'), *unmöglich* ('impossible'), and the copula verb *sein* (see 6.3.2). In general, if a German verb induces PR it goes without the infinitival complementizer particle *zu* (Eng. *to*, Dutch *te*), and if it does not induce PR but only SD it will take *zu*. The only exceptions found so far are the verbs *wagen* and *scheinen*, which induce PR but nevertheless require *zu*.

The long list of verbs inducing SD but no PR, and thus requiring *zu*, includes:

versuchen ('try')	*es wagen* ('dare (it)')	*veranlassen* ('cause')
lernen ('learn')	*lehren* ('teach')	*verbieten* ('forbid')
bitten ('request')	*sich entschließen* ('decide')	*behaupten* ('assert')
etc., etc.		

We thus generate (7a), with the SA (7b) and the shallow structure (7c):

(7)a.   ... daß ich versucht habe zu tanzen
        ... that I   tried   have to dance
        '... that I have tried to dance'

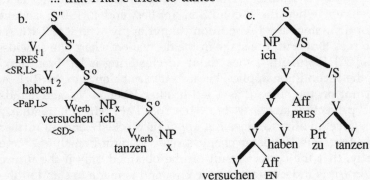

b.

c.

In the postcyclic treatment of (7c) the rule V-FINAL, to be applied after AFFIX HANDLING, has no visible effect when the V-cluster is made to stop before the embedded /S. But, as has been said, German does, under certain stylistic restrictions, allow the V-cluster to jump across an embedded /S. This gives the corresponding (8a), with near-surface structure (8b) (after application of AFFIX HANDLING, but before MINCE):

(8)a.   ... daß ich zu tanzen versucht habe
        ... that I to dance   tried   have
        '... that I have tried to dance'

b.

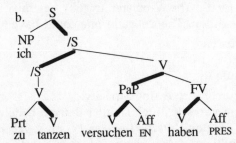

One notes the superficial similarity between (8a) and (2a) — *dass ich dich tanzen gesehen habe*. In terms of the present analysis, however, they reflect very different constructions. That they must be different appears, for one thing, from the fact that (2a) lacks a corresponding **daß ich dich gesehen habe, (zu) tanzen*, or **daß ich gesehen habe, dich (zu) tanzen*.

Let us now try out the various possible forms of a clause with multiple embeddings. Consider (9a-d) (German spelling, remarkably, follows the convention of putting a comma before an embedded /S when there is non-verbal lexical material preceding the verb form):

(9)a. ... weil   er versuchte, Maria zu lehren, den Hund die Zeitung holen zu
   ... because he   tried   Maria to teach   the dog   the   paper   fetch to

   lassen
   let

   '... because he tried to teach Maria to let the dog fetch the newspaper

 b. ... weil er Maria zu lehren versuchte, den Hund die Zeitung holen zu
    lassen

 c. ??... weil er Maria zu lehren, den Hund die Zeitung holen zu lassen
    versuchte

 d. ??... weil er Maria den Hund die Zeitung holen zu lassen zu lehren
    versuchte

All have the common SA (10a), and the common shallow structure (10b). One
notes that *versuchen* and *lehren* take SD, but *lassen* takes PR. There are no
optional applications of cyclic rules. But the postcyclic rule of V-FINAL leaves
the option of moving the V-cluster across an embedded /S (with a connotation
of elevated style).

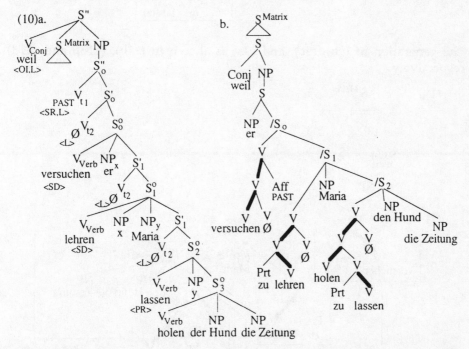

Clause (9a) is generated by not applying the extra option of moving V-FINAL
across an embedded /S at all, as demonstrated in (11a), where Ø-DELETION
and AFFIX HANDLING have applied, and the V-FINAL movement is indicated
by means of arrows:

(11)a.

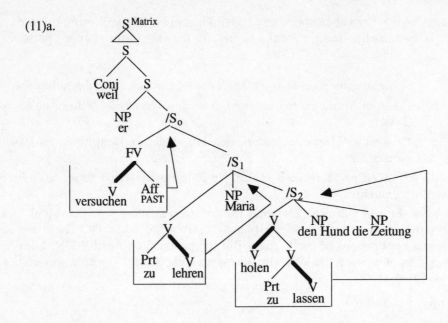

The generation of (9b), (9c), and (9d) is shown in (11b), (11c), and (11d), respectively:

(11)b.

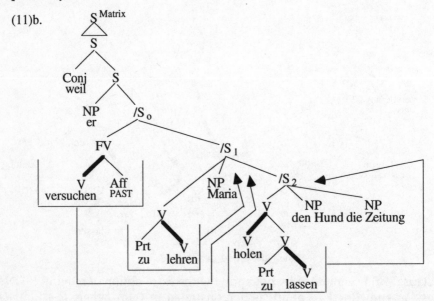

(11c) and (11d) are judged less acceptable or even unacceptable by German speakers. They have in common that the first V-cluster has jumped across two embedded /Ss, which, apparently, amounts to making somewhat too liberal a use of the option of moving across an embedded /S.

(11)c.

(11)d.

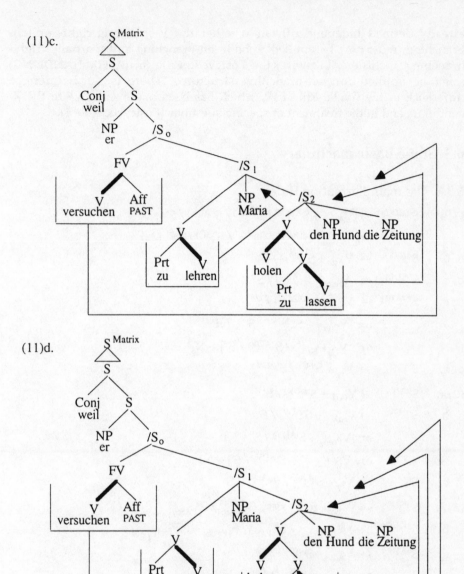

We shall now have a look at the rule system for German. After the systems for English, French, and Dutch, it has a familiar appearance. New elements are the introduction of the subjunctive in Formation Rule (1a), expanded in (1c), and the Postcyclic Rule (2) of *werden*-DELETION. Some comment on the subjunctive is given in section 6.6 below. Then, the Corollary for AUX-FORMATION, already defined independently of whether the V-cluster is right- or left-branching, must now be applied to both left-branching and (partially) right-branching V-clusters. Likewise, the Postcyclic Rule (6) (AFFIX HANDLING) must be applied for left-branching structures. There is, furthermore, a difference in the Cyclic Rule PaP, which has been made sensitive to the R-condition, and in the treatment of specific questions (Postcyclic Rule 4).

6.3 Some basic machinery

6.3.1 The main Formation Rules

(1)a. $\quad S''^{ADV_0} \rightarrow V_{Adv_0} + S''^{ATTR}/S''^{SUBJ}/S''^{ADV_1}/S''$

$\qquad$ **or:** $V_{Prep_0} + S''^{ATTR}/S''^{SUBJ}/S''^{ADV_1}/S'' + NP$

or b. $\quad S''^{ATTR} \rightarrow V_{Attr} + S''^{ADV_1}/S''$

or c. $\quad S''^{SUBJ} \rightarrow V_{Subj} + S''^{ADV_1}/S''$

or d. $\quad S''^{ADV_1} \rightarrow V_{Adv_1} + S''^{ADV_1}/S''$

$\qquad$ **or:** $V_{Prep_1} + S''^{ADV_1}/S'' + NP$

$\qquad$ **or:** $V_Q + {}_{NP}[^\wedge x + S''^{ADV_1}/S''] + NP$

or e. $\quad S'' \rightarrow V_{t_1} + S'^{FUT}/S'^{ADV_2}/S'$

(2)a. $\quad S'^{FUT} \rightarrow V_{FUT} + S'^{ADV_2}/S'$

b. $\quad S'^{ADV_2} \rightarrow V_{Adv_2} + S'^{ADV_2}/S'$

$\qquad$ **or:** $V_{Prep_2} + S'^{ADV_2}/S' + NP$

$\qquad$ **or:** $V_Q + {}_{NP}[^\wedge x + S'^{ADV_2}/S'] + NP$

c. $\quad S' \rightarrow V_{t_2} + S^{oPASS}/S^{oADV_3}/S^o$

(3)a. $\quad S^{oPASS} \rightarrow V_{Pass} + S^{oPASS}Prep/S^{oADV_3}_{[PASS]}/S^o_{[PASS]}$

b. $\quad S^{oPASS}Prep \rightarrow V_{PrepPass} + S^{oADV_3}_{[PASS]}/S^o_{[PASS]} + NP_{[SU_{V_{LEX}}]}$

c. $\quad S^{oADV_3} \rightarrow V_{Adv_3} + S^{oADV_3}/S^o$

$\qquad$ **or:** $V_{Prep_3} + S^{oADV_3}/S^o + NP$

d. $\quad S^o \rightarrow V_{LEX} + <lex.arg.frame>$ **or:** $V_{NP} + NP$

(4)a. $\quad NP \rightarrow :x/^\wedge x + S^{NOM}$ **or:** x **or:** X_{QU}

b. $\quad S^{NOM} \rightarrow V_{Nom} + {}_{NP}[x]$ **or:** $V_{Adj} + S^{NOM}$

6.3.2 Some lexicon

SA-cat	Fillers	Surface cat	Cyclic rules
V_{Adv_0}	und, denn, aber, übrigens, außerdem, ...	Adverb	L_S

V_{Attr}	Q$_{ue}$, Foc, ...	X: see 3.2.1; 5.2.6	L_S
V_{Subj}	SUBJ	Affix	L_V
V_{Adv_1}	also, glücklicherweise, morgen, gestern, ...	Adverb	L_{right}
V_{Adv_2}	also, glücklicherweise, morgen, gestern, außerdem, vielleicht, oft, deswegen, immer, fast, nie, †nicht, †schon, ...[2]	Adverb	L_{right}
V_{Adv_3}	schnell, gut, schlecht, dort, hier, ...	Adverb	L_{right}
V_{Prep_0}	in Bezug auf, ...	Prep	OI,L_S
V_{Prep_1}	in, mit, für, während, nach, ...	Prep	OI,L_{right}
V_{Prep_2}	in, mit, für, an, während, nach, ohne, ...	Prep	OI,L_{right}
V_{Prep_3}	in, mit, auf, ...	Prep	OI,L_{right}
$V_{Prep_{Pass}}$	von	Prep	OI,L_{right}
V_{t_1}	PRES, PAST	Affix (AH→FV)[3]	SR,L_V
V_{FUT}	werden	Verb	L_V
V_{t_2}	Ø	Verb	L_V
	haben/sein	Verb	PaP,L_V
V_{Pass}	*werden[4]	Verb	PaP,L_V
V_{Cop}	*sein	Verb	PR
V_Q	jede, alle, sämtliche, ein, einige, die meisten, ...	Det(erminer)	OI,L_{var}

V_{LEX}:

SA-cat	Fillers	Argument frame	Surface cat	Cyclic rules
V_{Nom}	Haus, Katze, Kind, Maus, Buch, Tisch, Frau, Mann, ...	+ NP	Noun	— —
V_{Adj}	klein, rot, alt, rund, groß, ...	+ NP	Adj	— —
V_{Adj}	treu, bekannt, ...	+ NP (+ NP$_{[IO]}$)	Adj	— —
V_{Adj}	wahrscheinlich, möglich, wahr, ...	+ NP/$_{NP}$[S'']	Adj	— —
V_{Adj}	leicht$_1$, schwierig$_1$, unmöglich$_1$, ...	+ NP/$S^o_{[PASS]}$	Adj	PR
V_{Adj}	leicht$_2$, schwierig$_2$, unmöglich$_2$, ...	+ NP$_x$ + $S^o_{[PASS]}$	Adj	SD

[2] For the meaning of † see LOWERING and FRONTING (= Postcyclic Rule (5)).

[3] With the postcyclic rule of AFFIX HANDLING the V-node directly above Aff is relabelled FV ('finite verb').

[4] As in the Dutch rule system, the asterisk indicates that the verb in question takes the perfective auxiliary *sein*. Moreover, the past participle form of this verb is *worden*, not, as would be expected, **geworden*. One remembers that the Dutch past participle of the passive auxiliary is the zero form.

V_{Verb} lachen, schlafen, tanzen, ...	+ NP	Verb	— —
V_{Verb} *sein, *gehen$_1$, *kommen$_1$, ...	+ NP	Verb	——
V_{Verb} *gehen$_2$, *kommen$_2$, ...	+ NP$_x$ + S^o	Verb	SD,PR
V_{Verb} essen, trinken, schreiben, ...	+ NP (+ NP)	Verb	— —
V_{Verb} $_V[_{VPrt}[auf]_V[essen]]$, ...			
$_V[_{VPrt}[auf]_V[trinken]]$,			
$_V[_{VPrt}[auf]_V[schreiben]]$, ...	+ NP + NP	Verb	— —
V_{Verb} geben, verkaufen, ...	+ NP (+ NP) + NP	Verb	— —
V_{Verb} überlassen,			
$_V[_{VPrt}[vor]_V[stellen]]$, ...	+ NP +NP + NP	Verb	— —
V_{Verb} $_V[_{VPrt}[zu]_V[vertrauen]]$, ...	+ NP +NP + NP/$_{NP}$[S"]	Verb	— —
V_{Verb} scheinen, ...	+ S'	Verb	PR,[+ZU]
V_{Verb} $_V[_{VPrt}[an]_V[fangen]]_1$, ...	+ S$'_\varnothing$	Verb	SD
V_{Verb} $_V[_{VPrt}[an]_V[fangen]]_2$, ...	+ NP$_x$ + S$'_\varnothing$	Verb	SD
V_{Verb} helfen, ...	+ NP + NP$_{x[IO]}$ + (S^o)	Verb	SD
V_{Verb} verbieten, ...	+ NP + NP$_x$ + S^o	Verb	SD
V_{Verb} lernen, ...	+ NP$_x$ + NP/S$'_\varnothing$/$_{NP}$[S"]	Verb	SD
V_{Verb} lehren, ...	+ NP + NP$_{x[DO]}$ + NP/S$'_\varnothing$/$_{NP}$[S"]	Verb	SD
V_{Verb} glauben, ...	+ NP$_x$ + NP$_{[IO]}$/S'/$_{(NP)}$[S"]	Verb	SD
V_{Verb} denken, ...	+ NP$_x$ + (S$'_\varnothing$/S")	Verb	SD
V_{Verb} wissen (-Pass), ...	+ NP + $_{NP}$[S"]/$_{NP}$[Q$_{ue}$+S"]	Verb	——
V_{Verb} wollen (-Pass), ...	+ NP$_x$ + NP/S$'_\varnothing$/S"	Verb	SD,PR
V_{Verb} bitten, ...	+ NP + NP$_{x[DO]}$ + S$'_\varnothing$	Verb	SD
V_{Verb} versprechen, ...	+ NP$_x$ + NP + NP/S$'_\varnothing$/$_{NP}$[S"]	Verb	SD
V_{Verb} versuchen, ...	+ NP$_x$ + S$'_\varnothing$	Verb	SD
V_{Verb} zögern, ...	+ NP$_x$ + S^o	Verb	SD
V_{Verb} entscheiden, ...	+ NP$_x$ + S$'_\varnothing$/$_{NP}$[S"]	Verb	SD
V_{Verb} befehlen, ...	+ NP + NP$_x$ + S$'_\varnothing$	Verb	SD
V_{Verb} müssen, können, sollen, ...	+ S'	Verb	PR
V_{Verb} lassen$_1$, ...	+ NP + S^o	Verb	PR
V_{Verb} lassen$_2$, ...	+ NP + NP$_{x[DO]}$ + S^o	Verb	SD,PR
V_{Verb} sehen, hören, ... + NP + NP/S^o/$_{(NP)}$[S"]/$_{NP}$[Q$_{ue}$+S"] Verb			PR

6.3.3 Cyclic rules

But for LOWERING and PaP, the rules of the Cycle are identical to those of 3.1.3, except for directionality: PR is always left-branching, i.e. left-adopting, and L$_V$ is left-branching and thus right-adopting except for the R-condition. There are, moreover, lexical differences: (a) The rule IT is now called ES, and $_{NP}$[es] is inserted. (b) For COPULA INSERTION V_{Cop}[sein] is inserted. Finally, LOWERING to the far right is subject to stricter conditions than those that apply in English and French (probably as a result of the overwhelming number of cases where L$_{right}$ applies in German). The conditions are identical to those in Dutch, and are stated as follows:

L_{right} does not cross an embedded S or /S, nor an adverbial to the right of V. Except for adverbials marked †, an Adv_2 lowered by L_{right} may stop before $NP_{[DO]}$.

The rule PAST PARTICIPLE is subject to the R-condition:

PAST PARTICIPLE:

The highest lexically filled non-spine V-node in the V-cluster of the argument-S right-adopts $_{Aff}$[EN]. With postcyclic AFFIX HANDLING the V-node directly above Aff is relabelled 'PaP'. If the left brother of PaP is labelled 'Prt' (verbal particle) the parent V is also relabelled 'PaP'. The rule is inoperative when the R-condition applies.

6.3.4 Corollaries

But for *to*-INSERTION and a lexical difference, the corollaries are identical to those of 3.1.4. For *that*-INSERTION $_{Comp}$[daß] is inserted. AUX-FORMATION is as in 3.1.4, but note that $_{Aff}$[SUBJ] also forms AUX (as specified in 2.10). *To*-INSERTION is replaced by *zu*-INSERTION, which functions differently: German *zu* is more closely connected with the lexical infinitive than English *to*, and its occurrence is predictable from the cyclic rules employed: PR normally blocks *zu*-INSERTION (except with *scheinen*), and SD requires it, unless coupled with PR:

Zu-INSERTION is a corollary of any cycle inducing [+zu] or SD without PR: The highest lexically filled V-node, except $_V$[Ø], in the V-cluster of the argument-S left-adopts $_{Prt}$[zu]. If there are two lexically filled V-nodes of equal height in the cluster, not counting $_V$[Ø], the non-spine V left-adopts $_{Prt}$[zu].

6.3.5 Some postcyclic rules (to be applied in the order given)

(1) Ø-DELETION: Delete $_V$[Ø]. Redefine AUX according to the Corollary.

(2) *Werden*-DELETION: If in a V-cluster $_{Aff}$[SUBJ] C-commands $_{Aff}$[PAST], which C-commands $_V$[werden], which C-commands $_V$[haben/sein], then delete $_V$[werden]. Optional when this part of the V-cluster is left-branching; obligatory when it is right-branching.

(3) CLITIC MOVEMENT (CM): Move 3rd ps [-animate] DO pronoun to immediate right of V-cluster.

(4) QUESTION FORMATION:

If $_C$[QU] is in the same clause:

a. $_X$[Q_{ue}] right-adopts $_C$[QU] (any QU-constituent up to phrase level in scope of $_X$[Q_{ue}], but not in embedded S). If no $_C$[QU] is found, $_X$[Q_{ue}] right-adopts $_{y-n}$[Ø] in main questions and $_{y-n}$[ob] in complement questions. X is $_C$[QU]/AUX//S or $_C$[QU]/$_C$[QU] (see 3.2.1; 5.2.6).

b. AUX//S right-adopts the nearest AUX.

If $_C$[QU] is in a complement *daß*-clause, but not in $_{NP}$[S]:

a. $_{Comp}$[daß] is changed into $_C$[QU]/$_C$[QU][Q_{ue}].

b. Insert direct-object-$_{NP}$[was$_{QU}$] into the S in the scope of $_X Q_{ue}$].

(5) **FRONTING:**[5]

    a. $_X$[Foc] right-adopts any major constituent $_C$[+Foc], except S, /S, AUX, and adverbs marked '†'. The category X is: $_C$[+Foc]/AUX//S (see 3.2.1 and 5.2.6).

    b. AUX//S right-adopts the nearest AUX.

    NB1: If $_C$[+Foc] is a PP$_3$ or a locative Adv$_3$, existential or passive $_{NP}$[es] is deleted.

    NB2: If $_C$[+Foc] is any adverbial and existential or passive $_{NP}$[es] — rb = locative adverb, $_{NP}$[es] is deleted.

    NB3: If $_C$[+Foc] is a subject *daß*-clause dummy subject $_{NP}$[es] is deleted.

(6) **AFFIX HANDLING (AH):** As in 3.1.5 (lexical differences as in 6.3.3).

(7) **V-FINAL:** Main clauses (S$_0$): move the non-AUX part of the V-cluster to the far right of /S, but not across an embedded S and preferably not across an embedded /S. The cluster may stop before a PrepPhrase. Non-main S or /S: move the whole V-cluster to the far right under the same conditions.

(8) **MINCE:** As in 3.1.5.

6.4 FRONTING and QUESTION FORMATION in German

As regards FRONTING, German does not seem to differ from Dutch, so that a simple reference to 5.2.6 will suffice. QUESTION FORMATION, however, shows at least one important difference. Whereas in English and Dutch a question word can be fronted directly from an embedded complement clause without further ado (provided the clause is not itself an embedded question and is not headed by NP), in German this is not possible. In German, when a QU-word occurs in a complement *daß*-clause not headed by an NP while the $_X$[Q$_{ue}$]-constituent stands over the main clause, a twofold strategy is followed. First, $_{Comp}$[daß] is changed into $_C$[QU]/$_C$[QU][Q$_{ue}$] (as if the *daß*-clause were a complement question), and subsequently the main clause under $_X$[Q$_{ue}$] acquires a dummy direct object NP filled by the question word *was* ('what'). The process is illustrated in sentence (12a), with SA (12b) and shallow structure (12c). Then the postcyclic rules (1) and (4) apply, resulting first in (12d) then in (12e) (with DOWNGRADING 2). Final treatment gives the surface structure (12f):

(12)a. Was glaubst du, wer es getan hat?
      what believe you who it done has
      'who do you believe has done it?'

---

[5] The three NBs attached to this rule are as inelegant and unsatisfactory as their counterparts in the Dutch system of chapter 5. We shall not try to create order in this apparent hodge-podge now, but will leave the question to future research. In Dutch and German, as in English, the question of 'its and theres' has not been resolved satisfactorily in any existing grammatical theory.

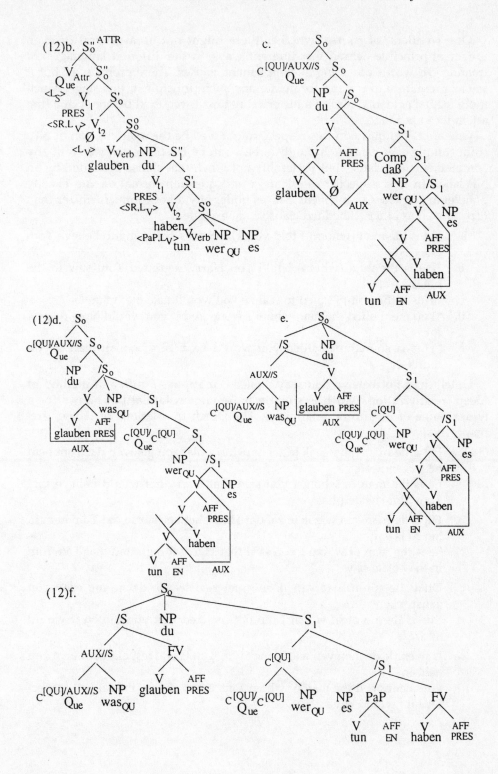

One wonders, of course, whether there might not be a general or even universal principle behind the different ways, in the different languages, of treating QU-words occurring in complement clauses. There probably is, but it seems premature to try and formulate any such principle at this stage. Much more factual evidence, also of a historical nature, is required before even a first attempt can be made.

One area of enquiry, in this respect, might well be the relativization of NPs from complement clauses. In English, NPs can be freely relativized from any complement *that*-clause, but preferably not when that clause is headed by an NP label. In this respect, relativization and question formation run exactly parallel in English. Complement clauses under any other complementizer than *that*, as well as other embedded clauses, are excluded:

(13)a.   He is the man (whom) I told you Harry was not going to believe Tom cheated

   b.   ?He is the man (whom) I told you Harry regretted Tom saw in the house

   c.   ?This is the point I failed to realize you would take me up on

   d.   *You mentioned the man whom I wondered if you would have respect for

   e.   *This is something which you would be a very foolish man if you didn't do

Dutch does not behave that way. Instead, it applies a different method of 'deep' relativization, which is slightly more circumstantial but allows for a wider range of NPs to be relativized. The Dutch translations of (13a-e) are, respectively:

(14)a.   Hij is de man van wie ik je zei dat Harry niet zou geloven dat Tom hem bedrogen heeft
        he is the man of whom I you said that Harry not would believe that Tom him cheated has

   b.   Hij is de man van wie ik je zei dat Harry het betreurde dat Tom hem in het huis zag
        he is the man of whom I you said that Harry it regretted that Tom him in the house saw

   c.   Dit is het punt waarvan ik me niet realiseerde dat je me erop zou aanspreken
        this is the point of which I me not realized that you me on-it would address

   d.   Je noemde de man van wie ik me afvroeg of je wel respekt voor hem zou hebben
        you mentioned the man of whom I me asked if you (modal prt) respect for him would have

e. *Dit is iets waarvan/wat je een domme man zou zijn als je het niet deed
this is something of which/which you a foolish man would be if you it
not did

The relativization of a 'deep' NP in complement clauses, no matter whether it
is a *dat*-clause or a dependent question, or whether it is headed by an NP
label, is made possible by adding an adjunct 'of which/whom' to the main
relative clause and a resumptive pronoun in the position of the relativized NP.
But, as shown by the ungrammatical (14e), this device does not work for
embedded clauses that are not complement clauses.

German behaves very much like Dutch in this respect:

(15)a. Er ist der Mann, von dem ich dir sagte, daß Harry nicht glauben würde,
daß Tom ihn betrogen hat
he is the man of whom I you said that Harry not believe would that
Tom him cheated has

b. Er ist der Mann, von dem ich dir sagte, daß Harry es bedauerte, daß
Tom ihn im Haus sah
he is the man of whom I you said that Harry it regretted that Tom
him in-the house saw

c. Dies ist der Punkt, über den ich mir nicht im klaren war, daß du mich
darum ansprechen würdest
this is the point about which I me(DAT) not in-the clear was that you
me(ACC) for-it address would

d. Du nanntest den Mann, von dem ich mir nicht sicher war, ob du ihn
respektieren würdest
you mentioned the man of whom I me(DAT) not sure was if you him(ACC)
respect would

e. *Dies ist etwas, von dem/was du ein dummer Kerl sein würdest, wenn
du es nicht tätest
this is something of which/which you a foolish man be would if you it
not did

We will, however, not pursue this matter any further here, as relativization
processes, being part of NP-grammar, are left out of account in this chapter (but
see 7.2.1 for some suggestions).

6.5 CLITIC MOVEMENT and the position of the subject

Not unlike Dutch and English, German moves third person pronouns (*es, ihn,
sie*) to a position right after the V-cluster, turning underlying *ich gegeben habe
ihr sie* ('I have given them to her') into *ich gegeben habe sie ihr*. V-FINAL then
produces the correct *Ich habe sie ihr gegeben* for main clauses, and ... *daß ich
sie ihr gegeben habe* for subordinate clauses. So far there is nothing special.

There is, however, a phenomenon in German not shared by English, French
or Dutch: in a main or subordinate clause containing a pronominal direct or

indirect object term and a non-pronominal subject term, the latter is often preferably, but not obligatorily, found in a position normally reserved for the oblique object. This phenomenon occurs only in subordinate clauses and in main clauses where FRONTING has taken place, not in 'canonical' main clauses. Moreover, for quantified subjects, as in (20a,b), the restrictions are laxer: here the 'irregular' position of the subject is found also when the clause contains no pronominal oblique terms. The following examples will give an idea:

(16)a.   Gestern noch wollte   ihm   in jener Hinsicht niemand   glauben
         yesterday still would   him(DAT) in that respect nobody(NOM) believe
         'only yesterday nobody would believe him in that respect'

   b.   Gestern noch wollte   ich   in jener Hinsicht niemandem glauben
         yesterday still would   I(NOM) in that respect nobody(DAT) believe
         'only yesterday I would believe nobody in that respect'

(17)a.   ... weil   mich   Gott-sei-Dank   (der) Karl   nicht gesehen hat
         ... because me(ACC) God-be-thanks   (the) Karl(NOM) not   seen has
         '... because, thank God, Karl did not see me'

   b.   ... weil   ich   Gott-sei-Dank   (den) Karl   nicht gesehen habe
         ... because I(NOM) God-be-thanks (the) Karl(ACC) not   seen have
         '... because, thank God, I I did not see Karl'

(18)a.   ... weil   es   doch   jeder   seit vielen Jahren weiß
         ... because it (MODAL PRT) everyone(NOM) since many years knows
         '... because everyone has known this for many years'

   b.   ... weil   ich   doch   jeden   seit vielen Jahren kenne
         ... because I(NOM) (MODAL PRT) everyone(ACC) since many years know
         '... because I have known everyone for many years'

(19)a.   Gestern hat es   mir   (der) Karl   versprochen
         yesterday has it me(DAT) (the) Karl(NOM)   promised
         'yesterday' Karl promised it to me

   b.   Gestern habe ich   es   (dem) Karl versprochen
         yesterday have I(NOM) it(ACC)   (the) Karl(DAT) promised
         'yesterday I promised it to Karl'

(20)a.   Bisher konnte den Jungen noch niemand   der Mutter   übergeben
         so far could the boy(ACC) still nobody(NOM)   the mother(DAT) hand over
         'so far, nobody has yet been able to hand the boy over to the mother'

   b.   Vermutlich hat die Bombe   dem Politiker   ein Terrorist geschickt
         probably has the bomb(ACC) the politician(DAT) a terrorist(NOM) sent
         'presumably it was a terrorist that sent the politician the bomb'

These phenomena are remarkable and, as yet, ill-understood. The relevant facts are carefully listed in Duden (Eisenberg et al. 1995:793-4; (20a,b) are from p.794), but without any explanatory rule system. None of the existing theories of grammar can account for them in a non-ad-hoc way. The connecting factor seems to be the position of AUX: if, after V-FINAL, a lexical or quantified subject T is not immediately followed by AUX, T seeks a position closer to the main lexical verb, but only, in most cases, if it does not have to jump across full lexical oblique objects. Given the uncertainties, however, and the lack of supportive data from other languages, we must leave the matter to later probing. The postcyclic rules in 6.3.5 do not take these phenomena into account.

6.6 Counterfactual and subjunctive in the four languages

In the previous chapters we have neglected counterfactual and subjunctive phenomena, mainly in order not to overwhelm the reader with too much at the time. At this point, however, we may venture a first exploratory look.

When we speak of 'counterfactual' we mean that a proposition is presented as being part of an imagined scenario whose realization is made dependent on the fulfilment of certain conditions which, however, are taken as unfulfilled, now or in the past. The conclusion is, therefore, that the proposition in question is not true but would have been if the conditions in question were or had been fulfilled. The simplest way to represent a counterfactual semantically is by means of a high sentence operator, say 'CF', which takes scope over the proposition in question and plays a role in the grammar.

From a semantic point of view, there are two main categories of counterfactual, the present and the past counterfactual, illustrated in (21a) and (21b), respectively:

(21)a. If he were rich he would pay
   b. If he had been rich he would have paid

(21a) is a present counterfactual, as appears from the fact that it allows for adverbials like *now* or *today*, which indicate the present time and thus go with the simple present or present perfect. It does not allow for past time adverbials like *yesterday*. The condition is stated in the *if*-clause, and the actual counterfactual in the main clause. Note that the *if*-clause has the simple past, whereas the main clause has the modal verb *will* in the simple past, followed by an untensed infinitive. (21b) is, in its most normal reading, a past counterfactual, as is shown by the fact that it makes sense to say, for example, *Last year, if he had been rich he would have paid*, but not *!Nowadays, if he had been rich he would have paid*. For the past counterfactual the *if*-clause has the pluperfect while the main clause has the modal verb *will* in the simple past, followed by a past infinitive.

One should note, however, that a sentence like (22) is ambiguous between a present and a past counterfactual reading:

(22)   If he had eaten his breakfast he would not have been so hungry.

The counterfactual operator can be removed from this sentence in two ways, either by saying *But he has eaten his breakfast and·he is not hungry* or by saying *But he did eat his breakfast and he was not hungry*. In fact, sentence (22) can be followed both by a present time adverbial like *now* and by a past time adverbial like *last Thursday*. This kind of ambiguity can arise because of

the fact that the CF operator changes present into past, and past into pluperfect in *if*-clauses. It follows that, in *if*-clauses, the present perfect also becomes
a pluperfect under the CF operator. In the main clause of (22) one might expect
the untensed infinitival *be so hungry*, which is also possible and disambiguates the sentence. Apparently, however, the pluperfect of the *if*-clause may
be transferred to the main clause as a past infinitive, without semantic consequences.

We now also see that (21b) is really ambiguous as well, as it allows for an
extended form like *If he had been rich for such a long time, as you say, he
would have paid by now*, which makes it a present counterfactual, though its
non-counterfactual analogue is not in the simple present but in the present
perfect tense. Semantically, however, that still means that the proposition is
presented as being part of what is the case now.

While discussing the syntax of English, in chapter 3, we did not go into
these matters, and we will not do so any further here either, leaving the
sorting out of details to future investigation. What we do want to show here is,
first, the fact that, from the point of view of universal semantics, there are
these two kinds of counterfactual, the present and the past, and, secondly, that
their syntactic and morphological realization differs considerably from
language to language, though there is a clear common pattern in the European
languages.

In most languages it is common for counterfactuals to occur under a possibility
operator, as in the following English sentences:

(23)a   He could escape if he tried harder
    b.   He could have escaped if he had tried harder

Obviously, the main clauses here do not mean, literally, that now or at the
contextually defined period in the past his escape is (was) in fact possible.
They mean that now or at the contextually defined period in the past it is
(was) possible for him to escape but he does (did) not.[6]

From a semantic point of view such cases are interesting because the CF
operator cannot by itself be given a place in the semantic analysis, since it
refuses to define its scope with respect to the possibility operator (POSS). That
is, it is inadequate to place CF above POSS, since that would imply that it is
(would have been) but is (was) in fact not possible that *p*, which is not what
the sentence means. Nor can CF be placed under POSS since that would say that
it is (was) possible that it is (was) counterfactually true that *p*, which is again
not what the sentence means. All one can do is unite CF and POSS into one
combined CF-POSS operator which says that it is (was) possible but does (did)
not happen that *p*. (It would seem that the best semantic definition of such an
operator would be to ascribe to it the normal satisfaction conditions of the

---

[6] A similar variant of the counterfactual in many languages is exemplified in English *She
was going to sing* or Dutch *Zij had zullen zingen*. Here the meaning is that it had somehow
been arranged or agreed that the person referred to by *she* would sing but that in fact she
didn't. That is, a 'has been arranged'-operator takes the place of POSS in these cases. We
will not investigate this counterfactual variety here, but leave it to future research.

natural language possibility operator, coupled with the precondition — leading to a presupposition — that the proposition p in the scope of the operator is counterfactual.)

Apart, however, from the semantic peculiarities involved, there are also purely syntactic complications. These appear when we compare the main clauses of (23) with their translations in other European languages. Let us consider the English, French, Dutch and German versions, isolating the semantic elements of the complex predicate ('HAV' is the cover term for the t_2 auxiliary of the perfect tenses; 'SUBJ' stands for 'subjunctive):

(24)a$_1$. He could escape
PAST-POSS-ESCAPE

a$_2$. He could have escaped
PAST-POSS-HAV-ESCAPE

b$_1$. Il pourrait s'enfuire
PAST-FUT-POSS-ESCAPE

b$_2$. Il aurait pu s'enfuire
PAST-FUT-HAV-POSS-ESCAPE

c$_1$. Hij zou kunnen ontsnappen
PAST-FUT-POSS-ESCAPE

c$_2$. Hij had kunnen ontsnappen
PAST-HAV-POSS-ESCAPE

d$_1$. Er könnte entkommen
SUBJ-PAST-POSS-ESCAPE

d$_2$. Er hätte entkommen können
SUBJ-PAST-HAV-ESCAPE-POSS

This comparison is instructive in a number of ways. One notices immediately the different syntactic make-up of the expressions in the different languages, despite their semantic identity. Some differences are immediately transparent. Thus, the fact that the Dutch (24c$_{1,2}$) has the order POSS-ESCAPE while the German (24d$_2$) has the order ESCAPE-POSS is due to the fact that Dutch V-clusters are right-branching but German V-clusters (but for the R-condition) are left-branching. In the respective SAs the order is the same: POSS-ESCAPE. This difference is, therefore, irrelevant with regard to SA-structure, and we shall consider German as also having the order POSS-ESCAPE.

More interesting, in this connection, is the fact that French, Dutch and German have the order HAV-POSS while only English has POSS-HAV. This is no doubt related to the fact that the verb expressing the POSS operator is a full lexical verb in the former three languages but an intertense modal in English, where it is, so to speak, forced into the position between the two tenses. In this case the SA-structure of the English sentence differs from those in the other three languages, apparently, however, without any semantic consequences.

A further difference consists in the fact that French and Dutch have the FUT operator, which is missing in English. In French this operator is the future tense. In Dutch it is the future main verb *zullen*, as in (25c,d). Both are normally used to express present and past counterfactuals in combination with t_1[PAST], as shown in (25a-d):

(25)a. Je mangerais
I PAST-FUT-Ø-eat
'I would eat'

c. Ik zou eten
I PAST-Ø-zullen Ø eat

b. J' aurais mangé
I PAST-FUT-HAV eaten
'I would have eaten'

d. Ik zou gegeten hebben
I PAST-Ø-zullen eaten HAV

Note, moreover, that (24c$_2$) has the variant *Hij zou hebben kunnen ontsnappen*, i.e. PAST-FUT-HAV-POSS-ESCAPE, and that (24d$_1$) has the variant *Er würde entkommen können*, i.e. SUBJ-PAST-FUT-POSS-ESCAPE, both with FUT. German, moreover, has the obligatory extra operator SUBJ in addition to the future auxiliary *werden*, to express counterfactuality, as in (26a-c):

(26)a. Er   würde   es   mir   sagen
        he SUBJ-PAST-FUT it(ACC) me(DAT) say
        'he would say it to me'

b. Er   würde   es   mir   gesagt haben
    he SUBJ-PAST-FUT   it(ACC) me(DAT) said   HAV
    'he would have said it to me'

c. ... daß er es   mir   gesagt haben   würde
    ... that he it(ACC) me(DAT) said   HAV   SUBJ-PAST-FUT
    '... that he would have said it to me'

We thus see that the element FUT is commonly used to express the counter-factual. However, it is often possible, and sometimes mandatory, to leave out the element FUT, as in (24c$_2$) and (24d$_{1,2}$). For German this is shown again in (26d,e), which are synonymous with (26b,c):

(26)d. Er   hätte   es   mir   gesagt
        he SUBJ-PAST-HAV it(ACC) me(DAT) said
        'he would have said it to me'

e. ... daß er es   mir   gesagt hätte
    ... that he it(ACC) me(DAT) said   SUBJ-PAST-HAV
    '... that he would have said it to me'

In German, the deletion of *werden* is obligatory in two separate classes of cases: (a) in temporal and conditional *wenn*-clauses (not unlike *will*-deletion in English *when*- and *if*-clauses — this class of cases does not concern us here), and (b) when the R-condition is fulfilled. We thus encounter the R-condition of section 6.2 again here, in a different context. Let us consider a few examples (whether main or subordinate clause is immaterial). *Werden*-DELETION is obligatory in these examples, as (28a,b) are ungrammatical:

(27)a. ... weil er   es   hätte   tun müssen
        ... because he it(ACC) SUBJ-PAST-HAV do   must
        '... because he should have done it'

b. ... daß wir weiter keinen Wein mehr   hätten   trinken dürfen
    ... that we further no   wine more SUBJ-PAST-HAV drink   may
    '... that we would not have been allowed any longer to drink wine'

(28)a. *... weil er es würde haben tun müssen
    b. *... daß wir weiter keinen Wein mehr würden haben trinken dürfen

If we assume that there is indeed a rule of *werden*-deletion, optional in most cases but obligatory when the R-condition is fulfilled (besides the obligatory deletion of *werden* in *wenn*-clauses), then the ungrammatical forms of (28a,b) are taken to underlie the grammatical forms of (27a,b), respectively. The underlying form of (24d₂) would then be the ungrammatical (29), which has the SA-structure SUBJ-PAST-FUT-HAV-POSS-ESCAPE (see above):

(29)   *Er würde haben entkommen können
        SUBJ-PAST-FUT-HAV-ESCAPE-POSS

As it does for German, it makes sense for Dutch to assume a rule of *zullen*-DELETION. English also uses *will* regularly to express the counterfactual, except in combination with POSS (clearly because English allows for only one modal at the time), but English does not have a rule of counterfactual *will*-DELETION. Nor does French. At SA-level, therefore, German counterfactuals have just one extra operator compared with English, French and Dutch, viz. SUBJ.

As regards German, Postcyclic Rule (2) accounts for both optional and obligatory *werden*-DELETION. We repeat the rule here for conventience (the notion 'C-command' is standard: *a node A C-commands a node B just in case the first node up from A dominates B*):

> ***Werden*-DELETION:** If in a V-cluster $_{Aff}$[SUBJ] C-commands $_{Aff}$[PAST], which C-commands $_V$[werden], which C-commands $_V$[haben/sein], then delete $_V$[werden]. Optional when this part of the V-cluster is left-branching; obligatory when it is right-branching.

To illustrate the rule let us consider two cases, (30) and (31). The SA-structure underlying (30a,b) is (30c), leading to the shallow structure (30d). The result of *Werden*-DELETION is shown in (30e). The surface structure of (30b), i.e. with *werden*-DELETION, is (30f). The surface structure of (30a), without *werden*-DELETION, is obvious.

(30)a. Er   würde   es   weiter ausgearbeitet haben
        he SUBJ-PAST-will   it(ACC) further out-worked   have
        'he would have worked it out further'

    b. Er   hätte   es   weiter ausgearbeitet
        he SUBJ-PAST-have   it(ACC) further out-worked
        'he would have worked it out further'

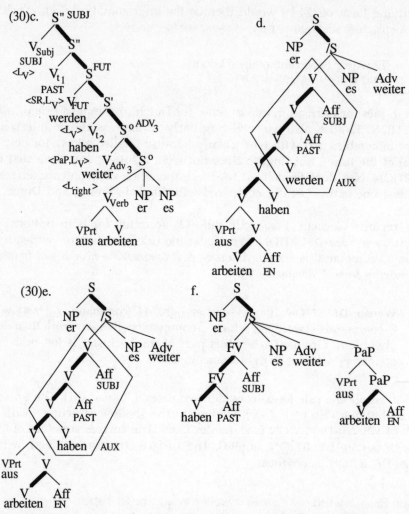

The second example, (31), involves obligatory *werden*-DELETION because the R-condition is fulfilled. The SA-structure underlying (31a) is (31b), leading to the shallow structure (31c). *Werden*-DELETION is now obligatory because the relevant part of the V-Cluster is right-branching. The result of *werden*-DELETION is shown in (31d); the surface structure is (31e):

(31)a. ... daß er es   hätte   sagen können
        ... that he it SUBJ-PAST-have   say   can
        '... that he could have said it'

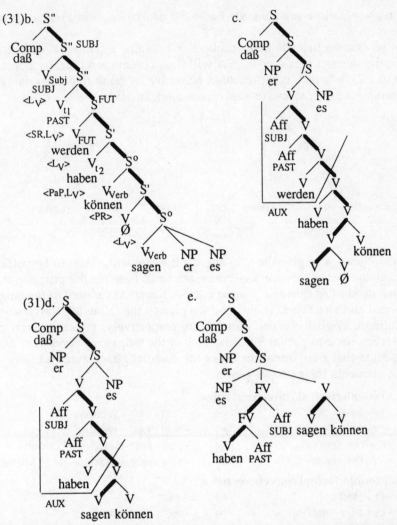

The comparison made above of the structural means by which the different languages in question express the counterfactual suggests that it makes sense to postulate a level of semantic representation which is neutral between the languages concerned and at wich it is specified that a given sentence is counterfactual, present or past (the latter with or without the POSS operator). A separate set of rules will then determine how this information is to be expressed in the SA-structures of the specific languages concerned. In section 1.4.4 the desirablility of such a limited language-neutral system of deeper semantic analysis (DSA) was adumbrated; a further elaboration, with some examples, is given in section 7.5 below. Let us, as a prelude to section 7.5, consider in rough outline how we may envisage DSA to represent counterfactuals, and how the

DSA representations are converted into the SAs of English, French, Dutch and German.

Let us assume that the DSA in question contains a sentential operator 'CF', taking the tenses in its scope. DSA will thus contain structural schemata like those in (32), where t_2 is represented either by SIM (simultaneous), i.e. $_V[\emptyset]$ in the grammars given above, or PREC (preceding), i.e. HAV.

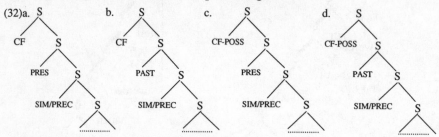

(32)a. b. c. d.

Such schemata as given in (32) are, for the moment, taken to be sufficiently language-neutral to serve as a common semantic base for the purpose at hand. We now need rules converting these into SA schemata for each of the languages concerned and vice versa. To this end we present the following conversion rules for German, English, French and Dutch, respectively, which convert partial DSA-structures into partial SA-structures of the languages concerned and vice versa. Note that the Formation Rules for each language automatically assign the SA-elements their proper place:

German counterfactual conversion rules:

a. ... - CF - PRES - ...   ↔   ... - SUBJ - PAST - werden - ...
b. ... - CF - PAST - SIM/PREC - ...   ↔   ... - SUBJ - PAST - werden - HAV - ...
c. ... - CF-POSS - PRES - ...   ↔   ... - SUBJ - PAST - werden - können - ...
d. ... - CF-POSS - PAST - ...   ↔   ... - SUBJ - PAST - werden - HAV - können - ...

English counterfactual conversion rules:

a. ... - CF - PRES - ...   ↔   ... - PAST - will - ...
b. ... - CF - PAST - SIM/PREC - ...   ↔   ... - PAST - will - HAV - ...
c. ... - CF-POSS - PRES - ...   ↔   ... - PAST - can - ...
d. ... - CF-POSS - PAST - SIM/PREC - ...   ↔   ... - PAST - can - HAV - ...

French counterfactual conversion rules:

a. ... - CF - PRES - ...   ↔   ... - PAST - FUT - ...
b. ... - CF - PAST - SIM/PREC - ...   ↔   ... - PAST - FUT - HAV - ...
c. ... - CF-POSS - PRES - ...   ↔   ... - PAST - FUT - pouvoir - ...
d. ... - CF-POSS - PAST - ...   ↔   ... - PAST - FUT - HAV - pouvoir - ...

Dutch counterfactual conversion rules:

a. ... - CF - PRES - ...   ↔   ... - PAST - Ø - zullen - ...
b. ... - CF - PAST - SIM/PREC - ...   ↔   ... - PAST - Ø - zullen - HAV - ...
c. ... - CF-POSS - PRES - ...   ↔   ... - PAST - Ø - zullen - kunnen - ...
d. ... - CF-POSS - PAST - ...   ↔   ... - PAST - Ø - zullen - HAV - kunnen - ...

One notes that the operator of futuricity is present in all cases, whether only underlyingly or also in surface structures, except in the cases of English CF-POSS, where *can* has, so to speak, ousted *will*. For Dutch and German, but not for English and French, we assume the existence of a rule of counterfactual FUTURE-DELETION, though not under identical conditions. English[7] and French[8] do not seem to delete counterfactual *will* or FUT, respectively (except in *if-* and *when-*, or *si-* and *quand*-clauses, but that is a separate matter).

The picture is now a great deal more regular. Allowing for the constraints imposed by the Formation Rules of each language, the SA-structures involved are very uniform for all languages. English shows an irregularity for the CF-POSS cases, where it is best assumed that *will* does not figure at all at SA-level. Moreover, the order of HAV and the possibility operator *can* is different in English from the other languages as *can* is allowed to occur only in intertense position. German, furthermore, has the subjunctive everywhere as an extra element. Then, the Ø-tense occurring in the Dutch versions is due to the fact that the futuricity verb *zullen* is, other than in the other three languages, not part of the auxiliary system but a main verb taking its own complement subject-S. The remaining differences are taken care of by the respective grammars.

Let us consider the German sentence (33a), with the DSA-structure (33b) and the corresponding SA-structure (33c). The surface structure is (33d), with obligatory *werden*-DELETION.

(33)a. Er   hätte   entkommen können
      he SUBJ-PAST-HAV   escape   can
      'he could have escaped'

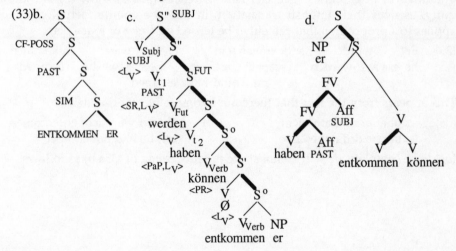

---

7 The English construction as in the first clause of *Had he told the truth he would not hang* is best considered a variant of an *if*-clause.

8 It is probably a general, perhaps universal, phenomenon that deletion of counterfactual FUT does not occur in languages that express FUT morphologically, i.e. by means of an affix.

With PREC for SIM in the DSA-structure we get (34). Note that the English translation does not differ from that of (33a), as English neutralizes the distinction between SIM and PREC in this case:

(34)a. Er   hätte   entkommen sein können
        he SUBJ-PAST-HAV escaped   HAV can
        'he could have escaped'

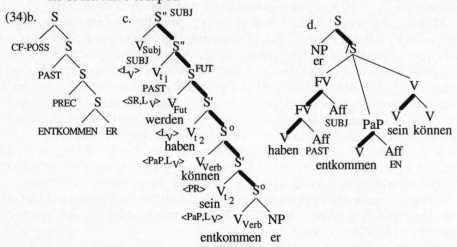

(34)b.   c.   d.

   Now consider the (b)-cases in the conversion rules. They have in common that the semantic distinction between SIM and PAST is neutralized, for lack of grammatical possibilities. The German sentences (35a,b) show a mild ambiguity, as does their English translation, in that the counterfactual operator applies to a proposition that can either be tensed PAST - SIM or PAST - PREC:

(35)a. Er   würde   entkommen sein   b. Er   wäre   entkommen
        he SUBJ-PAST-werden   escaped   be   he SUBJ-PAST-be escaped
                              'he would have escaped'

This appears from the fact that there are two possible continuations:

(36)a. ... aber er entkam nicht   b. ... aber er war nicht entkommen
        '... but he did not escape'   '... but he had not escaped'

Just to be complete we will demonstrate the processing of (35a,b) as follows:

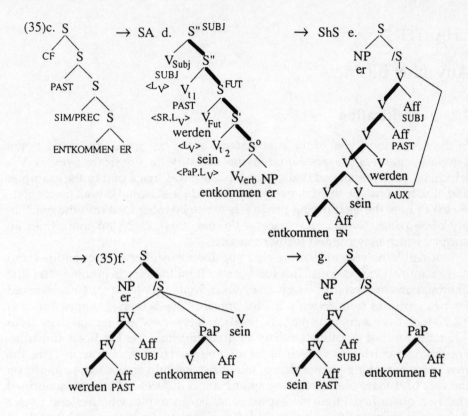

SS without FUT-DELETION   SS with FUT-DELETION

With this we conclude the chapter about German syntax. There are, obviously, many further questions and details to be sorted out, but one must know where to stop.

CHAPTER 7

Any other business

7.1 Quantification

In the Formation Rules of the rule systems of the languages discussed in the previous chapters we encountered the quantifying predicate symbol V_Q, which, however, remained undiscussed. No use was made of it in the examples and illustrations. In the following we provide a schematic and incomplete sketch of how the quantifying predicates are to be integrated into the machinery of Semantic Syntax. As space is limited, this can be no more than an outline, which may suggest further research.

Normally, theories of grammar do not distinguish between quantified and non-quantified expressions. This has been so from the very beginning. The first grammarians in western history, the Alexandrinian philologists (who worked for two centuries from roughly 280 BC onwards; see Seuren (to appear) section 2.2.2), took over a great deal of grammatical know-how and terminology from Aristotle, but not Aristotle's theory of quantification, his Predicate Calculus. For the Alexandrinians as well as for all later generations of grammarians the reason for not taking phenomena of quantification into account was simple: on the face of it there seems to be no grammatical difference between quantified and non-quantified linguistic expressions. For example, whether one uses a definite (non-quantified) or an indefinite (existentially quantified) NP in one's example sentences seems to make no difference. We shall see in a moment that this is due to the specific way in which quantifiers are processed: their treatment is such that the quantificational element is disguised as much as possible. A little probing, however, soon reveals that there are real syntactic differences between quantified and non-quantified expressions. Yet even if there were none, some account of quantification would have to be given in Semantic Syntax, in view of the fact that the semantics of quantified expressions is subject to scope constraints whereas the semantics of non-quantified expressions is not, as was noted above in section 3.5, in connection with ex. (16). And since scope is expressed as C-command in SA-structures, quantifiers must be factorized out.

That there are real syntactic differences between quantified and non-quantified expressions appears, for example, when we look at the placement of the negation word in Dutch and German. The observations made there then soon carry over to English and French. As has been shown, the negation in Dutch and German is lowered to the far right (as it was once in English):

(1)a. Michael kent   het boek niet   b. Michael kennt das Buch nicht
        Michael knows the book not   Michael knows the book not
        'Michael does not know the book'

The sentences (1a,b) are the logical (semantic) negation of *Michael kent het boek* and *Michael kennt das Buch*, respectively. They can be paraphrased as 'it is not the case that Michael knows the book'. But when we replace the definite direct object NP with an indefinite one, there is a difference. The logical (semantic) negation of *Michael kent een boek* and *Michael kennt ein Buch*, i.e. 'it is not the case that Michael knows a book', has the negation not at the far right but before the direct object. (*Geen* and *kein* are portmanteaus for 'niet-een' or 'nicht-ein' (i.e. 'not a').)

(2)a. Michael kent geen boek   b. Michael kennt kein Buch
      Michael knows no book   Michael knows no book
            'Michael does not know any book

In these two sentences, the negation has stopped short of crossing the indefinite NP. Not that it is ungrammatical to place the negation at the far right, as in:

(3)a. Michael kent een boek niet   b. Michael kennt ein Buch nicht
      Michael knows a book not   Michael knows a book not
            'there is a book Michael does not know'

But then the sentences have a different meaning. Now the negation does not take the whole sentence in its scope: they do not mean 'it is not the case that Michael knows a book', but rather, as shown in the gloss, 'there is a book Michael does not know'. In terms of the surface structures (3a,b) it is not possible to say what part of the sentence is in the scope of the negation. To do that one needs an analysis in terms of Predicate Calculus.

Apart from strongly marked intonation, English does not allow for a structure-preserving translation of (3a,b). Neither does French, which requires something like *Il y a un livre que Michel ne connaît pas*. Why English and French are thus restricted can only be shown in a non-ad-hoc way if elementary Predicate Calculus is incorporated into the machinery of syntax. The reason is that in English and French the negation is not allowed to go to the far right. It normally lands on the verbal cluster, though English negation may, under certain conditions, cluster with a quantified NP or adverbial. That being so, the negation is forced, in English and French, to stay left of the direct object, whereas the principles of QUANTIFIER LOWERING require that, under unmarked negation, the scope relation between the negation and the quantified direct object be expressed by surface structure left-to-right order. When the negation is in the scope of the quantified direct object it has to land to the right of the quantifier, and vice versa, on pain of misconstrual. Unless the machinery responsible for such phenomena is incorporated into the syntax no principled explanation can be provided for them. (Needless to say, such phenomena are a nightmare for any theory of automatic translation, unless, again, Predicate Calculus structures are accounted for syntactically.)

By way of introduction, let us generate the Dutch sentence (2a), complete with the quantificational apparatus. The SA-structure is (4a).[1] (4b) shows the effect of OBJECT INCORPORATION on the V_Q-cycle. The whole complex V_Q is now to be lowered onto the subject-S, the landing site being defined by the position of the variable (see 2.7.4.2), in this case the direct object position. This is shown in (4c). (4d) shows the LOWERING of *niet*, which has to stop short of crossing the quantified expression *een boek*. (4e) is the shallow structure. (For convenience all scope-sensitive elements have been flagged with the symbol '©' before and after LOWERING.)

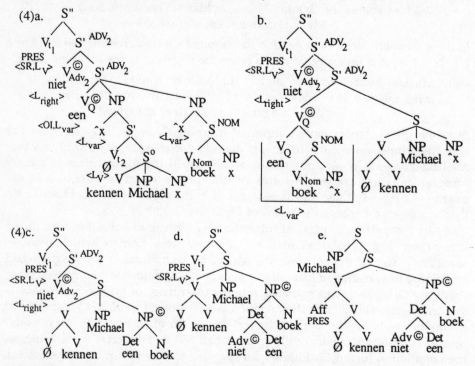

Some comment is in order. First some semantics. In the SA-structure (4a) the existential quantifier *een* figures as a binary predicate, with a subject and an object NP. The subject NP is to be read as 'the set of things that Michael knows', the object NP as 'the set of x such that x is a book', i.e. 'the set of books'. The operator ^x is similar to the lambda operator: model-theoretically, it yields the class of all elements that satisfy the propositional function (they yield truth when their names are substituted for the variable). The meaning of the existential quantifier *een* is: 'the intersection of the subject term denotation and the object term denotation is non-empty'. In this case: 'there is

---

[1] The reader will remember that the Formation Rules for Dutch generate the negation word and generally all class 2 adverbials (and quantifiers) between the two tenses, the reason being that far-right-LOWERING must result in /S-membership, and not in right-attachment to the main S-node (since V-FINAL makes the V-cluster jump across the class 2 adverbials).

at least one entity that is both a book and a thing Michael knows'. This particular way of analysing quantifiers was developed in the theory of *generalized quantification*, which is now widely recognized as being the most adequate system of logical analysis available for natural language quantification. This is, however, not the place to go into the technical details of quantification theory. It suffices to see that the meaning of *een* as specified above does indeed render the meaning of 'Michael knows a book'. It is also clear that the quantifier is a binary predicate over pairs of sets, i.e. a higher order predicate.

From a syntactic point of view the treatment of the quantifier *een* is similar to that of prepositions: OBJECT INCORPORATION followed by LOWERING. The difference is mainly that the landing site of LOWERING is the position of the variable bound by the quantifier. There is, moreover, an intermediate step, the LOWERING of the $\hat{}$x-operator inside the subject and object NPs. This process is part of NP-grammar, which is not discussed in detail in this book (for some discussion on definite NPs see 7.2.1). Nor is a full account given, in (4a-e), of the transition of the complex V_Q to the simpler $_{NP}[_{Det}[een]_N[boek]]$, again because this is NP-grammar. Yet a tentative sketch is provided in (5), where the cyclic processes are not part of S-syntax but are restricted to the complex V_Q. After LOWERING of the operator $\hat{}$x onto the variable we have (5a). Then $\hat{}$x is deleted due to SD induced by *een*, during which process *boek* is relabelled 'N', as in (5b), and $/S^{NOM}$ is erased in accordance with DOWNGRADING 2 (2.7.1.4). The final step is the LOWERING of *een* onto $_N[boek]$. *Een* is relabelled 'Det', yielding $_{NP}[_{Det}[een]_N[boek]]$, as in (5c). Obviously, this treatment will have to be reconsidered in the light of NP-grammar in general, but for now it will do.

(5)a. ... SD → b. ... L_N → c. ...

The next move is the LOWERING of *niet*. The rule prescribes LOWERING to the far right. However, for scope-sensitive elements like the negation, the instruction 'to the far right' is overruled by a general, probably universal, constraint which forbids movement across a scope-sensitive element that has been lowered earlier.

In SA-structures, scope is naturally expressed in terms of tree hierarchy. In the SA corresponding to a sentence like (6a) the Prepositional Phrase *because of the weather* will be placed above *not*, but in the SA corresponding to (6b) or (6c) the relation will be inverted:

(6)a.   John did not leave because of the weather
   b.   Because of the weather John did not leave
   c.   John did not leave, because of the weather

The semantic difference is clear and crucial: according to (6a) John left, though not because of the weather, whereas according to (6b,c) John did not leave, and the reason was the weather. In general, languages make sure that an operator with larger scope (higher in the SA-tree) precedes, in surface structure left-to-right order, operators with smaller scope (lower in the SA-tree). As was said in 5.7, the term we use for this constraint is *Scope Ordering Constraint* or SOC.

SOC is not absolute and can often be mitigated or even neutralized by secondary means such as a marked intonation or a special lexical choice, but globally speaking it holds. It ensures that the scope relations among scope-sensitive elements are mirrored in surface structure in terms of left-to-right order. Surface structure hierarchy seems to be able to override SOC to some extent and depending on the language in question. For example, if in English a scope-bearing element occurs outside and after the /S-constituent in surface structure it may have larger scope than elements inside /S, even though its temporal occurrence in surface structure is later. An intonational break, conveniently written as a comma, is then often used, as in (6c) above. Apparently, higher constituent status in surface structure can compensate for incongruous left-to-right order. Other factors may intervene as well, such as the selection of *some* instead of *any*, in English:

(7)a.   I have never forgotten any birthday
   b.   I have never forgotten some birthday

In (7a) the scope relation between *never* and *any* is unambiguous: *never* takes larger scope and *any*, which represents the existential quantifier, takes smaller scope. But (7b) has at least one natural reading where the relation is the other way round: 'there is at least one birthday which I have never forgotten'.

As regards the lowering of *niet* in (4c), SOC overrules the 'far right' instruction, and makes the negation stop short of any scope-sensitive element lowered earlier. In the familiar European languages the standard procedure, in such cases, appears to be for the negation to be left-adopted by the quantifier-determiner. This explains the complex Det-constituent in (4d). The shallow structure (4e) is then self-evident, and so is the further derivation to surface structure.

In section 5.7 above SOC was briefly discussed in connection with the Queuing Principle (QP) of Dutch and German adverbials, and the following example was given:

(8)a.   Nobody here speaks two languages
   b.   Two languages are spoken by nobody here

The former corresponds to 'not - $\exists$x:person here - $\exists$2y:language - [speak (x,y)]', the latter to '$\exists$2y:language - not - $\exists$x:person here - [speak (x,y)]' ('$\exists$' is, of course, the standard logical symbol for the existential quantifier). In many situations (8a) will be false, but (8b) true. As tree diagrams (8a,b) come out as (9a,b), respectively:

(9)a.
```
        S
       / \
      V©   S
     not  / \
        /   _____
       V©  NP            NP
     some  / \          / \
          ^x  S        ^x  S
         / _____   / \
        V©  NP         \ V   NP
       two  NP      person x
           / \      /\
         ^Y   S    ^Y  S
        / \        V  NP
       V   S    language y
      PRES / \
          V   S
          Ø  /|\
            V NP NP
          speak x y
```

b.
```
            S
           / _____
          V©  NP                NP
         two / \               / \
            ^Y  S             ^Y  S
               / \              / \
              V©  S           V   NP
             not / \      language y
                /   \
               V©   NP
             some  / \
                  ^x  S
                 / \
                V   S
              PRES / \
                  V   S
                  Ø  /|\
                    V NP NP
                  speak x y
```
(NP / x S / V NP person x)

The set-forming operator ^Y, with capital Y, differs from the ^y-operator with small y in that it forms the plural power set of its argument set, i.e. the standard power set minus Ø and minus all singletons. The object NP under *two* in (9a,b) thus stands for 'the set of all subsets of all languages, with cardinality > 1'. Analogously, the subject NP in (9a) stands for 'the set of all subsets of things x speaks, with cardinality > 1'. In (9b) it stands for 'the set of all subsets of things that nobody speaks, with cardinality > 1'. The operator *two* requires for truth that the two plural power sets have at least one element in common with cardinality 2: if John speaks two languages then there must be a set of two languages such that this set is an element of the plural power set of the things John speaks. The point of introducing this plural power-set-forming operator is that this keeps the meaning of the existential quantifier constant through singulars and plurals: it simply requires a non-empty intersection for truth. Syntactically, it is assumed that it induces LOWERING just like the ordinary set-forming operator.

It is easily seen that (9a) poses no problems with regard to SOC. By the time the three scope-sensitive operators are to be lowered, the tensed S has the standard NP-/S-structure. The existential operator *two languages* then lands at the position of ^Y (after ^Y-LOWERING), i.e. as direct object. Then *some person* lands at the ^x-position (after ^x-LOWERING), i.e. as subject. Finally, *not* is to be lowered onto the V-cluster but is stopped by *some person* which has been lowered earlier. Therefore, *not* is left-adopted by *some* to form a complex Det-constituent Det[Adv[not]Det[some]], which then becomes the portmanteau determiner *no*.

(9b), however, cannot be processed. After the standard formation of the NP-/S-structure S[NP[x]/S[speak y]], *some person* must be lowered and must land at the ^x-position, i.e. at the far left of the NP-/S-structure. After this, *not* can still be **lowered** to form the complex Det-constituent $_{Det}[_{Adv}[not]_{Det}[some]]$, but the highest operator, *two languages*, is now stranded: it has to land at the position of the ^Y-variable, a technical necessity that not even SOC can override. But in order to get to the ^Y-position it has to cross over two previously lowered scope-sensitive operators, which it cannot do. So (9b) is blocked and cannot be realized. Fortunately, English has a passive construction that solves the problem. The reader will have no difficulty figuring out that with a passive nuclear S SOC does not have to be violated. As a result (8b) has the primary meaning '∃2y:language - not - ∃x:person here - [speak (x,y)]', i.e. 'there are two languages not spoken by anybody here'.

Let us now consider (3a) or its isomorphic German equivalent (3b). Its derivation runs smoothly without any complication, as shown in (10a,b):

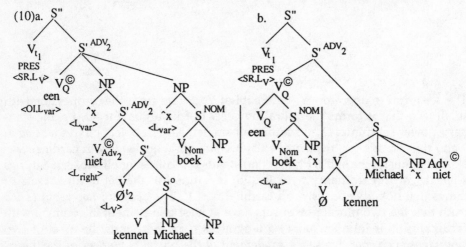

The SA-structure is (10a). In (10b) *niet* has been lowered to the far right, without any problem. Also, OBJECT INCORPORATION has taken place on the quantifier cycle. Further LOWERING of the complex quantifier to the x-position takes place without a hitch, since the ^x-position is safely to the left of the new position of *niet*. The further processing of this sentence is now obvious.

But now consider (11a), the English version of (10a). Here, the trouble is obvious. In (11b) *not* has been lowered onto the V-cluster, since it has found nothing in its way. Now the complex quantifier must be lowered, and its only possible landing site is the ^x-position, which is well to the right of lowered *not*. This is disallowed by SOC, so that the generation process is blocked. There are alternatives, such as the selection of accented *some* instead of weak *a*, or else, as in (8b), the passive may be chosen: *A (some) book is not known by Michael*. But as it stands, English does not permit a surface structure resulting from (11a). The same goes for French, as is easily checked.

(11)a. S''^{ADV_2} b. S''^{ADV_2}

```
(11)a.  S"ADV2

        V©Q   NP          NP
        a                      NOM
      <OI,Lvar>  ^x  S"ADV2
                <Lvar>        ^x   S
                                        NOM
              V©Adv2  S"        VNom  NP
              not               book   x
             <Lright>
                    Vt1      S'
                    PRES
                   <SR,Lv>  V      S°
                            Ø t2
                           <Lv>
                                V    NP    NP
                              know Michael  x
```

```
b.   S"ADV2

     V©Q      SNOM              S
     a   VQ   S
         a  VNom  NP     NP      /S
            book  ^x    Michael
        <Lvar>                V       NP
                                        ^x
                             Adv©  V
                             not
                                 Aff    V
                                 PRES
                                      V    V
                                      Ø   know
```

We shall not go into the detailed semantics of the quantifiers, nor into the syntactic phenomenon of 'quantifier floating', as in *They were all celebrating victory*, with *all* occupying the place of an adverb. But we will analyse again the sentences (16a,b) of section 3.5, now with the quantifier fully factorized out. The sentences are repeated here as (12a,b), respectively:

(12)a. He always snores during some arias
   b. During some arias, he always snores

We remember that (12a) is ambiguous between a reading where at every opera performance there are some arias during which he snores (=13a), and one in which there are specific arias during which he always snores (=13b). (12b) corresponds to (13b) only. Note that the object-NP term of the quantifier now has the plural-power-set-forming operator ^{X}. The quantifying predicate (plural) *some* requires for truth that the intersection of the two plural power sets be non-empty. What is needed now is one derivation from (13a) leading to (12a), and two derivations from (13b), one leading to (12a) and one to (12b). This will show up the ambiguity of (12a) and the non-ambiguity of (12b).

Consider first (13a). The treatment of S" gives the NP-/S structure $_S[_{NP}[he]$ $_{/S}[_V[PRES-Ø-snore]]]$. OBJECT INCORPORATION on the *during*-cycle gives the complex $_V[_V[during]_{NP}[x]]$, which is to be lowered. This LOWERING may take two forms, to the far right, or adoption by the parent S, i.e. to the left. It is already clear now that the latter option will block the LOWERING of *always*, since the *during*-PP will incorporate the quantifier *some*, and if this PP is on the extreme left of the sentence there is no way for *always* to get at the V-cluster but across the quantified PP. (Unlike *not*, *always* cannot cluster with a quantified determiner.) The grammar is thus forced to take the option LOWERING to the far right. Now OI is shown in (14a). LOWERING of the quantifier replaces the (modified) bound variable ^{X} with *some arias*, as in (14b). Subsequent LOWERING of *always* results in (14c). The surface structure is obvious.

(13)a. — (tree diagram with labels: S" ADV₂, V_Adv₂ *always* ⟨L_V⟩, S" ADV₂, V_Q *some* ⟨OI,L_var⟩, NP, ^X ⟨L_var⟩, S" ADV₂, NP, ^X ⟨L_var⟩, S NOM, V_Prep₂ *during* ⟨OI,L S/right⟩, S" NP x, NP V_Nom *aria* NP x, V_PRES¹ ⟨SR,L_V⟩, S', V Ø²t ⟨L_V⟩, S°, V_Verb *snore*, NP *he*)

b. — (tree diagram with labels: S" ADV₂, V_Q *some* ⟨OI,L_var⟩ ⟨L_var⟩, NP, ^X S" ADV₂, NP, ^X ⟨L_var⟩ S NOM, V_Prep₂ *during* ⟨OI,L S/right⟩, S" ADV₂ NP V_Nom NP, x *aria* x, V_Adv₂ *always* ⟨L_V⟩, S", V_PRES¹t ⟨SR,L_V⟩, S', V Ø²t ⟨L_V⟩, S°, V_Verb *snore*, NP *he*)

(14)a. — (tree diagram: S" ADV₂, V_Adv₂ *always* ⟨L_V⟩, S" ADV₂, V_Q, V_Q *some*, S NOM, V_Nom NP *aria* ^X ⟨L_var⟩, S, NP *he*, /S, V, AFF PRES, V, V, P NP, Ø *during* ^X, V *snore*)

b. — (tree diagram: S" ADV₂, V_Adv₂ *always* ⟨L_V⟩, S, NP *he*, /S, V, PP, AFF PRES, V, P NP© *during*, V V, Det N, Ø *snore*, *some arias*)

c. — (tree diagram: S, NP *he*, /S, V, PP, ADV© *always*, V, P NP© *during*, AFF PRES, V, Det N, *some arias*, V V, Ø *snore*)

It is thus clear that (13a) allows for only one derivation, which leads to (12a). Now to (13b). Here, LOWERING of *always* and OI on the *during*-cycle gives (15a). Now *during x* is to be lowered, in two possible ways. LOWERING on S will be all right, since when *some* is to be lowered it does not have to cross *always*. But LOWERING to the far right is all right as well, since it attaches ₚₚ[during x] to S and not to /S, and SOC may be overridden if the previously lowered operator is part of /S and the offending constituent is directly attached to S (see also (93a-f) in 7.4). LOWERING on S is shown in (15b), with shallow structure (15c). LOWERING to the far right is shown in (16a), with shallow structure (16b). One notes the difference between (14c) and (16b): in the latter the PP is attached to S, in the former to /S.

(15)a.

(16)a.

So far we have considered scope-sensitive versus scope-insensitive operators. It seems, however, that some operators are *weakly scope-sensitive*. By this we mean that SOC is weakened for these operators when they have been lowered into subject position. *When they are in subject position weakly scope-sensitive operators allow crossing by a higher negation to a position further to the right.* Universal quantifiers are typically weakly scope-sensitive, as appears from sentences like *All that glitters is not gold*, which means 'it is not the case that all that glitters is gold' and not 'for all that glitters it is not the case that it is gold'. The same meaning can also be expressed as *Not all that glitters is gold*, but this has not become the canonical form of the saying, perhaps for rhythmical reasons. Also, as will be shown in 7.2.2 below, lowered comment-NPs seem to be typically characterized by weak scope sensitivity.

Much more can be said about quantification, but we shall leave it at this.

7.2 Clefting, deep accent and WH-questions

7.2.1 A preliminary exercise in NP-grammar

Since it is impossible to say anything substantial about the grammar of clefts, pseudoclefts and WH-questions, and about contrastive and/or emphatic accents, without going into the syntax of NPs to at least some detail, we shall now have a cursory and tentative glance at some possible ways of treating the internal syntax of definite noun phrases. Something was said already, in a very global way, in section 3.2. Here we shall be a little more explicit. The reader is asked, however, to keep in mind that the present section is tentative and provisional.

Consider first the simple definite NP *the man*. The assumed SA-structure is shown in (17a), generated by the Formation Rules (4a) and (4b) for English (3.1.1). This structure is to be read as: 'the x such that x is a man'.

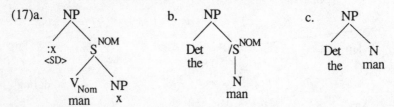

What the Formation Rules do not specify is the NP-syntax rule SD induced by the definite operator :x. The result of SD is shown first in (17b), then in (17c). In (17b) one sees that V_{Nom} has been renamed N, and that ':x' has been replaced with $_{Det}$[the]. In (17c) /S^{NOM} has been deleted due to DONWGRADING 2 (section 2.7.1.4), which automatically erases all nodes S or /S not dominating a V-node.

Let us now introduce an attributive adjective: *the old man*. The proposed SA-structure is (18a), which is to be understood, perhaps in an unorthodox fashion, as something like 'the x such that x mans oldly'. The main reasons for this analysis are the following. First, there is a clear parallelism between NPs consisting of an attributive adjective and a noun on the one hand, and sentences with a manner adverb and a verb on the other: a *good teacher* is one who *teaches well*, and a *fast runner* is one who *runs fast*. In a similar fashion we now say that an *old man* is one who *mans oldly* (following Montague's maxim that one should generalize from the most difficult case). Secondly, most attributive adjectives suffer from the widely known semantic problem that they do not denote a well-defined set of entities. Consequently, it is semantically inadequate to assign to a structure like *old man* a semantic value which consists of the intersection of men and old things. Yet, for lack of a better solution, most formal semantic theories do precisely that. This is fundamentally wrong, as there is no set of old entities: what is old to you may be young (or new) to me. This problem is well-known in semantics, but no satisfactory answer has so far been proposed. It is usually said that these adjectives imply some average or standard, but no non-ad-hoc structural account of such a standard has been proposed. The present analysis is an attempt at providing a more satisfactory account. By treating attributive adjectives as operators over S^{NOM} the semantic restriction that the quality of being old is related to the fact of being a man is automatically observed. To preserve unity, this analysis is extended to all attributive adjectives.

(18)a.
```
        NP
       /  \
     :x    S^NOM
    <SD>   /  \
         V_Adj  S^NOM
         old    /  \
        <L_V>  V_Nom  NP
               man    x
```

b.
```
        NP
       /  \
     :x    S^NOM
    <SD>   /  \
        V_Nom  NP
         /\     x
       Adj  V_Nom
       old  man
```

c.
```
        NP
       /  \
     Det    N
     the   /  \
         Adj    N
         old    man
```

LOWERING of $_V$[old] onto $_V$[man] gives the cluster shown in (18b). Note that, as in S-syntax, surface structure relabelling is applied at this stage: V_{Adj}[old] has been relabelled $_{Adj}$[old]. (18c) shows the result of SUBJECT DELETION induced by :x. The node $/S^{NOM}$ is again erased, as it does not dominate a V-node (DOWNGRADING 2).

It is easily seen that this analysis allows for unrestricted recursion of attributive adjectives. It is well-known that there are restrictions on the order and selection of series of adjectives. We say, for example, *that lovely old 18th century English cottage*, and not *that English old 18th century lovely cottage*. But this does not seem to be a matter for syntax to take care of. The order and selection of serially ordered adjectives seems, rather, a question to be dealt with by semantics. Syntactically, a phrase like *the sly old man* can be considered to be generated as in (19):

(19)a.
```
         NP
        /  \
      :x    S^NOM
     <SD>   /  \
          V_Adj  S^NOM
          sly    /  \
         <L_V>  V_Adj  S^NOM
                old    /  \
               <L_V>  V_Nom  NP
                      man    x
```

b.
```
         NP
        /  \
      :x    S^NOM
     <SD>   /  \
          V_Adj   S^NOM
          sly     /  \
         <L_V>  V_Nom  NP
                 /\     x
               Adj  V_Nom
               old  man
```

c.
```
         NP
        /  \
      :x    S^NOM
     <SD>   /  \
          V_Nom   NP
           /\      x
         Adj  V_Nom
         sly   /\
             Adj  V_Nom
             old  man
```

d.
```
        NP
       /  \
     Det    N
     the   /  \
         Adj    N
         sly   /  \
             Adj    N
             old    man
```

In languages where attributive adjectives follow their noun essentially the same account can be maintained. The only difference consists in the directionality of the LOWERING process. Whereas in English the LOWERING of NP-internal adjectives is right-branching, in cases where the adjective must follow the noun the LOWERING is left-branching.

Now consider noun phrases containing an NP-internal prepositional phrase, such as *the man in the house*. Here the S^{NOM} required by the :x-operator is more deeply embedded in the corresponding SA-structure, as shown in (20a). In (20b) the NP *the house* has been processed. Moreover, OBJECT INCORPORATION and far right LOWERING have taken place on the S-cycle, putting S^{NOM} directly under the :x-operator, thus enabling the implementation of SD. The result of SD is shown in (20c).

(20)a. [tree diagram] b. [tree diagram] c. [tree diagram]

Now the generation of *the old man in the house* is straightforward: the adjective *old* is placed directly above $_{S^{NOM}}[[man]_{NP}[x]]$ in a higher S^{NOM}, and the processing runs analogously:

(21)a. [tree diagram] b. [tree diagram] c. [tree diagram]

We are now ready for relative clauses. In (20) and (21) we saw that an S^{NOM} can be more deeply embedded, thereby complicating the NP. We apply the same principle to relative clauses, and posit (22a) as the SA-structure of the relative clause NP *the man who left the house*. After the standard cyclic processing of S" the structure looks like (22b).

(22)a. [tree diagram] b. [tree diagram]

Now, however, application of SD is not possible, since (22b) does not satisfy the structural criteria for the application of SD. In (20) and (21) we were lucky, as the processing of the prepositional phrase automatically led to the right conditions. But not here. Yet the structure can be processed, due to a specific set of relativization rules.

The first rule to apply now is the RAISING of the remote S^{NOM}. This means that this S^{NOM} fills the position of its own parent S. This S, or what remains of it, is shifted one position to the right. The NP that remains empty after this RAISING is not left dangling but receives the new filler PRO_{rel}. This is shown in (22c). One sees that (22c) does satisfy the structural criteria for the application of SD induced by the :x-operator. The remaining problem is what to do with PRO_{rel}, which has to be fronted. The fronting of PRO_{rel} is realized in a way analogous to the fronting technique we have applied to WH-questions and focused elements. A new constituent, labelled $c[rel]/c[rel]$ and with the filler 'Rel' is introduced, left-adopted by the S which is the right brother of S^{NOM}. (Actually, one might consider, for the sake of elegance, the introduction of a V_{Attr} with filler 'Rel', to be lowered in the Cycle onto its argument-S, and then relabelled $c[rel]/c[rel]$.) This new constituent $c[rel]/c[rel]$ will then attract PRO_{rel}, which will eventually become a relative pronoun (in this case *who*). The attraction of PRO_{rel} is shown in (22e), where one S-node has been pruned, according to TREE PRUNING 1 (2.7.1.3). (22f) shows the near-final product.

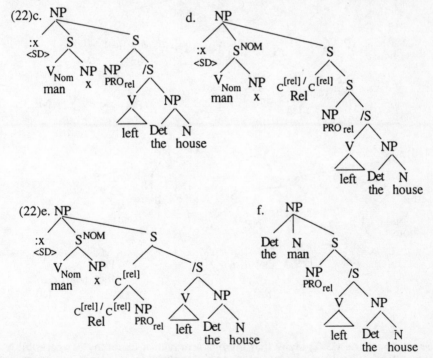

English allows for relative extraction (the RAISING of S^{NOM}) from any NP-position in a given S, provided it is not inside an island (Ross 1986(=1967)). As we saw in 6.4, English even permits relative extraction from embedded *that-*

clauses (but preferably not under an NP). (We saw, too, that Dutch, German and French are more restricted in this respect.)[2]

Let us, finally, consider relative extraction from the position of a direct-object-NP, as in *the house which the man left*. This is demonstrated in (23):

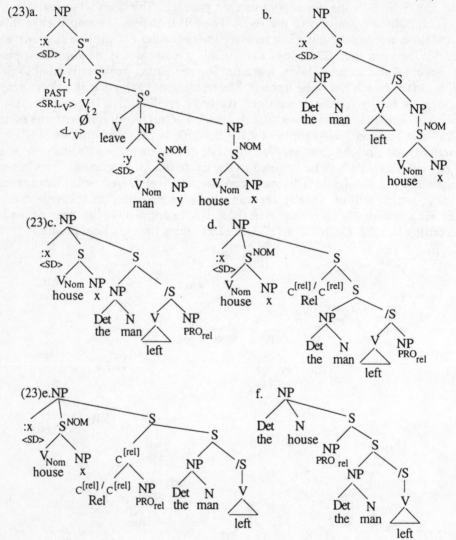

[2] Keenan & Comrie (1977) show that there is a universal hierarchy of accessibility to relative extraction: subject-NPs are most easily extractable: if a language has relative pronoun extraction, leaving behind an empty position, then this is always possible for subject-NPs. Direct-object-NPs are not always extractable: of the languages that have relative pronouns, many but not all allow for the extraction of direct-object-NPs. Indirect-object-NPs are again harder to extract, and NPs from prepositional phrases even more so. (Keenan and Comrie did not investigate accessibility from embedded clauses.)

This concludes our tentative exercise in NP-syntax. We now turn to clefting and accent.

7.2.2 Clefting, pseudoclefting and deep accent

Clefting and contrastive or emphatic accent form a cluster of phenomena that are relatively ill-understood yet felt to be important. They are to do with the way information is presented in actual discourse. What they have in common is the presupposition that the class of elements mentioned in the topic-constituent is non-empty. For example, in (24c) there is the existential pre-supposition that there is something the speaker can heal, and in (25b) the presupposition is that there is something he likes to eat. Yet although this presupposition must be taken to be a central discriminating factor in the discourse functions carried by the phenomena at hand, it is far from the only one. So far, no convincing theory has been presented that will account satisfactorily for the whole range of phenomena concerned. That being so, we must make do with what we have.

Clefting, in the European languages, takes two forms, ordinary clefting and pseudoclefting, illustrated in (24) and (25), respectively:

(24)a. It is the students who protested
    b. It is not your accent that irritates me, it's whát you say
    c. It is your body that I can heal, not your soul

(25)a. Whom I don't like is (I don't like) the deputy chairman
    b. What he likes to eat is (he likes to eat) chocolate
    c. What I won't do is (I won't) give in to her demands

Though both forms of clefting are clearly related to discourse structure there are both grammatical and discourse-semantic differences between the two kinds of clefting. Ordinary clefting seems appropriate when a speaker wants to correct an impression that has or may have been created. Hence the natural-ness of negated clefts and of polar oppositions, as in (24b,c). But clefts have other discourse functions as well, as appears from the following natural exchange taking place over the telephone between two friends both living in London:

(26)   A: Hallo Dick, I am ringing from Stavanger, so I can't be too long.
        B: Stavanger? What on earth are you doing there?
        A: We have a branch here, didn't you know? I've been here regularly over the past two years. *It was from Stavanger that I sent you that nice wooden sculpture, remember?*

What exactly the discourse function is of the cleft in the last sentence is not immediately clear, and it is not our purpose to sort that question out here. At this point we must be content with the general statement that there is a variety of discourse functions carried by clefts and pseudoclefts, and it is the task of discourse theory to account for them.

In English (but not, for example, in French), clefts correspond regularly with contrastive or emphatic accent, depending on whether there is or is not a polar contrast:

(27)a.   The STUDENT protested
    b.   Your ACCENT doesn't irritate me, WHAT YOU SAY does
    c.   I can heal your BODY, not your SOUL

Many non-European languages allow for the clefting of adjectives and/or predicates, usually with a copy left in what corresponds to the *that*-clause. Thus we have, for example, the following sentences from Sranan, the Creole language of Surinam:

(28)a.   Na   bigi yu   futu bigi, a no doti
         it-is big your feet big it-is not dirty
         'your feet are BIG, not DIRTY'

    b.   Na   fufuru a fufuru en, a no bay
         it-is steal he stole it it-is not buy
         'He STOLE it, he didn't BUY it'

In such cases English does not allow for clefting, only for contrastive accent. Pseudoclefting is marginally possible, as in:

(29)a.   What your feet are is BIG, not DIRTY
    b.   What he did was STEAL it, not BUY it

Pseudoclefts are naturally interpreted as answers to (explicit or implicit) questions that have or may have arisen in the context. Hence the lesser naturalness of negated pseudoclefts. The (explicit or implicit) question is resumed in the *wh*-clause, and the answer is given in the main clause. (25a), for example, is a natural answer to the question 'Who is it you don't like?', and (25b) to 'What does he like to eat?' It is very typical for pseudoclefts, especially in spoken English, to repeat the full sentence form of the question in the answer. In the examples of (25) this is indicated by the words in brackets.

One must be careful to avoid confusion between pseudocleft *wh*-clauses and relative clauses. In *Whom you don't like is damned*, for example, the *wh*-clause is a relative, not a pseudocleft, clause, and the sentence is of the canonical NP-/S form, with the *wh*-clause as the subject term.

In older forms of transformational grammar it was assumed that clefts and pseudoclefts are transformationally derived (derivable) from what we shall call the canonical form of the sentence in question. Attempts were made, for example, to derive (24b) from a structure underlying the canonical *Your accent does not irritate me, what you say irritates me*. Analogously, emphatic and contrastive accents were assumed to be assigned (assignable) by a late phonological rule, which would be free to select any morpheme, word or phrase for special accentuation. On the whole, however, these attempts have not been very successful. Nor have there been many proposals for alternative treatments. In fact, one has not heard much about clefts and pseudoclefts lately in the literature on transformational grammar.

One reason why it was found hard to derive (pseudo)clefts from canonical sentences was the fact that the transformational operations needed for such a derivation seemed wildly ad hoc and out of proportion with better-behaved grammatical rule systems. Apart from that, it must be observed that there are cases where both contrastive accent assignment and clefting are blocked, as is shown in (30). (30a) is all right, but (30b-d) are not, although *I don't think Harry will visit us any more* is a well-formed sentence. It is clear intuitively that the ungrammaticality of (30b-d) is connected with the negative polarity item *any more*, which requires a negation. But then, the negation is there, yet not in a structural position from where it can link up properly with the negative polarity item. And the conditions for a proper link-up were (and are still largely) unknown.

(30)a. I don't think HARRY should go, I think LARRY should
  b. *I don't think HARRY will visit us any more, I think LARRY will
  c. *It isn't HARRY I think will visit us any more, it's LARRY
  d. *Who I think will visit us any more is not HARRY, but LARRY

In view of these and related facts it seems appropriate to assume that clefts and pseudoclefts are not transformationally derived from the corresponding canonical sentence forms but reflect different, though related, structures at SA-level. Let us consider sentence (30a), together with its cleft and pseudocleft variants (31b-d) and the ungrammatical (31e):

(31)a. The STUDENT protested
  b. Wo protested was the STUDENT (protested)
  c. The one who protested was the STUDENT
  d. It is/was the STUDENT who protested
  e. *It is/was the STUDENT the one who protested

Despite their different discourse functions we will assume, for the moment that their SA-structures share important identical elements. Perhaps a discourse marker will have to be added, determining the syntactic treatment the sentence is to undergo. But we will leave that aspect unconsidered. Let us assume that (32a) is the SA-structure underlying (31a). The complex NP-predicate under the top-S we call the *comment*, the subject-NP we call the *topic*.

This overall S-structure, with the high comment-NP predicate and the topic NP-subject, is not accounted for in the Formation Rules given, but there should be no great problem in doing so. A novelty is V_{Nom}[PRO] in S^{NOM}. If undeleted this will end up as the neutral filler noun *one*, giving the NP *the one who protested*. But normally, this V_{Nom}[PRO] will be deleted, leaving just $_{NP}$[x], as the subject term of $_V$[protest] (S^{NOM} is erased due to DOWNGRADING 2). When V_{Nom}[PRO] is deleted, the comment-NP undergoes LOWERING onto the x-variable, as shown in (32b). The lowered NP will now carry along the extra accent it has on account of being the main predicate of the sentence. It is taken to be part of this NP-LOWERING process that all higher structure, i.e. the :x-operator and its immediately dominating NP, is deleted. But if V_{Nom}[PRO] is not deleted, no LOWERING can take place because in that case the normal procedure for the formation of relative clauses is followed (7.2.1). Since the variable x disappears during that procedure there is no landing place left for the LOWERING process, which is accordingly blocked.

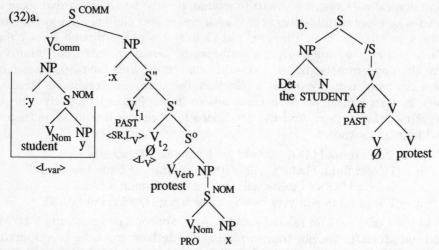

Note, incidentally, that the negation of (32a) is simply the SA (32a) under a higher negation operator. When this *not* is lowered after (32b) it can go directly to the V-cluster, resulting in the standard negation: *The STUDENT did not protest (somebody else did)*. This suggests that lowered comment-NPs should count as *weakly scope-sensitive* (see the end of section 7.1 above). In many languages, in fact, including Dutch and German, the previously lowered comment-NP is free to block crossing by the negation or to let it pass. Dutch and German thus have two forms corresponding to the negation of (31a):

(33)a. De STUDENT protesteerde niet
    b. Niet de STUDENT protesteerde

(34)a. Der STUDENT protestierte nicht
    b. Nicht der STUDENT protestierte

In English, preposed negation is possible only when the contrasting element comes under the same complex NP:

(35)a. Not the STUDENT but the PROFESSOR protested
    b. *Not the STUDENT protested

The weak scope-sensitivity of lowered comment-NPs appears also from the difference between (36a), with the quantified subject term *many people*, and (36b), with the definite term *my neighbours*:

(36)a, Many people don't like STRAWBERRIES but CHERRIES
    b. My neighbours don't like STRAWBERRIES but CHERRIES

(36b) simply means 'it is not the case that my neighbours like stráwberries; they like chérries'. But in (36a) the negation comes in the scope of the quantifier *many*, which is strongly scope-sensitive and therefore does not allow crossing by *not*. For that reason this sentence cannot mean 'it is not the case that many people like stráwberries; many people like chérries', but only 'for many people it is not the case that they like stráwberries; these people like chérries', i.e. with *many* over *not*.

This LOWERING analysis of comment-NPs opens up an enormous extension of the number of possible structural analyses for sentences, as long as these are considered without their intonational contour. A simple sentence like *The driver pushed the car into the garage* is now suddenly multiply ambiguous, depending on any emphatic or contrastive accent or combination of accents. The fact that sentence analysis thus becomes highly sensitive to intonational features is to be welcomed, as it shows the effect of discourse structure upon sentence structure and integrates, to some extent, the study of sentence intonation into the study of sentence syntax. This analysis will take away the temptation to assign intonational features to 'performance', or even 'pragmatics', while reserving classical grammar, which takes no account of intonation and topic-comment structure, for the language or competence system. If the present analysis is viable it shows that this division of labour is incorrect or counterproductive: topic-comment modulation is as much part of sentence grammar as is the standard analysis in terms of predicate-argument structure.

As was adumbrated in section 1.4.2, there are also truth-conditional differences between various contrastive accent assignments. In formal semantics this is standardly denied, yet the facts force one to conclude that formal semantics is wrong in this respect. There are clear differences between, for example, (37a) and (37b), and (37c) is not at all inconsistent:

(37)a. She was surprised that the DRIVER pushed the car into the garage
    b. She was surprised that the driver pushed the car into the GARAGE
    c. She was not surprised that the DRIVER pushed the car into the garage, what surprised her was that he pushed it into the GARAGE

This further supports the position that topic-comment modulation is part of the language system, and thus of sentence grammar, and should not be relegated to performance or pragmatics.

We now pass on to (31b) and (31c). These cannot be generated directly from (32a), since the highest S of (32a) is untensed, while both (31b) and (31c) have a tensed copula-verb. The same goes for the cleft sentence (31d).

Two possible answers can be given here. Either we assume, for clefts and pseudoclefts, an SA-structure, with the normal tense system above the highest S. Or else we call upon the Precycle and let it supply the missing tenses. The latter option can be defended on the grounds that there seems to be a dependency relation from the tense of the topic-S to the tense required by the comment-NP. When the topic-S is in the simple present, so must the comment be: (38a) and (39a) are ungrammatical. But, as shown in (38b,c) and (39b,c), when the topic-S of a cleft sentence is in the simple past, the comment allows for both the simple present and the simple past, depending on discourse factors:

(38)a. *It was Mary who writes novels   (39)a. *Who writes novels was Mary
    b. It is Mary who wrote novels   b. Who wrote novels is Mary
    c. It was Mary who wrote novels   c. Who wrote novels was Mary

So far, however, no thorough study exists of this dependency relation. It must be observed also that similar tense dependencies are found elsewhere in the grammar. For example, (40a) seems less correct than (40b), and (40c) is clearly ungrammatical:

(40)a. ?*I knew all along that you live there
    b. I knew all along that you lived there
    c. *By that time I had realized that you live there

Without wishing to take a definite stand on the issue we shall assume, for the present purpose, that the first of the two options is correct, and posit (41a) as the SA-structure for the cleft and the pseudocleft versions. If V_{Nom}[PRO] of S^{NOM} is not deleted the topic-NP will follow the normal rules for the formation of relative clauses (see 7.2.1) and come out as *the one who protested*. COPULA INSERTION is now required for the comment-NP, and subsequent TENSE ROUTINE will give (31c): *The one who protested was the STUDENT*.

(41)a.

b.

But let us now consider the case where V_{Nom}[PRO] of S^{NOM} is deleted. We assume that this deletion takes the place of the RAISING required for relative clause formation (7.2.1), the rest remaining equal. This produces the structure (41b). Now the relative clause will duly become *who protested*, and the whole sentence, with COPULA INSERTION and the selection of PAST for the highest t_1, will be (31b): *Who protested was the STUDENT*. (To get *Who protested was the STUDENT protested* one would have to fall back on some precyclic remodelling of (41a), to the effect that the comment-NP is extended with a copy of S" of the topic-NP minus $_{NP}$[S^{NOM}].)

What remains is the cleft sentence (31d), and the ruling out of the ungrammatical (31e). Clearly, (31d) involves the cyclic rule IT (repeated here for convenience):

IT: (structure-driven: applies when V of S° has subject (original) S" or $_{NP}$[S"]): Create new constituent $_{NP}$[it]. Attach $_{NP}$[it] to the immediate right of V. The S" or $_{NP}$[S"] to the immediate right of $_{NP}$[it] is moved to object position, still marked [SU].

And indeed, we see that after the deletion of V_{Nom}[PRO] of S^{NOM}, as in (41b), the conditions for IT are fulfilled: the subject term of the nominal comment predicate has the status of S", as it is a copy of the original S" of the topic-NP. After insertion of $_{NP}$[it] COPULA INSERTION and the selection of either PRES or PAST will do the rest. However, without the deletion of V_{Nom}[PRO] the conditions for IT are not fulfilled, which rules out the ungrammatical (31e).

7.2.3 Specific or WH-questions

This brings us to specific or WH-questions. In our treatment of WH-questions we have, so far, assumed that WH-elements are generated by the Formation Rules in the NP-position from which they are extracted to link up with the incomplete symbol in sentence-initial position.[3] This will now be changed. From now on we will generate WH-elements as comment-NPs in topic-comment structures like (32a) or (41a). A WH-question like (42a) will thus have a topic-comment-type SA-structure corresponding with (42b):

(42)a.   What did John say?
   b.   the x [John said x] is/was WHAT?

The reasons for this treatment are plentiful. First, besides (42a) we also have the cleft question form (43a) and the pseudocleft (43b):

(43)a.   What is/was it that John said?
   b.   What John said was WHAT?

Then, French specific (and yes-no) questions are often cast into the mould of a cleft. Non-cleft questions, such as (44a-c), are more common in spoken French:[4]

(44)a.   Où est l'Opéra?   b.   Pourquoi n'a-t-il pas mangé?
       where is the Opera   why has-he not eaten

   c.   Qu'a-t-il dit?
       what has-he said

Literary French often prefers a cleft form, as in (45a-d):

---

[3] Adverbial WH-expressions like *when, where, why* are considered to reflect underlying PPs: 'at what time', 'in what place', 'for what reason'.

[4] Yes-no questions also usually allow for a cleft version: *Est-ce que tu pourras venir ce soir?* (lit.: 'is-it that you will be able to come tonight?'). This suggests a structural link between yes-no questions and specific questions. This aspect, however, is not pursued here.

(45)a.   Où est-ce que je peux garer ma voiture?
         where is-it that I can park my car

   b.   Pourquoi est-ce que Jean n'a pas mangé?
        why is-it that Jean has not eaten

   c.   Qu'est-ce qu'il a dit?
        what is-it that he has said

   d.   Qu'est-ce qui a pris mon mari?
        what is-it that has taken (possession of) my husband

These facts about questions correspond with similar facts about contrastive and/or emphatic accents. The LOWERING of the comment-NP, as in (31a) above, is marginally allowed in colloquial but avoided in written French:

(46)a.   C'est l'étudiant qui a protesté   b.   ?L'ÉTUDIANT a protesté
         it is the student who has protested

Only in those far-fetched cases where the contrasted element is a bound morpheme is LOWERING of the comment-NP mandatory. The cleft (47b) is ridiculously ungrammatical:

(47)a.   Dieu DISpose, il ne PROpose pas!
         God DISposes, he does not PROpose!

   b.   *C'est DIS que Dieu pose, ce n'est pas PRO!
        it is DIS that God poses, it is not PRO

Moreover, as is well-known, specific questions have in common with clefts, pseudoclefts and contrastive or emphatic accent sentences that they presuppose the non-emptiness of the class of elements denoted by the S" in the non-accented topic (see the beginning of section 7.2.2). In other words, they presuppose the existence of some entity satisfying the semantic conditions set by the topic-NP.

Finally, there is the consideration that under this analysis the answer to a WH-question has, in principle, the same structure as the question itself, the only difference being that where the question has a question word the answer replaces that with the information required. When the question has the SA-form 'the x [John said x] is/was WHAT?' the answer has the SA-form 'the x [John said x] is/was "BLIMEY" '.

For these and similar reasons it seems appropriate to treat WH-elements as comment-NPs. Thus, the question *What did John say?* (=(42a)) is generated in the following way. Allowing for the appropriate adaptations in the Formation Rules we assume (48a) as the SA-structure underlying the sentence. Deletion of $V_{Nom}[PRO]$ must take place or else the LOWERING of PRO_{WH} is blocked (see (32)). Cyclic treatment of the S" under the topic-NP gives (48b). (48c) is the shallow structure: it shows the completion of the cyclic treatment. (48d) shows the effect of Postcyclic Rule (3a) for English: the WH-element has been attracted and fronted. Now Postcyclic Rule (3b) must be applied, attracting and fronting AUX. This is shown in (48e). Subsequent *Do*-SUPPORT will then replace $_V[\emptyset]$ with $_V[do]$. AFFIX HANDLING and MINCE will finish off the process.

(48)a.

b.

c.

(48)d.

e.

This treatment of specific questions does not contradict the treatment given in chapter 3. It just adds to it at a deeper and more explanatory level of syntax. One also sees that the cleft form of *What did John say?*, viz. *What is/was it that John said?*, is easily generated.

We must leave the discussion of specific questions at this, and move on to another issue.

7.3 CONJUNCTION REDUCTION

Conjunction reduction (CR) is an old sore in the theory of grammar, not only because the rules required seem out of step with what is normally found in the way of rules of syntax, but also because the facts have proved hard to pin down. As with other refractory areas of grammar, not much has been heard lately of CR in the grammatical literature. The following is an outline attempt at coming to terms with CR in its different forms. As the reader will notice, the format of the rules required is indeed rather different from what we have seen so far. On the other hand, the coverage of the facts seems close to adequate.

We shall first present a quick and global survey of the existing state of affairs, mainly based on Van Oirsouw (1987). Then we shall present our rule system for those cases of CR where a reconstruction in terms of two (or more) S-structures seems appropriate, i.e. cases that allow for *both ... and*, leaving out cases of *symmetrical CR*, like *John and Mary are a lovely pair*, which cannot be resolved in terms of **John is a lovely pair and Mary is a lovely pair* and do not allow for the insertion of *both*.[5]

Standardly, three forms of CR are distinguished. The first (generally known as CONJUNCTION REDUCTION; we shall speak of PAIRING, to avoid confusion) pairs non-identical constituents of otherwise the same Ss, with the necessary adaptation of number and other agreement features:

(49)a. John was at home and Mary was at home ⇒
   b. John and Mary were at home

This form of CR is generally considered to be limited to cases where the non-identical part (NID) of the Ss concerned is just one constituent (the subject-NP in (49a)), and where there is only one NID. Cases with more than one NID are marginal, and are, though inelegantly, treatable by means of a *respectively-*transformation, a variant of PAIRING:

(50)a. John bought a car for Mary and Harry bought a horse for Sue ⇒
   b. John and Harry bought a car and a horse for Mary and Sue, respectively

The precise status of PAIRING is much discussed. Yet it is generally distin-guished from GAPPING and RIGHT NODE RAISING (RNR). GAPPING typically occurs when two Ss, conjoined by *and*, have an identical part (ID) containing the finite verb. GAPPING then allows for the second occurrence of ID to be dropped (Neijt 1979):

(51)a. John ate the fish and Mary ate the meat ⇒
   b. John ate the fish and Mary the meat

RNR is said to occur when the conjoined full Ss contain only one ID-consti-tuent, which occurs at the far right of both Ss. A form of RAISING is then assumed for ID, resulting in a superior status of ID with regard to the two Ss:

(52)a. John likes fish and Joan hates fish ⇒
   b. John likes and Joan hates fish

It is to be noted immediately that if RNR is indeed a rule of syntax (which is denied here) it should apply also to cases where the far right ID contains more than one constituent, as in:

---

[5] We shall not go into questions of symmetrical conjunction here, as we do not, on the whole, deal with NP-grammar. It seems that, in principle, symmetrical conjunction can be treated as an NP-internal form of S-conjunction. NP[John and Mary] in *John and Mary are a lovely pair* can be regarded as derived from something like :X[John ε X AND Mary ε X], i.e. 'the set X of individuals such that John is a member of X and Mary is a member of X'.

(53)a. John read the news to Joe yesterday and Fred wrote the news to Joe
     yesterday ⇒
  b. John read and Fred wrote the news to Joe yesterday

where *the news to Joe yesterday* consists of three constituents.

Van Oirsouw (1987) argues that the standard triad of CR-rules can be replaced by one unified set of rules that will cover all cases (except symmetrical CR).
Although Van Oirsouw's analysis, for English and for Dutch, achieves a high
degree of adequacy there are some problems. First, it has not been integrated
into an overall conception of grammar but stands, more or less, on its own. Then
there are semantic problems, mainly to do with the scope of lowered operators.
Van Oirsouw is of course right in saying that one single rule or system of rules is
methodologically preferable, but it does seem that this ideal cannot be
realized without allowing the transformations to change the meaning of the
sentence. Consider, for example, the following cases:

(54)a. Someone looked at the frame and someone looked at the picture
  b. Someone looked at the frame and (at) the picture

(55)a. Many girls admire Harry and many girls detest Larry
  b. Many girls admire Harry and detest Larry

(56)a. John often went to the pub and he often went to the movies
  b. John often went to the pub and (to) the movies

(57)a. Some vegetables are boiled by Bea and some vegetables are fried by
     Fred
  b. Some vegetables are boiled by Bea and fried by Fred

Many authors have noted that the (a)-sentences differ systematically from
the (b)-sentences in that the latter exclude a reading involving double quantification, whereas the former impose such a reading. Fewer authors have noted
that this difference vanishes when the quantifier follows the occurrence of
and, as in:

(58)a. John has killed someone and Bill has killed someone
  b. John and Bill have killed someone

(59)a. Bea boils some vegetables and Fred fries some vegetables
  b. Bea boils and Fred fries some vegetables

(60)a. Harry is admired by many girls and Larry is detested by many girls
  b. Harry is admired and Larry is detested by many girls

(61)a. She wants to introduce Fred to someone and she has to introduce Ted to
     someone
  b. She wants to introduce Fred and has to introduce Ted to someone

Here the (b)-sentences allow for both the single and the multiple quantification reading, whereas the latter is obligatory for the (a)-sentences.[6]

---

[6] Yet the order of the scope-bearing elements does not seem to be the only factor determing
scope. When two finite verbs are conjoined and followed by an existential operator in the
singular, as in:

· These facts are clearly reminiscent of the SOC-phenomena discussed in 7.1 above. It therefore seems natural to propose that CR is likewise subject to SOC. If that is correct, these cases are naturally solved by the assumption that this form of CR is cyclic and interacts with the LOWERING of quantifiers and other scope-sensitive operators. There are, however, also cases where CR does not seem to be sensitive to scope differences and SOC seems to have no effect:

(62) a. John often went to the pub and Harry often went to the movies
     b. John often went to the pub and Harry to the movies

Here, despite the fact that the surface position of *and* follows that of the quantifier *often*, the structure is freely reduced under the reading of (62a) implying that the occasions on which John went to the pub and those on which Harry went to the movies need not coincide. Or consider:

(63) a. John killed someone for money and Harry killed someone by accident
     b. John killed someone for money and Harry by accident

Here two quantifications are made, no matter whether CR takes place or not.

These observations suggest that not all cases of CR should be handled by cyclic CR and thus be subject to SOC, and that there are at least two forms of CR, one cyclic and one postcyclic. This suggestion is supported by the fact that those cases where CR seems insensitive to SOC seem to be precisely the cases where GAPPING has always been assumed. On these grounds it is proposed here that there are two forms of CR, one cyclic, to be called CR-MAPPING, and one postcyclic, to be called CR-GAPPING. Let us consider CR-MAPPING first, limiting ourselves to English.

The underlying idea of CR-MAPPING is that the conjunction *and* is a weakly scope-sensitive binary operator, taking two Ss as arguments. It should be introduced by the Formation Rules as an adverbial at the level of Adv_1 or Adv_2, Adv_1 being the default.option. During the Cycle this *and*-operator is obligatorily lowered in the following way. The two argument Ss of *and*, S_1 and S_2, are mapped onto each other and the non-identical part (NID) is defined. This NID can be kept to a minimum, so that no identical parts are included, but it may also comprise identical elements (taking into account, of course, restrictions imposed by constituent structure), even to the point of declaring the two Ss non-identical in their entirety.[7] NID must, however, be continuous. (A

      (i)   Harry robbed and killed someone

there seems to be only the single quantification reading: 'there is one specific person who was both robbed and killed by Harry'. The intuitive feeling is that *robbed and killed* somehow forms one complex predicate specifying what happened to the person meant by *someone*. On the other hand, however, the multiple quantification reading is there again when the object term is plural:

      (ii)   Harry robbed and killed some people

Here, it does not have to be the same people who were robbed and who were killed. Facts such as these have so far escaped any theory.

[7] Complement Ss are minimal NIDs. From 'AND [I know that you lied][I know that you cheated]' the CR-form with minimal NID is *I know that you lied and that you cheated*. The form *I know that you lied and cheated* is derived from 'I know [that AND [you lied][you cheated]]. Likewise for infinitivals, as, for example, in (70d) below.

discontinuous NID can be handled but requires an awkward operation involving *respectively*.) Then, when NID has been established, the complement of NID, i.e. the part or parts that are treated as identical, is made to merge into one S in which the non-identical parts are subsumed under one overarching node and separated by an empty space symbolized as '-', defining the landing site of the lowered *and*.

This, however, is not all. Given the notion of CR-MAPPING in the wider context of Semantic Syntax, the facts force us to stipulate that S_1 and S_2 undergo not only the standard cyclic treatment they will have been through when the point arrives at which *and* is to be lowered, but also, in addition, the full Postcycle to the extent that this is possible. Only then, when the Postcycle is, as far as possible, completed for both argument Ss of *and*, will CR-MAPPING be allowed to apply, including the LOWERING of *and*. If there are any further operators to be lowered after *and*, the Cycle will then resume its path and carry on with the lowerings.

Consider, for example, sentences like (64a,b) (the constituent consisting of the conjuncts that have been placed together under CR-MAPPING is surrounded by square brackets):

(64)a.   [Can we and must we] leave now?
   b.   [Will John and can Harry] find the key?

These cannot be cases of CR-GAPPING, since the finite verbs are non-identical. They clearly look like cases of CR-MAPPING, but it cannot be CR-MAPPING applied to Ss as they are treated in the Cycle. QUESTION FORMATION must have applied before CR-MAPPING. Cases like these, which are perhaps not so prominent in English but abound in Dutch, make it inevitable to decide that postcyclic treatment must be completed before CR-MAPPING can take place.

The operation of mapping two Ss onto each other and the interruption of the Cycle by the Postcycle are elements we have not, so far, encountered. From a formal point of view, CR-MAPPING is, though well-defined, very different from the transformational operations that we have become familiar with. And the interruption of the Cycle by the Postcycle seems to run counter to the general architecture of the theory. This much may be unwelcome news. Yet one should take into account that so far no analysis has been able to cover the facts to a sufficient degree of adequacy, let alone to do so in terms of a seemingly well-behaved rule system. What we have gained with our analysis is that, at least, it is coming to real grips with the facts. The apparent unorthodoxy of the means by which this is achieved will, for the moment, have to be taken for granted. It may help if one takes into account the possibility that the grammar of conjunction reduction is perhaps to be regarded less as sentence grammar than as supra-sentence grammar, transcending the boundaries of ordinary S-grammar and therefore subject to different constraints. Yet this suggestion, though perhaps intuitively appealing, will have to be supported by a wider and empirically more solid theoretical context.

But let us first have a look at the proposed rule system. A few examples will show more clearly what is meant. Take (65a,b):

(65)a. [John left and Mary left]   b. [John and Mary] left

The SA-structure posited for these sentences is (65c). (65d) shows the stage at which both S"$_1$ and S"$_2$ have been through the Postcycle. In (65d) the minimal NID has been selected. Now CR-MAPPING is to apply. In (65e) S$_1$ and S$_2$ have been mapped onto each other and have merged, with the exception of the (minimal) NID-elements, which have been subsumed under a superordinate node and separated by '-', the landing site of *and*. After the LOWERING of *and* the structure is (65f=65b). With non-minimal NID the result is (65g=65a).

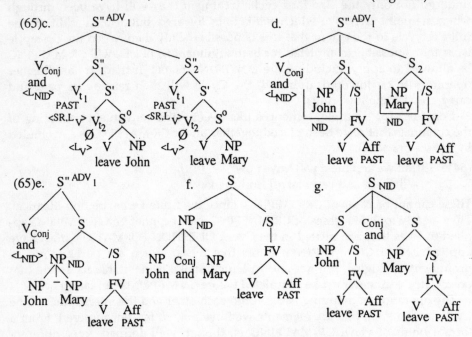

Now consider (53a,b) given above and repeated here:

(53)a. [John read the news to Joe yesterday and Fred wrote the news to Joe
        yesterday]   ⇒
    b. [John read and Fred wrote] the news to Joe yesterday

(66a-c) are analogous to (65c-e). (66d) has *and* in place (for minimal NID).

It will be noted that RIGHT NODE RAISING is no longer called for: its effects are produced by CR-MAPPING, which makes RNR superfluous. Semantically, this is correct as cases of RNR seem to obey SOC, as appears from (59)-(61) above. In those sentence pairs, the reduced version has the preferred reading where multiple quantification is involved (because the quantifier follows the conjunction), and the less preferred reading with single quantification (so that the quantifier has jumped across *and*, which is weakly scope-sensitive).

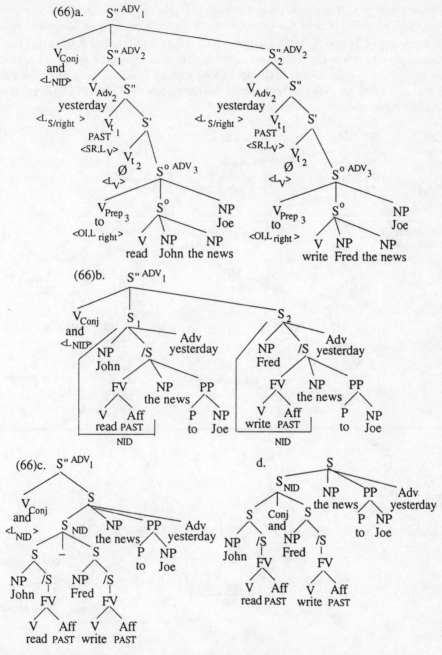

Let us now consider (54a,b) again, repeated here as (54a-c):

(54)a. [Someone looked at the frame and someone looked at the picture]
   b. Someone looked [at the frame and at the picture]
   c. Someone looked at [the frame and the picture]

and see why (54a) is not synonymous with (54b,c). The SA-structure underlying (54a) is (67a). (67b) shows the effect of the Postcycle on S_1'' and S_2''. (67c) shows the merging of S_1 and S_2 with minimal NID. Now *and* has to be lowered but is blocked by the strongly scope-sensitive existential operator *some*. Therefore, this form of CR is blocked. (54b) and (54c) can be realized only if *and* comes under *some*, as in (68a), which leads to (68b) after CR-MAPPING. In (68b) LOWERING of *someone* is unproblematic.

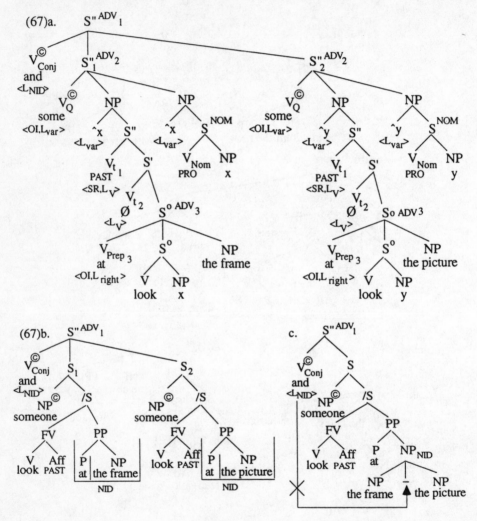

(68)a.

```
          S"ADV₁
        /   |    \
      V©Q   NP      NP
      some  / \    / \
   <OI,L var> x  S"ADV₂   x   S NOM
      <L var>  |      <L var>  / \
           V©Conj S₁    S₂    V Nom NP
           and   / \   / \    PRO    x
          <L NID> NP /S  NP /S
                  x        x
                  / \      / \
                FV   PP   FV   PP
               / \  / \  / \  / \
              V Aff P NP V Aff P NP
           look PAST at the frame look PAST at the picture
```

b.

```
          S"ADV₁
        /   |    \
      V©Q   NP      NP
      some  / \    / \
   <OI,L var> x  S     x   S NOM
      <L var>  / \  <L var> / \
            NP  /S       V Nom NP
            x    \       PRO    x
            FV    PP
           / \    |
          V  Aff  P  NP NID
       look PAST  at  / | \
                    NP Conj© NP
              the frame and the picture
```

Since the *and*-operator is weakly scope-sensitive it allows for crossing by another operator, as in:

(69)   [John and Harry] hate someone

which is scope-ambiguous between a multiple quantification reading where each hates someone, and a single quantification reading where there is someone hated by both. In the latter reading *someone* has crossed the weakly scope-sensitive *and*-operator. This case is thus analogous to (58)-(61) given above.[8]

CR-MAPPING often allows for the insertion of *both* before the first conjunct. This is possible only if CR-MAPPING is not maximal, i.e. if the conjuncts are not main S's (**Both John was ill and Harry had gone to the movies*). With complement-taking verbs *both* therefore indicates scope (see note 7). (70a) is ambiguous: either it is believed that the man has dual nationality or there are different beliefs about his nationality. *Both* in (70b) and (70c,d) disambiguates. In (70b) *and* comes under *believe*, i.e. the man is believed to have dual nationality. In (70c,d) *believe* comes under *and*, i.e. there are varying beliefs. In (70c) CR-GAPPING has applied in addition to CR-MAPPING (see below, especially (74c)). Without CR-GAPPING (70c) has the form (70d):

(70)a.   The man was believed to be [Spanish and Italian]
   b.   The man was believed to be [both Spanish and Italian]
   c.   The man was [both believed to be Spanish and [believed to be] Italian]
   d.   The man was [both believed to be Spanish and believed to be Italian]

Both is considered to be lowered after *and*, as an extra option when non-maximal NID has been chosen. The surface category is 'Adv', and the landing site is just left of NID, provided it is a site that can be filled by an adverb in S-syntax. English has adverb landing sites (a) sentence-initially, which allows for, e.g. *Both John and Harry left* (cf. *Normally she said nothing*), (b) on the

---

[8] Note that NID in (61a) comprises the ID-element *to introduce*. No use can be made of this ID-element, however, since NID has to be continuous — unless one is happy with the extremely stilted *She wants and has to introduce Fred and Ted, respectively, to someone.*

V-cluster, which explains *She both talked and gestured* (cf. *She quickly left*), and (c) at the far right, though stopped by flagged operators (see 7.1), which explains *He killed both the burglar and the policeman*. In Dutch, adverbs never land on the V-cluster, so that (71a) is ungrammatical (cf. 71b). (71c) is grammatical due to V-FINAL in subordinate clauses, which makes the V-cluster move across any far-right adverbial (cf. 71d):

(71)a. *Jan zowel lachte als huilde   b. *Jan hard lachte
        Jan both laughed and cried   Jan loudly laughed

    c. ... dat Jan zowel lachte als huilde d. ... dat Jan hard lachte
        ... that Jan both laughed and cried   ... that Jan loudly laughed

So much, for the moment, for CR-MAPPING. We now pass on to CR-GAPPING. CR-GAPPING is a postcyclic rule, to be ordered at the very end of the Postcycle, after the application of CR-MAPPING. It is applicable regardless of whether (obligatory) CR-MAPPING has been minimal or not minimal. Roughly speaking, the main condition for CR-GAPPING to apply is that ID contains the finite verb of the conjoined Ss. The effect of CR-GAPPING is that the second, identical, occurrence of FV is deleted, together with all other identical material, so that only non-identical material remains in S_2.

In principle, the deletion of ID under CR-GAPPING is maximal and ID does not have to be continuous. A further condition for English (but not for Dutch: cf. (86c) below) is that there must be non-identical material, usually the subject, to the left of the identical FV. (Anaphoric uptakes count as identical, but phonologically identical quantifiers, like *sometimes* in (72a,b), which have not been deleted by CR-MAPPING due to SOC, count as non-identical.) A case of non-subject NID preceding the identical FV is presented in (72a,b). If ID comprises the whole remainder of the second conjunct after the initial NID element, and both conjuncts are understood to be true at the same time, the adverb *too* is obligatorily added, as in (72d).[9] (The gapped elements are in smaller font and between square brackets; the sentence should therefore be read without the small-print bracketed text.)

(72)a. [Sometimes I find her attractive and sometimes I find her repulsive]
    b. [Sometimes I find her attractive and sometimes [I find her] repulsive]
    c. [Harry left the house yesterday and Pete left the house yesterday]
    d. [Harry left the house yesterday and Pete [left the house yesterday] too]

There are further stipulations and restrictions, not all of which can be fully dealt with here. First, if ID contains the FV and the FV is one of the auxiliary verbs (of modality, tense, aspect or voice) introduced by the Formation Rules in the Auxiliary System, CR-GAPPING is either blocked or applies only with

---

[9] *Too* cannot be added when the conjunction is understood as expressing two alternatives that will not or cannot be true at the same time, as in (i). Now the gapped version (ii) does not allow for *too*:
        (i)   Today I will cook and tomorrow you will cook
        (ii)   Today I will cook and tomorrow you [will cook] *too
Cases like these typically involve a topic-comment profile: 'today the one who will cook is me and tomorrow the one who cook is you'.

difficulty, as is shown by (73a-f).[10] The copula verb is all right for CR-GAPPING, as shown by (73g). In (73h) CR-GAPPING applies normally, because *wants* is not an auxiliary but a main FV. Finally, negation words cannot be made part of ID, as shown in (73j).

(73) a. *Fred will fry the fish and Ted [will] boil the chicken
 b. *Fred has fried the fish and Ted [has] boiled the chicken
 c. *?The fish was fried by Fred and the chicken [was] boiled by Ted
 d. ?Fred has to fry the fish and Ted [has] to boil the chicken
 e. ?Fred is to fry the fish and Ted [is] to boil the chicken
 f. ?Fred is frying the fish and Ted [is] boiling the chicken
 g. Fred is mad and Ted [is] just silly
 h. Fred wants to fry the fish and Ted [wants] to boil the chicken
 i. Fred always wants to stay and Ted [always wants] to leave
 j. *Fred never wants to stay and Ted [never wants] to leave

Moreover, CR-GAPPING applies as well when FV has been removed by CR-MAPPING but there is an identical embedded verb form, as in (74). (74a) shows maximal and (74b) minimal CR-MAPPING. Since NID is discontinuous and CR-MAPPING requires a continuous NID, the ID-element occurring between the discontinuous NID-elements has been taken along in (74b). Since ID in (74b) is the embedded verb form *painted*, CR-GAPPING now applies, giving (74c):

(74) a. [I had the door painted for Pete and I had the floor painted for Gene]
 b. I had [the door painted for Pete and the floor painted for Gene]
 c. I had [the door painted for Pete and the floor [painted] for Gene]

But note that this form of CR-GAPPING is not allowed when FV has not been deleted by CR-MAPPING. This is illustrated in (75) (which takes up (61)). (75a) represents maximal and (75b) minimal CR-MAPPING. Now CR-GAPPING does not apply to (75b) to delete *to introduce*, as the FVs are still present in both conjuncts and are not identical. Hence the ungrammaticality of (75c):

(75) a. [She wants to introduce Fred to someone and she has to introduce Ted to someone]
 b. [She wants to introduce Fred and has to introduce Ted] to someone
 c. *[She wants to introduce Fred and has [to introduce] Ted] to someone

(The condition on CR-GAPPING had therefore better be reformulated, with the restrictions mentioned above, to the effect that ID must contain the highest ranking verb form of the two conjuncts. But in order to do so we must first define the notion of verb ranking, which we shall not do here.)

The interaction of CR-MAPPING and CR-GAPPING, which (74) is an example of, is illustrated further in (76). (76a) shows maximal CR-MAPPING (the second

---

[10] This restriction does not hold for Dutch, where CR-GAPPING applies freely even if FV is an auxiliary of tense, aspect or voice. Note, moreover, that (73a-f) are a great deal better in question form:

  (i) Will Fred fry the fish and [will] Ted boil the chicken?
  (ii) Was the fish fried by Fred and [was] the chicken boiled by Ted?
  (iii) Does Fred have to fry the fish and [does] Ted [have] to boil the chicken?

occurrence of *textbook* may be pronominalized to *one*), and (76b) shows minimal CR-MAPPING. (76c) shows CR-GAPPING from (76a), and (76d) from (76b):

(76)a. [Fred had a good textbook and Ted had a bad textbook/one]
    b. [Fred had a good and Ted had a bad] textbook
    c. [Fred had a good textbook and Ted [had] a bad textbook/one]
    d. [Fred had a good and Ted [had] a bad] textbook

Then, CR-GAPPING does not apply when a complementizer or subordinating conjunction is part of the NID-constituent. Thus, although the (a)-sentences in (77) and (78) have the (b)-sentences as minimal variants (see note 7), the (c)-sentences are ungrammatical. In the (d)-sentences, however, *and* comes inside the subordinate clause. Now CR-GAPPING is possible, as shown in the (e)-sentences:

(77)a. [I believe that Harry eats meat and I believe that Larry eats fish]
    b. I believe [that Harry eats meat and that Larry eats fish]
    c. *I believe [that Harry eats meat and that Larry [eats] fish]
    d. I believe that [Harry eats meat and Larry eats fish]
    e. I believe that [Harry eats meat and Larry [eats] fish]

(78)a. [She left because Ted was rude and she left because the wine was awful]
    b. She left [because Ted was rude and because the wine was awful]
    c. *She left [because Ted was rude and because the wine [was] awful]
    d. She left because [Ted was rude and the wine was awful]
    e. She left because [Ted was rude and the wine [was] awful]

Finally, Constituent structure conditions differ for CR-MAPPING and for CR-GAPPING. As shown in Neijt (1979), CR-GAPPING does not maximize ID beyond main constituent boundaries. Thus (Neijt 1979:19,40,46), prepositions cannot be isolated under CR-GAPPING, as shown by (79b,c) and (80a). But under CR-MAPPING they can be, as shown in (80b):

(79)a. Charley writes with a pencil and John [writes] with a pen
    b. *Charley writes with a pencil and John [writes with] a pen
    c. *Charley writes with a pencil and John [writes with a] pen

(80)a. *John is confident of a successful outing and Peter [is] dependent on
        [a successful outing] at the track
    b. John is [confident of and dependent on] a successful outing at the track

Embedded /Ss are optionally subsumed under ID for the purpose of CR-GAPPING (Ross 1970b:250), but once it has been decided for an embedded /S whether or not it will be reckoned to be part of ID that decision will count for that entire embedded /S, including possible further embedded /Ss. That is, the decisions are made from the top down. Hence the grammaticality of (81a-e) and the ungrammaticality of (81f):

(81)a. I want to try to begin to write a novel and you want to try to begin to write a play

   b.   I want to try to begin to write a novel and you [want] to try to begin to write a play

   c.   I want to try to begin to write a novel and you [want to try] to begin to write a play

   d.   I want to try to begin to write a novel and you [want to try to begin] to write a play

   e.   I want to try to begin to write a novel and you [want to try to begin to write] a play

   f.   *I want to try to begin to write a novel and you [want] to try [to begin to write] a play

One great advantage of this analysis of CR is that it applies equally (the differences concern only minor details) to English and Dutch, despite the fact that Dutch sentence structure, with its V-FINAL rule and its END CLUSTER ARRANGEMENT, differs considerably from English sentence structure. In fact, none of the analyses presented in the context of Transformational Grammar is applicable to both English and Dutch, with the exception of Van Oirsouw (1987). Let us consider some examples.

A simple example is the following. (82a) represents maximal CR-MAPPING (with *and* inside the complement-clause). (82b) shows minimal CR-MAPPING, and (82c) shows the effect of CR-GAPPING on the basis of (82a):

(82)a.   Ik geloof dat [Henk een PC gekocht heeft en Karel een printer gekocht heeft]
       (I believe that Henk a PC bought has and Karel a printer bought has)

    b.   Ik geloof dat [Henk een PC en Karel een printer] gekocht heeft

    c.   Ik geloof dat [Henk een PC gekocht heeft en Karel een printer [gekocht heeft]]

Now consider:

(83)a.   Ik geloof dat [Lia blijven wil en Frans weggaan wil]
       (I believe that Lia stay wants-to and Frans away-go wants-to)

    b.   Ik geloof dat [Lia blijven wil en Frans weggaan [wil]]

    c.   Ik geloof dat [Lia blijven en Frans weggaan] wil

(84)a.   Ik geloof dat [Lia wil blijven en Frans wil weggaan]

    b.   Ik geloof dat [Lia wil blijven en Frans [wil] weggaan]

    c.   *Ik geloof dat [Lia blijven en Frans wil weggaan]

(85)a.   Ik geloof dat [Lia wil blijven en Frans weg wil gaan]

    b.   Ik geloof dat [Lia wil blijven en Frans weg [wil] gaan]

    c.   *Ik geloof dat [Lia blijven en Frans weg wil gaan]

All nine sentences mean 'I believe that Lia wants to stay and Frans wants to leave'. The (a)-sentences represent maximal CR-MAPPING. They differ only in that the postcyclic rule of END CLUSTER ARRANGEMENT has had different effects. These effects make for different CR possibilities. Due to the different word-orders in the (a)-sentences, non-maximal CR-MAPPING is possible only for (83a), as shown in (83c). Attempts at non-maximal CR-MAPPING for (84) and

(85) fail since NID has to be continuous. CR-GAPPING, however, as shown in the (b)-sentences, is possible regardless of the word order resulting from END CLUSTER ARRANGEMENT, as CR-GAPPING is insensitive to the continuity parameter.

Non-subject ID-material preceding FV is found in (86) (Van Oirsouw 1984). (86b) represents non-maximal CR-MAPPING. (86c) shows CR-GAPPING based on (86a), with the subject *ik* included in ID. (86d) is ungrammatical because CR-GAPPING has not applied maximally:

(86)a. [Ik heb kaas voor Piet gekocht en ik heb vlees voor Jan gekocht]
        (I have cheese for Piet bought and I have meat for Jan bought)
    b. Ik heb [kaas voor Piet en vlees voor Jan] gekocht
    c. [Ik heb kaas voor Piet gekocht en [ik heb] vlees voor Jan [gekocht]]
    d. *[Ik heb kaas voor Piet gekocht en [ik heb] vlees voor Jan gekocht]

An interesting point of comparison between English and Dutch is embedded /Ss under CR-GAPPING. As was shown in (81), Ross's example, English embedded verbal /S-material is included optionally in ID under CR-GAPPING, the options being made from the top down. The same goes for Dutch embedded /Ss, but not for V-clusters resulting from PREDICATE RAISING. The latter must always be included entirely in ID under CR-GAPPING, as shown in (87):

(87)a. [Lia heeft een roman kunnen lezen en Frans heeft een dissertatie kunnen lezen]
        (Lia has a novel be able read and Frans has a dissertation be able read)
    b. [Lia heeft een roman kunnen lezen en Frans [heeft] een dissertatie [kunnen lezen]]
    c. *[Lia heeft een roman kunnen lezen en Frans [heeft] een dissertatie kunnen [lezen]]
    d. *[Lia heeft een roman kunnen lezen en Frans [heeft] een dissertatie [kunnen] lezen]]

This calls for testing on those cases where PREDICATE RAISING is optional. In the lexicon of 5.2.2 there are three verbs with optional PR: *beginnen*$_2$ ('begin') and *proberen* or *trachten* ('try'). All three take the particle *te* with or without PR. We can thus consider the four variants of the subordinate clause given in (88)-(91), all meaning '... that I try to start to do this and you try to start to do that'. (Embedded /Ss are enclosed in labelled brackets.) With the help of chapter 5 the reader will be able to work out that (88) represents the case where PR has applied both on *beginnen* and on *proberen*. This sentence thus has one large V-cluster, which must not be interrupted by CR-GAPPING. In (89) PR has not applied on *beginnen*, which is therefore followed by an embedded /S, but it has applied on *proberen*. In (90) the reverse is the case: PR has applied on *beginnen* but not on *proberen*. And in (91) PR has not applied at all, so that there are two embedded /Ss. Given the rules and principles as formulated above, this leads to precisely the following predictions of grammaticality and ungrammaticality:

(88)a. ... dat ik dit probeer te beginnen te doen en jij dat probeert te beginnen te doen

b. ... dat ik dit probeer te beginnen te doen en jij dat [probeert te beginnen te doen]

c. *... dat ik dit probeer te beginnen te doen en jij dat [probeert te beginnen] te doen

d. *... dat ik dit probeer te beginnen te doen en jij dat [probeert] te beginnen [te doen]

e. *... dat ik dit probeer te beginnen te doen en jij dat [probeert] te beginnen te doen

(89)a. ... dat ik probeer te beginnen /S[dit te doen] en jij probeert te beginnen /S[dat te doen]

b. ... dat ik probeer te beginnen /S[dit te doen] en jij [probeert te beginnen] /S[dat [te doen]]

c. ... dat ik probeer te beginnen /S[dit te doen] en jij [probeert te beginnen] /S[dat te doen]

d. ... *dat ik probeer te beginnen /S[dit te doen] en jij [probeert] te beginnen /S[dat [te doen]]

e. ... *dat ik probeer te beginnen /S[dit te doen] en jij [probeert] te beginnen /S[dat te doen]

(90)a. ... dat ik probeer /S[dit te beginnen te doen] en jij probeert /S[dat te beginnen te doen]

b. ... dat ik probeer /S[dit te beginnen te doen] en jij [probeert] /S[dat [te beginnen te doen]]

c. ... *dat ik probeer /S[dit te beginnen te doen] en jij [probeert] /S[dat [te beginnen] te doen]

d. ... *dat ik probeer /S[dit te beginnen te doen] en jij [probeert] /S[dat te beginnen [te doen]]

e. ... dat ik probeer /S[dit te beginnen te doen] en jij [probeert] /S[dat te beginnen te doen]

(91)a. ... dat ik probeer /S[te beginnen /S[dit te doen]] en jij probeert /S[te beginnen /S[dat te doen]]

b. ... dat ik probeer /S[te beginnen /S[dit te doen]] en jij [probeert /S[te beginnen] /S[dat [te doen]]]

c. ... dat ik probeer /S[te beginnen /S[dit te doen]] en jij [probeert /S[te beginnen] /S[dat te doen]]

d. ... *dat ik probeer /S[te beginnen /S[dit te doen]] en jij [probeert] /S[te beginnen /S[dat [te doen]]]

e. ... dat ik probeer /S[te beginnen /S[dit te doen]] en jij [probeert] /S[te beginnen /S[dat te doen]]

Note that the analysis predicts that (89e) is ungrammatical but (91e) is not, even though they consist of exactly the same words in the same order. But they have different surface structures: in (89e) there is only one embedded /S, whereas in (91e) there are two. This, of course, makes testing on native speakers' intuitive grammaticality judgements impossible, and one has to conclude that (89e=91e) is grammatical as a clause. Other than that, all predictions on (un)grammaticality made in (88)-(91) match native speakers' judgements.

This shows in a dramatic fashion the correctness of the PREDICATE RAISING analysis presented in section 5.4. It also confirms the essential correctness of the CR analysis presented here, even if this analysis is still fragmentary and has to be left with many ends fraying.

7.4 Subordinate clauses and prepositional participial clauses

Nothing, or nothing much, has been said so far about the syntax of subordinate clauses other than complement clauses. Subordinate clauses are standardly headed by a subordinating conjunction, such as *because, while, when, although, after, now that*. It has been observed traditionally that subordinating conjunctions correspond regularly with prepositions. Thus, *because* corresponds with *because of, while* with *during*, etc. This correspondence is exploited in Semantic Syntax, in that subordinating conjunctions are treated on a par with prepositions, the only difference being that for subordinating conjunctions the object-NP obligatorily dominates an S''. Thus the sentence (92a) has the SA-structure (92b), assuming that the *because*-clause is of rank 2. The treatment is obvious: OBJECT INCORPORATION under *because* leads to a complex V consisting of $_V$[because] on the one hand and $_S$[he left] on the other. LOWERING (to the far right) then gives the subordinate clause $_S$[Sub-Conj[because] $_S$[he left]].

(92)a.   She cried because he left

b.

The negative sentence (93a) is scope-ambiguous (cf. (6a-c) above) between the readings (93c) and (93d). Without the comma and with a rising sentence-final intonation reading (93c) is expressed. In this reading the person denoted by *she* actually did cry and the person denoted by *he* did leave, but the reason she cried was not that he left. In (93a) with the comma, and in (93b), with the *because*-clause preposed, she did in fact not cry, the reason being that he left. These readings are better understood when one realizes that the conjunction *because* is *factive* in the sense of Kiparsky and Kiparsky (1971): it presupposes the truth of its object-clause. Since presuppositions are normally preserved under negation the presupposition that he did in fact leave is preserved in (93c), even though the whole sentence is placed under the negation operator. The inference that she did not cry in (93d) follows from the fact that the subject S"ADV2 of *because* contains *not*. The inference that she did cry in (93c) follows from the property of negation to affect primarily the highest lexical predicate in its scope (cf. p. 31 above), leaving the truth of lower Ss intact. (A cleft analysis like 'it is not because he left that she cried' reinforces this inference on presuppositional grounds.)

(93)a. She did not cry$_{(,)}$ because he left
   b. Because he left she did not cry

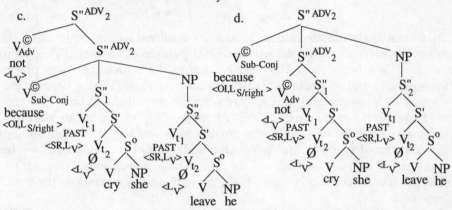

c. [tree labelled S"ADV2 ...] d. [tree labelled S"ADV2 ...]

(93c) must lead to just (93a), and (93d) to both (93a) and (93b), so that (93a) is ambiguous (barring the comma). The surface structure of (93c) is (93e=93a). That of (93d) is either (93e=93a) or (93f=93b). It will be noted that in generating (93e) from (93c) SOC has been observed, since the higher scope-sensitive operator *not* stays to the left of the lower scope-sensitive operator *because*. But in the generation of (93e) from (93d) the left-to-right order has been disturbed, as the higher *because* has crossed the lower *not* and stands to its right. Here the reader is referred to (12a,b) in section 7.1, repeated here for convenience:

(12)a. He always snores during some arias
   b. During some arias, he always snores

This sentence pair shows exactly the same ambiguity pattern as (93a,b). (12a) is scope-ambiguous between a specific and a non-specific reading for *some* and a corresponding smaller or larger scope reading for *always*. There, too, in order to get the specific reading for (12a), i.e. with large scope for *some*, the Prep-Phrase *during some arias* had to cross the *always*-operator lowered earlier. In connection with this case it was said that SOC may be overridden and LOWERING to the far right is all right for adverbials when the adverbial is attached to S and not to /S and if the previously lowered operator is part of /S. The path from (93d) to (93b) is again straightforward, as no exception to the strict left-to-right order principle has to be invoked.

(93)e.

```
            S                                              f.              S
        ╱  ╲                                                          ╱      ╲
      ╱  ╱  ╲                                                       ╱          ╲
    NP   /S    S                                              S                   S
    she  │   ╱ ╲                                           ╱   ╲              ╱    ╲
        FV  ©  V  Sub-Conj NP                          ©           NP    /S
       ╱╲  Adv cry because  │                    Sub-Conj NP       she   │  ╲
      V  Aff not            S                    because  │            FV   ©   V
      do PAST            ╱  ╲                             S          ╱╲  Adv cry
                       NP   /S                          ╱ ╲        V  Aff not
                       he   │                         NP  /S      do PAST
                           FV                         he   │
                          ╱ ╲                             FV
                         V  Aff                          ╱ ╲
                      leave PAST                        V  Aff
                                                     leave PAST
```

Apart from subordinate clauses headed by a subordinating conjunction we also have what may be called prepositional participial clauses (PPC), as in *By working hard he got rich*. They are an intermediate form between prepositional phrases and subordinate clauses headed by a subordinating conjunction. We speak of 'prepositional' clauses even though not all the expressions concerned are prepositions in the accepted sense. English *while*, for example, functions as the head of a PPC, as in *He died while drinking beer*, even though it is not a normal preposition. Moreover, not all normal prepositions allow for use as head of a PPC. We shall use the term *clausal prepositions* ('Cl-prep') to denote the class of possible heads of PPCs, but nothing much hangs on the terminology used.

As was indicated in section 2.7.4.3 and at the beginning of section 4.4.2, the structure proposed for PPCs is the following:

$$V_{Cl\text{-}prep}[X] + S'' + {}_{NP}[S^o/S']$$

where $V_{Cl\text{-}prep}$ is a clausal preposition and can be of rank 1, 2, or 3. The cyclic rules induced are SD, PrP, OI and $L_{S/right}$. Depending on the clausal preposition concerned, the object-S is either S' or S^o. *While*, for example, takes S^o, but *in virtue of* takes S': *in virtue of having worked* , but **while having worked*.

A sentence like (94a) is thus generated in the following manner. The SA-structure is (94b). After the standard cyclic treatment of S'' SD applies on the *while*-cycle. This is horizontal SD, not the vertical SD we have encountered so far (see 2.7.4.3). This eliminates $_{NP}[x]$ in the object S^o, turning it into /S. PrP and OI then produce (94c). Subsequent far right LOWERING of the *while*-phrase gives (94d), and postcyclic treatment results in the surface structure (94e).

(94)a. Socrates died while drinking hemlock

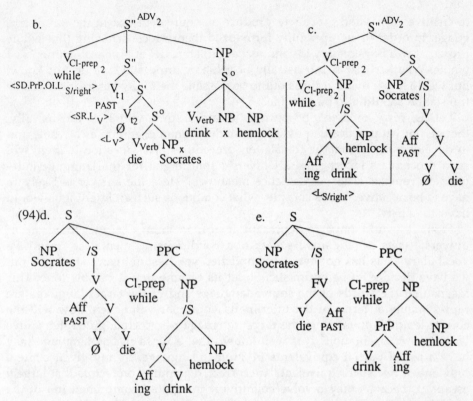

Given limitations of space we shall leave the discussion of subordinate clauses and PPCs at this point, leaving the elaboration of further elements of this part of the grammar to later work.

7.5 Deeper Semantic Analysis (DSA)

In section 1.4.4, and again in section 6.6, the possibility was anticipated of setting up a level of meaning representation that is less bound up with specific languages and could serve as a bartering counter for certain translation equivalents which would otherwise be hard to handle formally. At this point it is perhaps useful to discuss the question of language-independent meaning representation in more general terms. The question is: is it possible to develop a level or system of meaning representation that could serve as a general formally well-defined Universal Interlingua to be associated with formally well-defined reciprocal translation procedures for all human languages?

If what is expected is a strictly scientific, theoretically austere answer it is more likely to be negative than positive. We know that a correct translation of texts from one language into another often requires not only linguistic but also world knowledge. Correct translation of non-trivial texts is a deep process requiring full cognitive integration of the source language text and a full re-creative expression process to produce an equivalent text in the target language. In order to set up a fully formalized theory reconstructing that whole process it will be necessary to construct a formal model of human cognition as a whole. Whether that is intrinsically possible or impossible we do not know. But we do know that if it turns out to be possible then fully automatic machine translation should also be possible.

Let us, for a moment, be optimistic and assume that it is intrinsically, though not yet practically, possible to model human cognition as a whole and to develop fully automatic translation procedures. The question is then: will such procedures incorporate a Universal Interlingua for the language-independent representation of sentence meanings? Here the answer is likely to have to be negative. Let us consider what conditions such an Interlingua would have to satisfy.

First, it would have to represent lexical meanings. How? In terms of universal (sets of) cognitive satisfaction conditions, a 'mentalese' primitive vocabulary. This has not been accomplished yet, despite many attempts. But we have decided to be optimistic. So let us assume that it can be done. This means that the words of the source language and of the target language are representable in terms of the Interlingua vocabulary. But then, how will the correct lexical equivalent in the target language be selected, given the source language representation? It is well-known that a word in one language may have a list of partial equivalents in another language. In any given context only one or two such equivalents are correct, depending on factors that largely escape us because they involve cognitively integrated comprehension of the source text. The German verb *steuern*, for example, has at least the following partial equivalents in English: *steer, direct, navigate, pilot, drive, control, manipulate, manœuvre*, and probably a few more. Conversely, the English verb *drive* has at least the following partial equivalents in German: *treiben, zwingen, jagen, hetzen, lenken, fahren, führen, bohren, schlagen, rammen*, and, again, probably a few more. Let us assume, for the sake of simplicity, that both *steuern* and *drive* should be reckoned to be non-ambiguous so that one single meaning representation for each in the Interlingua will do. How can a formal translation procedure take the supposed Interlingua representation of, say, *steuern* in a given context of use and find the or a correct equivalent for English? Procedures have been worked out to do this on the basis of adjacent words. For example, if the direct object of *steuern* is a word for 'car' then the English *drive* should be appropriate. But this is not always the case, because sometimes *drive* is inappropriate and, say, *manœuvre* should be used. Humans decide these things on the basis of integrated comprehension of the source language text and reformulation in the target language. An algorithmic program would have to do the same, improbable as it may sound. But then there is no need for a separate level of universal interpretation in terms of an Interlingua. The cognitive machinery itself will do the job.

The same applies to the items occurring in the auxiliary system. The perfect tense auxiliary, for example, shows considerable semantic differences in

English and Dutch. English *have* has, besides (a) a meaning implying existential quantification over events, with the implication that the set of events can still be augmented ('there have been one or more occasions such that ...') also (b) a resultative meaning relevant to the present situation (*the car has been stolen*), and (c) a meaning implying continuation from the past into the present (*we have known for a long time that* ...). Note that the extra implication in meaning (a) makes the English perfect tense unfit for reference to a definite closed past: *!*Yesterday I have been unwell*.

Dutch *hebben/zijn* differs roughly in the following way. It shares the meaning (a) but without the extra implication. Though it is possible to use the perfect tense in a context where a set of events can still be augmented, it is not necessary to do so. It is, therefore, perfectly natural to say *Gisteren ben ik ziek geweest* (lit. 'yesterday I have been unwell'). The resultative meaning (b) is equally valid in Dutch. Meaning (c), however, does not exist in Dutch, which, like most languages, uses the simple present for such cases. Then the Dutch perfect tense has a meaning unknown in English: it is typically used to take distance from a narrative and to present a proposition as a comment on a series of past events or a past situation. Typically, at the end of a story, an English-speaking child will ask *Did it really happen?* whereas a Dutch-speaking child will say *Is het echt gebeurd?* ('has it really happened?'). This the Dutch child does because it takes distance from the narrative and is asking for comment on it.

In light of such facts it is difficult to see what the function could be of a separate meaning representation in terms of an Interlingua. Interlingua will represent, for example, the question *Did it really happen?* as asked by an English child at the end of a story. But how will it guarantee the correct selection of the present perfect tense for the Dutch equivalent without recourse to the whole cognitive machinery of integrated comprehension? It does not seem realistic to expect that this can be done solely at some level of meaning representation. This means that the prospect of an Interlingua level of meaning representations does not seem realistic. It is more realistic, though still very far away, to expect that any empirically adequate fully formal theory of translation will draw on the entire cognitive machinery, and will do so without the intervention of a universal Interlingua.

It should be observed, in this connection, that a theory of translation is in fact much more than a theory accounting only for actual translation processes. The interest of what we call a translation theory lies in the fact that it encompasses (a) a theory of the comprehension process and (b) a theory of the process of linguistic expression, the production process leading from the conception of a thought to an actual utterance. A translation theory, moreover, has the additional advantage of taking the output of (a) as input to (b), but in different languages. It is thus forced to look at semantic and grammatical linguistic universals under strict conditions of empirical adequacy. It is in this sense that we are speaking of a translation theory here.

The non-viability of an Interlingua stands out more clearly when we concentrate for a moment on the production process. In formulating a sentence in any language the speaker has, so to speak, to go through a *semantic question-naire* presented to him by the language in question. For example, when the language is Dutch and the speaker wants to make an assertion regarding the past, then in order to be able to use the Dutch language properly, the speaker has to answer the question whether the reference to the past is part of the (or a) narrative, or is to be presented as a metastatement providing a comment on the narrative. When the language is English this question does not arise but other questions will have to be answered. Likewise, if one wants to make a statement in Turkish involving the present, one must answer the question whether the statement is meant in a generic or habitual sense, in which case the aorist tense is to be used (see section 7.6). If not, the ordinary present tense will do. But this question does not arise for English, or for Dutch. Malay does not ask too many questions about time. It wants to know if the proposition to be formulated is to be interpreted as still having to take place. If so it prescribes the use of the particle-verb *akan*. If the proposition describes a state of affairs, rather than an event, it wants to know if the state of affairs in question is the recent result of past activity. If so, the particle-verb *sudah* is inserted.

Then there are questions of style and/or register. A Turkish newspaper contained the headline *Grip öldürdü*, which is literally 'The flu has caused to die' or 'the flu has killed' (see (101a) below). But that literal translation would hardly do for an English-language newspaper, which would rather have something like *Flu claims victims*. A formal theory that would account for such differences is, obviously, still a very far way off.

Questions of this nature form a language-specific semantic questionnaire. For a translation procedure this means that if the answers to the questions are not provided by the source language input, as very often they are not, they have to come from cognition as a whole. The fact that the questions differ widely from language to language, with the result that a semantic representation of a sentence in the source language often fails to contain the information needed for its translation into the target language, is one of the reasons why it is so hard to achieve an adequate translation theory and a formal translation procedure. For example, translating a Malay sentence into its English equivalent regular-ly involves time questions whose answers are not provided by the Malay sentence. To find the answers there is nothing one can do but consult one's own cognitively integrated comprehension.

Does this mean that it is pointless to look for levels of semantic analysis that are less language-specific than the SA-structures of our grammars and go beyond them, away from specific language structures and in the direction of universal cognition? Here the answer has to be that it is far from pointless to do so. On the contrary, as we saw in section 6.6. above in connection with counterfactuals in German, English, French and Dutch, we can achieve greater generality and discover regularities of linguistic expression by formulating deeper levels of semantic analysis or representation. Not all translation equivalents are to be fetched from the deep. Some can be handled at more superficial levels. And it seems that we are now in a position to begin to define a level at which certain translation equivalents that have so far escaped a principled and formally precise solution can be handled adequately. We have tentatively conceived of a level of Deeper Semantic Analysis or DSA, a perhaps areally restricted counter for negotiating certain translation equivalents in the four languages concerned. And we have seen that the surface differences of German, English, French and Dutch counterfactuals can be reduced to virtually complete identity only at the level of DSA, not at SA-level or any level nearer to the surface.

It must be remembered, however, that we are still some way off a full specification of the DSA for the four languages concerned and others that could be served by it. To the extent that the notion of DSA seems useful it will not provide a systematic analysis of lexical meaning but keep, in principle, lexical items intact and leave the search for their translation equivalents to other areas of cognition. Furthermore, it seems obvious that a distinction will have to be made between scope-sensitive and scope-insensitive operators. The former will have to maintain their mutual scope relations throughout, while the latter must be allowed the freedom to move up or down the auxiliary ladder of the SA-structures of the languages concerned, according to their Formation Rules. We will not consider this general question further here, and leave that to future research. But we will look at two further cases, besides the counterfactual in the four languages. The first seems to be a good candidate for treatment at DSA-level, the other less so.

Consider first the case of the French MAUX-verb *venir (de)*, discussed in 4.1.3 and 4.4.1. We will compare it, at SA-level, with its English equivalent *just have*. Consider the translation equivalents (95a,b), with their respective SA-structures (95c,d):

(95) a. Il vient de partir
    b. He has just left

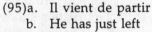
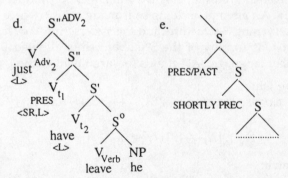

By means of a DSA-structure it is now fairly simple to formulate the translation equivalence. Suppose DSA contains structures like (95e) to express the fact that something has taken place shortly before the time referred to by the highest tense, PRES or PAST, with the operator SHORTLY PREC as a variant of PREC. Now we can formulate the following conversion rules for French and English, respectively:

French:

... - PRES/PAST - SHORTLY PREC - ...   ↔   ... - PRES/PAST - V_{Maux}[venir] - ...

English:

... - PRES/PAST - SHORTLY PREC - ...   ↔   ... - V_{Adv2}[just] - PRES/PAST - have - ...

It is easy to see that the Formation Rules of the two languages concerned will now take care of all that needs to be taken care of to get the correct surface structures.

Now, however, consider the English and Dutch sentences (96a,b), with the SA-structures (96c,d):

(96)a.   He likes to write well
 b.   Hij schrijft graag goed

c. [tree structure:]
S_0'' — V_{t1} (PRES <SR,L> ∅ <L>), S_0' — V_{t2} (∅ <L>), S_0^o — V_{Verb} (like <SD/SR> ∅ <L>) NP_x (he), S_1' — V_{t2} (∅ <L>), S_1^o ADV$_3$ — V_{Adv3} (good <L>), S_1^o — V_{Verb} (write) NP (x)

d. [tree structure:]
S'' — V_{t1} (PRES <SR,L>), S' ADV$_2$ — V_{Adv2} (graag <L>), S' — V_{t2} (∅$_2$ <L>), S^o ADV$_3$ — V_{Adv3} (goed <L>), S^o — V_{Verb} (schrijven) NP (hij)

e. [tree structure:]
S — SIM/PREC, S — PLEASE (S) — S — V_{LEX} NP (A, B), NP (B), ... <rest of arg. frame>

We may now try to devise a possible DSA-structure like (96e) and formulate conversion rules for English and Dutch to produce the correct translation either way. An attempt at doing so is made below (where '(S)' stands for any optional intervening S-structure, and the superscript 'I' over S^o in the English and Dutch versions for any of the S^o-superscripts allowed by the Formation Rules for either language; 'AF' stands for 'argument frame').

English:

...-SIM/PREC-PLEASE-(S)-NP[B]   ↔   ...-∅/HAV-V_{Verb}[like]+NP_x[B]+$_s\{V_{t2}[∅]+(S^{oI})\}$

$_s[v_{LEX}[A]+_{NP}[B]+\langle\text{rest of AF}\rangle]$ $_{s^o}[v_{LEX}[A]+_{NP}[x]+\langle\text{rest of AF}\rangle]$

Dutch:

...-SIM/PREC-PLEASE-(S)-NP[B]   ↔   ...-V_{Adv2}[graag]+$_{s'}[v_{t2}[∅/HAV]+(S^{oI})]$

$_s[v_{LEX}[A]+_{NP}[B]+\langle\text{rest of AF}\rangle]$ $_{s^o}[v_{LEX}[A]+_{NP}[B]+\langle\text{rest of AF}\rangle]$

Although it is probably possible to make these conversion rules work, perhaps with some necessary adjustments here and there, they are complex and lack the directness of the conversion rules for the counterfactual as given in 6.6 or those given for French *venir de* versus English *just have*. What we would like to have instead, is a simple dictionary translation of the form:

$$\text{V}_{\text{Verb}}[\text{like}] \leftrightarrow \text{V}_{\text{Adv2}}[\text{graag}]$$

without the intervention of any DSA at all. To achieve this, however, a system must be devised to ensure that *like* and *graag* are 'plugged in' at the right spot in the English and Dutch SA-structures, all the rest remaining equal. This system will also have to ensure that the translation of the subject-NP of *like*, say $_{\text{NP}_x}[\text{A}]$, ends up in the Dutch sentence in the position analogous to the position occupied by $_{\text{NP}}[x]$, the NP controlled by $_{\text{NP}_x}[\text{A}]$, in the English complement clause of *like*. It would take us too far, however, to pursue these possibilities any further here.

7.6 A glance at Turkish

7.6.1 Introductory observations on Turkish

We have, in this book, concentrated mainly on standard European languages, which, as we know, share many grammatical properties despite their large differences. In order to take away the impression that Semantic Syntax is tailored to the European languages and therefore less suitable for languages with a very different structure, the method of description we have employed for the European languages should be applied to a language with a very different structure. For this purpose, Turkish seemed a good candidate. In the following section we shall have a look at the central elements of the Turkish auxiliary system (the reference book used is Lewis 1984). The reader will be struck not only by the fact that our method of analysis seems to fit Turkish as naturally as it does the European languages, but also by the similarities between the rule system for Turkish and the systems for the European languages dealt with in the chapters 3-6.

Turkish is a consistently left-branching language, both in its syntax and in its morphology. It is, therefore, strictly Verb-final, with basic word order SOV. It is often said by teachers and other practitioners of the Turkish language that Turkish is 'absolutely regular' and therefore (apart from vocabulary) easy to learn. The 'absolute regularity' of Turkish is, of course, part of the established mythology of the language, of the kind often created for languages by their speakers. Yet there is no denying that certain principles seem to be applied with an iron consistency. In our cursory and provisional analysis of the language we shall see that Turkish is remarkable in at least one way. To the extent that the rule system has been developed no more than three post-cyclic rules seem to be required, first the rule of PERSON AGREEMENT, which inserts person endings, then the rule of *mI*-PLACEMENT, which assigns the proper place to the question particle -*mI*- in the V-cluster, and finally the simple rule of Ø-DELETION. Most of the work is, therefore, done by the Cycle and the need for postcyclic adjustments is minimal.

A few preliminary remarks are in order before we can start looking at the rule system. Compared with most European languages, Turkish has a rich morphology, reflected by the large number of surface affixes. Turkish is also rich in morphophonological and phonological rules. The most obvious ones are those of VOWEL HARMONY, which penetrate the whole of the morphological system.

The Turkish vowel system is conveniently described in terms of the two parameters high-low and front-back. On the high-low parameter there are two values, on the front-back parameter there are four, as shown in table 1:

	front			back
high	i	ü	u	ı
low	e	ö	o	a

Table 1   *The eight vowels of Turkish*

Most vowels in Turkish affixes are harmonic: they change according to the vowel in the preceding syllable within the same word. Harmonic vowels come in two varieties, the weak and the strong ones. The weak ones appear as *e* or *a*, according to the principle shown in table 2:

i	ü	u	ı
e	ö	o	**a**

Table 2   *Weak vowel harmony*

That is, if the vowel of the preceding syllable within the same word belongs to the four front vowels the suffix takes *e* as target value. If the vowel of the preceding syllable within the same word belongs to the four back vowels the suffix takes *a* as target value. It is customary in the linguistic literature to use the small cap symbol 'E' to represent the weakly harmonic vowel that alternates between *e* and *a*. For example, the negation affix -*me*-/-*ma*- ('not') is usually written -*mE*- in linguistic writings. We shall follow this convention.

Strong harmonic affix vowels appear in four guises, according to table 3:

i	**ü**	**u**	**ı**
e	ö	o	a

Table 3   *Strong vowel harmony*

If the preceding syllable within the same word has a far-front vowel the suffix takes the value *i*. If the preceding syllable has a mid-front vowel the target value of the suffix is *ü*. If it has a mid-back vowel the target value is *u*.

If it has a far-back vowel the value is *ı* (i.e. an unrounded [u] as in English *book*; Turkish *u* corresponds to the rounded English [u] as in *rule*). In the linguistic literature the small capital symbol I is standardly used to represent the alternation according to strong vowel harmony. Thus, the question morpheme is written -*mI-*, i.e. it occurs as -*mi-*, -*mü-*, -*mu-* or -*mı-*, depending on the vowel of the preceding syllable.

Furthermore, the small capital symbol 'D' is used for the sound that alternates between /d/ and /t/: /d/ between two vowels or preceded by a voiced consonant; otherwise /t/.

In many words and affixes the final voiceless stops /ç/, /p/, /t/ and /k/ are subject to a devoicing rule: they appear as /c/, /b/, /d/ and /ğ/, respectively, when followed by a suffix beginning with a vowel. (The letter *c* is pronounced as [dzj], *ç* as [tsj], *ş* as [sh].) For example, the dative of *çiçek* ('flower') is *çiçeğe* (the alphabet symbol *ğ* denotes a softened [g] which lengthens the preceding vowel). There are, however, also words that behave differently: the dative of *at* ('horse') is *ata*. We use the spelling *Ç, P, T, K* for those cases that follow this rule.

The semivowel -*y-* is inserted after the Postcycle whenever two vowels collide in a succession of bound morphemes (except -*Iyor-*), and between successive occurrences of *DI* in the pluperfect. Further morphophonological and phonological rules will not be discussed here.

Apart from the imperative and the subjunctive moods (which are left out of account here), Turkish has two sets of personal endings, often called the *primary* and the *secondary endings*. These endings always come at the very end of the conjugated form, except that the secondary endings can be followed by the question particle -*mI-*. In the rule system personal endings are added by the postcyclic rule of PERSON AGREEMENT. Whereas grammars of Turkish usually simply list the tenses that take the primary and those that take the secondary endings, it appears from the rule system that there is a regularity in that the primary endings are selected only if preceded by the Ø-symbol for the highest tense, that is, for the tenses selected under PRES. The primary and secondary person endings endings are as follows:

	I	you (sg.)	he,she,it	we	you (pl.)	they
primary	-Im	-sIn	Ø	-Iz	-sInIz	-lEr
secondary	-m	-n	Ø	-k	-nIz	-lEr

Table 4   *Primary and secondary person endings*

As regards the tenses in the indicative mood, it pays again to distinguish between a t_1 and a t_2. They do not, however, combine freely. The simplest and most principled solution seems to be to distinguish between a 'PRES-stream' and a 'PAST-stream'. The t_1 PRES is realized as Ø, the t_1 PAST as -*DI-*. When PRES is selected for t_1 the t_2-choices are limited to: -*Iyor-* ('simultaneous'), -*Er/Ir-* ('generic'), and -*EcEK-* ('future'). When PAST is selected the choices for t_2 are:

Ø ('simultaneous'), *-DI-* ('preceding'), *-Iyor-* (now restricted to 'simultaneous-narrative'), and again *-Er/Ir-* and *-EcEK-*. Tenses formed with *-Er/Ir-* are usually called 'aorist' in Turkish grammar. They express genericity and/or habitualness. The Turkish aorist is subject to a great deal of morphophonological alternation, especially in combination with the negation affix *-mE-*. Even the tense marker itself varies between weak and strong vowel harmony. This aspect is left out of account here.

Besides the PRES-stream and the PAST-stream there is a VERB-stream and a NOM-stream. Only the VERB-stream is sensitive to the distinction between PRES and PAST. In the NOM-stream the place of t_2 is taken by the copula verb, which becomes an affix *-I-* (from the archaic verb *i-mek* 'to be'; *-mEk* is the ending for infinitives), morphophonologically changed into *-y-* between a vowel and *-DI-*, and into *-Ø-* elsewhere. Moreover, there is an optional idiosyncratic primary ending *-DIr-* for 3rd person singular and *-DIr-lEr-* for 3rd person plural after the copula affix. The VERB-stream and the NOM-stream differ not only in that the former has a t_2 while the latter has a copula affix, but also in a few other respects. The VERB-stream places the negation, realized as the affix *-mE-*, right underneath t_2 (or right under the necessity predicate *-mElI-* when that is used), whereas the NOM-stream uses the verb *değil* for negation, placing it right underneath the copula affix *-I-*. Furthermore, in the VERB-stream the S° allows for further expansion, beyond the negation *-mE-*, by means of predicates (affixes) for possibility, causativity and passivity. These optional expansions are not available to the NOM-stream. The NOM-stream is thus rather restricted in its possibilities of expression. To the extent that expressions are needed for tenses, moods and modalities that are not available in the canonical NOM-stream, the verb *ol-mak* ('to be') is used. But we will not deal with this verb here.

In the VERB-stream it is thus possible to have sentences like (97a). (97b) contains the necessity operator -mElI-, which seems to be a hybrid between the VERB-stream and the NOM-stream in that it requires a copula verb (affix) but otherwise follows the rules of the VERB-stream ('LV': liaison vowel):

(97)a. Bu kitab-ı   yaz - dır - a - ma - y - acağ - ız
       this book-ACC write-CAUS-POSS-NEG - LV - FUT - 1pl
       'we will not be able to get someone to write this book'

   b. Bu kitab-ı   yaz - dır - a - ma - malı - y - dı
       this book-ACC write-CAUS-POSS-NEG - NEC-COPULA-PAST
       'it should not have been possible to get someone to write this book'

No such construction is available for a meaning like 'it should not have been possible for the book to be in your house', which requires generation entirely in the NOM-stream. To express that meaning one must have recourse to other, periphrastic, means.

A few more details are to be dealt with. First, the question particle *-mI-*. This is generated at the top of the auxiliary system in the highest adverbial expansion of S" (Formation Rule (1a)). It is normally lowered onto the V-cluster. There are, however, two complications. The first is that in sentences with a topic-comment profile (see 7.2) *-mI-* is not lowered onto the V-cluster but onto the comment-NP. We can thus have the following question forms:

(98)a. Bu adam cocuğ - a süt   ver - di - mi ?
        this man child-DAT milk give-PAST-QUESTION
        'did this man give milk to the child?'

   b. **Bu adam-mı** cocuğ-a süt ver-di ?
       'is it this man who gave milk to the child?'

   c. Bu adam **cocuğ-a-mı** süt ver-di ?
       'is it to the child that this man gave milk?'

   d. Bu adam cocuğ-a **süt-mü** ver-di ?
       'is it milk that this man gave to the child?'

Sentence (98a) is a neutral question but (98b-d) query the truth of whatever constituent is selected as the comment. This is why in the lexicon of 7.6.2 the question predicate *mI* is specified for LOWERING onto either the comment or V, depending on whether there is a topic-comment structure or not. In using the rule system given below to generate sentences, *mI*-LOWERING onto the comment is to be ignored as the rules contain no provision for topic-comment structure.

The second complication with *-mI-* is caused by its place in the V-cluster in neutral questions. It comes out of the Cycle at the top of the V-cluster, due to the standard LOWERING operation. The first postcyclic rule, PERSON AGREE-MENT, then adds person endings. The simplest way of formulating this rule is to make it sensitive to the highest tense t_1. When t_1 is Ø (PRES) the primary endings are selected, and the secondary endings are when t_1 is *DI* (PAST). The endings are then inserted just above the t_1 to which they are sensitive. This still leaves the question affix at the top of the V-cluster. In surface structures, however, it is not always found there but further down in the cluster. That is, when the cluster contains the copula affix *-I-*, whether realized as Ø or as *-y-*, the question affix *mI* is found just before the copula. If there is no copula (i.e. the sentence is in the VERB-stream), then, if there is a primary person ending except the 3rd person plural *-lEr*, *mI* is found just before the person ending. With secondary person endings, with *-lEr*, and, of course, when the ending is realized as Ø, *mI* is at the top of the V-cluster.

This state of affairs seems best described by means of a postcyclic rule of *mI*-PLACEMENT. Attempts to account for these phenomena directly in the Cycle result in chaotic rules, whereas a postcyclic treatment can deal with them in an orderly fashion. Moreover, given the grammars presented in the chapters 3-6 for the European languages, there is nothing strange in having a postcyclic rule which moves elements in a downward direction within the V-cluster.

The treatment of adverbials has been kept to a minimum. In fact, no class-1 adverbials have been introduced. What is important, however, is the fact that Turkish has postpositional phrases that occur as lexical predicates in S⁰s. With regard to prepositional phrases in the European languages we have left this question open (see note 18 in 3.7.3.2), but for Turkish there can be no doubt that postpositional phrases can function as lexical predicates in S⁰s, since they are treated as predicates in the NOM-stream, with copula, tense and other affixes attached to them:

(99)a. Siz   Mehmed-in   ev - in - de - mi - y - di - niz?
       you(pl) Mehmet-GEN house-his-in-QUESTION-COPULA-PAST-2pl
       'were you people in Mehmet's house?'

   b. Biz Mehmed-in   ev - in - de değil - Ø - di - k
       we Mehmet-GEN house-his - in   not - COPULA - PAST-1pl
       'we were not in Mehmet's house'

As far as the auxiliary system is concerned, Turkish makes no distinction between epistemic and agentive modals: both *-E(bil)-* (possibility) and *-mElI-* (necessity) are used epistemically ('it is possible/necessary that ...') and agentively ('have the ability/obligation to ...'). Lexical adjectives outside the auxiliary system may make this distinction, such as *lâzım*, which means 'necessary due to obligation or need', but the auxiliary system is indifferent to it. The expression for possibility, moreover, *-E(bil)-*, consists of the morpheme *-E-* which is the expression proper for possibility, optionally reinforced with *-bil-*, the verb stem for 'know', turned into an affix here. (When the possibility operator is followed by the negation *-mE-* the additional *-bil-* must be left out.) *MElI*, on the other hand, is, as has been said, a hybrid between the VERB-stream and the NOM-stream, in that it requires the copula *-I-* in t_2-position, but otherwise follows the VERB-stream. As the reader will notice, it jumps into the NOM-stream in Formation Rule (2c), only to jump out of it again in rule (3a).

As in the French *faire*-construction (see 4.4.3), the Turkish causative turns the subject of a lower transitive verb into a dative, as shown in (100), and the subject of a lower intransitive verb as well as the direct object of a lower transitive verb become accusative.

(100) ben cocuğ-a   mektub-u   yaz - dır - dı - m
       I   child-DAT   letter-ACC write-CAUS-PAST-1sg
       'I made the child write the letter'

This shift in case assignment is clearly due to the extra NP brought in by the causative in virtue of Formation Rule (3e), and the general format of SA-structures, which assigns dative case to a middle NP and accusative case to the last of two or three NPs. And like French, Turkish allows for multiple causatives.[11] The second causative predicate is then *t*, the third again *dIr*, etc. Theoretically speaking the process should be recursive, but more than two consecutive causatives are 'rarely if ever found outside the pages of grammar books, e.g. *öl-dür-t-dür-t* 'to get someone to get someone to get someone to make someone die', i.e. to kill through the agency of three intermediaries' (Lewis 1984:146). Clearly, multiple causatives may lead to 'constituent crowding', i.e. more NPs than the three argument positions allowed: nominative, dative,

---

[11] English has multiple lexical causatives, as in *Who is building over there?* or *This judge has hanged too many people*, where *build* and *hang*, respectively, are understood as involving at least one intermediary.

accusative. (PR under V_{Caus} may create new direct and indirect objects, as in French and Dutch.) To prevent crowding, lower verbs, possibly themselves causatives, may be selected without a subject-NP, as in *öl-dür-dü* 'he has caused (X) to die', 'he has killed (X)', or *mektub-u yaz-dır-dı* 'he caused (X) to write the letter'. To enable a subjectless verbal selection S^oCAUS produces a subscript feature [CAUS] that percolates downward till the lexical verb, allowing the selection of a lower verb without the subject-NP. It does not stop rule (3e) from being recursive, but at every new application a further subscript feature [CAUS] is added. Passive verbs are obligatorily selected without a subject-NP, the selection being induced by the subscript feature [PASS], as in *kitap yaz-ıl-dı* 'the letter was written'. However, there is no passive under causative or vice versa (see rules(3e,f)).

It is now time to look at the actual rule system. The cyclic rules need not be specified, as they function exactly as in the other languages discussed.

7.6.2 Some main Formation Rules

(1)a. $\quad S''ADV_1 \rightarrow S''ADV_2 \big/ S''PRES \big/ S''PAST + V_{Que}$

or b. $\quad S''ADV_2 \rightarrow S''ADV_2 \big/ S''PRES \big/ S''PAST + V_{Adv_2}$

$\qquad\qquad$ or: $\quad S''ADV_2 \big/ S''PRES \big/ S''PAST + NP + V_{Postp_2}$

or c. $\quad S''PRES \rightarrow S'PRES \big/ S'NOM + V_{t_1\text{-}Pres}$

or d. $\quad S''PAST \rightarrow S'PAST \big/ S'NOM + V_{t_1\text{-}Past}$

(2)a. $\quad S'PRES \rightarrow S^oNEG \big/ S^oPOSS \big/ S^oCAUS \big/ S^oPASS \big/ S^oVERB + V_{t_2\text{-}Pres}$

b. $\quad S'PAST \rightarrow S^oNEG \big/ S^oPOSS \big/ S^oCAUS \big/ S^oPASS \big/ S^oVERB + V_{t_2\text{-}Past}$

$\qquad\quad S'NOM \rightarrow S^oNEC \big/ S^oNOMNEG \big/ S^oNOM + V_{Cop}$

(3)a. $\quad S^oNEC \rightarrow S^oNEG \big/ S^oPOSS \big/ S^oCAUS \big/ S^oPASS \big/ S^oVERB + V_{Nec}$

b. $\quad S^oNOMNEG \rightarrow S^oNOM + V_{NomNeg}$

c. $\quad S^oNEG \rightarrow S^oPOSS \big/ S^oCAUS \big/ S^oPASS \big/ S^oVERB + V_{Neg}$

d. $\quad S^oPOSS \rightarrow S^oCAUS \big/ S^oPASS \big/ S^oVERB + V_{Poss}$

e. $\quad S^oCAUS \rightarrow NP + S^oCAUS_{[CAUS]} \big/ S^oVERB_{[CAUS]} + V_{Caus}$

f. $\quad S^oPASS \rightarrow S^oVERB_{[PASS]} + V_{Pass}$

g. $\quad S^oVERB \rightarrow \langle lex.arg.frame \rangle + V_{Verb}$

h. $\quad S^oNOM \rightarrow \langle lex.arg.frame \rangle + V_{Nom} \big/ V_{Adj} \big/ V_{Postp}$

7.6.3 Some lexicon

SA-cat	Fillers	Surface cat	Cyclic Rules
V_{Que}	mI	Affix	$L_{comment/V}$
V_{Adv_2}	bugün, dün, yarın, burda, ... today yesterday tomorrow here	Adverb	L_{left}

V_{Postp2}	dE, lE, sIz, dEn, ...	Affix	OI,L_{left}
	in,at with without from		
$V_{t_1\text{-}Pres}$	Ø (=PRES)	Affix	L_V
$V_{t_1\text{-}Past}$	DI (=PAST)	Affix	L_V
$V_{t_2\text{-}Pres}$	Iyor, Er/Ir, EcEK	Affix	L_V
	SIM AORIST FUT		
$V_{t_2\text{-}Past}$	Ø, DI, Iyor, Er/Ir, EcEK	Affix	L_V
	SIM PREC SIM(narrative) AORIST FUT		
V_{Neg}	mE	Affix	L_V
V_{Cop}	I	Affix	L_V
V_{NomNeg}	deği l	Verb	L_V
V_{Nec}	mElI	Affix	L_V
V_{Poss}	E(bil)	Affix	L_V
V_{Caus}	DIr, t (2nd causative)	Affix	PR
V_{Pass}	Il	Affix	L_V

V_{LEX}:

SA-cat	Fillers	Argument frame	Surface cat	Cyclic rules
V_{Nom}	ev, kedi, cocuK, house, cat, child, at, kitaP, adam, ... horse, book man	NP + —	Noun	— —
V_{Adj}	kücük, kırmızı, yeni, small, red, new, hasta, zengin, ... ill, rich	NP + —	Adj	— —
V_{Postp}	dE, lE, sIz, dEn, ... in/at, with, without, from	NP + NP + —	Affix	OI
V_{Verb}	gel, öl, uyu, uç, yüz... come., die, sleep, fly, swim	NP + —	Verb	— —
V_{Verb}	yaz, sev, yap, gör, al, bil, ... write, love, do, see, take/buy, know	NP + NP + —	Verb	— —

7.6.4 Some postcyclic rules (to be applied in the order given)

(1) **PERSON AGREEMENT:** Insert the person ending that corresponds with the subject just above the highest tense (Ø or *DI*) in the V-cluster (optionally between two successive occurrences of -*DI*-). Select the primary endings when t_1 is Ø, and the secondary tenses when t_1 is *DI*.

(2) *MI*-**PLACEMENT:** If the V-cluster contains the copula *I*, the question affix *mI* is lowered to just below *I*. If the V-cluster does not contain the copula but contains a PPE (primary person ending except -*lEr*-) *mI* is lowered to just below PPE. If the V-cluster contains two successive occurrences of -*DI*- *mI* is optionally inserted before the second -*DI*-. Otherwise *mI* stays in place.

(3) **Ø-DELETION:** Delete $_{Affix}$[Ø].

7.6.5 Some example sentences

Consider first sentence (101a), mentioned in the previous section. Its SA-structure is (101b). In virtue of the feature [CAUS] the lexical verb *öl* ('die') has been selected without the subject-NP. The shallow structure is (101c). Postcyclic rule (1) then adds the person ending Ø above $_{Aff}$[DI]. Rule (3) subsequently deletes both occurrences of Ø. The surface structure is (101d).

(101)a. Grip öl - dür - dü
       flu   die - CAUS - PAST
       the flu has killed'

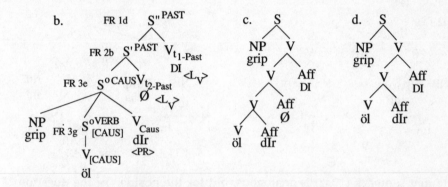

Next consider (102a), with the SA-structure (102b). (102c) shows the sentence half-way through the Cycle. (102d) represents the stage at which OBJECT INCORPORATION under *dE* has taken place. In (102e) the PostpPhrase has been lowered, and in (102f) the question affix is in place. (102g), finally, shows the effect of postcyclic PERSON AGREEMENT and Ø-DELETION:

(102)a. Ev -im-de   sen   oyna - dı- n - mı?
       house-my-in you   play-PAST-2sg-QUESTION
       'Did you play in my house?'

b.

FR 1a   S″ ADV₁

FR 1b   S″ ADV₂   V_Que
             mI
FR 1d   S″ PAST   NP   V_Postp₂   <L_v>
                dE
FR 2b   S′ PAST   V_t1-Past N   Aff   <OI,L_left>
            DI   ev   Im
FR 3g   S⁰VERB   V_t2-Past <L_v>
       NP   V   Ø
       sen oyna   <L_v>

c.

S″ ADV₁

S″ ADV₂   V_Que
             mI
S   NP   V_Postp₂   <L_v>
             dE
NP   V   N   Aff   <OI,L_left>
sen   ev   Im
   V   Aff
     DI
 V   Aff
oyna Ø

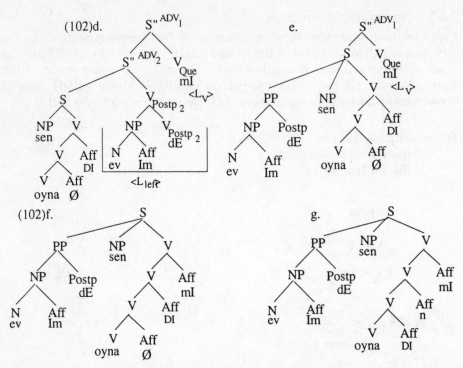

Note that sentence (103a) is analogous, but for the position of the question particle *-mI-* which is placed before the primary class person ending, according to Postcyclic Rule (2). (103b) and (103c) are now also obvious:

(103)a. Ev-im-de   sen   oyna - ıyor - mu - sun?
      house-my-in you play - SIM - QUESTION-2sg
      'are you playing in my house?'

   b. Ev-im-de   sen oyna - ma - dı - n - mı?
      house-my-in you play - NEG - PAST-2sg-QUESTION
      'did you not play in my house?'

   c. Ev - im - de   sen   oyna - ma - ıyor - mu - sun?
      house-my-in   you play - NEG - SIM - QUESTION-2sg
      'are you not playing in my house?'

Now consider (104a) with the SA-structure (104b). (104c) is the shallow structure. Note that V_{Postp}[dE] induces OI, resulting in *dE* being relabelled 'Aff', but the complex V remains V_{Postp}. (104d) is the surface structure, with the secondary person ending *nIz* and *mI* moved down to just below the copula:

(104)a Siz   ev - im - de - mi -   y - di - niz?
      you(pl) house-my-in-QUESTION-COPULA-PAST-2pl
      'were you people in my house?'

b.

```
                         FR 1a   S″ ADV₁
                       FR 1d   S″ PAST        V Que
                                               mI
                     FR 2c   S′ NOM     V t 1-Past   <L v>
                                         DI
                 FR 3h   S oNOM   V Cop   <L v>
                                   I
        NP    NP    V Postp   <L v>
        siz   /\    dE
           N   Aff  <OI>
           ev  Im
```

c.

```
              S
          NP      V
          siz    /\
               V      Aff
              /\       mI
            V    Aff
           /\    DI
      V Postp   Aff
               I
      NP    Aff
      /\    dE
    N   Aff
    ev  Im
```

d.

```
              S
          NP      V
          siz    /\
               V      Aff
              /\       niz
            V    Aff
           /\    DI
         V    Aff
        /\    I
   V Postp   Aff
              mI
      NP    Aff
      /\    dE
    N   Aff
    ev  Im
```

The Turkish pluperfect is, like in the European languages, composed of a double past: *DI + DI*, as in (105a-c), all three meaning 'had we come?'. Yet there are a few idiosyncrasies (cf. Lewis 1984:128-130), one of which has been mentioned above: between two successive occurrences of *DI* the liaison vowel *-y-* is inserted, as shown in (105a). Moreover, as appears from Postcyclic Rule (1), the secondary person ending, in this case *-k-*, may, exceptionally, be inserted between two successive occurrences of *DI*, as in (105b), in which case, of course, the liaison vowel is not inserted. Finally, as shown in (105b,c), the question particle *mI* is optionally inserted before the second occurrence of *DI*, but always followed by *-y-*.

(105)a. Biz gel-di-y-di-k-mi?
     b. Biz gel-di-k-mi-y-di?
     c. Biz gel-di-mi-y-di-k?

This combination of options and idiosyncrasies seems too much of a coincidence. It looks as if the Turkish pluperfect is developing from a nominal copula construction into a purely verbal one. We have interpreted the *-y-* in (105a-c) and in (106a₁) as the liaison vowel, but it is homophonous with the copula before *DI*. The copula, moreover, is phonologically extremely weak, which seems an invitation to change. If *-y-* is interpreted as a copula the fact that *mI* may occur just before it becomes regular, as the question particle is regularly placed just before the copula. Perhaps the pluperfect was expressed originally as something like 'we came, that's how it was', and in questions 'we came, is that how it was?', i.e. with a double past but not yet grammaticalized. This is, of course, speculation, but it shows how one can envisage the way irregularities and optional differences may arise in the course of linguistic change.

Let us generate (106a₁,₂). The common SA-structure is (106b). The shallow structure is (106c). Then Postcyclic Rule (1) adds the secondary person ending *-k-*, either, regularly, above the highest tense, as in (106d), or between the two occurrences of *DI*, as in (106e). Finally, in the morphophonology, the liaison vowel *-y-* is inserted between the two *DI*-s in (106d) but not in (106e):

(106)a₁. Biz gel - di - y - di - k   a₂. Biz gel - di - k - ti
         we come-PREC-LV-PAST-1pl   we come-PREC-1pl-PAST
                        'we had come'

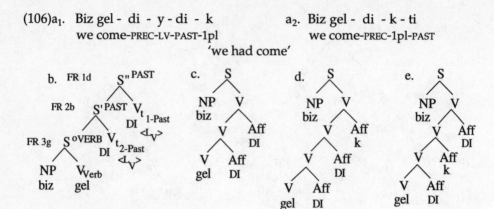

As a last example, consider (107a). The Cycle transforms the SA-structure (107b) into the shallow structure (107c). This becomes (107d) through Postcyclic Rule (1), which adds the primary ending *-Iz*. The copula verb takes the shape Ø. Postcyclic Rule (3) deletes the two occurrences of $_{Aff}$[Ø]:

(107)a. Biz hasta değil - iz
         we   ill   not-be-1pl
         'we are not ill'

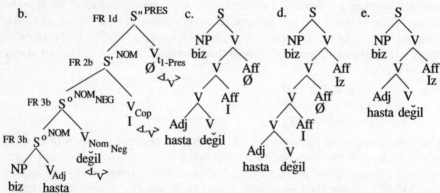

The reader will no doubt spend many more hours generating Turkish sentences from the rule system given above. I now take my leave.

List of French words

à	to, at	par	via, by (pass.)
absolu	absolute	paraître	appear
aimer	love	partir	leave, go away
aller	go	pendant	during
arriver	arrive	penser	think
avoir	have	petit	small, little
aussi	therefore	peu	little, few
avec	with	peut-être	maybe
beaucoup	much, many	possible	possible
boire	drink	pour	for
bon	good	pouvoir	can, be possible
chaque	every	préférer	prefer
chat	cat	premier	first
commencer	begin, start	présenter	present, introduce
continuer	continue	presque	almost
courir	run	probable	probable
croire	believe	promettre	promise
dans	in	quelque	some
devoir	must, have to	quant à	as regards, as for
dire	say	rire	laugh
donc	therefore	rond	round
donner	give	rouge	red
dormir	sleep	sans	without
en	while	savoir	know
en outre	moreover	se pouvoir	be possible
enfant	child	sembler	seem, appear
entendre	hear	soigneux	careful
être	be	souris	mouse
faire	make, do	souvent	often
falloir	be necessary	tenter	try
fidèle	faithful	toujours	always
heureux	happy	tout	all
laisser	let, make	un	a, one
lire	read	un peu	a little
livre	book	vendre	sell
maison	house	venir	come
malheureux	unhappy	vers	towards
manger	eat	vieux	old
mauvais	bad	vite	fast, quickly
mourir	die	voir	see
ne-jamais	never	volontiers	with pleasure, gladly
ne-pas	not	vouloir	want
obliger	oblige	vrai	true

List of Dutch words

aan	to, at	lachen	laugh
a l	already	laten	let, make
altijd	always	leren	1. learn 2. teach
bedriegen	deceive	lijken	appear, seem
beginnen	begin, start	liggen	lie, be prostrate
bekend	known	lopen	walk, go
beloven	promise	maar	but
besluiten	decide	makkelijk	easy
bijna	almost	man	man
boek	book	met	with
bovendien	moreover	misschien	maybe
daar	there	moeilijk	difficult, hard
daarom	therefore	moeten	must, be necessary
de meeste	most	mogelijk	possible
denken	think	morgen	tomorrow
doen	do	muis	mouse
door	through, by (pass.)	naar	to, towards
drinken	drink	niet	not
dus	so, therefore	nooit	never
een	a, one	onmogelijk	impossible
elk	each, every	op	on, at
en	and	oud	old
eten	eat	proberen	try
eten-op	eat up	reeds	already
gaan	go	rennen	run
geloven	believe	rond	round
gelukkig	happy	rood	red
geven	give	schijnen	seem, appear
gisteren	yesterday	schrijven	write
goed	good	slapen	sleep
groot	big	slecht	bad
hebben	have	sommige	some
helpen	help	staan	stand, be erect
hier	here	stellen-voor	introduce
horen	hear	tafel	table
huis	house	tijdens	during
ieder	each, every	trachten	try
in	in	trouw	faithful
kat	cat	vaak	often
kind	child	vallen	be humanly possible
klein	small	verbieden	prohibit, forbid
komen	come	verkiezen	prefer
kunnen	can, be possible, be able	verkopen	sell

vertrekken	leave. go away
verzoeken	request
vlug	quickly
voor	1. for 2. before
vrouw	woman
waar	true
waarschijnlijk	probable
wachten	wait
want	for, because
wat betreft	as regards, as for
weten	know
willen	want
worden	become, be (pass.)
zien	see
zijn	be
zitten	sit
zonder	without
zorgvuldig	careful
zullen	will

List of German words

aber	but	Katze	cat
alle	all	Kind	child
also	therefore, so	klein	small, little
alt	old	kommen	come
an	at, to	können	be able/possible
an-fangen	begin, start	lachen	laugh
auf	on, at	lassen	let, make
auf-essen	eat up	lehren	teach
auf-schreiben	write up	leicht	easy
auf-trinken	drink up	lernen	learn
außerdem	moreover	Mann	man
befehlen	order	Maus	mouse
bekannt	known	mit	with
bitten	request	mögen	like, may
Buch	book	möglich	possible
denken	think	morgen	tomorrow
denn	for, because	müssen	must
deswegen	for that reason	nach	after
die meisten	most	nicht	not
dort	there	nie	never
ein	a, one	oft	often
einige	some	ohne	without
entscheiden	decide	rot	red
essen	eat	rund	round
fast	almost	sämtliche	all taken together
Frau	woman	scheinen	seem, appear
für	for	schlafen	sleep
fühlen	feel	schlecht	bad
geben	give	schnell	fast, quickly
gehen	go	schon	already
gestern	yesterday	schreiben	write
glauben	believe	schwierig	difficult
groß	big, large	sehen	see
gut	good	sein	be
haben	have	sollen	must, will
Haus	house	tanzen	dance
helfen	help	Tisch	table
hier	here	trinken	drink
hören	hear	treu	faithful
immer	always	überlassen	leave to
in	in	übrigens	for the rest
in Bezug auf	as regards, as for	und	and
jede	every, each	unmöglich	impossible

vielleicht	maybe, perhaps
verbieten	prohibit, forbid
verkaufen	sell
versprechen	promise
versuchen	try
von	of, by (pass.)
vor-stellen	introduce
wahr	true
während	during
wahrscheinlich	probable
werden	become, will, be (pass.)
wissen	know
wollen	want, wish
zögern	hesitate
zu-vertrauen	entrust

Bibliography

Aarsleff, H.
  1970   The history of linguistics and Professor Chomsky. *Language* 46.3:
          570-585.

Abraham, W.
  1995   *Deutsche Syntax im Sprachenvergleich. Grundlegung einer typo-
          logischen Syntax des Deutschen.* Narr, Tübingen.

Asher, R.E. and J.M.Y. Simpson (eds)
  1994   *The Encyclopedia of Language and Linguistics.* 10 vols. Pergamon
          Press, Oxford.

Baker, C.L.
  1970   Double negatives. *Linguistic Inquiry* 1.2:169-186.
  1991   The syntax of English *not*: the limits of core grammar. *Linguistic
          Inquiry* 22.3:387-429.

Baker, Ph. and Chr. Corne
  1982   *Isle de France Creole. Affinities and Origins.* Karoma, Ann Arbor.

Berwick, R.C., S.P. Abney and C. Tenny (eds)
  1992   *Principle-Based Parsing: Computation and Psycholinguistics.*
          Studies in Linguistics and Philosophy 44. Kluwer, Dordrecht-
          Boston-London.

Bickerton, D.
  1981   *Roots of Language.* Karoma, Ann Arbor.

Blanche-Benveniste, Cl. and K. van den Eynde
  1987   Analyse morphologique et syntaxique des formes QUI, QUE, QUOI.
          Leuven University, Linguistics Department. Preprint 114.

Bloomfield, L.
  1914   *An Introduction to the Study of Language.* Henry Holt & Company,
          New York.
  1933   *Language.* Henry Holt & Company, New York.

Breva-Claramonte, M.
  1983   *Sanctius' Theory of Language. A Contribution to the History of
          Renaissance Linguistics.* Benjamins, Amsterdam.

Bybee, J.L. and Ö. Dahl
  1989   The creation of tense and aspect systems in the languages of the
          world. *Studies in Language* 13.1:51-103.

Chomsky, N.
  1957   *Syntactic Structures.* Mouton, The Hague.

1959a   Review of B.F. Skinner, *Verbal Behavior*, Appleton-Century-Crofts Inc., New York, 1957. *Language* 35.1:26-58.

1959b   On certain formal properties of grammars. *Information and Control* 2:137-167.

1959c   A note on Phrase Structure Grammars. *Information and Control* 2:393-395.

1965   *Aspects of the Theory of Syntax*. MIT Press, Cambridge Mass.

1966   *Cartesian Linguistics. A Chapter in the History of Rationalist Thought*. Harper & Row, New York-London.

1972   *Studies on Semantics in Generative Grammar*. Mouton, The Hague.

Chomsky, N. and G.A. Miller

1958   Finite State languages. *Information and Control* 1:91-112.

1963   Introduction to the formal analysis of natural languages. In: R.D. Luce, R.R. Bush & E. Galanter (eds), *Handbook of Mathematical Psychology, Vol.II*, John Wiley & Sons, New York. Pp. 269-321.

Chomsky, N. and M.P. Schützenberger

1963   The algebraic theory of Context-Free languages. In: P. Braffort & D. Hirschberg (eds), *Computer Programming and Formal Systems*, North-Holland, Amsterdam. Pp. 118-161.

Clifford, P.M.

1973   *Inversion of the Subject in French Narrative Prose from 1500 to the Present Day*. Publications of the Philological Society XXIV. Blackwell, Oxford.

Comrie, B.

1981   *Language Universals and Linguistic Typology*. Blackwell, Oxford.

1985   *Tense*. Cambridge University Press, Cambridge.

Coolen, Riet

1995   *The Semantic Processing of Isolated Novel Nominal Compounds*. PhD-diss. Nijmegen University.

Dahl, Ö.

1985   *Tense and Aspect Systems*. Blackwell, Oxford.

De Rijk, R.P.G.

1974   A note on prelexical Predicate Raising. In: Seuren (ed.) 1974:43-74.

De Saussure, F.

1916   *Cours de Linguistique Générale*. Payot, Paris.

Den Besten, H. and J. Rutten

1989   On Verb Raising, Extraposition and free word order in Dutch. In: D. Jaspers, W. Klooster, Y. Putseys and P. Seuren (eds), *Sentential Complementation and the Lexicon. Studies in Honour of Wim de Geest*. Foris, Dordrecht. Pp. 41-56.

Eisenberg, P., H. Gelhaus, H. Wellmann, H. Henne and H. Sitta
    1995   *Grammatik der deutschen Gegenwartssprache.* Duden Vol. 4. 5th
            Edition. Dudenverlag, Mannheim-Leipzig-Vienna-Zürich.

Elffers-Van Ketel, E.
    1991   *The Historiography of Grammatical Concepts. 19th and 20th cen-
            tury changes in the subject-predicate conception and the problem of
            their historical reconstruction.* Rodopi, Amsterdam-Atlanta, GA.

Evers, A.
    1971   The syntactic motivation of Predicate Raising. Unpublished
            paper, Department of General Linguistics, Utrecht University.
    1975   *The Transformational Cycle in Dutch and German.* PhD-Diss.
            Utrecht University.

Fodor, J.A.
    1975   *The Language of Thought.* Harvester Press, Hassocks, Sussex.

Fraser, B.
    1974   An examination of the performative analysis. *Papers in Linguis-
            tics* 7:1-40.

Frege, G.
    1906   Ueber die Grundlagen der Geometrie. *Jahresberichte der deutschen
            Mathematiker-Vereinigung* 15:293-309, 377-403, 423-430.

Gardiner, A.H.
    1932   *The Theory of Speech and Language.* Clarendon Press, Oxford.

Green, G.M.
    1974   *Semantics and Syntactic Regularity.* Indiana University Press,
            Bloomington, Ind.

Greenberg, J.H., Ch.A. Ferguson & E.A. Moravcsik (eds),
    1978   *Universals of Human Language.* 4 vols. Stanford University Press,
            Stanford, Cal.

Grevisse, M.
    1986   *Le bon usage. Grammaire française.* 12th edition revised by A.
            Goosse. Duculot, Paris-Gembloux.

Hajičová, E., and J. Panevová
    1993   Topic, focus and valency in the Praguian context. In: E. Hajičová
            (ed.), *Functional Description of Language.* Faculty of Mathematics
            and Physics, Charles University, Prague. Pp. 55-66.

Harris, Z.S.
    1951   *Methods in Structural Linguistics.* The University of Chicago
            Press, Chicago.

Hashimoto, M.J.
    1976   Language diffusion on the Asian Continent. Problems of typo-
            logical diversity in Sino-Tibetan. *Computational Analyses of
            Asian & African Languages* 3:49-65. National Inter-University

Research Institute of Asian & African Languages & Cultures, Tokyo.

Heidolph, K.E., W. Flämig and W. Motsch
1981   *Grundzüge einer deutschen Grammatik.* Akademie-Verlag, Berlin.

Hellwig, F.
1991   *Negation in Finnish. A Study in Semantic Syntax.* MA-thesis Nijmegen University.

Horn, L.R.
1985   Metalinguistic negation and pragmatic ambiguity. *Language* 61.1: 121-174.

Hornstein, N.
1977   Towards a theory of tense. *Linguistic Inquiry* 8.3:521-557.

Huck, G. J. and J. A. Goldsmith
1995   *Ideology and Linguistic Theory. Noam Chomsky and the Deep Structure Debates.* Routledge, London & New York.

Hutchins, W.J.
1986   *Machine Translation: Past, Present, Future.* Ellis Horwood, Chichester - Halsted Press (John Wiley & Sons), New York-Chichester-Brisbane-Toronto.

Jackendoff, R.
1977   *X̄-Syntax. A Study of Phrase Structure.* Linguistic Inquiry Monograph 2. MIT Press, Cambridge, Mass.

Janssen, T.M.V.
1993   The principle of compositionality. In: *Encyclopedia of Language and Linguistics.* Pergamon Press & University of Aberdeen Press, Oxford-Edinburgh. Pp. 654-656.

Jespersen, O.
1924   *The Philosophy of Grammar.* Allen & Unwin, London.

Joseph, B.D.
1983   *The Synchrony and Diachrony of the Balkan Infinitive. A Study in Areal, General, and Historical Linguistics.* Cambridge University Press, Cambridge.

Joshi, A.K., L. Levy and M. Takahashi
1975   Tree Adjunct Grammars. *Journal of the Computer and System Sciences* 10:136-163.

Kalepky, Th.
1928   *Neuaufbau der Grammatik als Grundlegung zu einem wissenschaftlichen System der Sprachbeschreibung.* Teubner, Leipzig.

Karttunen, L.
1970   On the semantics of complement sentences. *Papers from the Sixth Regional Meeting, Chicago Linguistic Society*, Linguistics Department, University of Chicago. Pp. 328-339.

1973   Presuppositions of compound sentences. *Linguistic Inquiry* 4.2:169-193.

1974   Presupposition and linguistic context. *Theoretical Linguistics* 1.1/2:181-194.

Katz, J.J.
1964   Mentalism in linguistics. *Language* 40:124-137.

Katz, J.J. and J.A. Fodor
1963   The structure of a semantic theory. *Language* 39:170-210.

Katz, J.J. and P.M. Postal
1964   *An Integrated Theory of Linguistic Descriptions.* MIT Press, Cambridge Mass.

Kayne, R.S.
1969   *The Transformational Cycle in French Syntax.* PhD-Diss. MIT.

1975   *French Syntax. The Transformational Cycle.* MIT Press, Cambridge, Mass.

1991   Romance Clitics, Verb Movement, and PRO. *Linguistic Inquiry* 22.4: 647-686.

Keenan, E.L. and B. Comrie
1977   Noun Phrase accessibility and Universal Grammar. *Linguistic Inquiry* 8.1:63-100.

Kiparsky, P. and C. Kiparsky
1971   Fact. In: Steinberg & Jakobovits:345-369.

Koster, J.
1975   Dutch as an SOV-language. *Linguistic Analysis* 1:111-136.

Kühner, R. and C. Stegmann
1955[3]   *Ausführliche Grammatik der lateinischen Sprache. Satzlehre.* 2 Vols. Gottschalk, Leverkusen.

Lakoff, G.
1971   On generative semantics. In: Steinberg & Jakobovits:232-296.

Langacker, R.
1973   Predicate Raising: some Uto-Aztecan evidence. In: B.B. Kachru, R.B. Lees, Y. Malkiel, A. Pietrangeli, S. Saporta (eds), *Issues in Linguistics. Papers in Honor of Henry and Renée Kahane.* University of Illinois Press, Urbana, Illinois. Pp. 468-491.

Levelt, W.J.M.
1974   *Formal Grammars in Linguistics and Psycholinguistics.* 3 Vols. Mouton, The Hague.

1989   *Speaking. From Intention to Articulation.* MIT Press, Cambridge Mass.

Lewis, G.L.
1984   *Turkish Gramnmar.* Clarendon Press, Oxford.

Li, Ch. and S.A. Thompson
1974   An explanation of word order change: SVO→SOV. *Foundations of Language* 12.2:201-214.

Lindholm, J.M.
1969   Negative-Raising and sentence pronominalization. *Papers from the Fifth Regional Meeting, Chicago Linguistic Society.* Linguistics Department, University of Chicago. Pp. 148-158.

Lyons, J.
1977   *Semantics.* 2 vols. Cambridge University Press, Cambridge.

Martinon, Ph.
1927   *Comment on parle en français.* Larousse, Paris.

McCawley, J.D.
1968   Lexical insertion in a Transformational Grammar without Deep Structure. *Papers from the Fourth Regional Meeting, Chicago Linguistic Society.* Linguistics Department, University of Chicago. Pp. 71-80. (Also in McCawley 1973:155-166)

1970   English as a VSO-Language. *Language* 46.2:286-299. (Also in McCawley 1973:211-228, and in Seuren (ed.) 1974:75-95)

1973   *Grammar and Meaning. Papers on Syntactic and Semantic Topics.* Taishukan Publishing Company, Tokyo.

1980   Review of Newmeyer 1980. *Linguistics* 18.9/10:911-930.

Meillet, A and M. Cohen
1952   *Les langues du monde.* Champion, Paris.

Meyer-Lübke, W.
1899   *Romanische Syntax.* (=Grammatik der romanischen Sprachen III) Reisland, Leipzig.

Montague, R.
1970   English as a formal language. In: B. Visentini et al. (eds), *Linguaggi nella Società e nella Tecnica*, Edizioni di Comunità, Milan. Pp.189-224.

1973   The proper treatment of quantification in ordinary English. In: J. Hintikka, J. Moravcsik and P. Suppes (eds), *Approaches to Natural Language*, Reidel, Dordrecht. Pp.221-242.

Muravyova, I.A.
1992   The Paleosiberian model of incorporation in comparison with the Oceanic one. In: *Pan-Asiatic Linguistics. Proceedings of the Third International Symposium on Language and Linguistics.* Chulalongkorn University, Bangkok, January 8-10, 1992. Vol. 1. Pp. 205-215.

Neijt, A.H.
1979   *Gapping. A Contribution to Sentence Grammar.* Foris, Dordrecht.

Newmeyer, F.J.
  1980   *Linguistic Theory in America. The First Quarter-Century of Trans-*
          formational Generative Grammar. Academic Press, New York-San
          Francisco-London.

Obenauer, H.-G.
  1976   *Études de syntaxe interrogative du français. QUOI, COMBIEN et le*
          complémenteur. Niemeyer, Tübingen.

Palmer, F.R.
  1979   *Modality and the English Modals*. Longman, London.

Partee, B.H., A. ter Meulen and R.E. Wall
  1990   *Mathematical Methods in Linguistics*. Kluwer, Dordrecht.

Paul, H.
  1880   *Prinzipien der Sprachgeschichte*. Niemeyer, Halle.

Perlmutter, D.M.
  1970   The two verbs begin. In: R. Jacobs & P. Rosenbaum (eds), *Readings*
          in English Transformation Grammar. Ginn & Co., Boston. Pp. 107–
          119.
  1971   *Deep and Surface Structure Constraints*. Holt, Rinehart & Win-
          ston, New York.

Peters, P.S. and R.W. Ritchie
  1973   On the generative power of transformational grammars. *Infor-*
          mation Sciences 6:49-83.

Postal, P.M.
  1974   *On Raising. One Rule of English Grammar and its Theoretical Im-*
          plications. MIT Press, Cambridge, Mass.

Renchon, H.
  1969   *Études de syntaxe descriptive II: la syntaxe de l'interrogation*.
          Palais des Académies, Brussels.

Reichenbach, H.
  1947   *Elements of Symbolic Logic*. Macmillan, London.

Rosenbaum, P.S.
  1967   *The Grammar of English Predicate Complement Constructions*.
          MIT Press, Cambridge, Mass.

Ross, J.R.
  1967   *Constraints on Variables in Syntax*. PhD-diss. MIT. (=Ross 1986)
  1969   A proposed rule of Tree Pruning. In: D.A. Reibel & S.A. Schane
          (eds), *Modern Studies in English. Readings in Transformational*
          Grammar. Prentice-Hall, Englewood Cliffs, N.J. Pp. 288-299.
  1970a   On declarative sentences. In: R. Jacobs & P. Rosenbaum (eds),
          Readings in English Transformational Grammar, Ginn & Co, Bos-
          ton. Pp. 222-272.

1970b   Gapping and the order of constituents. In: M. Bierwisch & K. Heidolph (eds), *Progress in Linguistics.* Mouton, The Hague. Pp. 249-259.

1986   *Infinite Syntax!* Ablex, Norwood N.J. (=Ross 1967)

Ruwet, N.
1972   *Théorie syntaxique et syntaxe du français.* Du Seuil, Paris.

1991   *Syntax and Human Experience.* The University of Chicago Press, Chicago-London.

Sasse, H.-J.
1987   The thetic/categorical distinction revisited. *Linguistics* 25.3:511-580.

Schachter, P.
1974   A non-transformational account of serial verbs. *Studies in African Linguistics,* Supplement 5:253-270

Schotel, H.
1994   SeSynPro. Towards a workbench for Semantic Syntax. In: G. Bouma & G. van Noord (eds), *CLIN IV: Papers from the Fourth CLIN Meeting.* Vakgroep Alfa-Informatica, Rijksuniversiteit Groningen, PO Box 716, 9700 AS Groningen, The Netherlands. Pp. 135-147.

Sechehaye, Ch.A.
1926   *Essai sur la structure logique de la phrase.* Champion, Paris.

Seuren, P.A.M.
1967   Negation in Dutch. *Neophilologus* 51.4:327-363.

1969   *Operators and Nucleus. A Contribution to the Theory of Grammar.* Cambridge University Press, Cambridge.

1972a   Autonomous versus Semantic Syntax. *Foundations of Language* 8:237-265. (Also in Seuren (ed.) 1974:96-122)

1972b   Predicate Raising and Dative in French and sundry languages. Magdalen College, Oxford / L.A.U.T. Trier. Unpublished.

1974   Negative's travels. In: Seuren (ed.) 1974:183-208.

1975   Referential constraints on lexical items. In: E.L. Keenan (ed.), *Formal Semantics of Natural Language.* Cambridge University Press, Cambridge. Pp. 84-98.

1976   Clitic pronoun clusters. *Italian Linguistics* 2:7-35.

1981   Tense and aspect in Sranan. *Linguistics* 19:1043-1076

1984   Operator Lowering. *Linguistics* 22:573-627.

1985   *Discourse Semantics.* Blackwell, Oxford.

1986   Helpen en helpen is twee. *Glot* 9.1/2:110-117.

1989   A problem in English subject complementation. In: D. Jaspers, W.G. Klooster, Y. Putseys & P.A.M. Seuren (eds), *Sentential Comple-*

mentation and the Lexicon. Studies in Honour of Wim de Geest. Foris, Dordrecht. Pp. 355-375.

1990 Verb Syncopation and Predicate Raising in Mauritian Creole. *Linguistics* 28.4:809-844

1994 Presupposition. In: Asher & Simpson:3311-3320.

1995 Notes on the history and syntax of Mauritian Creole. *Linguistics* 33:531-577.

(to appear) *The Linguist's Progress. A Historical and Systematic Introduction to the Study of Language.*

Seuren, P.A.M. (ed.)
1974 *Semantic Syntax*, Oxford University Press, Oxford.

Seuren, P.A.M. and H.Chr. Wekker
1985 Semantic transparency as a factor in Creole genesis. In: P. Muysken & N. Smith (eds), *Substrata versus Universals in Creole Genesis.* Benjamins, Amsterdam. Pp. 57-70.

Shannon, C.E. and W. Weaver
1949 *The Mathematical Theory of Communication.* University of Illinois Press, Urbana, Ill.

Sommer, B.A.
1972 *Kunjin Syntax: A Generative View.* Australian Institute of Aboriginal Studies. Canberra A.C.T. Australian Aboriginal Studies 45.

Sowa, J.F.
1984: *Conceptual Structures: Information Processing in Mind and Machine.* Addison-Wesley Publishing Cy, Reading,Mass.-Menlo Park,Calif.-London-Amsterdam-Don Mills,Ontario-Sydney.

Starosta, S.
1971 Lexical derivation in Case Grammar. *Working Papers in Linguistics* 3.8, Dept. of Linguistics, University of Hawaii, Honolulu.

Stassen, L.
1985 *Comparison and Universal Grammar.* Blackwell, Oxford.

Steinberg, D.D. and L.A. Jakobovits (eds)
1971 *Semantics. An Interdisciplinary Reader in Philosophy, Linguistics and Psychology.* Cambridge University Press, Cambridge.

Steinthal, H.
1860 *Charakteristik der hauptsächlichsten Typen des Sprachbaues.* (Neubearbeitung von Dr. Franz Misteli). Dümmler, Berlin.

Ultan, R.
1978 The nature of future tenses. In: Greenberg, Ferguson & Moravcsik (eds), vol.3:83-123.

Van Kuppevelt, J.
1991 *Topic en Comment. Expliciete en impliciete vraagstelling in discourse.* PhD-diss. Nijmegen University.

1993   About a uniform conception of S- and D-topics. In: E. Hajičová (ed.), *Functional Description of Language*. Faculty of Mathematics and Physics, Charles University, Prague. Pp. 133-147.

Van Oirsouw, R.R.
1984   Accessibility of deletion in Dutch. *Journal of Semantics* 3.3:201-227.

1987   *Syntax of Coordination*. Routledge, Chapman & Hall, London.

Weerman, F.
1989   *The V-2 Conspiracy. A Synchronic and a Diachronic Analysis of Verbal Positions in Germanic Languages*. Publications in Language Sciences 31. Foris, Dordrecht.

Wegener, Ph.
1885   *Untersuchungen über die Grundfragen des Sprachlebens*. Niemeyer, Halle.

Wilson, K.
1954   The Information Theory approach. In: Ch.E. Osgood & Th.A. Sebeok (eds), *Psycholinguistics. A Survey of theory and research problems*, Waverly Press, Baltimore. Pp. 35-49.

Wundt, W.
1880   *Logik. Eine Untersuchung der Prinzipien der Erkenntnis und der Methoden Wissenschaftlicher Forschung*. Enke, Stuttgart.

1900   *Völkerpsychologie. Eine Untersuchung der Entwicklungsgezetze von Sprache, Mythus und Sitte. Part 1, Die Sprache* (2 vols.) Engelmann, Leipzig.

1901   *Sprachgeschichte und Sprachpsychologie*. Engelmann, Leipzig.

Index